THE
RA

# THE LIMITS OF RATIONALITY

EDITED BY

## Karen Schweers Cook

AND

## Margaret Levi

THE UNIVERSITY OF CHICAGO PRESS
Chicago and London

Karen Schweers Cook is professor of sociology at the University of Washington and is the editor of *Social Exchange Theory.* Margaret Levi is professor of political science at the University of Washington and is the author of *Of Rule and Revenue.*

The University of Chicago Press, Chicago 60637
The University of Chicago Press, Ltd., London
© 1990 by the University of Chicago
All rights reserved. Published 1990
Printed in the United States of America
99 98 97 96 95 94 93 92 91 90                     5 4 3 2 1

Library of Congress Cataloging-in-Publication Data
The Limits of rationality / edited by Karen Schweers Cook and Margaret
Levi.
   p.  cm.
   Includes bibliographical references.
   ISBN 0–226–74238–5 (cloth). —ISBN 0–226–74239–3 (paper)
   1. Social change.  2. Social choice.  3. Decision-making.
   4. Reasoning.  I. Cook, Karen S.  II. Levi, Margaret.
   HM101.L495  1990                 90–30048
   303.4—dc20                            CIP

⊗ The paper used in this publication meets the minimum requirements of the American National Standard for Information Sciences—Permanence of Paper for Printed Library Materials, ANSI Z39.48-1984.

"Explain all that," said the Mock Turtle to Alice. "No, no! The adventures first," said the Gryphon in an impatient tone: "explanations take such a dreadful time."

—Lewis Carroll

# CONTENTS

# ACKNOWLEDGMENTS

The preparation of this book was made possible by various organizations and people. The College of Arts and Sciences and the Graduate School of the University of Washington provided the primary funding for the colloquium series which initiated this undertaking. Contributions to the colloquium series were also received from the departments of economics, philosophy, political science, psychology, and sociology. We especially appreciate the help of Dean Ernest Henley. Support from a National Science Foundation grant (SES8519319) to Karen Cook for related work made additional time and resources available for which we are grateful.

Jodi O'Brien served as the tireless and extremely competent research assistant in charge of the myriad details required to bring this project to fruition. Mary MacGregor, Peter Kelley, Pamela Oakes, and Hien Tran provided frequent staff support. Various graduate students provided input and encouragement along the way: Howard Faye, Jodi O'Brien, Malka Appelbaum-Maizel, Steve DeTray, Daniel Jackson, Peter Kollock, Sara Singleton, and Joseph Whitmeyer. The contributors not only provided the contents of the book, but also were patient, timely, and supportive. It has been a pleasure for us to work with each one.

# INTRODUCTION
# The Limits of Rationality
## Margaret Levi, Karen S. Cook,
## Jodi A. O'Brien, and Howard Faye

> It is only by the close consideration of reasons for failure that it will
> be possible to construct a more general account of human behavior
> in which the concept of rationality will have a privileged but not
> exclusive role.
>
> Elster 1986, 21

Our major aim in this volume is to evaluate the limits of social science
models based on rationality. Just what is it rational choice models can
and cannot do? Although we believe that practitioners of rational choice
theory already familiar with these issues will find this book useful, our
primary audience is scholars interested in the approach but still relatively
new to it. The book is organized to illuminate the paradigm itself as well
as to clarify the nature of the current controversies.

A second purpose is to enable the readers to understand what scholars
across disciplines have to say. Rational choice theory is deeply interdisciplinary. Its major theorists include political scientists, sociologists, philosophers, and psychologists, as well as economists. More often than
not, theorists from different disciplines speak different languages. This
presents a stumbling block to someone trying to discover what rational
choice theory has to offer. It also means that scholars in one discipline
sometimes fail to realize what ground has already proved fertile in another.

A third purpose is to make a case for a particular line of research. We
believe that it is possible to reduce the existing limits of models based on
rationality and that rational choice theory can produce even more powerful explanations of group processes, organizational behavior, and
other non-market behavior, that is, the stuff of political science and sociology. Such an enterprise, however, requires a careful investigation of
what the limits of the theory actually are and of the efficacy of proposed
solutions. In particular, we argue that the future of rational choice theory
lies in analyses of norms and institutions.

1

The volume itself is loosely based on a colloquium series organized by the co-editors at the University of Washington in the autumn of 1985. A primary motivation for the colloquium series and this book is to explore the "limits of rationality" conceived by those who possess some sympathy for the basic model but whose work raises questions meant to improve the approach. Papers were presented by Gary Becker, James Coleman, Jon Elster, Russell Hardin, Daniel Kahneman, Mark Machina, Charles Plott, and Michael Taylor, all of whom contributed chapters to the book. The coherence of the volume required the inclusion of several additional viewpoints; thus, papers were also solicited from Margaret Levi, Douglass North, Gary Miller, and Arthur Stinchcombe. Because our primary purpose is to evaluate the paradigm and to increase cross-disciplinary communication, we solicited comments from other scholars who have contributed to the debates surrounding rational choice theory. These scholars include Andrew Abbott, Robert Bates, William Bianco, Geoffrey Brennan, John Broome, Karen Cook, Robert Goodin, Michael Hechter, Carol Heimer, Stephen Majeski, and Jodi O'Brien. The commentaries broaden our treatment of the limits of rationality and help to extend the theory beyond its deep roots in economics.

The rational choice paradigm has benefited from, but is also limited by, its intellectual origins. Rational choice models are derived from utilitarian theory, neoclassical economics, and game theory. Utilitarianism supplies the ultimate concern with how to achieve overall social welfare. Neoclassical economics provides a theoretical model and a set of sophisticated methodologies for the investigation of social and political questions. Game theory introduces strategic behavior into the neoclassical model.

The emphasis on social welfare, especially the formulation of Pareto optimality, is sometimes problematic, however. "Efficient" solutions to utilitarian dilemmas are often impossible. Concern with democracy, justice, or some other value or principle can produce irresolvable conflicts with economic efficiency. Nor are there always determinant economic welfare solutions, as chaos theorems, the folk theorem, and other mathematical exercises have demonstrated.

Particularly in its "public choice" form, rational-choice theory was, for a long time, no more than an extension of neoclassical economic theory applied to political institutions and behavior. We find ourselves sharing an increasingly widespread concern that the rationality attributed to *homo economicus* is too simplistic or else simply wrong when applied to actors in many political and social situations. Economics assumes consumer sovereignty, equality of power, and a dynamic equilibrium. These assumptions are tenable in the realm of price theory. They are not always useful in understanding the state, protest behavior, conflict, and other dimensions of the political and social worlds we inhabit. Noncritical and straightforward applications of economic theory to nonmarket phenomena lead to a neglect of many of the most interesting aspects of those problems.

One response to the concern with the limits of economic theory is the introduction of strategic interaction into the model. Game theorists demonstrate that when the outcome depends upon an aggregation of individual choices, what each of us chooses affects and is affected by the choices others make. The interdependence of choices means that individual actions may have unintended consequences. Moreover, as the rules of the game change, so do the strategic interactions as well as the possible consequences, whether intended or unintended.

Although game theory has extended the power of rational choice models, it has not removed all the limitations inherent in these models. Rational choice remains a simplifying approach that does not always capture the complexity of political and social relationships. If this were solely a problem of filling in the detail, the critique would not be that consequential. The more disturbing claim is made that rational choice models produce misleading explanations of protest behavior, long-term secular change, social order, and other problems investigated by rational choice theorists. This key issue frames much of the debate and dialogue in *The Limits of Rationality*.

The book is organized into three parts: a critique of the basic theory; the introduction of preference formation and norms into the model; and the incorporation of institutional arrangements into the model.

## PART I: THE THEORY OF RATIONAL CHOICE

Is rational choice theory a version of utilitarian philosophy or is it a theory meant to produce testable hypotheses? To many of its practitioners it is both. Yet, the normative and descriptive/predictive models of rational choice derive from separate traditions. Each has its own corresponding research agenda.

The normative tradition of rational choice posits criteria by which to adjudge whether or not individual behavior is rational; it claims that, in principle, rational behavior enables individuals to achieve their goals; and then it deduces what must be the best institutional arrangements for the given ends. This is the stuff of theories of justice à la Rawls or arguments for citizen sovereignty à la Buchanan and Tullock.

The descriptive approach to rational choice focuses on the pattern of observable choices. Individuals are assumed to be rational actors whose choices and their outcomes can be predicted, given knowledge of the rules of the game and the set of alternative choices.

The question of what, exactly, constitutes the standard of rationality is the focus of major debate. For example, Elster argues for a definition based on internal consistency between actions and beliefs, while Machina focuses on the transitivity of preferences. Although both the normative and descriptive approaches seem to rest on specific definitions of rational action, occasional slippage between normative and descriptive elements tends to obscure important distinctions. Those economists who argue for the market as the model of all institutional arrangements confuse matters even further.

One fundamental issue raised about either variant of the theory is the extent to which rational choice assumptions are sufficiently "realistic." If the rational actor of the model bears little resemblance to those who actually make choices and decisions, the model "fails" both normatively and descriptively.

The many problems associated with determining what rational choice theory is and evaluating its standing led us to call on the major participants in this debate for background material. In part I, far more than the others, we have relied on previously published articles. Elster and Tversky and Kahneman argue that rational choice theory "fails" as a predictive theory. Brennan and Broome concur but argue for its important normative role. Machina defends the behavioral assumptions of utility theory once they have been modified to fit conditions of uncertainty. Plott demonstrates that, while the assumption of individual rationality may not hold, its predictions do in some important cases. Cook and O'Brien summarize additional empirical and theoretical issues that enable rational choice to retain some of its power as a descriptive theory.

Elster is specifically concerned with the extent to which rational motivations and choices underlie human behavior. For Elster, rationality is operative if beliefs and desires are logically consistent with the perceived environment and with each other and if the actions of the actors stand in an optimizing relationship to those beliefs and desires. Reasoning deductively and with this standard of rationality as his guide, he proceeds to evaluate applications of rational choice theory to a wide range of phenomena in a great diversity of disciplines. The general effort to delineate the appropriate scope of the theory suggests when and why rationality "fails."

There are two major sources of opposition to Elster's line of argument. One is reflected in Brennan's response that rationality fails long before we get to the conceptual complications Elster raises. Brennan argues that the standard version of rational choice theory requires a separate set of assumptions regarding preferences and is, therefore, logically incapable of predicting action based on the actor's attempts to maximize beliefs or desires. In Brennan's view, rational choice theory can predict actions only when it includes substantive claims concerning the content of the actor's utility function. The assumption of *homo economicus* in economics is illustrative here. Brennan concludes that rational choice is more suited to normative than descriptive theory.

Tversky and Kahneman come to similar conclusions about the limits of rational choice theory, but they bring to bear the perspective of psychologists concerned with the cognitive limitations. Certainly, rational choice theorists ignore at their peril the seminal contributions of Herbert Simon (1957), Leon Festinger (1957), and other major cognitive theorists.[1] Herbert Simon (1957) and his followers posit cognitive limitations on the computational capacity of actors and claim (Simon 1984) that these limits are quite distinct from the external information costs that concern economists.[2] Cognitive theories rest on models of bounded rationality in contrast to maximization. In the maximizing model, improved information will increase "rationality," and the lack of information is often the determinant of what seems to be irrational variations in preferences. For Simon, the causes of variation are the psychological constraints that affect choice even when information is easily obtained.

Tversky and Kahneman offer new evidence on and a new theory to account for the cognitive processes that make it difficult for individuals to reach rational decisions, even if that is their intention. In particular, Kahneman and Tversky demonstrate that the framing and transparency of choice sets influence decisions that lead to choices inconsistent with the assumed standards of rationality.

1. Elster (1983, esp. chap. 3) offers an interesting discussion of the relationship between cognitive processes and the theory of rationality.
2. For a review of the literature on information costs, see Moe (1984).

At first glance, the research of Tversky and Kahneman appears quite damaging to the standard theory of rational choice. Machina disagrees and presents one economist's reply to the challenges put forth by cognitive psychology. His nonexpected utility theory is a sophisticated, mathematically derived alternative model of rational behavior under conditions of uncertainty.

Machina concedes that one of the points at issue is whether economic analysis, or more generally rational choice, is best understood as predictive of rational behavior, a normative question, or of observed behavior, a descriptive problem. Broome focuses on this distinction to make the argument that the essays of both Tversky and Kahneman and Machina render quite plausible the conclusion that, in and of itself, expected utility theory is inadequate as a descriptive and predictive theory of people's actual preferences. Even more firmly than Brennan, he explicitly acknowledges the potential for the complete "failure" of the model. For him, the theory exists only for one reason: to guide actual decision making.

Plott, an economist, examines the role of rational choice theory in the experimental work on markets. The primary research objective for experimental economists, according to Plott, is "to construct simple markets that are special cases of the complicated phenomena to which the markets are ordinarily applied." In light of the findings these models are modified with the aim of improving their predictive accuracy when applied to increasingly complex phenomena.

Experimentalists typically evaluate alternative economic models rather than attempt to identify specific instances in which the rational choice axioms fail, the primary strategy adopted by cognitive psychologists. When results are obtained by economists that fail to fit their model of aggregate-level outcomes, elements of the model are revised or given new parameters (see Plott's discussion of the early oral auction experiments). Generally results are found to be consistent with market-level predictions even when violations of the individual-level postulates, upon which the model is based, occur.

Cook and O'Brien discuss the work on experimental economics in juxtaposition to the other pieces in this section, especially the work of Kahneman and Tversky which identifies instances in which the basic postulates fail. Even though Plott and Machina adopt a somewhat "defensive" tone, both argue that the pessimism regarding the utility of rational choice models is not justified. Cook and O'Brien emphasize that fundamental differences, not only in purpose, but also in levels of analysis and the scope of the theories at issue account for many of the discrepancies between the work of economists and psychologists; it is these discrepancies that form the bulk of the recent challenges to the rational choice paradigm.

## PART II: THE ROLE OF PREFERENCE FORMATION AND NORMS

The critiques of rational choice models in the first section suggest that a fuller theory of human action may require greater understanding of the formation and ordering of the preferences that constitute an individual's utility function. Two observations support this viewpoint. First, even putatively similar individuals vary significantly in their choices, presumably because of significant variations in their preferences or, at least, preference orderings. Second, despite the assumption of fixed and transitive preferences, individuals make inconsistent and nonrational decisions. These observations are problematic for rational choice theory because it claims to explain the outcome of aggregate decisions based on assumptions of individual rationality. If preferences vary for idiosyncratic reasons and if preferences are not transitive, then rational-choice theory will have little explanatory power.

The exploration of the role of preferences raises questions about the basic data of rational choice theories. Amartya Sen has suggested (1973) that the distinction between behavior, "true" preferences, and some other basis for utilities (such as "welfare") have not been clearly analyzed in the theoretical literature of rational choice. Despite the standard reliance on revealed preference as congruent with actual or "true" preference, the data on which to base an evaluation of the preferences and rationality of actors is not straightforwardly behavioral. The use of revealed preference blends the decision act with the preference that informs it. For example, Buridan's ass chose neither of two equally nourishing and equidistant haystacks and consequently died of starvation. If we accept this behavior as evidence of revealed preference, we conclude that the ass was indifferent between the two haystacks. Do we also conclude that it preferred death to life? A more satisfying hypothesis is that Buridan's ass had such serious problems in making decisions, any decisions, that its procrastination led to its death. Its choice was the result of cognitive factors that affected its preferences and not just the preferences themselves.

Dependence on behavioral data alone also obscures the importance of the social context of choice. The examples provided by Tversky and Kahneman in their chapter in part I emphasize the effects of "framing"

7

on a decision. An even more telling example is the Hobbesian world where rational individuals prefer security to war but cannot obtain their collective preference. Their behavior reflects their preferences within a particular context, that is, a world without enforceable contracts, but is not indicative of their preferences overall.

We argue for a theory of rational choice that includes the context of decisions as well as the decisions themselves. In particular, while acknowledging cognitive limitations, we wish to focus on the norms and institutions that constrain behavior. Currently there are three identifiable directions for significant theoretical development. The first is a more sophisticated elaboration of utility theory that would enable it to account for previously unexplained behavioral variation. The second is a fuller recognition of the cognitive limitations on individual decision-makers, that is, the case of Buridan's ass. The third is a more explicit recognition and modeling of the social context of choice, including the normative and institutional components.

George Stigler and Gary Becker have made the most persuasive case to date for maintaining the assumption of fixed and unchanging preferences, whatever the "frame" or context of the decision and whatever the cognitive limitations of the individual decision-maker. To explain variation in individual choice from their perspective requires only a more sophisticated account of relative price changes. They claim that tastes, which they merge with preferences, are stable over time and fairly invariant among people. For them, the crucial determinant of beneficial and harmful addictions, fads, and habits is the "accumulation of specific knowledge and skills" in the form of "consumption capital." Put simply, the more time and experience one invests in a taste, the more one will prefer the goods that cater to that taste. Alternatively, the less consumption capital one has invested, the less one is likely to prefer something that reflects that "taste."

Stigler and Becker are arguing against the need for a model of preference formation distinct from a theory of household production. Robert Goodin finds Stigler and Becker incapable of accounting for many of the kinds of phenomena a theory of endogenous preference formation would help to explain. The assumption of relatively invariant preferences does not do away with the fact of widely varying preferences. In Goodin's view, their failure to provide an account of the origin of the preferences that investments affect is a serious flaw. He does not find the Stigler and Becker model helpful in understanding even preferences for basic consumer staples; without a theory of preference formation, it is impossible to understand why the initial consumption decisions of individuals are so different.

In the division of labor academics practice, the problem of the origins of preference is probably best left to those who specialize in problems of cognitive development and to those concerned with the effects of culture and socialization on cognitive processes.[3] Other social scientists—for example, many political scientists, sociologists, economists, and anthropologists—specialize more in understanding the contexts in which choices are made. Before dismissing inconsistent and varying relationships between preferences and outcomes as outside the scope of rational-choice theory, however, it is useful to explore more carefully the capacities of models of rational choice. We have already discussed some fine-tuning of utility theory to encompass more sophisticated accounts of the effects of changes in investments and relative prices and of the role of information costs. Now we wish to turn to the role of norms.

Since the publication of Talcott Parson's magnum opus, *The Structure of Social Action* (1937), social scientists have tended to accept a dichotomy between explanations based on norms and those based on rational calculations.[4] In the last several decades, rational-choice theorists, particularly game theorists, have argued that some norms can be understood as the result of rational calculations. Two of the pioneers are James Coleman (1973) and Michael Taylor (1987 [1976]), although the general approach has been popularized most recently by Robert Axelrod (1984).

In their chapters, both Taylor and Coleman address the conditions under which actors will engage in cooperative behavior that resolves collective action problems. Collective action is considered a problem precisely because it represents a situation in which it is rational for each individual to refuse to cooperate even though the result will be the suboptimal provision of the collective good individuals desire. Taylor and Coleman perceive that cooperation does seem to emerge as a solution in some instances, but they reject the "sociological" characterization of cooperative behavior as an extrarational and exogenous solution to be labeled normative (see the discussion in Hechter 1987).

Taylor classifies the possible solutions to the collective action problem. He lays out the necessary conditions for internal, decentralized solutions

3. Some social exchange theorists, such as Homans (1974) offer operant conditioning as the source of preferences. On the other hand, there is an increasingly popular cultural approach as found in Wildavsky (1987) and others.
4. Hechter (1987, esp. chap. 2) provides a review, discussion, and critique of this dichotomy.

that will produce "spontaneous cooperation." These solutions require neither changes in the structure of the game nor the reliance on a central authority such as a state, but they do require individuals to discount the future at a relatively low rate and for the universe of potential cooperators to be of a size that permits knowledge of each other's choices.

Taylor goes on to discuss external solutions that require changes in the game through the restructuring of the perceptions, attitudes, or beliefs of the actors involved. In the Parsonian view, socially constructed norms constitute one such external solution. For Taylor, this is nonsensical since such a definition of norms either attaches them to sanctions for defection, which makes the sanctions and not the norms the explanatory factor, or internalizes them as preferences, which makes the solution internal and dependent on cognitive, not social, processes.

James Coleman also relies on game theory to explore the conditions under which norms of cooperation will emerge. He proposes that the "social structure of interaction," a notion borrowed from Axelrod (1984), determines the probability of the success of norms that induce cooperation. The more numerous the recollected interactions with the same players and the greater the degree of "closure," that is, the nonpermeability of a social structure to outsiders, the more likely is the emergence of norms that promote cooperation. One of his most interesting assertions is that a universe of freely associating individuals provides the poorest social structure for generating effective norms of cooperation.

Taylor and Coleman concur on the importance of iterated interactions among rational actors as a crucial precondition for cooperation. However, as Michael Hechter points out in his comments on Taylor, repeated plays of the game among the same players can produce multiple equilibria, not all of which solve collective action problems. Hechter also claims that internal solutions to the supergame, which are at the heart of both the Taylor and Coleman chapters, rest on several problematic assumptions: perfect information; the ability of the players to pick an appropriate discount rate given the uncertainty of the game's length; and the possibility of meeting the costs of monitoring.

Hechter proposes an alternative to the game theoretic formulation. He argues that cooperation evolves in two stages. First, individuals become dependent on a group that produces joint private goods the individuals desire. Second, the group is then able to establish formal controls and rules that inhibit defection.

Stephen Majeski also takes issue with the game theoretic approach.

Majeski argues that many rational-choice theorists tend to conflate norms with the behavior that is being identified as norm compliant. For instance, how does one distinguish between actions that are motivated by retaliation, strategic interest, or norms? In Majeski's view, norms are rules that are culturally specific. They are cognitively and socially constructed on the basis of precedent. They can be observed separately from the behaviors they are called on to explain. Most importantly, conceived this way, he argues, they have considerable explanatory power in accounting for an individuals' preference ordering and consequent decision making.

## Part III: Institutions

In the pieces by Michael Taylor and James Coleman, we see rational choice theorists turning to the explanation of the emergence of norms. Arthur Stinchcombe, Gary Miller, Russell Hardin, Douglass North, and Margaret Levi focus their attention on explanations of the emergence and transformation of institutions.

The investigation of institutions possesses a long and distinguished history in the social sciences, but in past decades it suffered a decline as behaviorism claimed center stage. Renewed interest has encouraged numerous scholars to include themselves or to find themselves included among the "new institutionalists" (March and Olsen 1984). Yet, despite the increasingly lengthy bibliography of institutional research, some of the crucial questions remain unanswered. Some even remain unasked.

One of the most important tasks of rational choice institutionalism is to account for the variation in institutional arrangements. There is the question of long-term secular change. Equally important is the question of diversity among the formalized structures that organize individual actors into collectivities. Firms can be vastly dissimilar from each other, but, even so, do they share similarities that markedly distinguish them from non-market institutions?

There are at least three forms of rational choice institutionalism. The first derives from the work of Max Weber. Its central concern is with rationalization, that is, with the formalization of decision making based on a few reasoned paradigms. Arthur Stinchcombe's article builds on this perspective. He is concerned with the long-term relationship between reason, defined as "a socially established method of calculating what should be authoritative in a particular case," and rationality, defined as "individual behavior that maximizes benefits and minimizes costs." In particular, he wants to understand what makes for "better" institutions of reason. In addition, he claims that modern institutions of reason tend to improve the rationality of the individuals within them by removing uncertainty and by permitting the individual to rely on the reasons established through time and experience. Thus, Stinchcombe is arguing that it is institutions rather than cognitive processes that, in many cases, account for variations in rationality. Institutions can remove some of the limits.

Andrew Abbott, also a sociologist, finds the Stinchcombe account attractive, but flawed. He takes Stinchcombe to task for both functionalism and an overemphasis on evolutionary processes. Abbott does not concur with Stinchcombe that "better" institutions necessarily evolve.

The second approach to institutions derives from Marxism and other macrohistorical approaches. The emphasis is on the economic, political, and social structures that affect each other as well as individual behavior. Douglass North, with his emphasis on property rights, and Russell Hardin, with his emphasis on the role of power, are both influenced by this perspective. It would be more accurate, however, to credit them with a crucial role in developing the third approach to institutions, one that derives from neoclassical economics, game theory, and other theories of rational choice. In this perspective, which Gary Miller shares, institutions are built by and change in response to the aggregation of individual actions. What distinguishes the perspective of these scholars from the more narrow approach of microeconomics, including its public choice variant, is their consideration of how institutions themselves, once established, affect choices.

Neoclassical economics traditionally ignored institutions. There are indeed some famous institutional economists such as John Commons, but they were the exceptions that proved the rule. Consumer sovereignty prevailed, and any arrangements that stood in the way of the market allocation of resources were considered "imperfections." Only recently have those imperfections undergone close scrutiny as recurring and normal aspects of economic, let alone political and social, life. Even today, there are those whose reaction is fundamentally normative; for them nearly all obstacles to pure freedom of choice should be eliminated.

It is really with Ronald Coase that the rational choice institutionalism began—although his insights were not fully explored until quite recently. The focus of his seminal paper on social costs (1960) was on specifying the conditions under which private costs and social costs diverged, given zero transaction costs and perfectly specified property rights. His concern with the sources of inefficient institutions began to cast doubt on the assumption of Pareto efficiency that lays at the base of most economic analyses.

A primary objective of rational choice institutionalism is to account for why institutions are sometimes efficient and sometimes not. The necessary building block for such an explanation derives from another important insight of Coase's (1937), the role of transaction costs.[5] Transaction costs refer to the costs of capturing, bargaining, measuring, monitoring, and enforcing property rights. They are among the costs associated with increasing productivity in the workplace or achieving compliance with state policies. Yet, they are costs economists have traditionally assumed to be zero.

Miller takes up a similar problem to Stinchcombe's, namely the conditions under which institutions enable people to act rationally, but he is also concerned with what makes institutions economically efficient. Miller's focus is on the firm and other organizations in which the laws of the market do not prevail but in which efficiency in the form of productivity is at issue. He starts with the paradoxical evidence that even when people do not act rationally as individuals, the outcome of their aggregate decision making can be rational. He finds that institutional arrangements with the proper mix of incentives and disincentives is only partially the answer. At least equally important, Miller finds, is leadership that motivates people to engage in greater effort.

Robert Bates and William Bianco applaud Miller's use of a rational choice perspective that is distinct from microeconomics and his integration of game theory and behavioralism. However, drawing on their own research on the same question, they claim that an overreliance on game theory blinds Miller to crucial institutional factors, incentives, and leadership characteristics that could change the predicted outcome. Even so, they credit Miller with leading the way toward an ultimately more satisfying and institutionally rich theory of rational choice.

Miller and Bates and Bianco place some emphasis on strategic interactions, that is, the ways in which the choices of one individual or one group of individuals affect the choices of others. It is Russell Hardin, however, who makes strategic behavior central to the investigation of institutional change. Hardin posits an explanation of the evolution of a particularly important institution: the state. Deriving his arguments from game theory, he claims that coordination logically precedes power as the essential tool of the state. Thus, for Hardin, Adam Smith is more suc-

5. See Coase's (1937) seminal article. Also, see more recent work by Alchian and Demsetz (1972); Williamson (1985); and Barzel (1989).

cessful than Thomas Hobbes in accounting for the theoretical origins of the state. Hardin, however, goes on to demonstrate that power can facilitate cooperation which in turn enhances the power of the state. As in Miller's account of institutional variation, leadership is crucial to the nature of institutional arrangements, but Hardin argues that the qualities of the person embodying the leadership role are less important than the resources available to any talented leader or than the likely strategic responses of the "led."

Carol Heimer's comments rest on the belief that Hardin may have uncovered in coordination an important and understudied aspect of power. Her aim is to make coordination susceptible to empirical investigation. She illuminates how geographical, status, and cultural variables may make coordination easier or harder. In the process of making coordination analyzable, Heimer contributes to one of the most crucial enterprises confronting the rational-choice paradigm: transforming its insights into testable hypotheses.

Douglass North focuses on how institutions evolve in order to reduce the transaction costs of interactions among individuals. For North, an institution represents a contractual relationship. Changes in relative prices lead to recontracting, which in turn leads to institutional change. Like Stinchcombe, he is concerned with change and development in institutions, but unlike Stinchcombe he does not claim that the result is steadily progressive. For North, institutions can deteriorate as well as get "better" over time.

The chapter by Margaret Levi investigates both what an institution is and one source of institutional change. Her emphasis is on the social interactions and relationships of power that comprise an institution. An institution rests on an ongoing set of bargains among the actors who set its rules, those who carry them out, and those who must comply. Their cooperation with each other is conditional; one actor's fulfillment of institutional responsibilities is contingent upon what others do. The breaking of the social bargain can lead to the withdrawal of consent or the refusal to comply, which can alter the distribution of resources of power within the institution and, consequently, precipitate institutional change.

The rational choice approach to institutions is certainly one form of the "new institutionalism." But, most of what passes for the "new institutionalism" represents a response to the behaviorism and behavioralism of the 1960s. It is a structuralism that pays little attention to the construction of choices. The essays in part III represent, in contrast, a re-

14

sponse to the neglect of factors that actually explain behavior and choice. An emphasis on context should not be confused with the structuralism that dominates so much of political science and sociology. We are not arguing that an understanding of context is sufficient. Rather, we are claiming that an adequate explanatory theory must begin with individuals whose choices, even within a given set of rules, affect the choices of others and, often, have unintended consequences.

The rational choice approach to institutions is concerned both with how human actions combine to create institutions and how existing institutions structure individual and aggregate choices. Moreover, the very origin of the norms and institutions that constrain behavior lie in individual choices. The recognition that the rules individuals establish affect the subsequent choices individuals make improves the model without sacrificing theoretical rigor.

A theory of rational choice provides the basis for both normative and empirical research. It is normative in the sense that the assumption of rationality provides a model of human identity and action from which is derived appropriate procedures for obtaining human objectives. It is empirical to the extent it offers predictive and explanatory accounts of human action. Given that both of the co-editors of this volume are committed to using the model to advance empirical research, we have selected articles and organized the volume to reflect a concern less with the design of policies and institutions than with the explanation of those that occur.

The major theoretical task this volume takes on is to strike a balance between the elements of the rational choice model that make it realistic with those that make it powerful. This requires a theory of choice that reflects, more or less accurately, how people make choices. More importantly it must explain, parsimoniously, what they actually do. It requires a theory that integrates individual-level analysis with the analysis of macro-phenomena. This means a theory in which rational, strategic actors both create and are constrained by the societal rules that are embedded in norms and institutions.

## REFERENCES

Alchian, Armen, and Harold M. Demsetz. 1972. "Production, Information Costs, and Economic Organization." *American Economic Review* 62 (December): 777–95.

Arrow, Kenneth. 1951, rev. 1963. *Social Choice and Individual Values*. New York: John Wiley & Sons.

Axelrod, Robert. 1984. *The Evolution of Cooperation.* New York: Basic Books.

Barzel, Yoram. 1989. *Economic Analysis of Property Rights.* New York: Cambridge University Press.

Black, Duncan. 1948. "The Decisions of a Committee Using a Special Majority." *Econometrica* 16 (July): 245–61.

Coase, Ronald. 1937. "The Nature of the Firm." *Economica* (November): 386–407.

———. 1960. "The Problem of Social Cost." *Journal of Law and Economics* 3:1–44.

Coleman, James S. 1973. *The Mathematics of Collective Action.* Chicago: Aldine.

Elster, Jon. 1983. *Explaining Technical Change.* New York and Cambridge: Cambridge University Press.

———, ed. 1986. *Rational Choice.* Oxford: Basil Blackwell.

Emerson, Richard. 1987. "Toward A Theory of Value in Social Exchange." In *Social Exchange Theory,* pp. 11–46 edited by Karen Cook. Beverly Hills: Sage.

Festinger, Leon. 1957. *A Theory of Cognitive Dissonance.* Stanford: Stanford University Press.

Hechter, Michael. 1987. *Principles of Group Solidarity.* Berkeley: University of California Press.

Hogarth, Robin, and Melvin Reder, eds. 1987. *Rational Choice.* Chicago: University of Chicago Press.

Homans, George. 1974 [1961]. *Social Behavior: Its Elementary Form,* 2d ed. New York: Harcourt Brace Jovanovich.

March, James, G. 1978. "Bounded Rationality, Ambiguity, and the Engineering of Choice." *Bell Journal of Economics* 9, no. 2: 587–608.

March, James G., and Johan P. Olsen. 1984. "The New Institutionalism: Organizational Factors in Political Life." *APSR* 78 (September): 734–49.

Moe, Terry M. 1984. "The New Economics of Organization." *American Journal of Political Science* 28, no. 4 (November): 739–77.

Olson, Mancur, Jr. 1965. *The Logic of Collective Action.* Cambridge: Harvard University Press.

Parsons, Talcott. 1937. *The Structure of Social Action.* New York: McGraw-Hill.

Sen, A. K. 1973. "Behavior and the Concept of Preference." *Econometrica* 40 (August): 241–59.

Simon, Herbert. 1957. *Models of Man.* New York: Wiley and Sons.

———. 1984. "Human Nature in Politics: The Dialogue of Psychology with Political Science." *APSR* 79, no. 2 (June): 293–304.

Taylor, Michael. 1987 [1976]. *The Possibility of Cooperation.* Cambridge and New York: Cambridge University Press.

Wildavsky, Aaron. 1987. "Choosing Preferences by Constructing Institutions: A Cultural Theory of Preference Formation." *APSR* 81, no. 1 (March): 3–21.

Williamson, Oliver E. 1985. *The Economic Institutions of Capitalism.* New York: The Free Press.

# PART ONE
# The Theory of
# Rational Choice

# 1

# When Rationality Fails

## Jon Elster

### Introduction

There are two ways in which theories can fail to explain: through indeterminacy and through inadequacy. A theory is indeterminate when and to the extent that it fails to yield unique predictions. It is inadequate when its predictions fail. Of these, the second is the more serious problem. A theory may be less than fully determinate and yet have explanatory power if it excludes at least one abstractly possible event or state of affairs. To yield a determinate prediction, it must then be supplemented by other considerations. The theory is weak, but not useless. It is in more serious trouble if the event or state of affairs that actually materializes is among those excluded by the theory. In saying this, I am not espousing naive falsificationism, but simply making the common-sense observation that it is worse for a theory to predict wrongly than to predict weakly but truthfully.[1] In the former case it must be replaced or modified, not supplemented.

My concern here is not with scientific theories in general, but with failures of rational choice theory. As argued below, rational choice theory is first and foremost a normative theory and only secondarily an explanatory approach. It tells people how to act and predicts that they will act in the way the theory tells them to. To the extent that it fails to give unambiguous prescriptions, it is indeterminate. To the extent that people fail to follow its prescriptions—to the extent, that is, that they behave irrationally—the theory is inadequate. The inadequacy of the theory is closely intertwined with that of indeterminacy. I argue, in fact, that *fail-*

This chapter also appeared, in somewhat extended form, as chapter one of the author's book, *Solomonic Judgements* (Cambridge: Cambridge University Press, 1989).

1. The Popperian view that it is better to predict strongly than weakly, because strong predictions are more likely to be falsified and therefore more surprising if not falsified, is quite consistent with this assertion. Popper was concerned with the *ex ante* choice of research strategy, whereas I am here discussing *ex post* properties of predictions.

*ure to recognize the indeterminacy of rational choice theory can lead to irrational behavior.*

The theory of rational choice is constrained at both ends. On the one hand, the notion of rationality has to be independently plausible as a normative account of human behavior. On the other hand, it has to yield prescriptions about particular cases that fit our preanalytical notions about what is rational in such cases. These notions are somewhat elastic. As we construct a theory of what is rational, some intuitions about what is rational in particular contexts may change. In particular, theory may force determinacy on our intuitions in situations where initially they were indeterminate. The theoretical notion of an equilibrium, for instance, can serve as guide to intuition and action when otherwise we would not know what to think or to do. Other, more recalcitrant, intuitions can force us to modify the theory.[2]

In what follows, I first set out the bare bones of rational choice theory (section II), including a discussion of whether desires can be rational. I then consider failures of rationality that are due to lack of determinacy (section III), and go on to discuss failures due to lack of adequacy (section IV). In the final section I briefly discuss how rationality can be supplemented or replaced by other guides to action.

## II. RATIONAL ACTION[3]

As I said, rational choice theory is first and foremost normative. It tells us what we ought to do in order to achieve our aims as well as possible. It does not, in the standard version, tell us what our aims ought to be. (Some nonstandard comments on this problem are offered below.) From the normative account we can derive an explanatory theory by assuming that people are rational in the normatively appropriate sense. The privileged but not exclusive status of this assumption is discussed in section V.

The central explananda of rational choice theory are *actions*. To explain an action, we must first verify that it stands in an optimizing relationship to the desires and beliefs of the agent. The action should be the best way of satisfying the agent's desires, given his beliefs. Moreover, we must demand that these desires and beliefs be themselves rational. At the very least, they must be internally consistent. With respect to beliefs we must also impose a more substantive requirement of rationality: they

2. For an example, see Elster (1984, 121, note 17). A recent debate of similar issues in Binmore (1987).
3. The following draws heavily on Elster (1983, chap. 1) and Elster (1986b).

20

should be optimally related to the evidence available to the agent. (The substantive rationality of desires is discussed below.) In forming their beliefs, the agents should consider all and only the relevant evidence, with no element being unduly weighted. As a logical extension of this requirement, we also demand that the collection of evidence itself be subject to the canons of rationality. The efficacy of action may be destroyed both by gathering too little evidence and by gathering too much. The optimal amount of evidence is partly determined by our desires. More important decisions make it rational to collect more evidence. Partly it is determined by our prior beliefs about the likely cost, quality and relevance of various types of evidence. Schematically, these relations can be represented as follows:

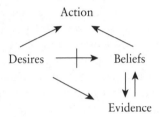

Rational action, then, involves three optimizing operations: finding the best action, for given beliefs and desires; forming the best-grounded belief, for given evidence; and collecting the right amount of evidence, for given desires and prior beliefs. Here, desires are the unmoved movers, reflecting Hume's dictum that "Reason is, and ought only to be the slave of the passions" (Hume [1739] 1960, 415). In saying this, he did not mean that reason ought to obey every whim and fancy of the passions. In particular, he would not have endorsed the direct shaping of reason by passion found in wishful thinking, illustrated by the blocked arrow in the diagram. To serve his master well, a slave must have some independence of execution: beliefs born of passion serve passion badly (Veyne 1976, 667).

It follows from this sketch that rational choice theory can go wrong at three levels and that in each case the failure may be due either to indeterminacy or to irrationality. There may not exist a uniquely optimal action, belief or amount of evidence. Or people may fail to carry out the action, form the belief, or collect the evidence as rationality requires them to do. Such failures of rationality are discussed in sections III and IV of this chapter. Here, I want to consider whether one can impose substantive rationality conditions on the desires of the agent.[4] The first idea that comes to mind is that it is rational to have the desires and emotions having which tends to make one happy. The proposal, however, turns out to be flawed.

To have a strong desire for something that is manifestly out of reach can make one desperately unhappy. Sometimes it seems natural to say that such desires are irrational. A person with moderate means who is tormented by violent desires for expensive luxury goods might well be called irrational. But we would not usually say that a person who lives in a totalitarian regime is irrational if he does not get rid of the desire for freedom that makes him deeply miserable.[5] Human beings are more than happiness machines.

*Example 1: Psychiatric Treatment of Soviet Dissidents*
The Serbsky Institute for Forensic Psychiatry in Moscow has become notorious for its treatment of political dissidents as mentally ill. "Some psychiatrists have buttressed their argument about the dissenter's poor adaptation by pointing to the tenacity with which he acts out his beliefs despite the odds . . . The dissenter does indeed operate in dangerous territory; the reaction of the regime is often harsh. But he is fully aware of the risks inherent in his nonconformist behavior; his moral integrity compels him to take them. Some dissenters have parried the psychiatrists on this point by asking whether Lenin and his colleagues were 'poorly adapted' when, in their struggle against the tsarist régime, they were constantly subject to harassment and arrest" (Bloch and Reddaway 1978, 255).

If anything, it is the conformist—the happy slave—rather than the dissident who appears to be irrational. Unconscious adaptation to the inevitable is a heteronomous mechanism, while rational desires must be autonomous (Elster 1983, chap. 3). One cannot be rational if one is the plaything of psychic processes that, unbeknownst to oneself, shape one's desires and values. This preanalytical idea is at least as strong as the intuition that rational desires are desires which make one happy. Sometimes the two ideas point in the same direction. People who always most

4. I discuss this question in Elster (1983, chapters I.4 and III.4). For the closely related question as to whether it makes sense to assess emotional reactions as rational or irrational, see Elster (1985a).

5. We might want to say that, however, if his desire for freedom is caused by the fact that he does not have it. For a brief discussion of such "counteradaptive preferences" see Elster (1983, 111–12).

want what they cannot get are neither autonomous nor happy. People who adapt to their environment by a process of conscious character planning are both autonomous and happy (Elster 1983, 117–19). At other times, as with the unconscious conformist and the autonomous dissident, the two ideas diverge. Tocqueville captures this ambiguity of conformism when he asks, "Should I call it a blessing of God, or a last malediction of His anger, this disposition of the soul that makes men insensible to extreme misery and often even gives them a sort of depraved taste for the cause of their afflictions?" (Tocqueville 1969, 317).

Could one entertain a similar proposal with respect to belief rationality? Could one argue, that is, that it is rational to have the beliefs having which tends to make one happy? In general, we would expect that one's happiness is best promoted by having beliefs which are well grounded in the evidence, since these are, by definition, the beliefs most likely to be true. Successful action requires correct factual beliefs. Yet in special cases this connection fails. To keep away from dangerous substances it may be necessary to have an exaggerated notion about the dangers of drug abuse (Winston 1980). High levels of level of motivation and achievement often require an unrealistically positive self-image, whereas people with more accurate self-perceptions tend to lose the motivation to go on with the business of living. They are sadder, but wiser.[6]

### Example 2: Stability of Marriage

"Expectations about divorce are partly self-fulfilling because a higher expected probability of divorce reduces investments in specific capital and thereby raises the actual probability" (Becker 1981, 224). "It is far from clear that a bride and a groom would be well advised to believe, on their wedding day, that the probability of their divorce is as high as .40" (Nisbett and Ross 1981, 271). The low-probability expectations of divorce are only partly self-fulfilling. Our misplaced confidence in ourselves motivates us to achievements that make it somewhat less misplaced, but still less than fully justified.

A belief which is unjustified and indeed false may well be instrumentally useful, but it seems odd to call it rational. Rationality, as usually understood, is a variety of intentionality. For something to be rational, it has to be within the scope of conscious, deliberate action or reflection.

---

6. Lewinsohn et al. (1980); see also Alloy and Abrahamson (1979) and, for a discussion of their findings, Elster (1985a).

Useful false beliefs obtain by fluke, not by conscious reflection upon the evidence. Although one cannot in the short run choose one's desires or one's emotional patterns, one can over time shape and bend them to some extent. Beliefs, by contrast, resist manipulation for instrumental purposes. Believing at will, for the sake of the good consequences of having the belief, is a self-defeating enterprise because one cannot—conceptually cannot—at one and the same time believe something and believe that the belief has been adopted on noncognitive grounds.[7] It is easy, therefore, to understand why exhortations to self-esteem, propagated by manuals on self-help therapy, have very limited success (Quattrone and Tversky 1986, 48).

## III. INDETERMINACY

To explain and predict events or states of affairs, a theory must have determinate implications about what will happen under given initial conditions. Ideally, the implications should be not only determinate, but unique. Among all the possible events or states, exactly one should be singled out by the theory. Outside of quantum mechanics, this is the explanatory ideal of science. A theory which does not yield unique predictions is incomplete. It may still, of course, be vastly superior to having no theory at all. It can be very valuable to know that certain things will *not* happen. Also, for practical purposes, it may not matter much which of the events consistent with the theory is actually realized. This said, the prospect of unique prediction dominates and guides scientific work.

In economics, and increasingly in the other social sciences, the neoclassical theory of choice holds out the promise of uniqueness. By its relentless insistence that all behavior is maximizing it can draw on a basic mathematical theorem that says every well-behaved function has exactly one maximum in a well-behaved set.[8] Moreover, in economic contexts many functions and sets are well behaved in the relevant sense. For the consumer, there is usually exactly one consumption bundle that maximizes utility within the set of purchases that satisfy his budget constraint. For the producer, there is exactly one combination of the factors of production which maximizes profit per unit of output.

Here I discuss a variety of circumstances under which rational choice

---

7. For this argument, see Williams (1973) and Elster (1984, chap. II.3). A recent challenge by Cook (1987) places too much weight on a hypothetical example in which the belief adopted at will is also the one that is better grounded in the evidence. A nonhypothetical example of a decision to adopt an unfounded belief would have been more convincing.

8. Technically, the function must be continuous and the set be compact and convex.

theory fails to yield unique predictions. There may be *several* options that are equally and maximally good. More importantly, there may be *no* option with the property that it is at least as good as any other.

The problem of multiple optima is, with one notable exception, relatively trivial. It arises when the agent is indifferent between two or more alternatives, each of which is deemed superior to all others. In such cases, rational choice theory must be supplemented by other approaches to predict which of the equi-optimal alternatives will actually be chosen or "picked" (Ullmann-Margalit and Morgenbesser 1977). If they are very similar to each other, it is not important to be able to make this prediction. Nobody cares which of two identical soup cans on the supermarket shelf is chosen. If the options differ from each other in offsetting ways, as when a consumer is indifferent between two cars with different strengths and weaknesses, the choice is more consequential. The car dealers will certainly care about the choice. I believe, however, that most cases of this kind are better described by saying that the consumer is unable to rank and compare the options. If he really were indifferent, a reduction of one dollar in the price of one car should induce a clear preference, but I don't believe it usually would.

The exception referred to is game theory, in which multiple optima abound. In noncooperative games with solutions in mixed strategies it can be shown that an agent will always be indifferent between the strategy prescribed to him by the solution and any other linear combination of the pure strategies that enter into the solution, always assuming that the other players stick to their solution behavior. John Harsanyi argues that the lack of a good reason for the agent to conform to the solution in such cases is a flaw in game theory as traditionally conceived. In his substitute solution concept, only "centroid" or equi-probabilistic mixed strategies are allowed. This proposal reflects the idea that when there are several optima, one is chosen at random by "what amounts to an unconscious chance mechanism inside [the agent's] nervous system" (Harsanyi 1977, 114). Here, rational choice is supplemented by a purely causal mechanism.

Nonexistence of rational choice is a more serious difficulty than nonunicity. The problem arises at all three levels distinguished above: when gathering evidence, when deriving beliefs from the given evidence, and when deriving an action from the given beliefs and desires. I shall consider them in the reverse order.

If the agent has an incomplete preference ordering, that is, he is unable to compare and rank all the options in his feasible set, there may be no action that is optimal.[9] It would be misleading to say that the agent is irrational: having complete preferences is no part of what it means to be rational. On the contrary, to insist that preferences must be complete and all pairs of alternatives be comparable can be a form of hyperrationality—that is, of irrationality. Other forms of hyperrationality are considered in section IV.

### Example 3: Choice of Career

"Life is not long, and too much of it must not pass in idle deliberation of how it shall be spent: deliberation, which those who begin it by prudence, and continue it with subtlety, must, after long expence of thought, conclude by chance. To prefer one future mode of life to another, upon just reasons, requires faculties which it has not pleased our Creator to give to us." [10] Suppose that I am about to choose between going to law school or to a school of forestry—a choice not simply of career but of life-style. I am attracted to both professions, but I cannot rank and compare them.[11] If I had tried both for a lifetime, I might have been able to make an informed choice between them. As it is, I know too little about them to make a rational decision. What often happens in such cases is that peripheral considerations move to the center. In my ignorance about the first decimal—whether my life will go better as a lawyer or as a forester—I look to the second decimal. Perhaps I opt for law school because that will make it easier for me to visit my parents on weekends. This way of deciding is as good as any—but it is not one that can be underwritten by rational choice as superior to, say, just tossing a coin.

The nonexistence of an optimal action can also arise because of peculiar features of the feasible set. In planning models with infinite horizons and no time-discounting, one can run into the paradox that "there is always an incentive to postpone consumption: on the other hand postponing consumption forever is clearly not optimal" (Heal 1973, 300). While a theoretical possibility, this problem is not central in actual decision-making. By contrast, the difficulties stemming from incomplete preferences are real and important. In addition to the problem of intra-

9. A special and important case is that of moral conflict, discussed in Levi (1986).

10. J. Boswell, *The Life of Samuel Johnson* A.D. 1766 (Aetat 57)—a letter from Johnson to Boswell dated 21 August 1766. I owe this reference to John Broome.

11. If I know myself well, I may be able to predict that whatever I do I shall end up preferring the occupation I choose, or perhaps the one that I do not choose, but this is not to know which choice will make me more happy.

personal comparisons of welfare referred to in example 3, the difficulty of making interpersonal comparisons can prevent us from ranking the options, if the ranking takes account of the welfare others derive from them (Sen and Williams 1982, 17).

At the next level, nonexistence of an optimal belief can arise in two ways: because of uncertainty and because of strategic interaction. Uncertainty here means radical ignorance, the lack of ability to assign numerical probabilities to the possible outcomes associated with the various options. If such assignments are possible, we face a problem of decision-making under risk, in which the rational decision rule—to maximize expected utility—can be counted on to yield an optimal choice. Farmers deciding on a crop mix or doctors deciding whether to operate act under risk. They can rely on well-defined probabilities derived from past frequencies. Stock-market speculators, soldiers, and others who have to act in novel situations cannot rely on frequencies. If they have sufficient information and good judgment, they may be able to make good probability estimates to feed into the expected utility calculus. If they have little information or poor judgment, rationality requires them to abstain from forming and acting upon such estimates. To attempt to do so would, for them, be a form of hyperrationality.

*Example 4: Nuclear Waste*
"Different geological mechanisms may be capable of generating the release of radioactive waste in the environment. Among these are groundwater flow, faulting, diapirism, erosion, fall of meteorites, magma intrusion, and modification of the drainage level of water. An approach to geological confinement is often sought by trying to quantify the probability of occurrence of any of these events and their nuisance value to man. Then, by combining these probabilities and nuisance values, one tries to assess the safety coefficient of the repository and to compare it to the accepted safety coefficients for present risks. This approach does not seem realistic to us *because basically the earth's development has not been a random phenomenon* (possibly apart from the fall of meteorites) and no geologist can seriously give reasonable figures for these probabilities (De Marsily et al. 1977, 521; my emphasis). Here is a case in which objective probabilities and judgmental subjective probabilities are equally out of reach.

When the situation is recognized as one of uncertainty, rational choice theory is limited but not powerless. Sometimes, we are able to dismiss an

THE THEORY OF RATIONAL CHOICE

option in the presence of another that, regardless of which state of the world obtains, has better consequences. Having done this, however, we are often left with several options for each of which there is some state in which it has better consequences than one of the others. Decision theory tells us that in choosing between these we are allowed to take account only of the best and the worst consequences of each action.[12] This may also narrow the field a bit, but often more than one option will be left. In choosing between these, one may adopt the rule of thumb to choose the option with the best worst-consequences (maximin), but there are no grounds for saying that this is more rational than to choose the option with best best-consequences (maximax).

Consider next, strategic interaction as an obstacle to rational belief formation. Often, rational choice requires beliefs about choices to be made by other people. These beliefs, to be rational, must take account of the fact that these others are similarly forming beliefs about oneself and about each other. Sometimes, these beliefs are indeterminate, when the situation has multiple equilibria with different winners and losers. The games of "Chicken" and "Battle of the Sexes" are well-known examples. Each of these games has two equilibria, each of which is better for both players than the worst outcome and preferred by one party to the other equilibrium. In the absence of enforcement or commitment devices, there is no way in which a player can form a rational belief about what the other will do.[13]

### Example 5: Rational Expectations

To make decisions about consumption and investment, economic agents must form expectations about the future state of the economy. According to an earlier view, these are "adaptive expectations" or extrapolations from current and past states. This view is unsatisfactory, because it assumes that people react mechanically without using all the information that is available to them. For instance, following the quadrupling of oil prices in 1973 we would expect expectations to change more radically and rapidly than what would be predicted by the theory of adaptive expectations. The theory of rational expectations, which emerged as a dominant para-

---

12. Luce and Raiffa (1957, 296); Arrow and Hurwicz (1971). Other proposals are discussed in I.5 below.

13. At least this holds for the symmetric version of these games. With asymmetries, tacit bargaining may lead the parties to converge to the equilibrium that favors the party who is least worried by the prospect of the worst outcome. The weak may accept a legal regime that favors the strong because, unlike the strong, they cannot survive in the state of nature.

digm in the 1970s, assumes that people are forward-looking, not backward-looking when forming their expectations and that, moreover, they make the best use of the information available to them. Essentially, people predict the future development of the economy using a correct economic model. Since expectations are part of the model, rational expectations must be self-fulfilling. The problem[14] is that often there are several sets of expectations about the economy that, if held by everybody, would be self-fulfilling. In the absence of government intervention to eliminate some of the equilibria, rational agents will not be able to form mutually supporting, self-fulfilling expectations.

Uncertainty and strategic interaction, taken separately, create problems for rational belief formation. When both are present, they wreak havoc. In planning for war, generals are hindered both by uncertainty about whether their sophisticated systems will work and by strategic complexities. The old dictum—don't base your plans on the enemy's intentions but on his capabilities—doesn't apply any more, if it ever did, since they are equally uncertain about the effectiveness of the weapons of the enemy (and about the degree of uncertainty among the generals on the other side).

### Example 6: Explaining Investment

"The outstanding fact is the extreme precariousness of the basis of knowledge on which our estimates of prospective yield will have to be made. Our knowledge of the factors which will govern the yield of an investment some years hence is usually very slight and often negligible. If we speak frankly, we have to admit that our basis of knowledge for estimating the yield ten years hence of a railway, a copper mine, a textile factory, the goodwill of a patent medicine, an Atlantic liner, a building in the city of London amounts to little and sometimes to nothing; or even five years hence" (Keynes 1936, 149–50). For the special case of investment in research and innovation, this lack of foreknowledge decomposes into the elements of uncertainty and strategic interaction. On the one hand, the outcome of innovative activities is inherently uncertain. One may strike gold, or find nothing. As Humphrey Lyttelton is reported to have said, "If I knew where jazz was going I'd be there already." But suppose one could know how

---

14. Actually, one of many problems that beset rational-expectations theory. For a survey, see Begg (1982, 61 ff.).

the chance of finding gold is related to the amount one has invested. Under the "winner-take-all" system of modern industry, it also matters to find it before others do. If other firms invest massively, the chances that a given firm will be first past the post may be too small to make the investment worthwhile. If other firms don't invest, the chances are much higher. But if it is true of each firm that it should invest if and only if others don't, it has no basis for anticipating what others will do (Dasgupta and Stiglitz 1980). Entrepreneurs might as well follow Keynes's advice and be guided by their "animal spirits."

Finally, determinacy problems arise with respect to the optimal amount of information one should collect before forming an opinion. Information is useful, but costly to acquire. Ideally, the rational agent would strike a balance between these two considerations: he would acquire information up to the point at which the marginal cost of acquiring information equals its expected marginal value. In some areas of decision-making these calculations can be carried out with great accuracy. Thus, "to detect intestinal cancer, it has become common to perform a series of six inexpensive tests ('guaiacs') on a person's stool. The benefits of the first two tests are significant. However, when calculations are done for each of the last four tests to determine the costs of detecting a case of cancer (not even curing it), the costs are discovered to be $49,150, $469,534, $4,724,695, and $47,107,214 respectively. To some these calculations suggest that the routine should be reduced, say, to a three-guaiac test." [15]

Sometimes it is impossible to estimate the marginal cost and benefit of information. Consider a general in the midst of battle who does not know the exact disposition of the enemy troops. The value of more information, while potentially great, cannot be ascertained. Determining the expected value would require a highly implausible ability to form numerical probability estimates concerning the possible enemy positions. (Indeterminacy of rational belief due to strategic interaction is important here.) The costs of acquiring information are equally elusive. The opportunity costs might be enormous, if the time spent gathering information offers the enemy a chance to attack or to prepare his defense, or they might be quite trivial. Under such circumstances, one might as well follow Napoleon's maxim, "On s'engage et puis on voit."

15. Menzel (1983, 6). The marginal value of the information is controversial, since it depends on an assessment of the value of life.

In between these extremes—medical diagnosis and the conduct of battle—fall most everyday situations. The observation that a rational person should make "greater investment in information when undertaking major than minor decisions," (Becker 1976, 7) while true, does not help him to decide *how* much to invest. That decision requires estimates about the probable costs and benefits of the search for information. Search theories of unemployment, for instance, assume that the unemployed worker knows the distribution of job offers or at least the general shape of the distribution. Using this knowledge, he can calculate the optimal time spent searching for well-paid jobs. This argument is of dubious value. The doctor carrying out a medical diagnosis finds himself *many* times in the *same situation*. Most persons are unemployed only once or, if more than once, under widely diverging circumstances. They have no way of learning by experience what the job distribution looks like. To be sure, they know something about the job market, but there is no reason to think that they can piece together their bits of information to a reliable subjective distribution.[16] Similar arguments apply to many consumer decisions, like the purchase of a car or an apartment. People know that it makes sense to spend some time searching and that it would be pointless to search forever, but between these lower and upper limits there is usually an interval of indeterminacy.

## IV. Irrationality

In this section I survey some main varieties of irrationality, including, as a special case, hyperrationality. The latter notion is defined as *the failure to recognize the failure* of rational choice theory to yield unique prescriptions or predictions. As in Kant's critique, the first task of reason is to recognize its own limitations and draw the boundaries within which it can operate. The irrational belief in the omnipotence of reason is what I call hyperrationality.

Failures to conform to well-defined prescriptions of rational choice theory arise at all three levels as distinguished in the first figure in this chapter. Consider first how actions can fail to relate optimally to the given desires and beliefs. The paradigm case is weakness of the will, characterized by the following features: (1) there is a prima facie judgment that $x$ is good; (2) there is a prima facie judgment that $y$ is good; (3) there is an all-things considered judgment that $x$ is better than $y$; (4) there

16. On the general point, see Tversky and Kahneman (1974); Lichtenstein, Fischhoff and Phillips (1982). For a devastating criticism of optimal-search theories, see Hey (1981).

is the fact that *y* is chosen. Often, *x* is an act that is in the long-term interest of the person or corresponds to his moral will, whereas *y* is a short-term impulse or a self-interested desire. There is no conceptual link, however, between weakness of the will, myopia, and selfishness (Elster 1985b).

There is another set of cases in which desires and beliefs can fail to bring about the end for which they provide reasons. They have been referred to as "excess of will," (Farber 1976) although they are not in any sense the contrary of weakness of will. Assume that if I do *x*, I shall bring about *y*, which is what I most desire. Moreover, I am able to do *x*, in the straightforward sense in which I am able to raise my arm. The snag, however, is that *x* will bring about *y* only if I do *x* without the intention to bring about *y*. Doing *x* for the purpose of bringing about *y* will not succeed. Examples of *x* and *y* could be: drinking hot tea at bedtime and falling asleep; working hard and forgetting a humiliating experience; looking at erotic pictures and becoming sexually aroused; joining a political movement and achieving self-respect.[17]

It might appear that someone who does *x* to achieve *y* acts rationally. He is doing what he believes is (let us assume) the best way of getting what he most desires. This would be true if the situation conformed to the standard scheme of action, depicted in the following figure.

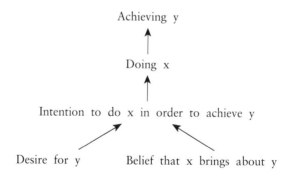

The scheme goes from beliefs and desires, through the intention to the action, and finally to the outcome of action. There is no guarantee, of course, that the intended outcome will occur. The belief that *x* brings about *y* could be mistaken. Extraneous factors might intervene. Actions

17. These examples and many others are extensively discussed in Elster (1983, chap. 2).

that fail to bring about their intended outcomes for such reasons are not irrational. They fail, as it were, honorably. Matters stand differently when the failure is intrinsic to the action, as when the very intention do *x* for the sake of *y* interferes with the efficacy of *x* to bring about *y*. This nonstandard scheme is shown in the following figure.

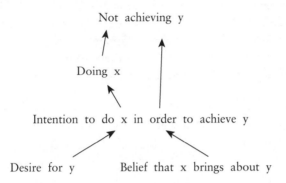

*Example 7: Don't Wait for Return of Husband*
This was the heading column in the *Miami Herald* (April 1987), in which Howard Halpern, a psychologist in private practice in New York City, answered the following question: "I am a 57-year-old woman whose husband of 36 years has decided to live alone. We've sold our house and are living in separate dwellings. He speaks of 'hope' and 'working things out,' while happily living the single life. I am unable to get on with my life in such an independent manner. We've had a great deal of joint and individual therapy, but it has not restored our relationship. We've lived together for a few months in the past two years. Each time I thought we would get back together, but then he would leave again. Is there something I should be doing besides waiting?" Mr. Halpern answered, "When you use the word 'waiting,' I get the impression that you have put your life on hold until your husband's hoped-for return. It is time to stop waiting. By that I don't mean you should make your separation legal—I'm not suggesting any action in particular. I think you must accept your situation as real, understand that your husband may not return and refuse to let your life be dependent on his decision. You have already made efforts to get him to return. Now you must pay attention to your own life and outline your own goals. Focusing

on yourself may make you more appealing to him, but that is not the reason to do it. You must do it for yourself." It is hard to think of advice that would be more misguided. The remark that focusing on herself might make her more appealing to him, while obviously intended to motivate her efforts, is sure to ruin their effect.

Consider next the varieties of irrationality that arise at the level of beliefs and desires. These can be subverted and distorted by causal forces in two main ways: by drives and motivations or by inadequate cognitive processing. Since the end result can be a motivational state (a desire) or a cognitive one (a belief), we have four categories that I now proceed to illustrate.

### The Motivational Basis of Motivations

By this phrase, I do not have in mind conscious character planning, the shaping of preferences by meta-preferences. Rather, it refers to nonconscious motivational mechanisms that shape our desires "behind our back." The best-known is what Festinger called "cognitive dissonance reduction," the natural tendency of the mind to rearrange its desires and beliefs so as to reduce the tension created by high valuations of objects believed to be unattainable or low valuations of objects believed to be inescapable.[18] Some applications of dissonance theory focus on the adjustment of beliefs, while others emphasize the motivated change in evaluations.

*Example 8: The Hungarian Black Market*[19]
One mechanism of dissonance reduction is "I paid a lot for it so it must be good." A Hungarian coffee shop begins to offer customers high-quality coffee to customers who are willing to pay a bit extra. As the shop has a limited quota of coffee beans, each customer who pays the high price creates an externality for the customers who pay the official price. The official cups of coffee being increasingly diluted, more and more customers are willing to pay the premium. Yet, as more and more do so, the quality of black-market coffee approaches the initial quality of the ordinary coffee. In the end, everybody

18. Festinger (1957, 1964); Wicklund and Brehm (1976). Economic applications include Akerlof and Dickens (1982) and Schlicht (1984).
19. The example draws upon Galasi and Kertesi (1987).

pays the higher price for coffee of ordinary quality. It would appear, therefore, that everybody has lost, in a standard $n$-person prisoner's dilemma. The twist to the story is that because of cognitive dissonance nobody experiences any subjective loss. Since they are paying more for the coffee, it must be better than it used to be. The prisoner's dilemma yields a Pareto-improvement: the shopkeeper gains more and the customers are happy.

It is not obvious that desires shaped by dissonance reduction are, *ipso facto,* irrational. They do, after all, make people happier. Desires shaped by dissonance-increasing mechanisms are more obviously irrational. Many people, for instance, have a preference for novelty that gets them into trouble.

### Example 9: What Father Does Is Always Right

In H. C. Andersen's story of this name a farmer goes to the market in the morning to sell or exchange his horse. First, he meets a man with a cow, which he likes so much that he exchanges it for the horse. In successive transactions, the cow is then exchanged for a sheep, the sheep for a goose, the goose for a hen and, finally, the hen for a sack of rotten apples. The farmers' road to ruin is paved with stepwise improvements.[20] (Actually he is not ruined, because a pair of English tourists make and lose a bet that his wife will be angry with him when he comes back with the apples.) Although the story doesn't say so, it is likely that the farmer would have refused to exchange his horse for a sack full of rotten apples. Curiosity and the thirst for novelty are triggered by options which are neither too similar nor too dissimilar from the current state (Middleton 1986). In Johannes V. Jensen's story of the same name—a take-off on Andersen's classic tale—the farmer goes to the market with a sack of rotten apples. By a series of lucky accidents, he comes back with a horse. When he tells his wife about the deals, she manages to see each of them in an unfavorable light. Although the story is not fully clear on this point, it appears she even thought a horse for a sack of apples a bad deal. Thus her perverse attitude is probably explicable by her belief that her husband cannot do anything right, not by an inherent conservatism that would be the converse of a

20. Von Weizsäcker (1971) offers a formal model of this process.

preference for novelty. If the latter was the case, she would probably prefer the end state over the initial state, while being opposed to each of the intermediate steps.

## The Motivational Basis of Cognitions

Dissonance reduction can also take the form of belief adjustment. Workers who take jobs in unsafe industries alter their estimated probabilities of accidents.[21] As a result, when safety equipment becomes available they may choose not to purchase it. Here, as in other cases, misinformation of private beliefs (or preferences) creates a case for government intervention.[22] In addition to direct motivational interference with the cognition, there can be indirect interference with the evidence on which cognition is based. People who dread having a dangerous disease put off seeing the doctor. People who fear they might be gaining weight avoid stepping on the scales.

Belief-oriented dissonance reduction is a form of wishful thinking. To the extent that it makes one feel happy, it might be thought to be a good thing. Usually, however, the pleasure of wishful thinking is of brief duration, like the warmth provided by pissing in one's pants. *Acting* on beliefs formed in this way can be disastrous and is likely to force a change in the beliefs. When action is not called for, the wishful beliefs can be more stable. The "just-world" theory, for instance, suggests that people adjust their beliefs about guilt and responsibility so as to preserve their belief that the world is fundamentally just (Lerner and Miller 1978). The best-known example is the "blame the victim" syndrome. While it would be perverse to say that blaming the victim is rational, it can certainly contribute to one's peace of mind. Some forms of motivated belief formation do not even have that effect. The congenital pessimist, who systematically believes that the world is as he would *not* like it to be, creates dissonance instead of reducing it. Dissonance reduction, while

21. This example is taken from Akerlof and Dickens (1982). This otherwise excellent article is marred by the idea that people can choose their own beliefs so that, for instance, they can weigh the psychic benefits of believing that their job is safe against the cost of increased chances of accidents. Although I am sure that both the costs and the benefits of dissonance reduction influence the extent to which it occurs, I don't think they do so by virtue of conscious comparison since, as argued above, beliefs cannot be deliberately chosen.

22. Sunstein (1986) has a general discussion of such cases.

a threat to autonomy and rationality, is at least intelligible in terms of the "wirings of the pleasure machine," as Amos Tversky has put it. Dissonance production indicates that the wires have been crossed and that something is radically wrong.

## The Cognitive Basis of Motivations

Under this heading fall the violations of expected utility theory that have been extensively studied over the last decade or so.[23] An important example is "framing," that is, preference reversal induced by redescription of the choice situation (Tversky and Kahneman 1981). People who would abstain from buying credit cards if firms impose a three-percent surcharge on card users, may be less deterred if firms offer a three-percent discount on cash purchases (Thaler 1980). Time preferences can be manipulated by presenting the difference between present and future consumption as a delay premium or as a speed-up cost (Loewenstein 1988). These are examples in which the reference points or frames are imposed from the outside. A more intriguing problem arises if we ask about the principles that regulate spontaneous choice of frames (Fischhoff 1983). It has been suggested that people choose the frame that induces the choice that makes them happy, (Machina 1987, 146) but it is far from obvious that nonconscious motivational mechanisms are capable of operating in this indirect manner.

Another set of deviations from expected utility theory arise because people do not treat known probabilities as the theory tells them to. (The problem comes on top of their difficulties in estimating unknown probabilities.) Thus, "low probabilities are overweighted, moderate and high probabilities are underweighted, and the latter effect is more pronounced than the former" (Tversky and Kahneman 1981, 454). In other words, people exaggerate the difference between impossible events and low-probability events and, especially, between near-certain and certain events. Attitudes toward nuclear accidents and other great disasters may, for this reason, include elements of irrationality. The point is *not* that it is irrational to feel anxiety at the prospect of a low-probability nuclear accident. What is irrational is that this attitude, when combined with other attitudes that may also appear unobjectionable in isolation, can be made to yield inconsistent choices. "It is not easy to determine whether people value the elimination of risk too much or the reduction of risk too

23. A recent summary is Machina (1987).

little. The contrasting attitudes to the two [logically equivalent] forms of protective action, however, are difficult to justify on normative grounds" (Tversky and Kahneman 1981, 456).

## The Cognitive Basis of Cognitions

There is by now a massive body of evidence showing how belief formation can fail because people rely on misleading heuristic principles or, more simply, ignore basic facts about statistical inference.[24] Securities and futures markets seem excessively sensitive to current information (Arrow 1982). Baseball trainers who notice that last season's star is not living up to his past performance are rapid to conclude that he has been spoilt by success, ignoring the statistical principle that, on the average, an outstanding performance is likely to be followed by one closer to average ("regression to the mean").[25] "Labeling" theorists of mental illness cite as evidence for their theory the fact that the longer people have been in mental hospitals, the less likely they are to get well, ignoring the alternative explanation that the probabilities of getting well may differ across people but be constant over time (Gullestad and Tschudi 1982).

### Example 10: Calvinism

The last two examples turn upon a confusion between causal and noncausal interpretation of the facts. Max Weber's interpretation of the affinity between Calvinism and economic activity invokes a similar tendency to infuse diagnostic facts with causal value. "Thus, however useless good works might be as a means of attaining salvation, for even the elect remain beings of the flesh, and everything they do falls infinitely short of divine standards, nevertheless, they are indispensable as a sign of election. They are the technical means, not of purchasing salvation, but of getting rid of the fear of damnation" (Weber 1904–5, 115). It has been argued that the mechanism invoked here is motivational, a form of dissonance reduction (Barry 1978, 41). It could, however, be a purely cognitive tendency to confuse diagnostic and causal efficacy. When people ask themselves, "If not now, when?" and "If not me, who?" they commit similar fallacies, albeit very useful ones.[26] People

24. Good summaries are Nisbett and Ross (1981) and Kahneman, Slovic, and Tversky (1982).
25. Nisbett and Ross (1981, 164), referring to "the sophomore slump."
26. See Quattrone and Tversky (1986) for the latter fallacy and Elster (1985b) for a discussion of the former.

who open only one box in Newcomb's Problem do the same.[27]

I conclude this section with a few remarks about hyperrationality. (1) Sometimes people attempt to eliminate uncertainty of beliefs or incompleteness of preferences, although the choice situation is essentially indeterminate. It is always possible to devise questions that will force a person to reveal his preferences or subjective probabilities, but often there is no reason to believe in the robustness of the results. Since the outcome may depend on the procedures of elicitation, there is nothing "out there" that is captured by the questions. (2) Sometimes people look to the second decimal when they are ignorant about the first. In some contexts, this method of problem-solving is as good as any other. In others, it can be very wasteful, if people differ in their assessment of the second decimal and spend resources arguing about it. (3) Sometimes, people will reframe an indeterminate decision problem so as to make it appear determinate. If one option stands out along one dimension, that dimension may take on increased importance so as to make the choice an easier one. (4) Sometimes, people seek out what is rational to do in any given situation instead of looking for more general rules that cover many similar cases. Focusing on rules rather than acts can economize on costs of decision and also have superior incentive effects.[28] (5) Sometimes, people ignore the costs of decision-making. They search for the solution that would have been best if found instantaneously and costlessly, ignoring the fact that the search itself has costs that may detract from optimality.

## V. ALTERNATIVES TO RATIONALITY

In light of earlier sections, several questions arise. How serious are these failures of rational choice theory? Is there any reason to think that the theory has a privileged status in the study of human action? What are the alternative accounts that could supplement or replace the theory?

The failures of indeterminacy appear to me to be quite serious. One way of assessing the power of the theory is to distinguish choice situa-

27. For exposition and discussion of this problem, see the articles collected in Campbell and Sowden (1985). A perfect illustration is a circular letter issued by English Baptists around 1770: "Every soul that comes to Christ to be saved . . . is to be encouraged . . . The coming soul need not fear that he is not elected, for non but such would be willing to come" (Thompson 1968, 38).
28. In addition, focusing on rules can protect one against weakness of will.

tions by two criteria: the importance of the problem and the number of agents involved. "Small" problems, that is problems in which the options do not differ much in value from each other, do not lend themselves to the rational approach. Either the options are equally good or it is not clear that it would pay to find out which is the better, or that it would pay to find out whether it will pay to find out. "Large" problems,[29] in which the choice can be expected to have wide-ranging consequences, also tend to fall outside the scope of the theory. Preference rankings over big chunks of life tend to be incomplete, and subjective probabilities over events in the distant future tend to be unreliable. The theory is more powerful when applied to medium-sized problems like the purchase of a car or of a house, but even here the question of optimal search is largely indeterminate.

Other things being equal, decision-problems with one agent or with many agents are more likely to yield determinate solutions than problems with a small number of agents. By definition, one-agent problems have no strategic indeterminacy. With many sellers and many buyers, competition forces a unique set of equilibrium prices. With one seller and one buyer, there is often a large range of mutually acceptable outcomes and much indeterminacy concerning which outcome will be realized.[30] A rough conclusion is that rational choice theory is applicable mainly to one-agent and many-agent problems of intermediate size. Although precise quantification is impossible, indeterminacy is not a marginal problem that can be assimilated to "friction" or "noise."

The factual importance of irrationality does not lend itself to a similarly systematic analysis. The central issue is whether people deal irrationally with important problems. The issue cannot be studied experimentally, since limitations on funding rarely allow stakes to be high enough and subjects to be numerous enough to get reliable results.[31] In-

29. See Ullmann-Margalit (1985) for an analysis of "big decisions" that nicely complements the analysis of "small" decisions in Ullmann-Margalit and Morgenbesser (1977).

30. Although noncooperative bargaining theory has done much to force determinacy in such problems (Rubinstein 1982), it is mainly of use in two-person contexts. Three-person bargaining problems remain largely indeterminate even in the noncooperative approach (Sutton 1986).

31. To get around this problem, it has been suggested that experiments be conducted in Third World countries, in which five-or ten-dollar rewards would represent high stakes. To get around any ethical problems, all subjects could receive the maximal reward when the experiment was completed, even though told beforehand that they would get it only if they performed well. For reasons explained in Barry (1986), severe ethical problems would still remain.

trospection, casual observation, historical case studies, and novels suggest that irrationality is quite widespread. Drug abuse is perhaps the most striking evidence. More generally, the widespread inability to be properly swayed by future consequences of present action points to a serious deficit in rationality.[32] Studies of "group think" (Janis 1972) suggest that political and military decisions are often made in disregard of the evidence. The motivated ignorance of the Holocaust is a massive example of irrational belief formation (Laqueur 1980). The vast sales of self-therapy manuals suggest that many people believe that they can talk themselves into self-confidence and self-respect. I could go on enumerating cases, but they would not add much to the general idea. Irrationality is neither marginal nor omnipresent.

Although indeterminacy and irrationality are widespread, they do not affect the normative privilege of rationality. First and foremost, rationality is privileged because we want to be rational (Føllesdal 1982). We take little pride in our occasional or frequent irrationality, although sometimes it has to be accepted as the price we pay for other things we value. In our dealings with other people, we are compelled to treat them as, by and large, rational. Communication and discussion rest on the tacit premise that each interlocutor believes in the rationality of the others, since otherwise there would be no point to the exchange (Midgaard 1980, and Habermas 1982). To understand others, we must assume that, by and large, they have rational desires and beliefs and act rationally upon them. If a person says that he wants $x$ and yet deliberately refrains from using the means that he knows to be most conducive to $x$, we usually conclude not that he is irrational, but that he does not really want $x$. Sometimes, of course, we may conclude that irrationality offers the best explanation of a given piece of behavior, but even then most of the evidence about the agent that goes into that conclusion is formed on the assumption that he is, by and large, rational (Davidson 1980).

The explanatory privilege of rationality rests on two grounds. As just observed, rationality is presupposed by any competing theory of motivation, whereas rationality itself does not presuppose anything else. On grounds of parsimony, therefore, we should begin by assuming nothing

32. Against those who say that discounting the future only shows a "taste for the present" and that *de gustibus non est disputandum*, I would reply, first, that much time discounting is inconsistent (Elster 1985b) and, second, that even consistent time discounting beyond what is justified by mortality tables is a failure of rationality.

but rationality.[33] Also, while rationality may have its problems, the opposition is in even worse shape. The dictum that you can't beat something with nothing applies here, with some modifications. As will be clear from what I shall say about the alternatives to rational choice theory, they are more than nothing, but they don't quite amount to something either.

Herbert Simon's theory of satisficing is intended to supplement rational choice theory when it is indeterminate.[34] It has been applied to technical change (Nelson and Winter 1982), consumer choice (Hey 1981, 1982), and numerous other problems. The strength and main weakness of the theory is its realism. On the one hand it is true and important that many people are happy once their aspiration level has been reached. They stop searching once they have found something that is good enough. On the other hand, there is to my knowledge no robust explanation of why people have the aspiration levels they do, nor of why they use the particular search rules they do. The theory describes behavior, but does not really explain it. Now, one might say that a similar criticism applies to rational choice theory, which does not, after all, explain why people have the preferences they do. The hypothesis that people behave rationally is nevertheless simpler, more general, and more powerful than the assumption that they are guided by their aspiration levels. In the theory of the firm, for instance, rational choice theory needs only one assumption, namely, that the firm maximizes profits. Satisficing theory needs many assumptions, stipulating one aspiration level for each of the many subroutines of the firm and, when that level is not attained, one search mechanism for each routine.

Simon's theory, and other theories in the same vein (notably Heiner 1983), are intended to *supplement* rational choice theory, both as a guide to and as an explanation of action. They are rarely intended to *replace* the rationality assumption. Proponents of these alternatives usually grant that rational choice theory has substantial explanatory power in the absence of uncertainty, but add that most real-life decision-making is char-

33. The situation is somewhat similar to the privileged status of the assumption of selfishness. We can consistently imagine a world in which everybody behaved selfishly all the time, but not a world in which everybody behaved altruistically all the time, because altruism presupposes some nonaltruistic pleasures that the altruist can promote.

34. I disregard the interpretation of satisficing as maximizing under constraints on information-processing capacities. Limited calculating ability is only one obstacle to first-best rationality. A more important obstacle, in my view, is our inherently limited knowledge about the value of information. Also, people with severely limited cognitive capacities may not be able to understand their limits and hence are not, subjectively, constrained by them.

acterized by a high degree of uncertainty that is costly or impossible to resolve. This is also the point of departure of the theory offered by Isaac Levi to guide and explain decision-making under value conflicts and uncertainty (Levi 1974, 1986). Under conditions of unresolved value conflict he recommends that we use lexicographically secondary values to decide among the options that are "admissible" according to the primary, conflicting values, an admissible option being one that is optimal according to one of these values (or to some weighted average of them). Under conditions of uncertainty he similarly recommends the use of *security* and *deferability* to supplement the expected-value criterion. Levi also argues that many apparent violations of rationality can be understood by assuming that the agents are acting in accordance with his prescriptions. Their choices reflect reasonable ways of coping with unresolved value conflicts and uncertainty rather than cognitive illusions of the kind discussed above.[35] Levi does not try, however, to account for all the apparent violations to expected-utility theory.

Other theories, offered squarely as alternatives to rational choice theory, aim to explain what they admit to be violations of rationality. They can be classified, very roughly, into psychological, biological, and sociological alternatives to the economic approach to behavior.

Psychological theories attempt to explain the observed violations of expected-utility theory referred to above by providing an account that (1) is simple and intuitively plausible, (2) explains all observed deviations from expected-utility theory, and (3) predicts no unobserved deviations. Attempts to achieve this goal include prospect theory (Kahneman and Tversky 1979; Tversky and Kahneman 1987), generalized expected-utility theory (Machina 1983), and regret theory (Loomes and Sugden 1982). This is a field where nonexperts should tread warily, and I abstain from evaluating the various proposals, beyond the presumably uncontroversial remark that only prospect theory appears to be capable of explaining framing phenomena. I note, below, however, an apparent example of irrationality through framing that is more plausibly explained by a sociological alternative to rational choice theory.

Biological alternatives take off from findings about animal behavior.

35. Levi (1986, 33) shows that a perfectly sensible way of handling unresolved value conflicts can lead to violation of Sen's "property alpha," which says that if *a* is chosen in the set (*a, b*), *b* should never be chosen in a larger set (*a, b, c*). Similarly he argues (Levi 1986, chap. 7) that the Ellsberg and Allais paradoxes of choice under risk can be handled without imputing irrationality to the agents who make these apparently inconsistent decisions.

Animals can be constrained to choose between two responses, each of which has a particular reward schedule. In variable-ratio (VR) schedules we set up a constant probability of reward for each response. The one-armed bandits of the Las Vegas variety illustrate this reward schedule. It is a mechanism with no memory: if we hit the jackpot on one occasion, we are just as likely to hit it again the next time. In variable-interval (VI) schedules, we set up a mechanism with memory, so that each unrewarded response increases the probability that the next response will be rewarded. In each period the experimenter uses a chance device, with constant probabilities, to decide whether food is to be made available. Once it has been made available, it stays available. The animal does not know, however, whether it is available. To find out, and to get the food, it must make the appropriate response.

The central question is whether animals allocate their attention optimally between the two responses, that is, whether they act to maximize their rewards. Faced with the choice between two VR-schedules, animals often do the rational thing and allocate all their attention to the response with the highest probability of reward. Sometimes, however, they commit the "gambler's fallacy" of distributing the stakes in proportion to the odds. With two VI-schedules, the findings are also ambiguous. In a VI/VR-schedule, animals usually do not optimize. Instead of equalizing the marginal return to the two responses, as rationality would require them to do, they equalize the average return. They forget, as it were, that most of the VI rewards come from a few responses and that it isn't really profitable to pay attention to this schedule beyond visiting it from time to time to collect any reward that might have come due after its last visit.

Richard Herrnstein argues that the principle of equalizing average returns ("the matching law") is a more fundamental principle than utility maximization.[36] In addition to explaining allocation of behavior across schedules, it can explain the allocation over time. Specifically, the matching law predicts that time discounting will be steeper than the exponential discount functions usually stipulated by economists. Although the empirical verdict is not yet in, there is evidence that much animal and human discounting is nonexponential (Ainslie 1975, 1982, 1984, 1986). On the other hand, the matching law explains only the most naive forms of human behavior. People can use conscious thought processes to analyze the structure of the choice situation. Unlike animals, they are not

---

36. Herrnstein and Vaughan (1980); Vaughan and Herrnstein (1987); A cautiously optimizing approach to animal behavior is Staddon (1983, 1987).

restricted to myopic learning. The matching law may describe "prerational" behavior, but is powerless to explain more sophisticated choice processes.

A sociological alternative to the economic approach is the theory of social norms.[37] I define social norms mainly by their nonoutcome-oriented character. Whereas rationality tells people, "If you want *y*, do *x*," many social norms simply say, "Do *x*." Some social norms are hypothetical, but they make the action contingent on past behavior of oneself or others, not on future goals. These norms say, "If others do *y*, do *x*" or, "If you have done *y*, do *x*." The norms are *social* if they satisfy two further conditions: they are shared with other members of the community and they are enforced in part by sanctions provided by others.

Here are some examples of social norms, chosen with a view to the contrast with rational action. (1) The norm of voting is very strong in Western democracies. It accounts for most voting in national elections (Barry 1979, 17–18; Wolfinger and Rosenstone 1980, 8 and passim). Selfish voters have virtually nothing to gain from voting, while the costs are non-negligible. Altruistic voters might find voting rational, were it not for problems of strategic interaction. Altruistic voting is a game with multiple equilibria, in each of which most, but not all, voters go to the polls.[38] (2) The norm of vengeance practiced in many traditional societies is triggered by an earlier offense, not motivated by future rewards. Indeed, from the future-oriented point of view vengeance is pointless at best, suicidal at worst. (3) In most Western societies there is a norm against walking up to someone in a cinema queue and asking to buy his place. The norm is puzzling, as nobody would lose and some could gain from the transaction. (4) Norms of dress and etiquette do not seem to serve any ulterior purpose, unlike, for instance, traffic rules that serve to prevent accidents.

Consider finally an example that could be explained both in terms of framing and in terms of social norms. Consider a suburban community where all houses have small lawns of the same size.[39] Suppose a houseowner is willing to pay his neighbor's son ten dollars to mow his lawn, but not more. He would rather spend half an hour mowing the lawn himself than pay eleven dollars to have someone else do it. Imagine now

---

37. I discuss this theory at some length in Elster (1989).

38. For the reasoning behind this statement, see Oliver, Marwell, and Teixeira (1985) or cases B, D, and E in Schelling (1978, 220).

39. I am indebted to Amos Tversky for suggesting this to me as an example of social norms.

that the same person is offered twenty dollars to mow the lawn of another neighbor. It is easy to imagine that he would refuse, probably with some indignation. But this has an appearance of irrationality. By turning down the offer of having his neighbor's son mow his lawn for eleven dollars, he implies that half an hour of his time is worth at most eleven dollars. By turning down the offer to mow the other neighbor's lawn for twenty dollars, he implies that it is worth at least twenty dollars. But it cannot both be worth less than eleven and more than twenty dollars.

The explanation in terms of framing suggests (Thaler 1980, 43) that people evaluate losses and gains foregone differently. Credit card companies exploit this difference when they insist that stores advertise cash discounts rather than credit card surcharges. The credit-card holder is less affected by the lost chance of getting the cash discount than by the extra cost of paying with the card. Similarly, the houseowner is more affected by the out-of-pocket expenses that he would incur by paying someone to mow his lawn than by the loss of a windfall income. But this cannot be the full story, because it does not explain why the houseowner should be indignant at the proposal. Part of the explanation must be that he doesn't think of himself as the kind of person who mows other people's lawns for money. It *isn't done*, to use a revealing phrase that often accompanies social norms.

Economists often argue that norms can be reduced to individual rationality. One version of the reductionist claim is that norms are "nothing but" raw material for strategic manipulation; that people invoke norms to rationalize their self-interest while not believing in them. But this is absurd: if nobody believed in the norms there would be nothing to manipulate (Edgerton 1985, 3). A more serious reductionist argument proceeds from the fact that norms are maintained by sanctions. Suppose I face the choice between taking revenge for the murder of my cousin and not doing anything. The cost of revenge is that I might, in turn, be the target of countervengeance. The cost of not doing anything is that my family and friends are certain to desert me, leaving me out on my own, defenselessly exposed to predators. A cost-benefit analysis is likely to tell me that revenge is the rational choice. More generally, norm-guided behavior is supported by the threat of sanctions that make it rational to obey the norm.

Against this argument, each of the following objections is a sufficient refutation. First, sometimes norms are followed in the absence of any observers who could sanction violations. Many people vote even when nobody would notice it if they didn't. Second, we have to ask why anyone would want to impose the sanctions. Perhaps they follow a meta-norm to sanction people who violate first-order norms, but then we have to ask whether it is rational to follow that norm. In the regress that now arises, there must come a point at which the cost of expressing disapproval is less than the cost of receiving disapproval for not expressing it, since the former cost is approximately constant while the second goes rapidly to zero. The chain of norms must have an unmoved mover, to which the rationalist reduction does not apply.

Among the alternatives to rational choice theory, the—as yet undeveloped—theory of social norms holds the most promise. It is radically different from rational choice theory, whereas the other alternatives are largely variations on the same consequentialist theme. They are different species of the same genus, whereas the theory of norms is of a different genus altogether. Other species of the genus might include the theory of neurotic behavior, which is similarly rigid, mechanical, and nonconsequentialist. Eventually, the goal of the social sciences must be to construct the family comprising both genera—to understand outcome-oriented motivations and nonconsequentialist ones as elements in a general theory of action. As long as this task is not accomplished, rational choice theory will probably remain privileged, by virtue of the simplicity and power of the maximizing assumption. And in the event that it should one day be accomplished, rationality would still retain its privilege as a normative account of action.

## References

Ainslie, G. 1975. "Specious Reward." *Psychological Bulletin* 82: 463–96.
———. 1982. "A Behavioral Economic Approach to the Defense Mechanisms: Freud's Energy Theory Revisited." *Social Science Information* 21: 735–79.
———. 1984. "Behavioral Economics II: Motivated Involuntary Behavior." *Social Science Information* 23: 247–74.
———. 1986. "Beyond Microeconomics." In *The Multiple Self*, pp. 133–76, edited by J. Elster. Cambridge: Cambridge University Press.
Akerlof, G., and W. T. Dickens. 1982. "The Economic Consequences of Cognitive Dissonance." *American Economic Review* 72: 307–19.
Alloy, L., and L. Abrahamson. 1979. "Judgment of Contingency in Depressed and Non-depressed Students: Sadder but Wiser?" *Journal of Experimental Psychology: General* 108: 441–85.
Arrow, K. 1982. "Risk Perception in Psychology and Economics." *Economic Inquiry* 20: 1–9.
Arrow, K., and L. Hurwicz. 1971. "An Optimality Criterion for Decision-making under Uncertainty." In *Uncertainty and Expectation in Economics*, pp. 1–11, edited by C. F. Carter and J. L. Ford. Clifton, NJ: Kelley.
Barry, B. 1978. "Comment." In *Political Participation*, pp. 37–48, edited by S. Benn et al. Canberra: Australian National University Press.

————. 1979. *Sociologists, Economists and Democracy.* 2d ed. Chicago: University of Chicago Press.

————. 1986. "Lady Chatterley's Lover and Doctor Fischer's Bomb Party." In *Foundations of Social Choice Theory,* pp. 11–44, edited by J. Elster and A. Hylland. Cambridge: Cambridge University Press.

Becker, G. 1976. *The Economic Approach to Human Behavior.* Chicago: University of Chicago Press.

————. 1981. *A Treatise on the Family.* Cambridge, MA: Harvard University Press.

Begg, D. K. H. 1982. *The Rational Expectations Revolution in Macroeconomics.* Oxford: Philip Allan.

Binmore, K. 1987. "Modeling Rational Players." *Economics and Philosophy* 3: 179–214.

Bloch, S., and P. Reddaway. 1978. *Russia's Political Hospitals.* London: Futura Books.

Campbell, R., and L. Sowden, eds. 1985. *Paradoxes of Rationality and Cooperation.* Vancouver: University of British Columbia Press.

Cook, J. T. 1987. "Deciding to Believe without Self-deception." *Journal of Philosophy* 84: 441–46.

Dasgupta, P., and J. Stiglitz. 1980. "Uncertainty, Industrial Structure, and the Speed of R & D." *Bell Journal of Economics* 11: 1–28.

Davidson, D. 1980. *Essays on Actions and Events.* Oxford: Oxford University Press.

Edgerton, R. B. 1985. *Rules, Exceptions and Social Order.* Berkeley: University of California Press.

Elster, J. 1983. *Sour Grapes.* Cambridge: Cambridge University Press.

————. 1984. *Ulysses and the Sirens.* Rev. ed. Cambridge: Cambridge University Press.

————. 1985a. "Sadder but Wiser? Rationality and the Emotions." *Social Science Information* 24: 375–406.

————. 1985b. "Weakness of Will and the Free-Rider Problem. *Economics and Philosophy* 1: 231–65.

————. ed. 1986a. *The Multiple Self.* Cambridge: Cambridge University Press.

————. 1986b. "Introduction." In *Rational Choice,* 1–33, edited by J. Elster. Oxford: Blackwell.

————. 1989. *The Cement of Society.* Cambridge: Cambridge University Press.

Farber, L. 1976. *Lying, Despair, Jealousy, Envy, Sex, Suicide, Drugs, and the Good Life.* New York: Basic Books.

Festinger, L. 1957. *A Theory of Cognitive Dissonance.* Palo Alto, CA: Stanford University Press.

————. 1964. *Conflict, Decision and Dissonance.* Palo Alto, CA: Stanford University Press.

Fischhoff, B. 1983. "Predicting Frames." *Journal of Experimental Psychology: Learning, Memory and Cognition* 9: 103–16.

Føllesdal, D. 1982. "The Status of Rationality Assumptions in Interpretation and in the Explanation of Action." *Dialectica* 36: 301–16.

Galasi, P., and G. Kertesi. 1987. "The Spread of Bribery in a Soviet-type Economy." Unpublished manuscript. Department of Economics, Karl Marx University, Budapest.

Gullestad, S., and F. Tschudi. 1982. "Labeling Theories of Mental Illness." *Psychiatry and the Social Sciences* 2: 213–26.

Habermas, J. 1982. *Zur Theorie des kommunikativen Handelns.* Frankfurt am Main: Suhrkamp.

Harsanyi, J. 1977. *Rational Behavior and Bargaining Equilibrium in Games and Social Situations.* Cambridge: Cambridge University Press.

Heal, G. 1973. *The Theory of Economic Planning.* Amsterdam: North-Holland.

Heiner, R. 1983. "The Origin of Predictable Behavior." *American Economic Review* 83: 560–95.

Herrnstein, R., and W. Vaughan. 1980. "Melioration and Behavioral Allocation." In *Limits to Action: The Allocation of Individual Behavior,* 143–76, edited by J. E. R. Staddon. New York: Academic Press.

Hey, J. D. 1981. "Are Optimal Search Rules Reasonable?" *Journal of Economic Behavior and Organization* 2: 47–70.

———. 1982. "Search for Rules of Search." *Journal of Economic Behavior and Organization* 3: 65–82.

Hume, D. [1739] 1960. *A Treatise of Human Nature,* edited by Selby-Bigge. Oxford: Oxford University Press.

Janis, I. 1972. *Victims of Group-Think.* Boston: Houghton-Mifflin.

Kahneman, D., P. Slovic, and A. Tversky, eds. 1982. *Judgment under Uncertainty.* Cambridge: Cambridge University Press.

Kahneman, D., and A. Tversky. 1979. "Prospect Theory." *Econometrica* 47: 263–91.

Keynes, J. M. 1936. *The General Theory of Employment, Interest and Money.* London: Macmillan.

Laqueur, W. 1980. *The Terrible Secret.* Boston: Little, Brown.

Lerner, M. J., and D. T. Miller. 1978. "Just World Research and the Attribution Process." *Psychological Bulletin* 85: 1030–51.

Levi, I. 1974. "On Indeterminate Probabilities." *Journal of Philosophy* 71: 391–418.

———. 1986. *Hard Choices.* Cambridge: Cambridge University Press.

Lewinsohn, P., W. Mischel, W. Chaplin, and R. Barton. 1980. "Social Competence and Depression: The Role of Illusory Self-Perception." *Journal of Abnormal Psychology* 89: 203–12.

Lichtenstein, S., B. Fischhoff, and L. D. Phillips. 1982. "Calibration of Probabilities: The State of the Art to 1980." In Kahneman, Slovic, and Tversky, eds. 1982, 306–34.

Loewenstein, G. 1988. "Frames of Mind in Intertemporal Choice." *Management Science* 34: 200–214.

Loomes, Graham, and Robert Sugden. 1982. "Regret Theory: An Alternative Theory of Rational Choice Under Uncertainty." *Economic Journal* 92: 805–24.

Luce, R. D., and H. Raiffa. 1957. *Games and Decisions.* New York: Wiley.

Machina, M. 1983. "Generalized Expected Utility Analysis and the Nature of Observed Violations of the Independence Axiom." In *Foundations of Utility and Risk Theory with Applications,* 263–93, edited by B. T. Stigum and F. Wenstøp. Dordrecht: Reidel.

———. 1987. "Choice under Uncertainty." *Journal of Economic Perspectives* 1(1): 121–54.

de Marsily, G., et al. 1977. "Nuclear Waste Disposal: Can the Geologist Guarantee Isolation?" *Science* 197: 519–27.

Menzel, P. T. 1983. *Medical Costs, Moral Choices.* New Haven: Yale University Press.

Middleton, E. 1986. "Some Testable Implications of a Preference for Subjective Novelty." *Kyklos* 39: 397–418.

Midgaard, K. 1980. "On the significance of Language and a Richer Concept of Rationality." In *Politics as Rational Action,* 83–97, edited by L. Lewin and E. Vedung. Dordrecht: Reidel.

Nelson, R., and S. Winter. 1982. *An Evolutionary Theory of Economic Change.* Cambridge, MA: Harvard University Press.

Nisbett, R., and L. Ross. 1981. *Human Inference: Strategies and Shortcomings of Social Judgment.* Engelwood Cliffs, NJ: Prentice Hall.

Oliver, P., G. Marwell, and R. Teixeira. 1985. "A Theory of the Critical Mass. I: Interdependence, Group Heterogeneity and the Production of Collective Action." *American Journal of Sociology* 91: 522–56.

Quattrone, G., and A. Tversky. 1986. Self-deception and the Voter's Illusion. In *The Multiple Self,* 35–58, edited by J. Elster. Cambridge: Cambridge University Press.

Rubinstein, A. 1982. "Perfect Equilibrium in a Bargaining Model." *Econometrica* 50: 97–109.

Schelling, T. C. 1978. *Micromotives and Macrobehavior.* New York: Norton.

Schlicht. E. 1984. "Cognitive Dissonance in Economics." *Schriften des Vereins für Sozialpolitik, Gesellschaft für Wirtschafts- und Sozialwissen-schaften.* N.S. 141: 61–81.

Sen, A., and B. A. O. Williams. "Introduction." In *Utilitarianism and Beyond,* 1–22, edited by A. Sen and B. A. O. Williams. Cambridge: Cambridge University Press.

Staddon, J. E. R. 1983. *Adaptive behavior and Learning.* Cambridge: Cambridge University Press.

———. 1987. "Optimality Theory and Behavior." In *The Latest on the Best,* 179–98, edited by J. Dupré. Cambridge, MA: The MIT Press.

Sunstein, C. 1986. "Legal Interference with Private Preferences." *University of Chicago Law Review* 53: 1129–74.

Sutton, J. 1986. "Non-cooperative Bargaining Theory: An Introduction." *Review of Economic Studies* 53: 709–24.

Thaler, R. 1980. "Towards a Positive Theory of Consumer Choice." *Journal of Economic Behavior and Organization* 1: 39–60.

Thompson, E. P. 1968. *The Making of the English Working Class.* Harmondsworth: Penguin Books.

Tocqueville, A. de. 1969. *Democracy in America.* New York: Anchor Books.

Tversky, A., and D. Kahneman. 1974. "Judgment under Uncertainty." *Science* 185: 1124–30.

———. 1981. "The Framing of Decisions and the Psychology of Choice." *Science* 211:453–58.

Ullmann-Margalit, E. 1985. "Opting: The Case of 'Big' Decisions." Unpublished manuscript. Department of Philosophy. Hebrew University, Jerusalem.

Ullmann-Margalit, E., and S. Morgenbesser. 1977. "Picking and choosing." *Social Research* 44: 757–85.

Vaughn, William, Jr., and Richard J. Herrnstein. 1987. "Choosing Among Natural Stimuli." *Journal of Experimental Analysis of Behavior* 47: 5–16.

Veyne, P. 1976. *Le pain et le cirque.* Paris: Editions du Seuil.

Weber, M. [1904–5] 1958. *The Protestant Ethic and the Spirit of Capitalism.* New York: Scribner.

Weizsäcker, C. C. von. 1971. "Notes on Endogenous Change of Tastes." *Journal of Economic Theory* 3: 345–72.

Wicklund, R. A., and J. W. Brehm. 1976. *Perspectives on Cognitive Dissonance.* Hillsdale, NJ: Lawrence Erlbaum.

Williams, B. A. O. 1973. "Deciding to Believe." In *Problems of the Self*, 136–51. Cambridge: Cambridge University Press.

Winston, G. 1980. "Addiction and Backsliding: A Theory of Compulsive Consumption." *Journal of Economic Behavior and Organization* 1: 295–324.

Wolfinger, R. E., and S. J. Rosenstone. 1980. *Who Votes?* New Haven: Yale University Press.

## COMMENT: *What Might Rationality Fail to Do?*
## Geoffrey Brennan

Whether, and in what sense, rational choice theory can be said to "fail" depends critically on what work one expects the theory to do. According to Elster, ". . . rational choice theory is first and foremost a normative theory and only secondarily an explanatory approach." In one sense, I agree with this sentiment—though the sense in which I agree is not Elster's. Moreover, I suspect that Elster and I are eccentric in this view. Certainly, within neoclassical economics, which is where rational choice theory (RCT) receives its most extensive application, rationality is seen almost exclusively as a premise from which propositions about human behavior can be derived—hardly at all as an ethical ideal for which agents should strive. Whether rationality is strictly *required* for the predictive/explanatory work economists want to do, and indeed whether it can—at least its standard version—do any predictive work at all will be matters I shall discuss briefly in what follows. My main object, however, is to clarify and distinguish, more sharply than Elster does, the alternative normative and predictive roles of RCT and to suggest both a connection between these roles and a normative purpose for RCT rather different from those Elster focuses on.

In order to isolate the different kinds of work RCT might do, let me point to three different contexts in which it might be used:

*Situation 1*
Your friend, A, comes to you for advice. He has been offered a position at the University of Chicago. Should he take it? Here, it might be helpful for you to help him clarify his objectives, or for you to inquire whether his beliefs about Chicago (and the status quo) and other relevant matters are properly connected to the evidence he has available, or for you to help him decide whether he needs additional information and what its likely value and cost will be. All these are tasks that

I am grateful to Alan Hamlin and Philip Pettit for conversations on this topic. Standard caveats apply.

RCT, in the "standard version" which Elster isolates, can be seen to provide.

*Situation 2*

You have a purpose you seek to promote that requires you to predict the behavior of a large number of people in your community. That is, the ability to predict citizens' behavior more accurately will be useful to you. You are looking to RCT to help you in this predictive task.

*Situation 3*

You find yourself in a position where you need to make decisions that will influence a large number of others. Either for ethical reasons, or by virtue of your eccentric tastes, you wish to promote the well-being of those others. You want to know how you might do this in the most effective way. You have basically two options. You could try to discern the outcome that is best for them and impose that outcome. Or you could establish a procedure whereby they could choose for themselves. Which procedure should you choose? The answer will, in part, depend on whether individuals can be trusted to pursue their own ends effectively—in other words, whether they are rational or not.

I shall begin my discussion of RCT from the perspective of situation 2. This is probably the most natural starting point for a social scientist—certainly for an economist—and it is, in any event, useful for my purposes.

The version of RCT described by Elster as "standard" amounts more or less to the requirement that actions be such as to promote the agent's purposes to the maximum possible extent. This requirement involves, in turn, optimal information-gathering (where this is well-defined) and optimal use of the information available. To use the language of economics, Elster's standard version of RCT amounts to no more than the assumption that the agent is utility-maximizing. As it happens, economists mean something more than this by rational choice. In the economist's version, restrictions are imposed on the *structure* of preferences (that is, utility functions) the most important of which are the so-called convexity requirements. These, rather loosely put, amount to the proposition that income-compensated demand curves are downward-sloping, so that one can predict the effect of changes in relative prices on quantities of goods demanded. Most of the important propositions in standard microeconomics are comparative static propositions of just this type: "price rises, demand falls."

As Elster notes, correctly in my view, this "standard version" involves no substantive restrictions on the agent's ends/purposes/desires. Given this, it is self-evident that RCT in its standard version is not sufficient to predict actions. Prediction would require not only the assumption that the agent is rational, but also knowledge of what the agent's ends or purposes actually are. Indeed, it is not merely that RCT on its own cannot predict which action the individual will undertake—that RCT involves an "underdetermination" of action. It is at least arguable that there is *no* action that RCT rules out. That is, for virtually any action, there exists some purpose for which that action is best. Even nontransitive choices can be rational if the agent's ends are sufficiently finely individuated. For example, suppose the agent is observed to choose *a* over *b* and *b* over *c* but *c* over *a*. No charge of irrationality can *stick* if *a* in the context of *b*, and *a* in the context of *c*, are different options to the agent. *Some* restriction on the agent's ends—whether provided by some (nonstandard) version of rationality, or otherwise—is required to give rationality any predictive bite at all. In economists' language, prediction of behavior requires not just the knowledge that agents are utility-maximizing, and not just knowledge of the *structure* of utility functions, but also knowledge of the *content* and *precise form* of utility functions. This is knowledge that RCT, either in the Elster "standard version" or the economist's version, does not provide. Rational choice theory, therefore, cannot predict actions.

There are three possible lines of response available to this charge. One is to claim that knowledge of agents' ends is *independently* available in sufficient detail to allow prediction of actions to follow, once rationality is assumed. I do not, however, see how such a claim can be seriously entertained. Agents' purposes are surely among the most complex and obscure aspects of the social landscape. Moreover, even apparently simple and psychologically plausible purposes—the desire for affection, or for prestige, or for survival, say—are hardly sufficiently concrete to permit anything except extremely rough and coarse-gained predictions. Much of Elster's work elsewhere can be interpreted precisely as emphasizing just how complex the connection between action and purpose in rational-actor-theory may be. Once one allows for even minimal psychological complexity, any suggestion that specific actions can be deduced from the assumption of rationality alone seems hopelessly farfetched. The sorts of ends relevant to immediate action can be expected to vary widely across persons and to be differentially weighted across persons, times, and places. They cannot be taken as self-evident.

The second line of response is to follow the behaviorist tradition in economics. This line involves exploiting the rationality assumption in a double role. First, once rationality is assumed, it is possible to induce something about preferences from the agent's previous actions; those previous actions "reveal" the agent's preferences. Then as a second step, the assumption of convexity is used to predict the effects on action of relative price changes. A sufficient history of previous such responses enables the analyst to predict what the behavioral response will be. In a typical example, estimates of price elasticities will be used to predict the change in consumption levels of particular goods in response to price changes. What is crucial in this line of reasoning is, however, not so much the notion of rationality per se but rather a sort of behavioral consistency. If the predicted behavior failed to eventuate, it would always be open to the economist to hypothecate that preferences had changed in the interim. The behaviorally derived preference function will only predict accurately if the behavior pattern remains the same. We need to ask therefore where rationality implies fixity of preferences. Clearly it does not. Perhaps a certain kind of feverish variation in agents' purposes might be seen to be ruled out by commonsense notions of rationality, but it is not ruled out by either the standard or the economist's version of RCT. Furthermore, the kind of rigid fixity that this behaviorist line requires would seem to rule out the possibility of psychological changes, or of perhaps a moderate taste for variety—both of which commonsense notions of rationality would presumably want to admit.

The behaviorist line invites a further question that I shall want to return to. If what is crucial to prediction is behavioral consistency, why is the language of "rationality," "purpose," and so on, with its patently psychological connotations, adopted? Why not simply talk of "behavior response"? In what way would it matter for the predictive story, for example, if the individual utility functions got all mixed up, so that A acted on the basis of B's utility function, B on the basis of C's and so on? Providing those "utility functions" and their allocation across persons remained fixed, there would be total behavioral regularity and the predictions derived from the "revealed preference" account would go through. But the actions of individuals would not be rational. None would be acting to fulfill his own ends: A's actions could not be explained in terms of A's purposes.

I turn briefly to a third possible line in establishing the usefulness of rationality assumptions in prediction—and that is to reject the standard version of RCT in favor of something more substantive. We might specifically want to define *some* ends, some preferences, as "irrational"—in short, to extend the rationality notion to include specification, to a greater or lesser degree, of the *content* of individual utility functions. This is certainly not an unknown move in economics: economists do it when they describe profit-maximization or wealth-maximization as "rational" behavior. The so-called "rational-actor" theory of politics, for example, is often characterized by its assumption of narrowly self-interested behavior (typically income-maximizing) on the part of voters, politicians, and bureaucrats. Sometimes the term "rational egoism" is used as if the notions of rationality and egoism are interchangeable or necessarily connected in some fundamental way. It needs to be emphasized that *this* use of "rationality" is entirely nonstandard, and though economists often move unannounced between this nonstandard use and their standard version, it is "loose talk" for them to do so.[1]

The general point here is that nonstandard versions of RCT will be capable of making predictions about behavior precisely to the extent that those versions involve substantive specifications of the content of agents' utility functions. Whether such specifications *ought* to be subsumed under the definition of "rationality" is a semantic issue and not, I suppose, a matter of great consequence, providing we understand what is meant. For example, excluding self-destruction as an "irrational" objective[2] would not seem to do serious violence to common usage. But any specification of the content of preferences sufficient to enable prediction of agent behavior will need to be much more detailed than this, and to include such detail under the rubric of "rationality" seems an entirely inappropriate use of language.

If all this is accepted, then RCT in anything remotely like the standard version "fails" *as a predictive device* long before we get to the conceptual complications that Elster raises. The problem, for example, that utility functions may generate multiple solutions to a given maximization problem seems a second-order one in the face of the fact that we cannot tell whether or not the agent has chosen the maximum solution even when it is unique, nor can we predict what that solution will be. RCT is intrinsically a *partial* theory of behavior: it is necessarily "indeterminate" in that sense. And if the purpose is to predict, if we are conceiving RCT in

1. There is one sense in which utility-maximization does imply "income or wealth maximization." This is when income is defined as "full income" in the economist's sense: that is, the sum of all valued goods the agent "consumes" weighted by their (shadow) prices. "Income" so defined bears only an incidental resemblance to income as the man in the street, or the tax expert, or even the economically literate accountant would perceive it.

2. Self-destruction could, of course, remain a rational *action* if it promoted some highly valued purpose.

a context like situation 2, then most of the real action is going to be performed by the motivational assumptions and not by the assumption of rationality.

Suppose, however, you conceive RCT in the normative role that Elster envisages—as a prescription telling you how to act. Suppose specifically that you are in situation 1. Then the opaqueness of the agent's purposes is not a problem. You do not need to know what your friend's purposes are to be helpful—as long as *he* knows them. And of course if the person you are to be helpful to happens to be yourself, then the issue is entirely internal. The admonition to behave rationally, together with a set of instructions as to what that involves (how much information to gather, how to use that which you have, how to calculate the best action) is quite complete. Or at least it is so, except in the case of those problems of indeterminacy that Elster isolates. It is in this setting then that Elster's discussion becomes central.

There are, though, three niggling doubts. First, the "inadequacy" test, the second strand of Elster's pathology, seems inappropriate for a prescriptive theory. It is presumably no critique of the normative force of "love they neighbor" that most of us find it impossible to do it much of the time. Even if my friend is not entirely rational, it may well be good for him to aspire to be so. At the same time (my second doubt), it is not obvious that many people would find RCT satisfactory as a normative theory of personal conduct. It is tempting to remark that it will be good for A to behave rationally only to the extent that his ends are "good." Which seems to land us in a normative analogue to the incompleteness/inadequacy bind that RCT exhibits in the predictive sphere—that is, with a requirement that something more than RCT be provided. Third, it should be noted that the view of RCT as a prescriptive device, at least as envisaged in situation 1, gives a specifically *calculative* role to the theory. It suggests that you should calculate the best action in such and such a way: by clarifying purposes, checking whether beliefs are consistent with evidence, and so on. But as Elster notes, the objects of attention (whether explanatory or prescriptive) in RCT are *actions*, not calculative mechanisms. What one should do under (prescriptive) RCT is choose the "right" action (that is, the utility-maximizing one); the theory does not say that one should adopt a particular procedure in choosing it. It may well be that in many cases one can choose the right action by quite a different calculative procedure—for example, by trusting one's habits or by fixing on certain salient features of the options. It may even be that to choose the rational action *rationally* (namely, with an eye to all the *costs* of calculation) will rule out the utility-maximizing calculus in some cases. And instances isolated by Elster elsewhere (and conundrums offered by Derek Parfit) illustrate the situation nicely. Selection of action by noncalculative processes does not represent a "failure" of rationality necessarily. It does so, if at all, only where the action undertaken differs from the one that maximizes utility. I should make it clear here that I do not want to insist that the use of RCT as a prescriptive theory of calculation is wrong or misconceived (though as a matter of fact I think it is). I simply wish to emphasize that there is a distinction between a prescriptive theory of action and a prescriptive theory of *calculation*, and I think that Elster moves excessively casually between the two. Elster is not unique in this: it is a common enough practice among decision theorists. But the distinction seems to me important, and Elster's work elsewhere is part of what has led me to believe so.

So much for situation 1. I want now to turn to a different normative use of the rationality assumption—its role in the defense of "liberal" institutions. I have already noted that the assumption of rationality per se does not help much if at all in predicting behavior and that RCT must be supplemented by substantive and often fairly detailed assumptions about motivations. But even RCT so supplemented may not predict any better than extrapolation from observed behavioral regularities. For some economists, at least, such extrapolation is really all that RCT amounts to. The theory is a sort of mnemonic device—a convenient way of keeping track of possible logical inconsistencies that might arise from a more radically inductive, atheoretical procedure. "Preference" in the "revealed preference" tradition simply means "behavior in previous periods" in settings presumed to be analogous, and "rationality" means mere behavioral consistency. Why, then, burden the theory with psychological terms like "preference," "ends," "rationality," and so on? Why not refer simply to "behavior," subscripted for time, and be done with it? What does all this decision-theoretical baggage add, except confusion?

Well there is *something* added at the predictive level: namely, the prediction that *beliefs* will play a role in determining behavior. In particular, *changes* in relevant beliefs will alter behavior, much as changes in relative prices do; though it is interesting to note that relative prices do most of the predictive work in economics and occupy most of the analytic space.

But a more significant role for the rationality assumption is that it serves to establish a connection between action and individual well-being that vests agent action with a normative authority it would otherwise lack. Clearly, whatever the inadequacies of RCT as a complete ethical theory, "rationality" does have some normative connotations: to be "irrational"—to act so as to subvert your true purposes—is something you ought to avoid, in general.[3] To claim that agents are rational is to claim that they act purposefully. A purpose is, here, something that is important to the agent that she fulfill. To the extent that what is important to agents is considered important more generally, then rationality provides reasons for allowing individuals to choose for themselves. In other words, the assumption that agents are rational is a significant ingredient in providing an ethical underpinning for the notion of citizen sovereignty.[4] Institutions ought to be arranged so that individuals choose for themselves, for in that way the outcomes that emerge will be those the individuals prefer. Or where, as in familiar prisoners' dilemma interactions, individual decentralized action does not lead to the preferred outcome, the outcome that individuals would choose collectively under some appropriate decision-making rule (unanimity, arguably) remains the conceptual ideal. It is, of course, on this generalized individual-sovereignty plank that modern welfare economics is built. The "failure" of any institution ("market failure," "political failure," and the like) is the failure of that institution to permit individuals to appropriate all possible mutual gains—"gains" as evaluated by those individuals, by reference to the preferences they would reveal in appropriately idealized choice settings.

Clearly, for this normative apparatus to be compelling, the connection between action and purpose must go through. The notion that the individual acts so as to bring about outcomes that he prefers is crucial, for example, to the standard welfare economics argument for market arrangements in provision of private goods. If the agent's actions cannot be relied on to further that agent's purposes, then the case for allowing maximal freedom of choice in private good consumption loses its quasi-utilitarian support.

3. Exceptions might occur where you, in acting contrary to your own purposes, incidentally fulfill the purposes of others, as, for example, might be the case if you had an irrational compulsion to cooperate in prisoners' dilemma interactions; or where trying to act contrary to your own purposes actually serves to promote them, as in several inventions of Derek Parfit's (1984).

4. A case for the claim that individuals should be free to choose for themselves can be made independently of whether individuals' purposes are being promoted—on direct libertarian lines, for example. Such a case, however, must be rather less compelling if this freedom subverts individuals' possessive purposes.

It is in this connection that I have always seen Elster's arguments about rational action[5] as having their force. The problem of "intrinsically incidental consequences," for example, is that in cases where the desired outcome cannot be promoted by action undertaken by the choosing agent, then standard arguments for allowing agents to choose for themselves are undone. The problem with the "multiple self" (Elster 1986) is that the notion of *the* agent's purposes are not well-defined: actions to promote the purposes of one persona of the self will subvert the purposes of the other persona(e). And so on.

To summarize. Rational choice theory can be applied—and hence can fail—in three different roles: in the prediction/explanation of agent behavior; in telling individual agents how to act; and in providing a normative defense of "liberal" institutions. Elster's discussion focuses on the first two roles. But in both, for different reasons, the sorts of anxieties he raises seem somewhat beside the point—not irrelevant exactly, but perhaps of second-order importance. In my view, it is in the third role that the assumption of "rationality" per se is most significant and where the kinds of failure that Elster isolates are the most telling. Since this third role is in my view an important one, I regard Elster's discussion as significant. But I find his *focus* strange. The paper encourages us to look at interesting material, but through the wrong lens. My aim here has been to draw attention to Elster's lens, and to show why I think it is the wrong one.

## REFERENCES

Elster, J. 1983. *Sour Grapes.* Cambridge: Cambridge University Press.
———. 1984. *Ulysses and the Sirens.* Rev. ed. Cambridge: Cambridge University Press.
———. 1986. *The Multiple Self.* Cambridge: Cambridge University Press.
Parfit, D. 1984. *Reasons and Persons.* Oxford: Clarendon Press.

5. As set out not only here, but also, for example, in Elster (1983; 1984; 1986a).

# 2

# Rational Choice and the Framing of Decisions

## Amos Tversky and Daniel Kahneman

The modern theory of decision making under risk emerged from a logical analysis of games of chance rather than from a psychological analysis of risk and value. The theory was conceived as a normative model of an idealized decision-maker, not as a description of the behavior of real people. In Schumpeter's words, it "has a much better claim to being called a logic of choice than a psychology of value" (1954, 1058).

The use of a normative analysis to predict and explain actual behavior is defended by several arguments. First, people are generally thought to be effective in pursuing their goals, particularly when they have incentives and opportunities to learn from experience. It seems reasonable, then, to describe choice as a maximization process. Second, competition favors rational individuals and organizations. Optimal decisions increase the chances of survival in a competitive environment, and a minority of rational individuals can sometimes impose rationality on the whole market. Third, the intuitive appeal of the axioms of rational choice makes it plausible that the theory derived from these axioms should provide an acceptable account of choice behavior.

The thesis of the present article is that, in spite of these a priori arguments, the logic of choice does not provide an adequate foundation for a descriptive theory of decision making. We argue that the deviations of actual behavior from the normative model are too widespread to be ignored, too systematic to be dismissed as random error, and too fundamental to be accommodated by relaxing the normative system. We first sketch an analysis of the foundations of the theory of rational choice and then show that the most basic rules of the theory are commonly violated by decision-makers. We conclude from these findings that the normative

Reprinted from *Journal of Business* 59 (no. 4, pt. 2): 251–78. ©1986 by The University of Chicago. All rights reserved. Most of the empirical demonstrations have been reported in earlier publications. Problems 3, 4, 7, 8, and 12 were published in this article for the first time.

and the descriptive analyses cannot be reconciled. A descriptive model of choice is presented, which accounts for preferences that are anomalous in the normative theory.

## I. A HIERARCHY OF NORMATIVE RULES

The major achievement of the modern theory of decision under risk is the derivation of the expected utility rule from simple principles of rational choice that make no reference to long-run considerations (von Neumann and Morgenstern 1944). The axiomatic analysis of the foundations of expected utility theory reveals four substantive assumptions—cancellation, transitivity, dominance, and invariance—besides the more technical assumptions of comparability and continuity. The substantive assumptions can be ordered by their normative appeal, from the cancellation condition, which has been challenged by many theorists, to invariance, which has been accepted by all. We briefly discuss these assumptions.

*Cancellation.* The key qualitative property that gives rise to expected utility theory is the "cancellation" or elimination of any state of the world that yields the same outcome regardless of one's choice. This notion has been captured by different formal properties, such as the substitution axiom of von Neumann and Morgenstern (1944), the extended sure-thing principle of Savage (1954), and the independence condition of Luce and Krantz (1971). Thus, if A is preferred to B, then the prospect of winning A if it rains tomorrow (and nothing otherwise) should be preferred to the prospect of winning B if it rains tomorrow because the two prospects yield the same outcome (nothing) if there is no rain tomorrow. Cancellation is necessary to represent preference between prospects as the maximization of expected utility. The main argument for cancellation is that only one state will actually be realized, which makes it reasonable to evaluate the outcomes of options separately for each state. The choice between options should therefore depend only on states in which they yield different outcomes.

*Transitivity.* A basic assumption in models of both risky and riskless choice is the transitivity of preference. This assumption is necessary and essentially sufficient for the representation of preference by an ordinal utility scale $u$ such that A is preferred to B whenever $u(A) > u(B)$. Thus transitivity is satisfied if it is possible to assign to each option a value that does not depend on the other available options. Transitivity is likely to hold when the options are evaluated separately but not when the consequences of an option depend on the alternative to which it is compared, as implied, for example, by considerations of regret. A common argument for transitivity is that cyclic preferences can support a "money pump," in which the intransitive person is induced to pay for a series of exchanges that returns to the initial option.

*Dominance.* This is perhaps the most obvious principle of rational choice: if one option is better than another in one state and at least as good in all other states, the dominant option should be chosen. A slightly stronger condition—called stochastic dominance—asserts that, for unidimensional risky prospects, A is preferred to B if the cumulative distribution of A is to the right of the cumulative distribution of B. Dominance is both simpler and more compelling than cancellation and transitivity, and it serves as the cornerstone of the normative theory of choice.

*Invariance.* An essential condition for a theory of choice that claims normative status is the principle of invariance: different representations of the same choice problem should yield the same preference. That is, the preference between options should be independent of their description. Two characterizations that the decision-maker, on reflection, would view as alternative descriptions of the same problem should lead to the same choice—even without the benefit of such reflection. This principle of invariance (or extensionality [Arrow 1982]), is so basic that it is tacitly assumed in the characterization of options rather than explicitly stated as a testable axiom. For example, decision models that describe the objects of choice as random variables all assume that alternative representations of the same random variables should be treated alike. Invariance captures the normative intuition that variations of form that do not affect the actual outcomes should not affect the choice. A related concept, called consequentialism, has been discussed by Hammond (1985).

The four principles underlying expected utility theory can be ordered by their normative appeal. Invariance and dominance seem essential, transitivity could be questioned, and cancellations has been rejected by many authors. Indeed, the ingenious counterexamples of Allais (1953) and Ellsberg (1961) led several theorists to abandon cancellation and the expectation principle in favor of more general representations. Most of these models assume transitivity, dominance, and invariance (e.g., Hansson 1975; Allais 1979; Hagen 1979; Machina 1982; Quiggin 1982; Weber 1982; Chew 1983; Fishburn 1983; Schmeidler 1984; Segal 1984; Yaari 1984; Luce and Narens 1985). Other developments abandon transitivity but maintain invariance and dominance (e.g., Bell 1982; Fishburn 1982, 1984; Loomes and Sugden 1982). These theorists responded to observed violations of cancellation and transitivity by weakening the normative theory in order to retain its status as a descriptive model. This strategy, however, cannot be extended to the failures of dominance and invariance that we shall document. Because invariance and dominance are normatively essential and descriptively invalid, a theory of rational decision cannot provide an adequate description of choice behavior.

We next illustrate failures of invariance and dominance and then review a descriptive analysis that traces these failures to the joint effects of the rules that govern the framing of prospects, the evaluation of outcomes, and the weighting of probabilities. Several phenomena of choice that support the present account are described.

## II. Failures of Invariance

In this section we consider two illustrative examples in which the condition of invariance is violated and discuss some of the factors that produce these violations.

The first example comes from a study of preferences between medical treatments (McNeil et al. 1982). Respondents were given statistical information about the outcomes of two treatments of lung cancer. The same statistics were presented to some respondents in terms of mortality rates and to others in terms of survival rates. The respondents then indicated their preferred treatment. The information was presented as follows.[1]

### Problem 1 (Survival frame)
Surgery: Of 100 people having surgery 90 live through the post-operative period, 68 are alive at the end of the first year and 34 are alive at the end of five years.
Radiation Therapy: Of 100 people having radiation therapy all live through the treatment, 77 are alive at the end of one year and 22 are alive at the end of five years.

### Problem 1 (Mortality frame)
Surgery: Of 100 people having surgery 10 die during surgery or the post-operative period, 32 die by the end of the first year and 66 die by the end of five years.
Radiation Therapy: Of 100 people having radiation therapy, none die during treatment, 23 die by the end of one year and 78 die by the end of five years.

1. All problems are presented in the text exactly as they were presented to the participants in the experiments.

The inconsequential difference in formulation produced a marked effect. The overall percentage of respondents who favored radiation therapy rose from 18 percent in the survival frame ($N = 247$) to 44 percent in the mortality frame ($N = 336$). The advantage of radiation therapy over surgery evidently looms larger when stated as a reduction of the risk of immediate death from 10 percent to 0 percent rather than as an increase from 9 percent to 100 percent in the rate of survival. The framing effect was not smaller for experienced physicians or for statistically sophisticated business students than for a group of clinic patients.

Our next example concerns decisions between conjunctions of risky prospects with monetary outcomes. Each respondent made two choices, one between favorable prospects and one between unfavorable prospects (Tversky and Kahneman 1981, p. 454). It was assumed that the two selected prospects would be played independently.

*Problem 2 (N = 150).*
Imagine that you face the following pair of concurrent decisions. First examine both decisions, then indicate the options you prefer.

Decision (i) Choose between:
A. a sure gain of $240 [84%]
B. 25% chance to gain $1000 and 75% chance to gain nothing [16%]

Decision (ii) Choose between:
C. a sure loss of $750 [13%]
D. 75% chance to lose $1000 and 25% chance to lose nothing [8%]

The total number of respondents is denoted by N, and the percentage who chose each option is indicated in brackets. (Unless otherwise specified, the data were obtained from undergraduate students at Stanford University and at the University of British Columbia.) The majority choice in decision i is risk averse, while the majority choice in decision ii is risk seeking. This is a common pattern: choices involving gains are usually risk averse, and choices involving losses are often risk seeking—except when the probability of winning or losing is small (Fishburn and Kochenberger 1979; Kahneman and Tversky 1979; Hershey and Schoemaker 1980).

Because the subjects considered the two decisions simultaneously, they expressed, in effect, a preference for the portfolio A and D over the portfolio B and C. However, the preferred portfolio is actually dominated by the rejected one! The combined options are as follows.

A & D: 25% chance to win $240 and 75% chance to lose $760.

B & C: 25% chance to win $250 and 75% chance to lose $750.

When the options are presented in this aggregated form, the dominant option is invariably chosen. In the format of problem 2, however, 73 percent of respondents chose the dominated combination A and D, and only 3 percent chose B and C. The contrast between the two formats illustrates a violation of invariance. The findings also support the general point that failures of invariance are likely to produce violations of stochastic dominance and vice versa.

The respondents evidently evaluated decisions i and ii separately in problem 2, where they exhibited the standard pattern of risk aversion in gains and risk seeking in losses. People who are given these problems are very surprised to learn that the combination of two preferences that they considered quite reasonable led them to select a dominated option. The same pattern of results was also observed in a scaled-down version of problem 2, with real monetary payoff (see Tversky and Kahneman 1981, 458).

As illustrated by the preceding examples, variations in the framing of decision problems produce systematic violations of invariance and dominance that cannot be defended on normative grounds. It is instructive to examine two mechanisms that could ensure the invariance of preferences: canonical representations and the use of expected actuarial value.

Invariance would hold if all formulations of the same prospect were transformed to a standard canonical representation (for example, a cumulative probability distribution of the same random variable) because the various versions would then all be evaluated in the same manner. In problem 2, for example, invariance and dominance would both be preserved if the outcomes of the two decisions were aggregated prior to evaluation. Similarly, the same choice would be made in both versions of the medical problem if the outcomes were coded in terms of one dominant frame (for example, rate of survival). The observed failures of invariance indicate that people do not spontaneously aggregate concurrent prospects or transform all outcomes into a common frame.

The failure to construct a canonical representation in decision problems contrasts with other cognitive tasks in which such representations are generated automatically and effortlessly. In particular, our visual experience consists largely of canonical representations: objects do not appear to change in size, shape, brightness, or color when we move around them or when illumination varies. A white circle seen from a sharp angle in dim light appears circular and white, not ellipsoid and grey. Canonical representations are also generated in the process of language comprehension, where listeners quickly recode much of what they hear into an abstract propositional form that no longer discriminates, for example, between the active and the passive voice and often does not distinguish what was actually said from what was implied or presupposed (Clark and Clark 1977). Unfortunately, the mental machinery that transforms percepts and sentences into standard forms does not automatically apply to the process of choice.

Invariance could be satisfied even in the absence of a canonical representation if the evaluation of prospects were separately linear, or nearly linear, in probability and monetary value. If people ordered risky prospects by their actuarial values, invariance and dominance would always hold. In particular, there would be no difference between the mortality and the survival versions of the medical problem. Because the evaluation of outcomes and probabilities is generally nonlinear, and because people do not spontaneously construct canonical representations of decisions, invariance commonly fails. Normative models of choice, which assume invariance, therefore cannot provide an adequate descriptive account of choice behavior. In the next section we present a descriptive account of risky choice, called prospect theory, and explore its consequences. Failures of invariance are explained by framing effects that control the representation of options, in conjunction with the nonlinearities of value and belief.

## III. FRAMING AND EVALUATION OF OUTCOMES

Prospect theory distinguishes two phases in the choice process: a phase of framing and editing, followed by a phase of evaluation (Kahneman and Tversky 1979). The first phase consists of a preliminary analysis of the decision problem, which frames the effective acts, contingencies, and outcomes. Framing is controlled by the manner in which the choice problem is presented as well as by norms, habits, and expectancies of the decision maker. Additional operations that are performed prior to evaluation include cancellation of common components and the elimination of options that are seen to be dominated by others. In the second phase, the framed prospects are evaluated, and the prospect of highest value is selected. The theory distinguishes two ways of choosing between prospects: by detecting that one dominates another or by comparing their values.

For simplicity, we confine the discussion to simple gambles with numerical probabilities and monetary outcomes. Let $(x, p; y, q)$ denote a prospect that yields $x$ with probability $p$ and $y$ with probability $q$ and that preserves the status quo with probability $(1—p—q)$. According to prospect theory, there are values $v(.)$, defined on gains and losses, and decision weights $\pi(.)$, defined on stated probabilities, such that the overall value of the prospect equals $\pi(p)v(x) + \pi(q)v(y)$. A slight modification is required if all outcomes of a prospect have the same sign.[2]

## The Value Function

Following Markowitz (1952), outcomes are expressed in prospect theory as positive or negative deviations (gains or losses) from a neutral reference outcome, which is assigned a value of zero. Unlike Markowitz, however, we propose that the value function is commonly S shaped, concave above the reference point, and convex below it, as illustrated in figure 2.1. Thus the difference in subjective value between a gain of $100 and a gain of $200 is greater than the subjective difference between a gain of $1,100 and a gain of $1,200. The same relation between value differences holds for the corresponding losses. The proposed function expresses the property that the effect of a marginal change decreases with the distance from the reference point in either direction. These hypotheses regarding the typical shape of the value function may not apply to ruinous losses or to circumstances in which particular amounts assume special significance.

A significant property of the value function, called *loss aversion*, is that the response to losses is more extreme than the response to gains. The common reluctance to accept a fair bet on the toss of a coin suggests that the displeasure of losing a sum of money exceeds the pleasure of winning the same amount. Thus the proposed value function is (1) defined on gains and losses, (2) generally concave for gains and convex for losses, and (3) steeper for losses than for gains. These properties of the value function have been supported in many studies of risky choice involving monetary outcomes (Fishburn and Kochenberger 1979; Kahneman and

---

2. If $p + q = 1$ and either $x > y > 0$ or $x < y < 0$, the value of a prospect is given by $v(y) + \pi(p)[v(x) - v(y)]$, so that decision weights are not applied to sure outcomes.

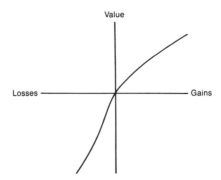

FIGURE 2.1 A Typical Value Function

Tversky 1979; Hershey and Schoemaker 1980; Payne, Laughhunn, and Crum 1980) and human lives (Tversky 1977; Eraker and Sox 1981; Tversky and Kahneman 1981; Fischhoff 1983). Loss aversion may also contribute to the observed discrepancies between the amount of money people are willing to pay for a good and the compensation they demand to give it up (Bishop and Heberlein 1979; Knetsch and Sinden 1984). This effect is implied by the value function if the good is valued as a gain in the former context and as a loss in the latter.

Framing Outcomes

The framing of outcomes and the contrast between traditional theory and the present analysis are illustrated in the following problems.

> *Problem 3 (N = 126):*
> Assume yourself richer by $300 than you are today. You have to choose between
> a sure gain of $100 [72%]
> 50% chance to gain $200 and 50% chance to gain nothing [28%]

> *Problem 4(N = 128):*
> Assume yourself richer by $500 than you are today. You have to choose between
> a sure loss of $100 [36%]
> 50% chance to lose nothing and 50% chance to lose $200 [64%]

As implied by the value function, the majority choice is risk averse in problem 3 and risk seeking in problem 4, although the two problems are essentially identical. In both cases one faces a choice between $400 for sure and an even chance of $500 or $300. Problem 4 is obtained from problem 3 by increasing the initial endowment by $200 and subtracting this amount from both options. This variation has a substantial effect on preferences. Additional questions showed that variations of $200 in initial wealth have little or no effect on choices. Evidently, preferences are quite insensitive to small changes of wealth but highly sensitive to corresponding changes in reference point. These observations show that the effective carriers of values are gains and losses, or changes in wealth, rather than states of wealth as implied by the rational model.

The common pattern of preferences observed in problems 3 and 4 is of special interest because it violates not only expected utility theory but practically all other normatively based models of choice. In particular, these data are inconsistent with the model of regret advanced by Bell (1982) and by Loomes and Sugden (1982) and axiomatized by Fishburn (1982). This follows from the fact that problems 3 and 4 yield identical outcomes and an identical regret structure. Furthermore, regret theory cannot accommodate the combination of risk aversion in problem 3 and risk seeking in problem 4—even without the corresponding changes in endowment that make the problems extensionally equivalent.

Shifts of reference can be induced by different decompositions of outcomes into risky and riskless components, as in the above problems. The reference point can also be shifted by a mere labeling of outcomes, as illustrated in the following problems (Tversky and Kahneman 1981, 453).

*Problem 5 (N = 152):*
Imagine that the U.S. is preparing for the outbreak of an unusual Asian disease, which is expected to kill 600 people. Two alternative programs to combat the disease have been proposed. Assume that the exact scientific estimates of the consequences of the programs are as follows:

If Program A is adopted, 200 people will be saved. [72%]

If Program B is adopted, there is 1/3 probability that 600 people will be saved, and 2/3 probability that no people will be saved. [28%]

In problem 5 the outcomes are stated in positive terms (lives saved), and the majority choice is accordingly risk averse. The prospect of certainly saving 200 lives is more attractive than a risky prospect of equal expected value. A second group of respondents was given the same cover story with the following descriptions of the alternative programs.

*Problem 6 (N = 155)*:
If Program C is adopted 400 people will die. [22%]

If Program D is adopted there is 1/3 probability that nobody will die, and 2/3 probability that 600 people will die. [78%]

In problem 6 the outcomes are stated in negative terms (lives lost), and the majority choice is accordingly risk seeking. The certain death of 400 people is less acceptable than a two-thirds chance that 600 people will die. Problems 5 and 6, however, are essentially identical. They differ only in that the former is framed in terms of the number of lives saved (relative to an expected loss of 600 lives if no action is taken), whereas the latter is framed in terms of the number of lives lost.

On several occasions we presented both versions to the same respondents and discussed with them the inconsistent preferences evoked by the two frames. Many respondents expressed a wish to remain risk averse in the "lives saved" version and risk seeking in the "lives lost" version, although they also expressed a wish for their answers to be consistent. In the persistence of their appeal, framing effects resemble visual illusions more than computational errors.

## Discounts and Surcharges

Perhaps the most distinctive intellectual contribution of economic analysis is the systematic consideration of alternative opportunities. A basic principle of economic thinking is that opportunity costs and out-of-pocket costs should be treated alike. Preferences should depend only on relevant differences between options, not on how these differences are labeled. This principle runs counter to the psychological tendencies that make preferences susceptible to superficial variations in form. In particular, a difference that favors outcome A over outcome B can sometimes be framed either as an advantage of A or as a disadvantage of B by suggesting either B or A as the neutral reference point. Because of loss aversion, the difference will loom larger when A is neutral and B-A is evaluated as a loss than when B is neutral and A-B is evaluated as a gain. The significance of such variations of framing has been noted in several contexts.

Thaler (1980) drew attention to the effect of labeling a difference between two prices as a surcharge or a discount. It is easier to forgo a discount than to accept a surcharge because the same price difference is valued as a gain in the former case and as a loss in the latter. Indeed, the credit card lobby is said to insist that any price difference between cash and card purchases should be labeled a cash discount rather than a credit surcharge. A similar idea could be invoked to explain why the price response to slack demand often takes the form of discounts or special concessions (Stigler and Kindahl 1970). Customers may be expected to show less resistance to the eventual cancellation of such temporary arrangements than to outright price increases. Judgments of fairness exhibit the same pattern (Kahneman, Knetsch, and Thaler, in this issue).

Schelling (1981) has described a striking framing effect in a context of tax policy. He points out that the tax table can be constructed by using as a default case either the childless family (as is in fact done) or, say, the modal two-child family. The tax difference between a childless family and a two-child family is naturally framed as an exemption (for the two-child family) in the first frame and as a tax premium (on the childless family) in the second frame. This seemingly innocuous difference has a large effect on judgments of the desired relation between income, family size, and tax. Schelling reported that his students rejected the idea of granting the rich a larger exemption than the poor in the first frame but favored a larger tax premium on the childless rich than on the childless poor in the second frame. Because the exemption and the premium are alternative labels for the same tax differences in the two cases, the judgments violate invariance. Framing the consequences of a public policy in positive or in negative terms can greatly alter its appeal.

The notion of a money illusion is sometimes applied to workers' willingness to accept, in periods of high inflation, increases in nominal wages that do not protect their real income—although they would strenuously resist equivalent wage cuts in the absence of inflation. The essence of the illusion is that, whereas a cut in the nominal wage is always recognized as a loss, a nominal increase that does not preserve real income may be treated as a gain. Another manifestation of the money illusion was observed in a study of the perceived fairness of economic actions (Kahneman, Knetsch, and Thaler, 1986b). Respondents in a telephone interview evaluated the fairness of the action described in the following vignette, which was presented in two versions that differed only in the bracketed clauses.

A company is making a small profit. It is located in a community experiencing a recession with substantial unemployment [but no inflation/and inflation of 12 percent]. The company decides to [decrease wages and salaries 7 percent/increase salaries only 5 percent] this year.

Although the loss of real income is very similar in the two versions, the proportion of respondents who judged the action of the company "unfair" or "very unfair" was 62 percent for a nominal reduction but only 22 percent for a nominal increase.

Bazerman (1983) has documented framing effects in experimental studies of bargaining. He compared the performance of experimental subjects when the outcomes of bargaining were formulated as gains or as losses. Subjects who bargained over the allocation of losses more often failed to reach agreement and more often failed to discover a Pareto-optimal solution. Bazerman attributed these observations to the general propensity toward risk seeking in the domain of losses, which may increase the willingness of both participants to risk the negative consequences of a deadlock.

Loss aversion presents an obstacle to bargaining whenever the participants evaluate their own concessions as losses and the concessions obtained from the other party as gains. In negotiating over missiles, for example, the subjective loss of security associated with dismantling a missile may loom larger than the increment of security produced by a similar action on the adversary's part. If the two parties both assign a two-to-one ratio to the values of the concessions they make and of those they obtain, the resulting four-to-one gap may be difficult to bridge. Agreement will be much easier to achieve by negotiators who trade in "bargaining chips" that are valued equally, regardless of whose hand they are in. In this mode of trading, which may be common in routine purchases, loss aversion tends to disappear (Kahneman and Tversky 1984).

## IV. The Framing and Weighting of Chance Events

In expected-utility theory, the utility of each possible outcome is weighted by its probability. In prospect theory, the value of an uncertain outcome is multiplied by a decision weight $\pi(p)$, which is a monotonic function of $p$ but is not a probability. The weighing function $\pi$ has the following properties. First, impossible events are discarded, that is, $\pi(0) = 0$, and the scale is normalized so that $\pi(1) = 1$, but the function is not well behaved near the end points (Kahneman and Tversky 1979). Second, for low probabilities, $\pi(p) > p$, but $\pi(p) + \pi(1 - p) \leq 1$ (sub-

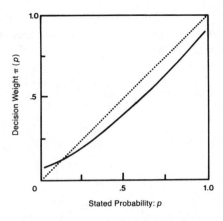

FIGURE 2.2 A Typical Weighting Function

certainty). Thus low probabilities are overweighted, moderate and high probabilities are underweighted, and the latter effect is more pronounced than the former. Third, $\pi(pr)/\pi(p) < \pi(pqr)/\pi(pq)$ for all $0 < p$, $q$, $r \leq 1$ (subproportionality). That is, for any fixed probability ratio $r$, the ratio of decision weights is closer to unity when the probabilities are low than when they are high, for example, $\pi(.1)/\pi(.2) > \pi(.4)/\pi(.8)$. A hypothetical weighting function that satisfies these properties is shown in figure 2.2. Its consequences are discussed in the next section.[3]

## Nontransparent Dominance

The major characteristic of the weighting function is the overweighting of probability differences involving certainty and impossibility, for example, $\pi(1.0) - \pi(.9)$ or $\pi(.1) - \pi(0)$, relative to comparable differences in the middle of the scale, for example, $\pi(.3) - \pi(.2)$. In particular, for small $p$, $\pi$ is generally subadditive, for example, $\pi(.01) + \pi(.06) > \pi(.07)$. This property can lead to violations of dominance, as illustrated in the following pair of problems.

3. The extension of the present analysis to prospects with many (nonzero) outcomes involves two additional steps. First, we assume that continuous (or multivalued) distributions are approximated, in the framing phrase, by discrete distributions with a relatively small number of outcomes. For example, a uniform distribution on the interval $(0, 90)$ may be represented by the discrete prospect $(0, .1; 10, .1; \ldots; 90, .1)$. Second, in the multiple-outcome case the weighting function, $\pi_p(p_i)$, must depend on the probability vector $p$, not only on the component $p_i$, $i = 1, \ldots, n$. For example, Quiggin (1982) uses the function $\pi_p(p_i) = \pi(p_i)/[\pi(p_i) + \ldots + \pi(p_i)]$. As in the two-outcome case, the weighting function is assumed to satisfy subcertainty, $\pi_p(p_1) + \ldots + \pi_p(p_n) \leq 1$, and subproportionality.

*Problem 7 (N = 88).*

Consider the following two lotteries, described by the percentage of marbles of different colors in each box and the amount of money you win or lose depending on the color of a randomly drawn marble. Which lottery do you prefer?

### Option A

| 90% white | 6% red | 1% green | 1% blue | 2% yellow |
|-----------|--------|----------|---------|-----------|
| $0 | win $45 | win $30 | lose $15 | lose $15 |

### Option B

| 90% white | 6% red | 1% green | 1% blue | 2% yellow |
|-----------|--------|----------|---------|-----------|
| $0 | win $45 | win $45 | lose $10 | lose $15 |

It is easy to see that option B dominates option A: for every color the outcome of B is at least as desirable as the outcome of A. Indeed, all respondents chose B over A. This observation is hardly surprising because the relation of dominance is highly transparent, so the dominated prospect is rejected without further processing. The next problem is effectively identical to problem 7, except that colors yielding identical outcomes (red and green in B and yellow and blue in A) are combined. We have proposed that this operation is commonly performed by the decision maker if no dominated prospect is detected.

*Problem 8 (N = 124).*

Which lottery do you prefer?

### Option C

| 90% white | 6% red | 1% green | 3% yellow |
|-----------|--------|----------|-----------|
| $0 | win $45 | win $30 | lose $15 |

### Option D

| 90% white | 7% red | 1% green | 2% yellow |
|-----------|--------|----------|-----------|
| $0 | win $45 | lose $10 | lose $15 |

The formulation of problem 8 simplifies the options but masks the relation of dominance. Furthermore, it enhances the attractiveness of C, which has two positive outcomes and one negative, relative to D, which has two negative outcomes and one positive. As an inducement to consider the options carefully, participants were informed that one-tenth of them, selected at random, would actually play the gambles they chose. Although this announcement aroused much excitement, 58 percent of the participants chose the dominated alternative C. In answer to another question the majority of respondents also assigned a higher cash equivalent to C than to D. These results support the following propositions. (1) Two formulations of the same problem elicit different preferences, in violation of invariance. (2) The dominance rule is obeyed when its application is transparent. (3) Dominance is masked by a frame in which the inferior option yields a more favorable outcome in an identified state of the world (for example, drawing a green marble). (4) The discrepant preferences are consistent with the subadditivity of decision weights. The role of transparency may be illuminated by a perceptual example. Figure 2.3 presents the well-known Müller-Lyer illusion: the top line appears longer than the bottom line, although it is in fact shorter. In figure 2.4, the same patterns are embedded in a rectangular frame, which makes it apparent that the protruding bottom line is longer than the top one. This judgment has the nature of an inference, in contrast to the perceptual impression that mediates judgment in figure 2.3. Similarly, the finer partition introduced in problem 7 makes it possible to conclude that option D is superior to C, without assessing their values. Whether the relation of dominance is detected depends on framing as well as on the sophistication and experience of the decision maker. The dominance relation in problems 8 and 1 could be transparent to a sophisticated decision maker, although it was not transparent to most of our respondents.

## Certainty and Pseudocertainty

The overweighting of outcomes that are obtained with certainty relative to outcomes that are merely probable gives rise to violations of the expectation rule, as first noted by Allais (1953). The next series of problems (Tversky and Kahneman 1981, 455) illustrates the phenomenon discovered by Allais and its relation to the weighting of probabilities and to the framing of chance events. Chance events were realized by drawing a single marble from a bag containing a specified number of favorable and unfavorable marbles. To encourage thoughtful answers, one-tenth of the participants, selected at random, were given an opportunity to play the gambles they chose. The same respondents answered problems 9–11, in that order.

*Problem 9 (N = 77).*
Which of the following options do you prefer?
A. a sure gain of $30 [78%]

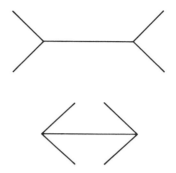

FIGURE 2.3 The Müller-Lyer Illusion

B. 80% chance to win $45 and 20% chance to win nothing
[22%]

*Problem 10 (N = 81).*
Which of the following options do you prefer?
C. 25% chance to win $30 and 75% chance to win nothing
[42%]
D. 20% chance to win $45 and 80% chance to win nothing
[58%]

Note that problem 10 is obtained from problem 9 by reducing the probabilities of winning by a factor of four. In expected utility theory a preference for A over B in problem 9 implies a preference for C over D in problem 10. Contrary to this prediction, the majority preference switched from the lower prize ($30) to the higher one ($45) when the probabilities of winning were substantially reduced. We called this phenomenon the *certainty effect* because the reduction of the probability of winning from certainty to .25 has a greater effect than the corresponding reduction from .8 to .2. In prospect theory, the modal choice in problem 9 implies $v(45)\pi(.80) < v(30)\pi(1.0)$, whereas the modal choice in problem 10 implies $v(45)\pi(.20) > v(30)\pi(.25)$. The observed violation of expected utility theory, then, is implied by the curvature of $\pi$ (see fig. 2.2) if

$$\frac{\pi(.20)}{\pi(.25)} > \frac{v(30)}{v(45)} > \frac{\pi(.80)}{\pi(1.0)}.$$

Allais's problem has attracted the attention of numerous theorists, who attempted to provide a normative rationale for the certainty effect by relaxing the cancellation rule (see, e.g., Allais 1979; Fishburn 1982,

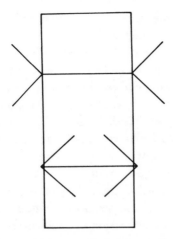

FIGURE 2.4 A Transparent Version of the Müller-Lyer Illusion

1983; Machina 1982; Quiggin 1982; Chew 1983). The following problem illustrates a related phenomenon, called the *pseudocertainty effect,*
that cannot be accommodated by relaxing cancellation because it also
involves a violation of invariance.

> *Problem 11 (N = 85):*
> Consider the following two stage game. In the first stage,
> there is a 75% chance to end the game without winning any-
> thing, and a 25% chance to move into the second stage. If
> you reach the second stage you have a choice between:
> E. a sure win of $30 [74%]
> F. 80% chance to win $45 and 20% chance to win nothing
> [26%]
> Your choice must be made before the outcome of the first
> stage is known.

Because there is one chance in four to move into the second stage,
prospect E offers a .25 probability of winning $30, and prospect F offers
a .25 × .80 = .20 probability of winning $45. Problem 11 is therefore
identical to problem 10 in terms of probabilities and outcomes. However, the preferences in the two problems differ: most subjects made a
risk-averse choice in problem 11 but not in problem 10. We call this
phenomenon the pseudocertainty effect because an outcome that is actually uncertain is weighted as if it were certain. The framing of problem
11 as a two-stage game encourages respondents to apply cancellation:
the event of failing to reach the second stage is discarded prior to evalu-

ation because it yields the same outcomes in both options. In this framing problems 11 and 9 are evaluated alike.

Although problems 10 and 11 are identical in terms of final outcomes and their probabilities, problem 11 has a greater potential for inducing regret. Consider a decision maker who chooses F in problem 11, reaches the second stage, but fails to win the prize. This individual knows that the choice of E would have yielded a gain of $30. In problem 10, on the other hand, an individual who chooses D and fails to win cannot know with certainty what the outcome of the other choice would have been. This difference could suggest an alternative interpretation of the pseudocertainty effect in terms of regret (e.g., Loomes and Sugden 1982). However, the certainty and the pseudocertainty effects were found to be equally strong in a modified version of problems 9–11 in which opportunities for regret were equated across problems. This finding does not imply that considerations of regret play no role in decisions. (For examples, see Kahneman and Tversky [1982, 710].) It merely indicates that Allais's example and the pseudocertainty effect are primarily controlled by the nonlinearity of decision weights and the framing of contingencies rather than by the anticipation of regret.[4]

The certainty and pseudocertainty effects are not restricted to monetary outcomes. The following problem illustrates these phenomena in a medical context. The respondents were 72 physicians attending a meeting of the California Medical Association. Essentially the same pattern of responses was obtained from a larger group ($N = 180$) of college students.

*Problem 12 ($N = 72$).*

In the treatment of tumors there is sometimes a choice between two types of therapies: (1) a radical treatment such as extensive surgery, which involves some risk of imminent death, (2) a moderate treatment, such as limited surgery or radiation therapy. Each of the following problems describes

4. In the modified version—problems 9'–11'—the probabilities of winning were generated by drawing a number from a bag containing 100 sequentially numbered tickets. In problem 10', the event associated with winning $45 (drawing a number between one and 20) was included in the event associated with winning $30 (drawing a number between one and 25). The sequential setup of problem 11 was replaced by the simultaneous play of two chance devices: the roll of a die (whose outcome determines whether the game is on) and the drawing of a numbered ticket from a bag. The possibility of regret now exists in all three problems, and problem 10' and 11' no longer differ in this respect because a decision-maker would always know the outcomes of alternative choices. Consequently, regret theory cannot explain either the certainty effect (9' vs. 10') or the pseudocertainty effect (10' vs. 11') observed in the modified problems.

the possible outcome of two alternative treatments, for three different cases. In considering each case, suppose the patient is a 40-year-old male. Assume that without treatment death is imminent (within a month) and that only one of the treatments can be applied. Please indicate the treatment you would prefer in each case.

### Case 1
Treatment A: 20% chance of imminent death and 80% chance of normal life, with an expected longevity of 30 years. [35%]
Treatment B: certainty of a normal life, with an expected longevity of 18 years. [65%]

### Case 2
Treatment C: 80% chance of imminent death and 20% chance of normal life, with an expected longevity of 30 years. [68%]
Treatment D: 75% chance of imminent death and 25% chance of normal life, with an expected longevity of 18 years. [32%]

### Case 3
Consider a new case where there is a 25% chance that the tumor is treatable and a 75% chance that it is not. If the tumor is not treatable, death is imminent. If the tumor is treatable, the outcomes of the treatment are as follows:
Treatment E: 20% chance of imminent death and 80% chance of normal life, with an expected longevity of 30 years. [32%]
Treatment F: certainty of normal life, with an expected longevity of 18 years. [68%]

The three cases of this problem correspond, respectively, to problems 9–11, and the same pattern of preferences is observed. In case 1, most respondents make a risk-averse choice in favor of certain survival with reduced longevity. In case 2, the moderate treatment no longer ensures survival, and most respondents choose the treatment that offers the higher expected longevity. In particular, 64 percent of the physicians who chose B in case 1 selected C in case 2. This is another example of Allais's certainty effect.

The comparison of cases 2 and 3 provides another illustration of pseudocertainty. The cases are identical in terms of the relevant outcomes and their probabilities, but the preferences differ. In particular, 56 percent of the physicians who chose C in case 2 selected F in case 3. The conditional framing induces people to disregard the event of the tumor not being treatable because the two treatments are equally ineffective in this case. In this frame, treatment F enjoys the advantage of pseudocertainty. It appears to ensure survival, but the assurance is conditional on the treatability of the tumor. In fact, there is only a .25 chance of surviving a month if this option is chosen.

The conjunction of certainty and pseudocertainty effects has significant implications for the relation between normative and descriptive theories of choice. Our results indicate that cancellation is actually obeyed in choices—in those problems that make its application transparent. Specifically, we find that people make the same choices in problems 11 and 9 and in cases 3 and 1 of problem 12. Evidently, people "cancel" an event that yields the same outcomes for all options, in two-stage or nested structures. Note that in these examples cancellation is satisfied in problems that are formally equivalent to those in which it is violated. The empirical validity of cancellation therefore depends on the framing of the problems.

The present concept of framing originated from the analysis of Allais's problems by Savage (1954, 101–4) and Raiffa (1968, 80–86), who reframed these examples in an attempt to make the application of cancellation more compelling. Savage and Raiffa were right: naive respondents indeed obey the cancellation axiom when its application is sufficiently transparent.[5] However, the contrasting preferences in different versions of the same choice (problems 10 and 11 and cases 2 and 3 of problem 12) indicate that people do not follow the same axiom when its application is not transparent. Instead, they apply (nonlinear) decision weights to the probabilities as stated. The status of cancellation is therefore similar to that of dominance: both rules are intuitively compelling as abstract principles of choice, consistently obeyed in transparent problems and frequently violated in nontransparent ones. Attempts to rationalize the preferences in Allais's example by discarding the cancellation axiom face a major difficulty: they do not distinguish transparent formulations in which cancellation is obeyed from nontransparent ones in which it is violated.

5. It is noteworthy that the conditional framing used in problems 11 and 12 (case 3) is much more effective in eliminating the common responses to Allais's paradox than the partition framing introduced by Savage (see, e.g., Slovic and Tversky 1974). This is probably due to the fact that the conditional framing makes it clear that the critical options are identical—after eliminating the state whose outcome does not depend on one's choice (that is, reaching the second stage in problem 11, an untreatable tumor in problem 12, case 3).

## V. Discussion

In the preceding sections we challenged the descriptive validity of the major tenets of expected utility theory and outlined an alternative account of risky choice. In this section we discuss alternative theories and argue against the reconciliation of normative and descriptive analyses. Some objections of economists to our analysis and conclusions are addressed.

### Descriptive and Normative Considerations

Many alternative models of risky choice, designed to explain the observed violations of expected utility theory, have been developed in the last decade. These models divide into the following four classes. (1) Nonlinear functionals (e.g., Allais 1953, 1979; Machina 1982) are obtained by eliminating the cancellation condition altogether. These models do not have axiomatizations leading to a (cardinal) measurement of utility, but they impose various restrictions (that is, differentiability) on the utility functional. (2) The expectations quotient model (axiomatized by Chew and MacCrimmon 1979; Weber 1982; Chew 1983; Fishburn 1983) replaces cancellation by a weaker substitution axiom and represents the value of a prospect by the ratio of two linear functionals. (3) Bilinear models with nonadditive probabilities (e.g., Kahneman and Tversky 1979; Quiggin 1982; Schmeidler 1984; Segal 1984; Yaari 1984; Luce and Narens 1985) assume various restricted versions of cancellation (or substitution) and construct a bilinear representation in which the utilities of outcomes are weighted by a nonadditive probability measure or by some nonlinear transform of the probability scale. (4) Nontransitive models represent preferences by a bivariate utility function. Fishburn (1982, 1984) axiomatized such models, while Bell (1982) and Loomes and Sugden (1982) interpreted them in terms of expected regret. For further theoretical developments, see Fishburn (1985).

The relation between models and data is summarized in table 2.1. The stub column lists the four major tenets of expected utility theory. Column 1 lists the major empirical violations of these tenets and cites a few representative references. Column 2 lists the subset of models discussed above that are consistent with the observed violations.

The conclusions of table 2.1 may be summarized as follows. First, all the above models (as well as some others) are consistent with the violations of cancellation produced by the certainty effect.[6] Therefore, Allais's

6. Because the present article focuses on prospects with known probabilities, we do not discuss the important violations of cancellation due to ambiguity (Ellsberg 1961).

Table 2.1 Summary of Empirical Violations and Explanatory Models

| Tenet | Empirical Violation | Explanatory Model |
|---|---|---|
| Cancellation | Certainty effect (Allais 1953, 1979; Kahneman and Tversky 1979) (problems 9–10, and 12 [cases 1 and 2]) | All models |
| Transitivity | Lexicographic semiorder (Tversky 1969) Preference reversals (Slovic and Lichtenstein 1983) | Bivariate models |
| Dominance | Contrasting risk attitudes (problem 2) Subadditive decision weights (problem 8) | Prospect theory |
| Invariance | Framing effects (Problems 1, 3–4, 5–6, 7–8, 10–11, and 12) | Prospect theory |

"paradox" cannot be used to compare or evaluate competing nonexpectation models. Second, bivariate (nontransitive) models are needed to explain observed intransitivities. Third, only prospect theory can accommodate the observed violations of (stochastic) dominance and invariance. Although some models (e.g., Loomes and Sugden 1982; Luce and Narens 1985) permit some limited failures of invariance, they do not account for the range of framing effects described in this article.

Because framing effects and the associated failures of invariance are ubiquitous, no adequate descriptive theory can ignore these phenomena. On the other hand, because invariance (or extensionality) is normatively indispensable, no adequate prescriptive theory should permit its violation. Consequently, the dream of constructing a theory that is acceptable both descriptively and normatively appears unrealizable (see also Tversky and Kahneman 1983).

Prospect theory differs from the other models mentioned above in being unabashedly descriptive and in making no normative claims. It is designed to explain preferences, whether or not they can be rationalized. Machina (1982, 292) claimed that prospect theory is "unacceptable as a descriptive model of behavior toward risk" because it implies violations of stochastic dominance. But since the violations of dominance predicted by the theory have actually been observed (see problems 2 and 8), Machina's objection appears invalid.

Perhaps the major finding of the present article is that the axioms of rational choice are generally satisfied in transparent situations and often violated in nontransparent ones. For example, when the relation of stochastic dominance is transparent (as in the aggregated version of problem 2 and in problem 7), practically everyone selects the dominant prospect. However, when these problems are framed so that the relation of dominance is no longer transparent (as in the segregated version of problem 2 and in problem 8), most respondents violate dominance, as predicted. These results contradict all theories that imply stochastic dominance as well as others (e.g., Machina 1982) that predict the same choices in transparent and nontransparent contexts. The same conclusion applies to cancellation, as shown in the discussion of pseudocertainty. It appears that both cancellation and dominance have normative appeal, although neither one is descriptively valid.

The present results and analysis—particularly the role of transparency and the significance of framing—are consistent with the conception of bounded rationality originally presented by Herbert Simon (see, e.g., Simon 1955, 1978; March 1978; Nelson and Winter 1982). Indeed, prospect theory is an attempt to articulate some of the principles of perception and judgment that limit the rationality of choice.

The introduction of psychological considerations (for example, framing) both enriches and complicates the analysis of choice. Because the framing of decisions depends on the language of presentation, on the context of choice, and on the nature of the display, our treatment of the process is necessarily informal and incomplete. We have identified several common rules of framing, and we have demonstrated their effects on choice, but we have not provided a formal theory of framing. Furthermore, the present analysis does not account for all the observed failures of transitivity and invariance. Although some intransitivities (e.g., Tversky 1969) can be explained by discarding small differences in the framing phase, and others (e.g., Raiffa 1968, 75) arise from the combination of transparent and nontransparent comparisons, there are examples of cyclic preferences and context effects (see, e.g., Slovic, Fischhoff, and Lichtenstein 1982; Slovic and Lichtenstein 1983) that require additional explanatory mechanisms (for example, multiple reference points and variable weights). An adequate account of choice cannot ignore these effects of framing and context, even if they are normatively distasteful and mathematically intractable.

## Bolstering Assumptions

The assumption of rationality has a favored position in economics. It is accorded all the methodological privileges of a self-evident truth, a reasonable idealization, a tautology, and a null hypothesis. Each of these interpretations either puts the hypothesis of rational action beyond question or places the burden of proof squarely on any alternative analysis of belief and choice. The advantage of the rational model is compounded because no other theory of judgment and decision can ever match it in scope, power, and simplicity.

Furthermore, the assumption of rationality is protected by a formidable set of defenses in the form of bolstering assumptions that restrict the significance of any observed violation of the model. In particular, it is commonly assumed that substantial violations of the standard model are (1) restricted to insignificant choice problems, (2) quickly eliminated by learning, or (3) irrelevant to economics because of the corrective function of market forces. Indeed, incentives sometimes improve the quality of decisions, experienced decision makers often do better than novices, and the forces of arbitrage and competition can nullify some effects of error and illusion. Whether these factors ensure rational choices in any particular situation is an empirical issue, to be settled by observation, not by supposition.

It has frequently been claimed (see e.g., Smith 1985) that the observed failures of rational models are attributable to the cost of thinking and will thus be eliminated by proper incentives. Experimental findings provide little support for this view. Studies reported in the economic and psychological literature have shown that errors that are prevalent in responses to hypothetical questions persist even in the presence of significant monetary payoffs. In particular, elementary blunders of probabilistic reasoning (Grether 1980; Tversky and Kahneman 1983) major inconsistencies of choice (Grether and Plott 1979; Slovic and Lichtenstein 1983), and violations of stochastic dominance in nontransparent problems (see problem 2 above) are hardly reduced by incentives. The evidence that high stakes do not always improve decisions is not restricted to laboratory studies. Significant errors of judgment and choice can be documented in real world decisions that involve high stakes and serious deliberation. The high rate of failures of small businesses, for example, is not easily reconciled with the assumptions of rational expectations and risk aversion.

Incentives do not operate by magic: they work by focusing attention and by prolonging deliberation. Consequently, they are more likely to prevent errors that arise from insufficient attention and effort than errors that arise from misperception or faulty intuition. The example of visual illusion is instructive. There is no obvious mechanism by which the mere introduction of incentives (without the added opportunity to make measurements) would reduce the illusion observed in figure 2.3, and the illusion vanishes—even in the absence of incentives—when the display is altered in figure 2.4. The corrective power of incentives depends on the nature of the particular error and cannot be taken for granted.

The assumption of the rationality of decision making is often defended by the argument that people will learn to make correct decisions and sometimes by the evolutionary argument that irrational decision makers will be driven out by rational ones. There is no doubt that learning and selection do take place and tend to improve efficiency. As in the case of incentives, however, no magic is involved. Effective learning takes place only under certain conditions: it requires accurate and immediate feedback about the relation between the situational conditions and the appropriate response. The necessary feedback is often lacking for the decisions made by managers, entrepreneurs, and politicians because (1) outcomes are commonly delayed and not easily attributable to a particular action; (2) variability in the environment degrades the reliability of the feedback, especially where outcomes of low probability are involved; (3) there is often no information about what the outcome would have been if another decision had been taken; and (4) most important decisions are unique and therefore provide little opportunity for learning (see Einhorn and Hogarth 1978). The conditions for organizational learning are hardly better. Learning surely occurs, for both individuals and organizations, but any claim that a particular error will be eliminated by experience must be supported by demonstrating that the conditions for effective learning are satisfied.

Finally, it is sometimes argued that failures of rationality in individual decision making are inconsequential because of the corrective effects of the market (Knez, Smith, and Williams 1985). Economic agents are often protected from their own irrational predilections by the forces of competition and by the action of arbitrageurs, but there are situations in which this mechanism fails. Hausch, Ziemba, and Rubenstein (1981) have documented an instructive example: the market for win bets at the racetrack is efficient, but the market for bets on place and show is not. Bettors commonly underestimate the probability that the favorite will end up in second or third place, and this effect is sufficiently large to sustain a contrarian betting strategy with a positive expected value. This inefficiency is found in spite of the high incentives, of the unquestioned level of dedication and expertise among participants in racetrack markets, and of obvious opportunities for learning and for arbitrage.

Situations in which errors that are common to many individuals are unlikely to be corrected by the market have been analyzed by Haltiwanger and Waldman (1985) and by Russell and Thaler (1985). Further-more, Akerlof and Yellen (1985) have presented their near-rationality theory, in which some prevalent errors in responding to economic changes (for example, inertia or money illusion) will (1) have little effect on the individual (thereby eliminating the possibility of learning), (2) provide no opportunity for arbitrage, and yet (3) have large economic effects. The claim that the market can be trusted to correct the effect of individual irrationalities cannot be made without supporting evidence, and the burden of specifying a plausible corrective mechanism should rest on those who make this claim.

The main theme of this article has been that the normative and the descriptive analyses of choice should be viewed as separate enterprises. This conclusion suggests a research agenda. To retain the rational model in its customary descriptive role, the relevant bolstering assumptions must be validated. Where these assumptions fail, it is instructive to trace the implications of the descriptive analysis (for example, the effects of loss aversion, pseudocertainty, or the money illusion) for public policy, strategic decision making, and macroeconomic phenomena (see Arrow 1982; Akerlof and Yellen 1985).

## REFERENCES

Akerlof, G. A., and Yellen, J. 1985. Can small deviations from rationality make significant differences to economic equilibria? *American Economic Review* 75:708–20.

Allais, M. 1953. Le comportement de l'homme rationnel devant le risque: Critique des postulats et axiomes de l'Ecole Américaine. *Econometrica* 21:503–46.

———. 1979. The foundations of a positive theory of choice involving risk and a criticism of the postulates and axioms of the american School. In M. Allais and O. Hagen (eds.), *Expected Utility Hypotheses and the Allais Paradox.* Dordrecht: Reidel.

Arrow, K. J. 1982. Risk perception in psychology and economics. *Economic Inquiry* 20:1–9.

Bazerman, M. H. 1983. Negotiator judgment. *American Behavioral Scientist* 27:211–28.

Bell, D. E. 1982. Regret in decision making under uncertainty. *Operations Research* 30:961–81.

Bishop, R. C., and Heberlein, T. A. 1979. Measuring values of extra-market goods: Are indirect measures biased? *American Journal of Agricultural Economics* 61:926–30.

Chew, S. H. 1983. A generalization of the quasilinear mean with applications to the measurement of income inequality and decision theory resolving the Allais paradox. *Econometrica* 51:1065–92.

Chew, S. H., and MacCrimmon, K. 1979. Alpha utility theory, lottery composition, and the Allais paradox. Working Paper no. 686. Vancouver: University of British Columbia.

Clark, H. H., and Clark, E. V. 1977. *Psychology and Language*. New York: Harcourt Brace Jovanovich.

Einhorn, J. J., and Hogarth, R. M. 1978. Confidence in judgment: Persistence of the illusion of validity. *Psychological Review* 85:395–416.

Ellsberg, D. 1961. Risk, ambiguity, and the Savage axioms. *Quarterly Journal of Economics* 75:643–69.

Eraker, S. E., and Sox, H. C. 1981. Assessment of patients' preferences for therapeutic outcomes. *Medical Decision Making* 1:29–39.

Fischhoff, B. 1983. Predicting frames. *Journal of Experimental Psychology: Learning, Memory and Cognition* 9:103–16.

Fishburn, P. C. 1982. Nontransitive measurable utility. *Journal of Mathematical Psychology* 26:31–67.

———. 1983. Transitive measurable utility. *Journal of Economic Theory* 31:293–317.

———. 1984. SSB utility theory and decision making under uncertainty. *Mathematical Social Sciences* 8:253–85.

———. 1985. Uncertainty aversion and separated effects in decision making under uncertainty. Working paper. Murray Hill, N.J.: AT&T Bell Labs.

Fishburn, P. C. and Kochenberger, G. A. 1979. Two-piece von Neumann-Morgenstern utility functions. *Decision Sciences* 10:503–18.

Grether, D. M. 1980. Bayes rule as a descriptive model: The representativeness heuristic. *Quarterly Journal of Economics* 95:537–57.

Grether, D. M., and Plott, C. R. 1979. Economic theory of choice and the preference reversal phenomenon. *American Economic Review* 69:623–38.

Hagen, O. 1979. Towards a positive theory of preferences under risk. In M. Allais and O. Hagen (eds.) *Expected Utility Hypotheses and the Allais Paradox*. Dordrecht: Reidel.

Haltiwanger, J., and Waldman, M. 1985. Rational expectations and the limits of rationality: An analysis of heterogeneity. *American Economic Review* 75:326–40.

Hammond, P. 1985. Consequential behavior in decision trees and expected utility. Institute for Mathematical Studies in the Social Sciences Working Paper no. 112. Stanford, Calif.: Stanford University.

Hansson, B. 1975. The appropriateness of the expected utility model. *Erkenntnis* 9:175–93.

Hausch, D. B.: Ziemba, W. T.; and Rubenstein, M. E. 1981. Efficiency of the market for racetrack betting. *Management Science* 27:1435–52.

Hershey, J. C., and Schoemaker, P. J. H. 1980. Risk taking and problem context in the domain of losses: An expected utility analysis. *Journal of Risk and Insurance* 47:111–32.

Kahneman, D., Knetsch, J. L., and Thaler, R. H. 1986a. Fairness and the assumptions of economics. *Journal of Business*. 1986a. 59 (4 pt. 2): 285–300.

———. 1986b. Perceptions of fairness: Entitlements in the market. *American Economic Review*.

Kahneman, D., and Tversky, A. 1979. Prospect theory: An analysis of decision under risk. *Econometrica* 47:263–91.

———. 1982. The psychology of preferences. *Scientific American* 246:160–73.

———. 1984. Choices, values, and frames. *American Psychologist* 39:341–50.

Knetsch, J. L., and Sinden, J. A. 1984. Willingness to pay and compensation demanded: Experimental evidence of an unexpected disparity in measures of value. *Quarterly Journal of Economics* 99:507–21.

Knez, P.; Smith, V. L.; and Williams, A. W. 1985. Individual rationality, market rationality and value estimation. *American Economic Review: Papers and Proceedings* 75:397–402.

Loomes, G., and Sugden, R. 1982. Regret theory: An alternative theory of rational choice under uncertainty. *Economic Journal* 92:805–24.

Luce, R. D., and Krantz, D. H. 1971. Conditional expected utility. *Econometrica* 39:253–71.

Luce, R. D., and Narens, L. 1985. Classification of concatenation measurement structures according to scale type. *Journal of Mathematical Psychology* 29:1–72.

Machina, M. J. 1982. "Expected utility" analysis without the independence axiom. *Econometrica* 50:277–323.

McNeil, B. J.; Pauker, S. G.; Sox, H. C., Jr.; and Tversky, A. 1982. On the elicitation of preferences for alternative therapies. *New England Journal of Medicine* 306:1259–62.

March, J. G. 1978. Bounded rationality, ambiguity, and the engineering of choice. *Bell Journal of Economics* 9:587–608.

Markowitz, H. 1952. The utility of wealth. *Journal of Political Economy* 60: 151–58.

Nelson, R. R., and Winter, S. G. 1982. *An Evolutionary Theory of Economic Change*. Cambridge, Mass.: Harvard University Press.

Payne, J. W.; Laughhunn, D. J.; and Crum, R. 1980. Translation of gambles and aspiration level effects in risky choice behavior. *Management Science* 26:1039–60.

Quiggin, J. 1982. A theory of anticipated utility. *Journal of Economic Behavior and Organization* 3:323–43.

Raiffa, H. 1968. *Decision Analysis: Introductory Lectures on Choices under Uncertainty*. Reading, Mass.: Addison-Wesley.

Russell, T., and Thaler, R. 1985. The relevance of quasi-rationality in competitive markets. *American Economic Review* 75:1071–82.

Savage, L. J. 1954. *The Foundations of Statistics*. New York: Wiley.

Schelling, T. C. 1981. Economic reasoning and the ethics of policy. *Public Interest* 63:37–61.

Schmeidler, D. 1984. Subjective probability and expected utility without additivity. Preprint Series no. 84. Minneapolis: University of Minnesota, Institute for Mathematics and Its Applications.

Schumpeter, J. A. 1954. *History of Economic Analysis*. New York: Oxford University Press.

Segal, U. 1984. Nonlinear decision weights with the independence axiom. Working Paper in Economics no. 353. Los Angeles: University of California, Los Angeles.

Simon, H. A. 1955. A behavioral model of rational choice. *Quarterly Journal of Economics* 69:99–118.

———. 1978. Rationality as process and as product of thought. *American Economic Review: Papers and Proceedings* 68:1–16.

Slovic, P.; Fischhoff, B.; and Lichtenstein, S. 1982. Response mode, framing, and information processing effects in risk assessment. In R. M. Hogarth (ed.), *New Directions for Methodology of Social and Behavioral Science: Question Framing and Response Consistency*. San Francisco: Jossey-Bass.

Slovic, P., and Lichtenstein, S. 1983. Preference reversals: A broader perspective. *American Economic Review* 73:596–605.

Slovic, P., and Tversky, A. 1974. Who accepts Savage's axiom? *Behavioral Science* 19:368–73.

Smith, V. L. 1985. Experimental economics: Reply. *American Economic Review* 75:265–72.

Stigler, G. J., and Kindahl, J. K. 1970. *The Behavior of Industrial Prices*. New York: National Bureau of Economic Research.

Thaler, R. H. 1980. Towards a positive theory of consumer choice. *Journal of Economic Behavior and Organization* 1:39–60.

Tversky, A. 1969. Intransitivity of preferences. *Psychological Review* 76:105–10.

———. 1977. On the elicitation of preferences: Descriptive and prescriptive considerations. In D. E. Bell, R. L. Keeney, and H. Raiffa (eds.), *Conflicting Objectives in Decisions*. New York: Wiley.

Tversky, A., and Kahneman, D. 1981. The framing of decisions and the psychology of choice. *Science* 211:453–58.

———. 1983. Extensional versus intuitive reasoning: The conjunction fallacy in probability judgment. *Psychological Review* 90:293–315.

von Neumann, J., and Morgenstern, O. 1944. *Theory of Games and Economic Behavior*. Princeton, N.J.: Princeton University Press.

Weber, R. J. 1982. The Allais paradox, Dutch auctions, and alpha-utility theory. Working paper. Evanston, Ill.: Northwestern University.

Yaari, M. E. 1984. Risk aversion without decreasing marginal utility. Report Series in Theoretical Economics. London: London School of Economics.

# 3

# Choice Under Uncertainty: Problems Solved and Unsolved

## Mark J. Machina

Fifteen years ago, the theory of choice under uncertainty could be considered one of the "success stories" of economic analysis: it rested on solid axiomatic foundations, it had seen important breakthroughs in the analytics of risk, risk aversion and their applications to economic issues, and it stood ready to provide the theoretical underpinnings for the newly emerging "information revolution" in economics.[1] Today choice under uncertainty is a field in flux: the standard theory is being challenged on several grounds from both within and outside economics. The nature of these challenges, and of our profession's responses to them, is the topic of this paper.

The following section provides a brief description of the economist's canonical model of choice under uncertainty, the expected utility model of preferences over random prospects. I shall present this model from two different perspectives. The first perspective is the most familiar and has traditionally been the most useful for addressing standard economic questions. However the second, more modern perspective will be the most useful for illustrating some of the problems which have beset the model, as well as some of the proposed responses.

Each of the subsequent sections is devoted to one of these problems. All are important, some are more completely "solved" than others. In each case I shall begin with an example or description of the phenomenon in question. I shall then review the empirical evidence regarding the

Reprinted, with permission, from *Journal of Economic Perspectives* 1, no. 1 (Summer 1987): 121–54. © 1987 American Economic Association. The author is grateful to Brian Binger, John Conlisk, Jim Cox, Vincent Crawford, Gong Jin Dong, Elizabeth Hoffman, Michael Rothschild, Carl Shapiro, Vernon Smith, Joseph Stiglitz, Timothy Taylor and especially Joel Sobel for helpful discussions on this material, and the Alfred P. Sloan Foundation for financial support.

1. E.g., von Neumann and Morgenstern (1947) and Savage (1954) (axiomatics); Arrow (1965), Pratt (1964), and Rothschild and Stiglitz (1970) (analytics); Akerlof (1970) and Spence and Zeckhauser (1971) (information).

uniformity and extent of the phenomenon. Finally, I shall report on how these findings have changed, or are likely to change, or ought to change, the way we view and model economic behavior under uncertainty. On this last topic, the disclaimer that "my opinions are my own" has more than the usual significance.[2]

## THE EXPECTED UTILITY MODEL
### The Classical Perspective: Cardinal Utility and Attitudes Toward Risk

In light of current trends toward generalizing this model, it is useful to note that the expected utility hypothesis was itself first proposed as an alternative to an earlier, more restrictive theory of risk-bearing. During the development of modern probability theory in the seventeenth century, mathematicians such as Blaise Pascal and Pierre de Fermat assumed that the attractiveness of a gamble offering the payoffs $(x_1, \ldots, x_n)$ with probabilities $(p_1, \ldots, p_n)$ was given by its expected value $\bar{x} = \Sigma x_i p_i$. The fact that individuals consider more than just expected value, however, was dramatically illustrated by an example posed by Nicholas Bernoulli in 1728 and now known as the *St. Petersburg Paradox:*

> Suppose someone offers to toss a fair coin repeatedly until it comes up heads, and to pay you $1 if this happens on the first toss, $2 if it takes two tosses to land a head, $4 if it takes three tosses, $8 if it takes four tosses, etc. What is the largest sure gain you would be willing to forgo in order to undertake a single play of this game?

Since this gamble offers a ½ chance of winning $1, a ¼ chance of winning $2, etc., its expected value is $(½) \cdot \$1 + (¼) \cdot \$2 + (⅛) \cdot \$4 + \ldots = \$½ + \$½ + \$½ + \ldots = \$\infty$, so it should be preferred to any finite sure gain. However, it is clear that few individuals would forgo more than a moderate amount for a one-shot play. Although the unlimited financial backing needed to actually make this offer is somewhat unrealistic, it is not essential for making the point: agreeing to limit the game to at most one million tosses will still lead to a striking discrepancy between most individuals' valuations of the modified gamble and its expected value of $500,000.

The resolution of this paradox was proposed independently by Gabriel Cramer and Nicholas's cousin Daniel Bernoulli (Bernoulli, 1738/1954).

---

2. References have been limited to the most significant examples of and/or most useful introduction to the literature in each area. For further discussions of these issues see Arrow (1982), Machina (1983a, 1983b), Sugden (1986) and Tversky and Kahneman (1986).

Arguing that a gain of $200 was not necessarily "worth" twice as much as a gain of $100, they hypothesized that the individual possesses what is now termed a *von Neumann-Morgenstern utility function* $U(\cdot)$, and rather than using expected value $\bar{x} = \Sigma x_i p_i$, will evaluate gambles on the basis of expected utility $\bar{u} = \Sigma U(x_i)p_i$. Thus the sure gain $\xi$ which would yield the same utility as the Petersburg gamble, that is, the certainty equivalent of this gamble, is determined by the equation

$$U(W + \xi) = (\tfrac{1}{2}) \cdot U(W + 1) + (\tfrac{1}{4}) \cdot U(W + 2) \qquad (1)$$
$$+ (\tfrac{1}{8}) \cdot U(W + 4) + \ldots$$

where $W$ is the individual's current wealth. If utility took the logarithmic form $U(x) \equiv \ln(x)$ and $W = \$50,000$, for example, the individual's certainty equivalent $\xi$ would only be about $9, even though the gamble has an infinite expected value.

Although it shares the name "utility," $U(\cdot)$ is quite distinct from the ordinal utility function of standard consumer theory. While the latter can be subjected to any monotonic transformation, a von Neumann-Morgenstern utility function is cardinal in that it can only be subjected to transformations of the form $a \cdot U(x) + b$ $(a > 0)$, namely, transformations which change the origin and/or scale of the vertical axis, but do not affect the "shape" of the function.[3]

To see how this shape determines risk attitudes, consider figures 3.1 and 3.2. The monotonicity of $U_a(\cdot)$ and $U_b(\cdot)$ in the figures reflects the property of stochastic dominance preference, where one lottery is said to stochastically dominate another one if it can be obtained from it by shifting probability from lower to higher outcome levels.[4] Stochastic dominance preference is thus the probabilistic analogue of the attitude that "more is better."

Consider a gamble offering a $\tfrac{2}{3}:\tfrac{1}{3}$ chance of the outcomes $x'$ or $x''$. The points $\bar{x} = (\tfrac{2}{3}) \cdot x' + (\tfrac{1}{3}) \cdot x''$ in the figures give the expected value of this gamble, and $\bar{u}_a = (\tfrac{2}{3}) \cdot U_a(x') + (\tfrac{1}{3}) \cdot U_a(x'')$ and $\bar{u}_b = (\tfrac{2}{3}) \cdot U_b(x') + (\tfrac{1}{3}) \cdot U_b(x'')$ give its expected utilities for $U_a(\cdot)$ and $U_b(\cdot)$. For the concave utility function $U_a(\cdot)$ we have $U_a(\bar{x}) > \bar{u}_a$, which implies that this individual would prefer a sure gain of $\bar{x}$ (which would yield utility

3. Such transformations are often used to normalize the utility function, for example to set $U(0) = 0$ and $U(M) = 1$ for some large value $M$.

4. Thus, for example, a $\tfrac{2}{3}:\tfrac{1}{3}$ chance of $100 or $20 and a $\tfrac{1}{2}:\tfrac{1}{2}$ chance of $100 or $30 both stochastically dominate a $\tfrac{1}{2}:\tfrac{1}{2}$ chance of $100 or $20.

$U_a(\bar{x})$) to the gamble. Since someone with a concave utility function will in fact always prefer receiving the expected value of a gamble to the gamble itself, concave utility functions are termed risk averse. For the convex utility function $U_b(\cdot)$ we have $\bar{u}_b > U_b(\bar{x})$, and since this preference for bearing the risk rather than receiving the expected value will also extend to all gambles, $U_b(\cdot)$ is termed risk loving. In their famous article, Friedman and Savage (1948) showed how a utility function which was concave at low wealth levels and convex at high wealth levels could explain the behavior of individuals who both incur risk by purchasing lottery tickets as well as avoid risk by purchasing insurance. Algebraically, Arrow (1965) and Pratt (1964) have shown how the degree of concavity of a utility function, as measured by the curvature index $- U''(x)/U'(x)$, determines how risk attitudes, and hence behavior, will vary with wealth or across individuals in a variety of situations. If $U_c(\cdot)$ is at least as risk averse as $U_d(\cdot)$ in the sense that $- U_c''(x)/U_c'(x) \geq - U_d''(x)/U_d'(x)$ for all $x$, then an individual with utility function $U_c(\cdot)$ would be willing to pay at least as much for insurance against any risk as would someone with utility function $U_d(\cdot)$.

Since a knowledge of $U(\cdot)$ would allow us to predict preferences (and hence behavior) in any risky situation, experimenters and applied decision analysts are frequently interested in eliciting or recovering their subjects' (or clients') von Neumann-Morgenstern utility functions. One method of doing so is termed the fractile method. This approach begins by adopting the normalization $U(0) = 0$ and $U(M) = 1$ (see note 3) and fixing a "mixture probability" $\bar{p}$, say $\bar{p} = \frac{1}{2}$. The next step involves finding the individual's certainty equivalent $\xi_1$ of a $\frac{1}{2}:\frac{1}{2}$ chance of $M$ or 0, which implies that $U(\xi_1) = (\frac{1}{2}) \cdot U(M) + (\frac{1}{2}) \cdot U(0) = \frac{1}{2}$. Finding the certainty equivalents of the $\frac{1}{2}:\frac{1}{2}$ chances of $\xi_1$ or 0 and of $M$ or $\xi_1$ yields the values $\xi_2$ and $\xi_3$ which solve $U(\xi_2) = \frac{1}{4}$ and $U(\xi_3) = \frac{3}{4}$. By repeating this procedure (i.e., $\frac{1}{8}$, $\frac{3}{8}$, $\frac{5}{8}$, $\frac{7}{8}$, $\frac{1}{16}$, $\frac{3}{16}$, etc.), the utility function can (in the limit) be completely assessed.

Our discussion so far has paralleled the economic literature of the 1960s and 1970s by emphasizing the flexibility of the expected utility model compared to the Pascal-Fermat expected value approach. However, the need to analyze and respond to growing empirical challenges has led economists in the 1980s to concentrate on the behavioral restrictions implied by the expected utility hypothesis. It is to these restrictions that we now turn.

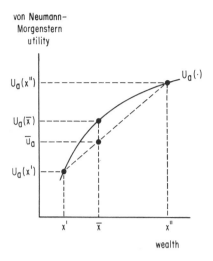

FIGURE 3.1 Concave Utility Function of a Risk Averter

## A Modern Perspective: Linearity in the Probabilities as a Testable Hypothesis

As a theory of individual behavior, the expected utility model shares many of the underlying assumptions of standard consumer theory. In each case we assume that the objects of choice, either commodity bundles or lotteries, can be unambiguously and objectively described, and that situations which ultimately imply the same set of availabilities (for example, the same budget set) will lead to the same choice. In each case we also assume that the individual is able to perform the mathematical operations necessary to actually determine the set of availabilities, for example, to add up the quantities in different sized containers or calculate the probabilities of compound or conditional events. Finally, in each case we assume that preferences are transitive, so that if an individual prefers one object (either a commodity bundle or a risky prospect) to a second, and prefers this second object to a third, he or she will prefer the first object to the third. We shall examine the validity of these assumptions for choice under uncertainty in some of the following sections.

However, the strongest implication of the expected utility hypothesis stems from the form of the expected utility maximand or preference function $\Sigma U(x_i)p_i$. Although this preference function generalizes the expected value form $\Sigma x_i p_i$ by dropping the property of linearity in the pay-

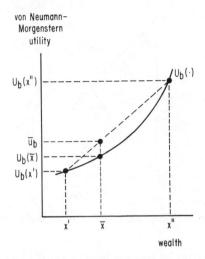

FIGURE 3.2 Convex Utility Function of a Risk Lover

offs (the $x_i$'s), it retains the other key property of this form, namely linearity in the probabilities.

Graphically, we may illustrate the property of linearity in the probabilities by considering the set of all lotteries or prospects over the fixed outcome levels $x_1 < x_2 < x_3$, which can be represented by the set of all probability triples of the form $P = (p_1, p_2, p_3)$ where $p_i = \text{prob}(x_i)$ and $\Sigma p_i = 1$. Since $p_2 = 1 - p_1 - p_3$, we can represent these lotteries by the points in the unit triangle in the $(p_1, p_3)$ plane, as in figure 3.3.[5] Since upward movements in the triangle increase $p_3$ at the expense of $p_2$ (that is, shift probability from the outcome $x_2$ up to $x_3$) and leftward movements reduce $p_1$ to the benefit of $p_2$ (shift probability from $x_1$ up to $x_2$), these movements (and more generally, all northwest movements) lead to stochastically dominating lotteries and would accordingly be preferred. Finally, since the individual's indifference curves in the $(p_1, p_3)$ diagram are given by the solutions to the linear equation

$$\bar{u} = \sum_{i=1}^{3} U(x_i)p_i = U(x_1)p_1 + U(x_2)$$  (2)

$$(1 - p_1 - p_3) + U(x_3)p_3 = \text{constant}$$

5. Thus, if $x_1 = \$20$, $x_2 = \$30$ and $x_3 = \$100$, the prospects in note 4 would be represented by the points $(p_1, p_3) = (\frac{1}{3}, \frac{2}{3})$, $(p_1, p_3) = (\frac{1}{2}, \frac{1}{2})$ respectively. Although it is fair to describe the renewal of interest in this approach as "modern," versions of this diagram go back at least to Marschak (1950).

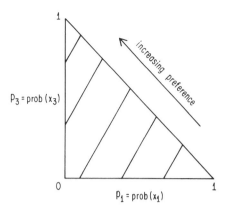

FIGURE 3.3 Expected Utility Indifference Curves in the Triangle Diagram

they will consist of parallel straight lines of slope $[U(x_2) - U(x_1)]/[U(x_3) - U(x_2)]$, with more preferred indifference curves lying to the northwest. This implies that in order to know an expected utility maximizer's preferences over the entire triangle, it suffices to know the slope of a single indifference curve.

To see how this diagram can be used to illustrate attitudes toward risk, consider figures 3.4 and 3.5. The dashed lines in the figures are not indifference curves but rather *iso-expected value lines,* that is, solutions to

$$\bar{x} = \sum_{i=1}^{3} x_i p_i = x_1 p_1 + x_2(1 - p_1 - p_3)$$
$$+ x_3 p_3 = \text{constant} \qquad (3)$$

Since northeast movements along these lines do not change the expected value of the prospect but do increase the probabilities of the tail outcomes $x_1$ and $x_3$ at the expense of the middle outcome $x_2$, they are examples of *mean preserving spreads* or "pure" increases in risk (Rothschild and Stiglitz 1970). When the utility function $U(\cdot)$ is concave (namely, risk averse), its indifference curves can be shown to be steeper than the iso-expected value lines as in figure 3.4,[6] and such increases in risk will lead to lower indifference curves. When $U(\cdot)$ is convex (risk loving), its indifference curves will be flatter than the iso-expected value lines

6. This follows since the slope of indifference curves is $[U(x_2) - U(x_1)] / [U(x_3) - U(x_2)]$, the slope of the iso-expected value lines is $[(x_2 - x_1] / [x_3 - x_2]$, and concavity of $U(\cdot)$ implies $[U(x_2) - U(x_1)] / [x_2 - x_1] > [U(x_3) - U(x_2)] / [x_3 - x_2]$ whenever $x_1 < x_2 < x_3$.

(as in figure 3.5) and increases in risk will lead to higher indifference curves. If we compare two different utility functions, the one which is more risk averse (in the above Arrow-Pratt sense) will possess the steeper indifference curves.

Behaviorally, we can view the property of linearity in the probabilities as a restriction on the individual's preferences over probability mixtures of lotteries. If $P^* = (p_1^*, \ldots, p_n^*)$ and $P = (p_1, \ldots, p_n)$ are two lotteries over a common outcome set $\{x_1, \ldots, x_n\}$, the $\alpha:(1 - \alpha)$ probability mixture of $P^*$ and $P$ is the lottery $\alpha P^* + (1 - \alpha)P = (\alpha p_1^* + (1 - \alpha)p_1, \ldots, \alpha p_n^* + (1 - \alpha)p_n)$. This may be thought of as that prospect which yields the same ultimate probabilities over $\{x_1, \ldots, x_n\}$ as the two-stage lottery which offers an $\alpha:(1 - \alpha)$ chance of winning either $P^*$ or $P$. Since linearity in the probabilities implies that $\Sigma U(x_i)(\alpha p_i^* + (1 - \alpha)p_i) = \alpha \cdot \Sigma U(x_i)p_i^* + (1 - \alpha) \cdot \Sigma U(x_i)p_i$, expected utility maximizers will exhibit the following property, known as the *Independence Axiom* (Samuelson 1952):

> If the lottery $P^*$ is preferred (resp. indifferent) to the lottery $P$, then the mixture $\alpha P^* + (1 - \alpha)P^{**}$ will be preferred (resp. indifferent) to the mixture $\alpha P + (1 - \alpha)P^{**}$ for all $\alpha > 0$ and $P^{**}$.

This property, which is in fact equivalent to linearity in the probabilities, can be interpreted as follows:

> In terms of the ultimate probabilities over the outcomes $\{x_1, \ldots, x_n\}$, choosing between the mixtures $\alpha P^* + (1 - \alpha)P^{**}$ and $\alpha P + (1 - \alpha)P^{**}$ is the same as being offered a coin with a probability of $1 - \alpha$ of landing tails, in which case you will obtain the lottery $P^{**}$, and being asked before the flip whether you would rather have $P^*$ or $P$ in the event of a head. Now either the coin will land tails, in which case your choice won't have mattered, or else it will land heads, in which case you are 'in effect' back to a choice between $P^*$ or $P$, and it is only 'rational' to make the same choice as you would before.

Although this is a prescriptive argument, it has played a key role in economists' adoption of expected utility as a descriptive theory of choice under uncertainty. As the evidence against the model mounts, this has lead to a growing tension between those who view economic analysis as the description and prediction of what they consider to be rational behavior and those who view it as the description and prediction of observed behavior. We turn now to this evidence.

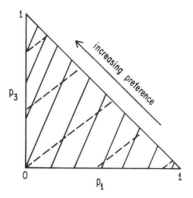

(solid lines are expected utility indifference curves)
(dashed lines are iso-expected value lines)

FIGURE 3.4 Relatively Steep Indifference Curves of a Risk Averter

## VIOLATIONS OF LINEARITY IN THE PROBABILITIES
### The Allais Paradox and "Fanning Out"

One of the earliest and best known examples of systematic violation of linearity in the probabilities (or equivalently, of the independence axiom) is the well-known *Allais Paradox* (Allais, 1953, 1979). This problem involves obtaining the individual's preferred option from each of the following two pairs of gambles (readers who have never seen this problem may want to circle their own choice from each pair before proceeding):

$$a_1: \left\{ 1.00 \text{ chance of } \$1,000,000 \quad \text{versus} \quad a_2: \left\{ \begin{array}{l} .10 \text{ chance of } \$5,000,000 \\ .89 \text{ chance of } \$1,000,000 \\ .01 \text{ chance of } \$0 \end{array} \right. \right.$$

and

$$a_3: \left\{ \begin{array}{l} .10 \text{ chance of } \$5,000,000 \\ .90 \text{ chance of } \$0 \end{array} \right. \quad \text{versus} \quad a_4: \left\{ \begin{array}{l} .11 \text{ chance of } \$1,000,000 \\ .89 \text{ chance of } \$0 \end{array} \right.$$

Defining $\{x_1, x_2, x_3\} = \{\$0; \$1,000,000; \$5,000,000\}$, these four gambles are seen form a parallelogram in the $(p_1, p_3)$ triangle, as in figures 3.6 and 3.7. Under the expected utility hypothesis, therefore, a preference for $a_1$ in the first pair would indicate that the individual's indifference curves were relatively steep (as in figure 3.6), and hence a preference for

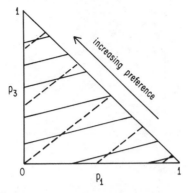

(solid lines are expected utility indifference curves)
(dashed lines are iso-expected value lines)

FIGURE 3.5 Relatively Flat Indifference Curves of a Risk Lover

$a_4$ in the second pair. In the alternative case of relatively flat indifference curves, the gambles $a_2$ and $a_3$ would be preferred.[7] However, researchers such as Allais (1953), Morrison (1967), Raiffa (1968) and Slovic and Tversky (1974) have found that the modal if not majority preferences of subjects has been for $a_1$ in the first pair and $a_3$ in the second, which implies that indifference curves are not parallel but rather fan out, as in figure 3.7.

One of the criticisms of this evidence has been that individuals whose choices violated the independence axiom would "correct" themselves once the nature of their violation was revealed by an application of the above coin-flip argument. Thus, while even Savage chose $a_1$ and $a_3$ when first presented with this example, he concluded upon reflection that these preferences were in error (Savage, 1954, 101–3). Although his own reaction was undoubtedly sincere, the hypothesis that individuals would invariably react in such a manner has not been sustained in direct empirical testing. In experiments where subjects were asked to respond to Allais-type problems and then presented with arguments both for and against the expected utility position, neither MacCrimmon (1968), Moskowitz (1974) nor Slovic and Tversky (1974) found predominant net swings toward the expected utility choices.

7. Algebraically, these cases are equivalent to the expression [.10 $U(5,000,000)$ − .11 · $U(1,000,000)$ + .01 · $U(0)$] being negative or positive, respectively.

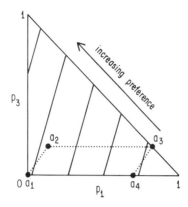

FIGURE 3.6 Expected Utility Indifference Curves and the Allais Paradox

## Additional Evidence of Fanning Out

Although the Allais Paradox was originally dismissed as an isolated example, it is now known to be a special case of a general empirical pattern termed the *common consequence effect*. This effect involves pairs of probability mixtures of the form:

$$b_1: \alpha\delta_x + (1 - \alpha)P^{**} \text{ versus } b_2: \alpha P + (1 - \alpha)P^{**}$$

and

$$b_3: \alpha\delta_x + (1 - \alpha)P^* \text{ versus } b_4: \alpha P + (1 - \alpha)P^*$$

where $\delta_x$ denotes the prospect which yields $x$ with certainty, $P$ involves outcomes both greater and less than $x$, and $P^{**}$ stochastically dominates $P^*$.[8] Although the independence axiom clearly implies choices of either $b_1$ and $b_3$ (if $\delta_x$ is preferred to $P$) or else $b_2$ and $b_4$ (if $P$ is preferred to $\delta_x$), researchers have found a tendency for subjects to choose $b_1$ in the first pair and $b_4$ in the second (MacCrimmon, 1968; MacCrimmon and Larsson, 1979; Kahneman and Tversky, 1979; Chew and Waller, 1986). When the distributions $\delta_x$, $P$, $P^*$ and $P^{**}$ are each over a common out-

8. The Allais Paradox choices $a_1$, $a_2$, $a_3$, and $a_4$ correspond to $b_1$, $b_2$, $b_4$ and $b_3$, where $\alpha$ = .11, $x$ = \$1,000,000, $P$ is a $^{10}/_{11}:^1/_{11}$ chance of \$5,000,000 or \$0, $P^*$ is a sure chance of \$0, and $P^{**}$ is a sure chance of \$1,000,000. The name of this phenomenon comes from the "common consequence" $P^{**}$ in $\{b_1, b_2\}$ and $P^*$ in $\{b_3, b_4\}$.

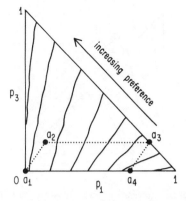

FIGURE 3.7 Indifference Curves that "Fan Out" and the Allais Paradox

come set $\{x_1, x_2, x_3\}$, the prospects $b_1$, $b_2$, $b_3$ and $b_4$ will again form a parallelogram in the $(p_1, p_3)$ triangle, and a choice of $b_1$ and $b_4$ again implies indifference curves which fan out, as in figure 3.7.

The intuition behind this phenomenon can be described in terms of the above "coin-flip" scenario. According to the independence axiom, preferences over what would occur in the event of a head should not depend upon what would occur in the event of a tail. In fact, however, they may well depend upon what would otherwise happen.[9] The common consequence effect states that the better off individuals would be in the event of a tail (in the sense of stochastic dominance), the more risk averse they become over what they would receive in the event of a head. Intuitively, if the distribution $P^{**}$ in the pair $\{b_1, b_2\}$ involves very high outcomes, I may prefer not to bear further risk in the unlucky event that I don't receive it, and prefer the sure outcome $x$ over the distribution $P$ in this event (that is, choose $b_1$ over $b_2$). But if $P^*$ in $\{b_3, b_4\}$ involves very low outcomes, I may be more willing to bear risk in the (lucky) event that I don't receive it, and prefer the lottery $P$ to the outcome $x$ in this case (that is, choose $b_4$ over $b_3$). Note that it is not my beliefs regarding the probabilities in $P$ which are affected here, merely my willingness to bear them.[10]

A second class of systematic violations, stemming from another early

9. As Bell (1985) notes, "Winning the top prize of $10,000 in a lottery may leave one much happier receiving $10,000 as the lowest prize in a lottery."
10. In a conversation with the author, Kenneth Arrow has offered an alternative phrasing of this argument: The widely maintained hypothesis of decreasing absolute risk aversion asserts that individuals will display more risk aversion in the event of a loss and less risk

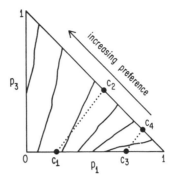

FIGURE 3.8 Indifference Curves that Fan Out and the Common Ratio Effect

example of Allais (1953), is known as the *common ratio effect*. This phenomenon involves pairs of prospects of the form:

$$c_1: \begin{cases} p \text{ chance of } \$X \\ 1 - p \text{ chance of } \$0 \end{cases} \text{ versus } c_2: \begin{cases} q \text{ chance of } \$Y \\ 1 - q \text{ chance of } \$0, \end{cases}$$

and

$$c_3: \begin{cases} rp \text{ chance of } \$X \\ 1 - rp \text{ chance of } \$0 \end{cases} \text{ versus } c_4: \begin{cases} rq \text{ chance of } \$Y \\ 1 - rq \text{ chance of } \$0 \end{cases}$$

where $p > q$, $0 < X < Y$ and $r \in (0, 1)$, and includes the "certainty effect" of Kahneman and Tversky (1979) and the ingenious "Bergen Paradox" of Hagen (1979) as special cases.[11] Setting $\{x_1, x_2, x_3\} = \{0, X, Y\}$ and plotting these prospects in the $(p_1, p_3)$ triangle, the segments $\overline{c_1 c_2}$ and $\overline{c_3 c_4}$ are seen to be parallel (as in figure 3.8), so that the expected utility model again predicts choices of $c_1$ and $c_3$ (if the individual's indifference curves are steep) or else $c_2$ and $c_4$ (if they are flat).

However, experimental studies have found a systematic tendency for choices to depart from these predictions in the direction of preferring $c_1$

---

aversion in the event of a gain. In the common consequence effect, individuals display more risk aversion in the event of an opportunity loss and less risk aversion in the event of an opportunity gain.

11. The former involves setting $p = 1$, and the latter consists of a two-step choice problem where individuals exhibit the effect with $Y = 2X$ and $p = 2q$. The name "common ratio effect" comes from the common value of prob$(X)$/prob$(Y)$ in the pairs $\{c_1, c_2\}$ and $\{c_3, c_4\}$.

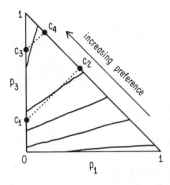

FIGURE 3.9 Indifference Curves that Fan Out and the Common Ratio Effect with Negative Payoffs

and $c_4$,[12] which again suggests that indifference curves fan out, as in the figure (Tversky, 1975; MacCrimmon and Larsson 1979; Chew and Waller 1986). In a variation on this approach, Kahneman and Tversky (1979) replaced the gains of $X and $Y in the above gambles with losses of these magnitudes, and found a tendency to depart from expected utility in the direction of $c_2$ and $c_3$. Defining $\{x_1, x_2, x_3\}$ as $\{-Y, -X, 0\}$ (to maintain the condition $x_1 < x_2 < x_3$) and plotting these gambles in figure 3.9, a choice of $c_2$ and $c_3$ is again seen to imply that indifferent curves fan out. Finally, Battalio, Kagel, and MacDonald (1985) found that laboratory rats choosing among gambles which involved substantial variations in their actual daily food intake also exhibited this pattern of choices.

A third class of evidence stems from the elicitation method described in the previous section. In particular, note that there is no reason why the mixture probability $\bar{p}$ must be $\frac{1}{2}$ in this procedure. Picking any other $\bar{p}$ and defining $\xi_1^*$, $\xi_2^*$ and $\xi_3^*$ as the certainty equivalents of the $\bar{p}$: $(1 - \bar{p})$ chances of M or 0, $\xi_1^*$ of 0, and M or $\xi_1^*$ yields the equations $U(\xi_1^*) = \bar{p}$, $U(\xi_2^*) = \bar{p}^2$, $U(\xi_3^*) = \bar{p} + (1 - \bar{p})\bar{p}$, etc., and such a procedure can also be used to recover $U(\ )$.

Although this procedure should recover the same (normalized) utility function for any mixture probability, researchers such as Karmarker (1974, 1978) and McCord and de Neufville (1983, 1984) have found a tendency for higher values of $\bar{p}$ to lead to the "recovery" of higher valued utility functions, as in figure 3.10. By illustrating the gambles used to obtain the values $\xi_1$, $\xi_2$, and $\xi_3$ for $\bar{p} = \frac{1}{2}$, $\xi_1^*$ for $\bar{p} = \frac{1}{4}$ and $\xi_1^{**}$ for $\bar{p}$

12. Kahneman and Tversky (1979), for example, found that 80 percent of their subjects preferred a sure gain of 3,000 Israeli pounds to a .80 chance of winning 4,000, but 65 percent preferred a .20 chance of winning 4,000 to a .25 chance of winning 3,000.

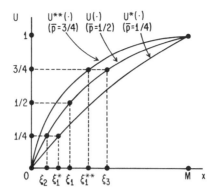

FIGURE 3.10 "Recovered" Utility Functions for Mixture Probabilities ¼, ½, and ¾

= ¾, figure 3.11 shows that, as with the common consequence and common ratio effects, this *utility evaluation effect* is precisely what would be expected from an individual whose indifference curves departed from expected utility by fanning out.[13]

### Non-Expected Utility Models of Preferences

The systematic nature of these departures from linearity in the probabilities has led several researchers to generalize the expected utility model by positing nonlinear functional forms for the individual preference function. Examples of such forms and researchers who have studied them include:

$$\Sigma v(x_i)\pi(p_i) \qquad\qquad \text{Edwards (1955)} \qquad (4)$$
$$\text{Kahneman and Tversky (1979)}$$

$$\frac{\Sigma v(x_i)\pi(p_i)}{\Sigma \pi(p_i)} \qquad\qquad \text{Karmarkar (1978)} \qquad (5)$$

$$\frac{\Sigma v(x_i)p_i}{\Sigma \tau(x_i)p_i} \qquad\qquad \begin{array}{c}\text{Chew (1983)}\\ \text{Fishburn (1983)}\end{array} \qquad (6)$$

13. Having found that $\xi_1$ which solves $U(\xi_1) = (\frac{1}{2}) \cdot U(M) + (\frac{1}{2}) \cdot U(0)$, choose $\{x_1,x_2,x_3\}$ = $\{0, \xi_1, M\}$, so that the indifference curve through $(0,0)$ (i.e., a sure gain of $\xi_1$) also passes through $(\frac{1}{2}, \frac{1}{2})$ (a $\frac{1}{2}$:$\frac{1}{2}$ chance of $M$ or $0$). The order of $\xi_1, \xi_2, \xi_3, \xi_1^*$ and $\xi_1^{**}$ in figure 3.10 is derived from the individual's preference ordering over the five distributions in figure 3.11 for which they are the respective certainty equivalents.

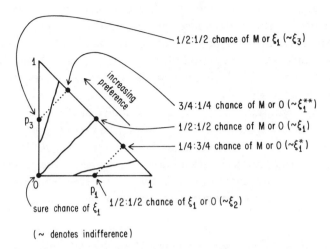

1/2:1/2 chance of M or $\xi_1$ ($\sim\xi_3$)

3/4:1/4 chance of M or 0 ($\sim\xi_1^{**}$)

1/2:1/2 chance of M or 0 ($\sim\xi_1$)

1/4:3/4 chance of M or 0 ($\sim\xi_1^*$)

1/2:1/2 chance of $\xi_1$ or 0 ($\sim\xi_2$)

sure chance of $\xi_1$

( $\sim$ denotes indifference )

FIGURE 3.11 Fanning Out Indifference Curves that Generate the Responses of Figure 3.10

$$\Sigma v(x_i)[g(p_1 + \ldots + p_i) - g(p_1 + \ldots + p_{i-1})] \qquad \text{Quiggin (1982)} \qquad (7)$$

$$\Sigma v(x_i)p_i + [\Sigma \tau(x_i)p_i]^2 \qquad \text{Machina (1982)} \qquad (8)$$

Many (though not all) of these forms are flexible enough to exhibit the properties of stochastic dominance preference, risk aversion/risk preference and fanning out, and (6) and (7) have proven to be particularly useful both theoretically and empirically. Additional analyses of these forms can be found in Chew, Karni and Safra (1987), Fishburn (1964), Segal (1984) and Yaari (1987).

Although such forms allow for the modelling of preferences which are more general than those allowed by the expected utility hypothesis, each requires a different set of conditions on its component functions $v(\cdot)$, $\pi(\cdot)$, $\tau(\cdot)$ or $g(\cdot)$ for the properties of stochastic dominance preference, risk aversion/risk preference, comparative risk aversion, etc. In particular, the standard expected utility results linking properties of the function $U(\cdot)$ to such aspects of behavior will generally not extend to the corresponding properties of the function $v(\cdot)$ in the above forms. Does this mean that the study of non-expected utility preferences requires us to abandon the vast body of theoretical results and intuition we have developed within the expected utility framework?

Fortunately, the answer is no. An alternative approach to the analysis of nonexpected utility preferences proceeds not by adopting a specific nonlinear function, but rather by considering nonlinear functions in general, and using calculus to extend the results from expected utility theory in the same manner in which it is typically used to extend results involving linear functions.[14]

Specifically, consider the set of all probability distributions $P = (p_1, \ldots, p_n)$ over a fixed outcome set $\{x_1, \ldots, x_n\}$, so that the expected utility preference function can be written as $V(P) = V(p_1, \ldots, p_n) \equiv \Sigma U(x_i)p_i$, and think of $U(x_i)$ not as a "utility level" but rather as the coefficient of $p_i = \text{prob}(x_i)$ in this linear function. If we plot these coefficients against $x_i$ as in figure 3.12 the expected utility results of the previous section can be stated as:

*Stochastic Dominance Preference:* $V(\cdot)$ will exhibit global stochastic dominance preference if and only if the coefficients $\{U(x_i)\}$ are increasing in $x_i$, as in the figure.

*Risk Aversion:* $V(\cdot)$ will exhibit global risk aversion if and only if the coefficients $\{U(x_i)\}$ are concave in $x_i$,[15] as in the figure.

*Comparative Risk Aversion:* The expected utility preference function $V^*(P) \equiv \Sigma U^*(x_i)p_i$ will be at least as risk averse as $V(\cdot)$ if and only if the coefficients $\{U^*(x_i)\}$ are at least as concave in $x_i$ as $\{U(x_i)\}$.[16]

Now take the case where the individual's preference function $\mathcal{V}(P) = \mathcal{V}(p_1, \ldots, p_n)$ is not linear (that is, not expected utility) but at least differentiable, and consider its partial derivatives $\mathcal{U}(x_i; P) \equiv \partial \mathcal{V}(P)/\partial p_i = \partial \mathcal{V}(P)/\partial \text{prob}(x_i)$. Pick some probability distribution $P_0$ and plot these $\mathcal{U}(x_i; P_0)$ values against $x_i$. If they are again increasing in $x_i$, it is clear that any infinitesimal stochastically dominating shift from $P_0$, such as a decrease in some $p_i$ and matching increase in $p_{i+1}$, will be preferred. If they are again concave in $x_i$, any infinitesimal mean preserving spread, such as a drop in $p_i$ and (mean preserving) rise in $p_{i-1}$ and $p_{i+1}$, will

14. Readers who wish to skip the details of this approach may proceed to the next section.
15. As in note 6, this is equivalent to the condition that $[U(x_{i+1}) - U(x_1)] / [x_{i+1} - x_i] < [U(x_1) - U(x_{i-1})]/[x_i - x_{i-1}]$ for all $i$.
16. As in note 6, this is equivalent to the condition that $U^*(x_i) \equiv p(U(x_i))$ for some increasing concave function $p(\cdot)$.

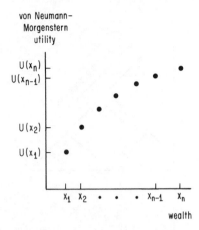

FIGURE 3.12 von Neumann-Morgenstern Utilities as Coefficients of the Expected Utility Preference Function $V(p_1,\ldots,p_n) = \Sigma U(x_i)p_i$

make the individual worse off. In light of this correspondence between the coefficients $\{U(x_i)\}$ of an expected utility preference function $V(\cdot)$ and the partial derivatives $\{\mathscr{U}(x_i; P_0)\}$ of the non-expected utility preference function $\mathscr{V}(\cdot)$, we refer to $\{\mathscr{U}(x_i; P_0)\}$ as the individual's local utility indices at $P_0$.

Of course, the above results will only hold precisely for infinitesimal shifts from the distribution $P_0$. However, we can exploit another result from standard calculus to show how "expected utility" results may be applied to the exact global analysis of non-expected utility preferences. Recall that in many cases, a differentiable function will exhibit a specific global property if and only if that property is exhibited in its linear approximations at each point. For example, a differentiable function will be globally nondecreasing if and only if its linear approximations are nondecreasing at each point. In fact, most of the fundamental properties of risk attitudes and their expected utility characterizations are precisely of this type. In particular, it can be shown that:

> *Stochastic Dominance Preference:* A non-expected utility preference function $\mathscr{V}(\cdot)$ will exhibit global stochastic dominance preference if and only if its local utility indices $\{\mathscr{U}(x_i; P)\}$ are increasing in $x_i$ at each distribution $P$.

> *Risk Aversion:* $\mathscr{V}(\cdot)$ will exhibit global risk aversion if and only if its local utility indices $\{\mathscr{U}(x_i; P)\}$ are concave in $x_i$ at each distribution $P$.

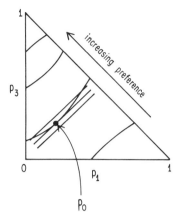

(solid lines are local expected utility approximation
to non-expected utility indifference curves at $P_0$)

FIGURE 3.13 Tangent "Expected Utility" Approximation to Non-expected Utility Indifference Curves

*Comparative Risk Aversion:* The preference function $\mathcal{V}^*(\cdot)$ will be globally at least as risk averse as $\mathcal{V}(\cdot)$[17] if and only if its local utility indices $\{\mathcal{U}^*x_i; P)\}$ are at least as concave in $x_i$ as $\{\mathcal{U}(x_i; P)\}$ at each $P$.

Figures 3.13 and 3.14 give a graphical illustration of this approach for the outcome set $\{x_1, x_2, x_3\}$. Here the solid curves denote the indifference curves of the non-expected utility preference function $\mathcal{V}(P)$. The parallel lines near the lottery $P_0$ denote the tangent "expected utility" indifference curves that correspond to the local utility indices $\{\mathcal{U}(x_i; P_0)\}$ at $P_0$. As always with differentiable functions, an infinitesimal change in the probabilities at $P_0$ will be preferred if and only if they would be preferred by this tangent linear (that is, expected utility) approximation. Figure 3.14 illustrates the above "risk aversion" result: It is clear that these indifference curves will be globally risk averse (averse to mean preserving spreads) if and only if they are everywhere steeper than the dashed iso-expected value lines. However, this is equivalent to all of their *tangents* being steeper than these lines, which is in turn equivalent to all of their local expected utility approximations being risk averse, or in other words, to the local utility indices $\{\mathcal{U}(x_i; P)\}$ being concave in $x_i$ at each distribution $P$.

17. For the appropriate generalizations of the expected utility concepts of "at least as risk averse" in this context, see Machina (1982, 1984).

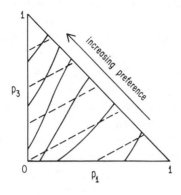

(dashed lines are iso-expected value lines)

FIGURE 3.14 Risk Aversion of Every Local Expected Utility Approximation is Equivalent to Global Risk Aversion

My fellow researchers and I have shown how this and similar techniques can be applied to further extend the results of expected utility theory to the case of non-expected utility preferences, to characterize and explore the implications of preferences which "fan out," and to conduct new and more general analyses of economic behavior under uncertainty (Machina 1982; Chew 1983; Fishburn 1984; Epstein 1985; Allen 1987; Chew, Karni, and Safra 1987). However, while I feel that they constitute a useful and promising response to the phenomenon of nonlinearities in the probabilities, these models do not provide solutions to the more problematic empirical phenomena of the following sections.

### THE PREFERENCE REVERSAL PHENOMENON
### The Evidence

The findings now known as the preference reversal phenomenon was first reported by psychologists Lichtenstein and Slovic (1971). In this study, subjects were first presented with a number of pairs of bets and asked to choose one bet out of each pair. Each of these pairs took the following form:

$$P\text{-bet:} \begin{cases} p \text{ chance of } \$X \\ 1 - p \text{ chance of } \$x \end{cases} \text{ versus } \$\text{-bet:} \begin{cases} q \text{ chance of } \$Y \\ 1 - q \text{ chance of } \$y, \end{cases}$$

where $X$ and $Y$ are respectively greater than $x$ and $y$, $p$ is greater than $q$, and $Y$ is greater than $X$ (the names "$P$-bet" and "$\$$-bet" come from the greater probability of winning in the first bet and greater possible gain in the second). In some cases, $x$ and $y$ took on small negative values. The subjects were next asked to "value" (state certainty equivalents for) each of these bets. The different valuation methods used consisted of (1) asking subjects to state their minimum selling price for each bet if they were to own it, (2) asking them to state their maximum bid price for each bet if they were to buy it, and (3) the elicitation procedure of Becker, De-Groot and Marschak (1964), in which it is in a subject's best interest to reveal his or her true certainty equivalents.[18] In the latter case, real money was used.

The expected utility model, as well as each of the *non*-expected utility models of the previous section, clearly implies that the bet which is actually chosen out of each pair will also be the one which is assigned the higher certainty equivalent.[19] However, Lichtenstein and Slovic found a systematic tendency for subjects to violate this prediction by choosing the $P$-bet in a direct choice but assigning a higher value to the $\$$-bet. In one experiment, for example, 127 out of 173 subjects assigned a higher sell price to the $\$$-bet in every pair in which the $P$-bet was chosen. Similar findings were obtained by Lindman (1971), and in an interesting variation on the usual experimental setting, by Lichtenstein and Slovic (1973) in a Las Vegas casino where customers actually staked (and hence sometimes lost) their own money. In another real-money experiment, Mowen and Gentry (1980) found that groups who could discuss their (joint) decisions were, if anything, more likely than individuals to exhibit the phenomenon.

Although the above studies involved deliberate variations in design in order to check for the robustness of this phenomenon, they were nevertheless received skeptically by economists, who perhaps not unnaturally felt they had more at stake than psychologists in this type of finding. In

18. Roughly speaking, the subject states a value for the item, and then the experimenter draws a random price. If the price is above the stated value, the subject forgoes the item and receives the price. If the drawn price is below the stated value, the subject keeps the item. The reader can verify that under such a scheme it can never be in a subject's best interest to report anything other than his or her true value.

19. Economic theory tells us that income effects could cause an individual to assign a lower bid price to the object that, if both were free, would actually be preferred. This reversal, however, should not occur for either selling prices or the Becker, DeGroot, and Marschak elicitations. For evidence on sell price/bid price disparities, see Knetsch and Sinden (1984) and the references cited there.

an admitted attempt to "discredit" this work, economists Grether and Plott (1979) designed a pair of experiments which, by correcting for issues of incentives, income effects, strategic considerations, ability to indicate indifference and other items, would presumably not generate this phenomenon. They nonetheless found it in both experiments. Further design modifications by Pommerehne, Schneider and Zweifel (1982) and Reily (1982) yielded the same results. Finally, the phenomenon has been found in experimental market transactions involving the gambles (Knez and Smith, 1986), or when the experimenter is able to act as an arbitrageur and make money off of such reversals (Berg, Dickhaut, and O'Brien 1983).

## Two Interpretations of this Phenomenon

How you interpret these findings depends on whether you adopt the worldview of an economist or a psychologist. An economist would reason as follows: Each individual possesses a well-defined preference relation over objects (in this case lotteries), and information about this relation can be gleaned from either direct choice questions or (properly designed) valuation questions. Someone exhibiting the preference reversal phenomenon is therefore telling us that he or she (1) is indifferent between the $P$-bet and some sure amount $\xi_p$, (2) strictly prefers the $P$-bet to the $\$$-bet, and (3) is indifferent between the $\$$-bet and an amount $\xi_\$$ greater than $\xi_p$. Assuming they prefer $\xi_\$$ to the lesser amount $\xi_p$, this implies that their preferences over these four objects are cyclic or intransitive.

Psychologists on the other hand would deny the premise of a common underlying mechanism generating both choice and valuation behavior. Rather, they view choice and valuation (even different forms of valuation) as distinct processes, subject to possibly different influences. In other words, individuals exhibit what are termed *response mode effects*. Excellent discussions of probabilistic beliefs and utility functions can be found in Hogarth (1975), Slovic, Fischhoff and Lichtenstein (1982), Hershey and Schoemaker (1985) and MacCrimmon and Wehrung (1986). In reporting how the response mode study of Slovic and Lichtenstein (1968) led them to actually predict the preference reversal phenomenon, I can do no better than quote the authors themselves:

> The impetus for this study [Lichtenstein and Slovic (1971)] was our observation in our earlier 1968 article that choices among pairs of gambles appeared to be influenced primar-

ily by probabilities of winning and losing, whereas buying and selling prices were primarily determined by the dollar amounts that could be won or lost. . . . In our 1971 article, we argued that, if the information in a gamble is processed differently when making choices and setting prices, it should be possible to construct pairs of gambles such that people would choose one member of the pair but set a higher price on the other. (Slovic and Lichtenstein 1983)

### Implications of the Economic Worldview

The issue of intransitivity is new neither to economics nor to choice under uncertainty. May (1954), for example, observed intransitivities in pairwise rankings of three alternative marriage partners, where each candidate was rated highly in two of three attributes (intelligence, looks, wealth) and low in the third. In an uncertain context, Blyth (1972) has adapted this approach to construct a set of random variables $(\tilde{x}, \tilde{y}, \tilde{z})$ such that $\text{prob}(\tilde{x} > \tilde{y}) = \text{prob}(\tilde{y} > \tilde{z}) = \text{prob}(\tilde{z} > \tilde{x}) = \frac{2}{3}$, so that individuals making pairwise choices on the basis of these probabilities would also be intransitive. In addition to the preference reversal phenomenon, Edwards (1954, 404–5) and Tversky (1969) have also observed intransitivities in preferences over risky prospects. On the other hand, researchers have shown that many aspects of economic theory, in particular the existence of demand functions and of general equilibrium, are surprisingly robust to dropping the assumption of transitivity (Sonnenschein 1971; Mas-Colell 1974; Shafer 1974).

In any event, economists have begun to develop and analyze models of nontransitive preferences over lotteries. The leading example of this is the "expected regret" model developed independently by Bell (1982), Fishburn (1982) and Loomes and Sugden (1982). In this model of pairwise choice, the von Neumann-Morgenstern utility function $U(x)$ is replaced by a *regret/rejoice function* $r(x, y)$ which represents the level of satisfaction (or if negative, dissatisfaction) the individual would experience if he or she were to receive the outcome $x$ when the alternative choice would have yielded the outcome $y$ (this function is assumed to satisfy $r(x, y) \equiv -r(y, x)$). In choosing between statistically independent gambles $P^* = (p_1^*, \ldots, p_n^*)$ and $P = (p_1, \ldots, p_n)$ over a common outcome set $\{x_1, \ldots, x_n\}$, the individual will choose $P^*$ if the expectation $\Sigma_i \Sigma_j r(x_i, x_j) p_i^* p_j$ is positive, and $P$ if it is negative.

Note that when the regret/rejoice function takes the special form $r(x,$

Choice Under Uncertainty

$y) \equiv U(x) - U(y)$ this model reduces to the expected utility model, since we have

$$\sum_i \sum_j r(x_i, x_j) p_i^* p_j \qquad (9)$$

$$\equiv \sum_i \sum_j \Big[ U(x_i) - U(x_j) \Big] p_i^* p_j \equiv \sum_i U(x_i) p_i^* - \sum_j U(x_j) p_j$$

so that the individual will prefer $P^*$ to $P$ if and only if $\Sigma_i U(x_i) p_i^* > \Sigma_j U(x_j) p_j$.[20] However, in general such an individual will neither be an expected utility maximizer nor have transitive preferences.

However, this intransitivity does not prevent us from graphing such preferences, or even applying "expected utility" analysis to them. To see the former, consider the case when the individual is facing alternative independent lotteries over a common outcome set $\{x_1, x_2, x_3\}$, so that we may again use the triangle diagram to illustrate their "indifference curves," which will appear as in figure 3.15. In such a case it is important to understand what is and is not still true of these indifference curves. The curve through $P$ will still correspond to the set of lotteries that are indifferent to $P$, and it will still divide the set of lotteries that are strictly preferred to $P$ (the points in the direction of the arrow) from the ones to which $P$ is strictly preferred. Furthermore, if (as in the figure) $P^*$ lies above the indifference curve through $P$, then $P$ will lie below the indifference curve through $P^*$ (that is, the individual's ranking of $P$ and $P^*$ will be unambiguous). However, unlike indifference curves for transitive preferences, these curves will cross,[21] and preferences over the lotteries, $P$, $P^*$ and $P^{**}$ are seen to form an intransitive cycle. But in regions where the indifference curves do not cross (such as near the origin) the individual will be indistinguishable from someone with transitive (albeit non-expected utility) preferences.

To see how expected utility results can be extended to this nontransitive framework, fix a lottery $P = (p_1, \ldots, p_n)$ and consider the question of when an (independent) lottery $P^* = (p_1^*, \ldots, p_n^*)$ will be preferred or not preferred to $P$. Since $r(y, x) \equiv -r(y, x)$ implies $\Sigma_i \Sigma_j r(x_i, x_j) p_i p_j \equiv 0$, we have that $P^*$ will be preferred to $P$ if and only if

---

20. When $r(x, y)$ takes the form $r(x, y) \equiv v(x)\tau(y) - v(y)\tau(x)$, this model will reduce to the (transitive) model of equation (6). This is the most general form of the model which is compatible with transitivity.

21. In this model the indifference curves will all cross at the same point. This point will thus be indifferent to all lotteries in the triangle.

113

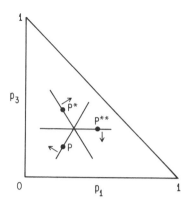

FIGURE 3.15 "Indifference Curves" for the Expected Regret Model

$$0 < \sum_i \sum_j r(x_i, x_j) p_i^* p_j$$
$$= \sum_i \sum_j r(x_i, x_j) p_i^* p_j - \sum_i \sum_j r(x_i, x_j) p_i p_j$$
$$= \sum_i \left[ \sum_j r(x_i, x_j) p_j \right] p_i^* - \sum_i \left[ \sum_j r(x_i, x_j) p_j \right] p_i \qquad (10)$$
$$= \sum_i \phi(x_i; P) p_i^* - \sum_i \phi(x_i; P) p_i$$

In other words, $P^*$ will be preferred to $P$ if and only if it implies a higher expectation of the "utility function" $\phi(x_i; P) \equiv \Sigma_j r(x_i, x_j) p_j$ than $P$. Thus if $\phi(x_i; P)$ is increasing in $x_i$ for all lotteries $P$ the individual will exhibit global stochastic dominance preference, and if $\phi(x_i; P)$ is concave in $x_i$ for all $P$ the individual will exhibit global risk aversion, even though he or she is not necessarily transitive (these conditions will clearly be satisfied if $r(x, y)$ is increasing and concave in $x$). The analytics of expected utility theory are robust indeed.

The developers of this model have shown how specific assumptions on the form of the regret/rejoice function will generate the common consequence effect, the common ratio effect, the preference reversal phenomenon, and other observed properties of choice over lotteries. The theoretical and empirical prospects for this approach accordingly seem quite impressive.

### Implications of the Psychological Worldview

On the other hand, how should economists respond if it turns out that the psychologists are right, and the preference reversal phenomenon really is generated by some form of response mode effect (or effects)? In that case, the first thing to do would be to try to determine if there were analogues of such effects in real-world economic situations.[22] Will individuals behave differently when determining their valuation of an object (for example, reservation bid on a used car) than when reacting to a fixed and non-negotiable price for the same object? Since a proper test of this would require correcting for any possible strategic and/or information-theoretic (such as signalling) issues, it would not be a simple undertaking. However, in light of the experimental evidence, I feel it is crucial that we attempt it.

Say we found that response mode effects did not occur outside of the laboratory. In that case we could rest more easily, although we could not forget about such issues completely: experimenters testing other economic theories and models (such as auctions) would have to be forever mindful of the possible influence of the particular response mode used in their experimental design.

On the other hand, what if we did find response mode effects out in the field? In that case we would want to determine, perhaps by going back to the laboratory, whether the rest of economic theory remained valid provided the response mode is held constant. If this were true, then with further evidence on exactly how the response mode mattered, we could presumably incorporate it as a new independent variable into existing theories. Since response modes tend to be constant within a given economic model, e.g. quantity responses to fixed prices in competitive markets, valuation announcements (truthful or otherwise) in auctions, etc., we should expect most of the testable implications of this approach to appear as cross-institutional predictions, such as systematic violations of the various equivalency results involving prices versus quantities or second price-sealed bid versus oral English auctions. In such a case, the new results and insights regarding our theories of institutions and mechanisms could be exciting indeed.[23]

22. It is important to note that neither the evidence of response mode effects (e.g., Slovic 1975) nor their implications for economic analysis are confined to the case of choice under uncertainty.

23. A final "twist" on the preference reversal phenomenon: Holt (1986) and Karni and Safra (1987) have shown how the procedures used in most of these studies will only lead to truthful revelation of preferences under the added assumption that the individual satisfies the independence axiom and has given examples of transitive non-expected utility preference rankings that lead to the typical "preference reversal" choices. How (and whether) experimenters will be able to address this issue remains to be seen.

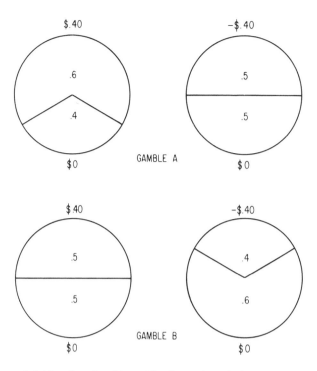

FIGURE 3.16 Duplex Gambles with Identical Underlying Distributions

## FRAMING EFFECTS
### Evidence

In addition to response mode effects, psychologists have uncovered an even more disturbing phenomenon, namely that alternative means of representing or "framing" probabilistically equivalent choice problems will lead to systematic differences in choice. An early example of this phenomenon was reported by Slovic (1969), who found that offering a gain or loss contingent on the joint occurrence of four independent events with probability $p$ elicited different responses than offering it on the occurrence of a single event with probability $p^4$ (all probabilities were stated explicitly). In comparison with the single-event case, making a gain contingent on the joint occurrence of events was found to make it more attractive, and making a loss contingent on the joint occurrence of events made it more unattractive.

In another study, Payne and Braunstein (1971) used pairs of gambles of the type illustrated in figure 3.16. Each of the gambles in the figure, known as a *duplex gamble,* involves spinning the pointers on both its "gain wheel" (on the left) and its "loss wheel" (on the right), with the individual receiving the sum of the resulting amounts. Thus an individual choosing Gamble A would win $.40 with probability .3 (that is, if the pointer in the gain wheel landed up and the pointer in the loss wheel landed down), would lose $.40 with probability .2 (if the pointers landed in opposite positions), and would break even with probability .5 (if the pointers landed either both up or both down). An examination of Gamble B reveals that it has an identical underlying distribution, so that subjects should be indifferent between the two gambles regardless of their risk preferences. However, Payne and Braunstein found that individuals in fact chose between such gambles (and indicated nontrivial strengths of preference) in manners which were systematically affected by the attributes of the component wheels. When the probability of winning in the gain wheel was greater than the probability of losing in the loss wheel for each gamble (as in the figure), subjects tended to choose the gamble whose gain wheel yielded the greater probability of a gain (Gamble A). In cases where the probabilities of losing in the loss wheels were respectively greater than the probabilities of winning in the gain wheels, subjects tended toward the gamble with the lower probability of losing in the loss wheel.

Finally, although the gambles in figure 3.16 possess identical underlying distributions, continuity suggests that a slight worsening of the terms of the preferred gamble could result in a pair of nonequivalent duplex gambles in which the individual will actually choose the one with the stochastically dominated underlying distribution. In an experiment where the subjects were allowed to construct their own duplex gambles by choosing one from a pair of prospects involving gains and one from a pair of prospects involving losses, stochastically dominated prospects were indeed chosen (Tversky and Kahneman, 1981).[24]

A second class of framing effects involves the phenomenon of a *reference point*. Theoretically, the variable which enters an individual's von Neumann-Morgenstern utility function should be total (that is, final) wealth, and gambles phrased in terms of gains and losses should be combined with current wealth and re-expressed as distributions over final wealth levels before being evaluated. However, economists since Mar-

---

24. Subjects were asked to choose either (A) a sure gain of $240 of or (B) a ¼:¾ chance of $1,000 or $0, and to choose either (C) a sure loss of $750 or (D) a ¾:¼ chance of −$1,000 or 0.84 percent chose A over B, and 87 percent chose D over C, even though B + C dominates A + D, and choices over the combined distributions were unanimous when they were presented explicitly.

kowitz (1952) have observed that risk attitudes over gains and losses are more stable than can be explained by a fixed utility function over final wealth, and have suggested that the utility function might be best defined in terms of changes from the "reference point" of current wealth. This stability of risk attitudes in the face of wealth variations has also been observed in several experimental studies.[25]

Markowitz (1952, 155) also suggested that certain circumstances may cause the individual's reference point to temporarily deviate from current wealth. If these circumstances include the manner in which a given problem is verbally described, then differing risk attitudes over gains and losses can lead to different choices depending upon the exact description. A simple example of this, from Kahneman and Tversky (1979), involves the following two questions:

> In addition to whatever you own, you have been given 1,000 (Israeli pounds). You are now asked to choose between a $\frac{1}{2}$:$\frac{1}{2}$ chance of a gain of 1,000 or 0 or a sure gain of 500.

and

> In addition to whatever you own, you have been given 2,000. You are now asked to choose between a $\frac{1}{2}$:$\frac{1}{2}$ chance of a loss of 1,000 or 0 or a sure loss of 500.

These two problems involve identical distributions over final wealth. However, when put to two different groups of subjects, 84 percent chose the sure gain in the first problem but 69 percent chose the $\frac{1}{2}$:$\frac{1}{2}$ gamble in the second. A nonmonetary version of this type of example, from Tversky and Kahneman (1981, 1986), posits the following scenario:

> Imagine that the U.S. is preparing for the outbreak of an unusual Asian disease, which is expected to kill 600 people. Two alternative programs to combat the disease have been proposed. Assume that the exact scientific estimate of the consequences of the programs are as follows:
> If program A is adopted, 200 people will be saved.
> If Program B is adopted, there is $\frac{1}{3}$ probability that 600 people will be saved, and $\frac{2}{3}$ probability that no people will be saved.

Seventy-two percent of the subjects who were presented with this form of the question chose Program A. A second group was given the same

---

25. See the discussion and references in Machina (1982, 285–86).

initial information, but the descriptions of the programs were changed to read:

> If Program C is adopted 400 people will die.
> If Program D is adopted there is ⅓ probability that nobody will die, and ⅔ probability that 600 people will die.

Although this statement of the problem is once again identical to the former one, 78 percent of the respondents chose Program D.

In other studies, Schoemaker and Kunreuther (1979), Hershey and Schoemaker (1980), McNeil, Pauker, Sox and Tversky (1982) and Slovic, Fischhoff, and Lichtenstein (1982) have found that subjects' choices in otherwise identical problems will depend upon whether they are phrased as decisions whether or not to gamble or whether or not to insure, whether the statistical information for different therapies is presented in terms of cumulative survival probabilities or cumulative mortality probabilities, etc. For similar examples of this phenomenon in nonstochastic situations, see Thaler (1980).

In a final class of examples, not based on reference point effects, Moskowitz (1974) and Keller (1982) found that the proportion of subjects choosing in conformance with or in violation of the independence axiom in examples like the Allais Paradox was significantly affected by whether the problems were described in the standard matrix form (e.g., Raiffa 1968, 7), decision tree form, or as minimally structured written statements. Interestingly enough, the form which was judged the "clearest representation" by the majority of Moskowitz's subjects (the tree form) led to the lowest degree of consistency with the independence axiom, the highest proportion of fanning out choices, and the highest persistency rate of these choices (pp. 234, 237–38).

## Two Issues Regarding Framing

The replicability and pervasiveness of the above types of examples is indisputable. However, before being able to assess their implications for economic modelling we need to resolve two issues.

The first issue is whether these experimental observations possess any analogue outside of the laboratory. Since real-world decision problems do not present themselves as neatly packaged as the ones on experimental questionnaires, monitoring such effects would not be as straightforward. However this does not mean that they do not exist, or that they cannot be objectively observed or quantitatively measured. The real-world example which comes most quickly to mind, and is presumably of no small importance to the involved parties, is whether gasoline price differentials should be represented as "cash discounts" or "credit surcharges." Similarly, Russo, Krieser and Miyashita (1975) and Russo (1977) found that the practice, and even method, of displaying unit price information in supermarkets (information which consumers could calculate for themselves) affected both the level and distribution of consumer expenditures. The empirical marketing literature is no doubt replete with findings that we could legitimately interpret as real-world framing effects.

The second, more difficult issue is that of the independent observability of the particular frame that an individual will adopt in a given problem. In the duplex gamble and matrix/decision tree/written statement examples of the previous section, the different frames seem unambiguously determined by the form of presentation. However, in instances where framing involves the choice of a reference point, which presumably include the majority of real-world cases, this point might not be objectively determined by the form of presentation, and might be chosen differently, and what is worse, unobservably, by each individual.[26] In a particularly thorough and insightful study, Fischhoff (1983) presented subjects with a written decision problem which allowed for different choices of a reference point, and explored different ways of predicting which frame individuals would adopt, in order to be able to predict their actual choices. While the majority choice of subjects was consistent with what would appear to be the most appropriate frame, Fischhoff noted "the absence of any relation within those studies between [separately elicited] frame preference and option preference." Indeed to the extent that frame preferences varied across his experiments, they did so inversely to the incidence of the predicted choice.[27] If such problems can occur in predicting responses to specific written questions in the laboratory, imagine how they could plague the modelling of real-world choice behavior.

Framing Effects and Economic Analysis:
Have We Already Solved this Problem?

How should we respond if it turns out that framing actually is a real-world phenomenon of economic relevance, and in particular, if individ-

26. This is not to say that well-defined reference points never exist. The reference points involved in credit surcharges vs. cash discounts, for example, seem unambiguous.

27. Fischhoff (1983, 115–16). Fischhoff notes, "If one can only infer frames from preferences after assuming the truth of the theory, one runs the risk of making the theory itself untestable."

uals' frames cannot always be observed? I would argue that the means of responding to this issue can already be found in the "tool box" of existing economic analysis.

Consider first the case where the frame of a given economic decision problem, even though it should not matter from the point of view of standard theory, can at least be independently and objectively observed. I believe that economists have in fact already solved such a problem in their treatment of the phenomenon of "uninformative advertising." Although it is hard to give a formal definition of this term, it is widely felt that economic theory is hard put to explain a large proportion of current advertising in terms of traditional informational considerations.[28] However, this has hardly led economists to abandon classical consumer theory. Rather, models of uninformative advertising proceed by quantifying this variable (such as air time) and treating it as an additional independent variable in the utility and/or demand function. Standard results like the Slutsky equation need not be abandoned, but rather simply reinterpreted as properties of demand functions holding this new variable constant. The amount of advertising itself is determined as a maximizing variable on the part of the firm (given some cost curve), and can be subjected to standard comparative static analysis.

In the case when decision frames can be observed, framing effects can presumably be modelled in an analogous manner. To do so, we would begin by adopting a method of quantifying, or at least categorizing, frames. The second step, some of which has of course already been done, is to study both the effect of this new independent variable holding the standard economic variables constant, and conversely, to retest our standard economic theories in conditions where we carefully held the frame fixed. With any luck we would find that, holding the frame constant, the Slutsky equation still held.

The next step in any given modelling situation would be to ask "who determines the frame?" If (as with advertising) it is the firm, then the effect of the frame upon consumer demand, and hence upon firm profits, can be incorporated into the firm's maximization problem, and the choice of the frame as well as the other relevant variables (for example, prices and quantities) can be simultaneously determined and subjected to comparative static analysis, just as in the case of uninformative advertising.

28. A wonderful example, offered by my colleague Joel Sobel, are milk ads which make no reference to either price or to a specific dairy. What could be a more well-known commodity than milk?

A seemingly more difficult case is when the individual chooses the frame (for example, a reference point) and this choice cannot be observed. Although we should not forget the findings of Fischhoff (1983), assume that this choice is at least systematic in the sense that the consumer will jointly choose the frame and make the subsequent decision in a manner which maximizes a "utility function" which depends both on the decision and the choice of frame. In other words, individuals make their choices as part of a joint maximization problem, the other component of which (the choice of frame or reference point) cannot be observed.

Such models are hardly new to economic analysis. Indeed, most economic models presume that the agent is simultaneously maximizing with respect to variables other than the ones being studied. When assumptions are made on the individual's joint preferences over the observed and unobserved variables, the well-developed *theory of induced preferences*[29] can be used to derive testable implications on choice behavior over the observables. With a little more knowledge on exactly how frames are chosen, such an approach could presumably be applied here as well.

The above remarks should not be taken as implying that we have already solved the problem of framing in economic analysis or that there is no need to adapt, and if necessary abandon, our standard models in light of this phenomenon. Rather, they reflect the view that when psychologists are able to hand us enough systematic evidence on how these effects operate, economists will be able to respond accordingly.

OTHER ISSUES: IS PROBABILITY THEORY RELEVANT?
The Manipulation of Subjective Probabilities

The evidence discussed so far has primarily consisted of cases where subjects have been presented with explicit (that is, "objective") probabilities as part of their decision problems, and the models which have addressed these phenomena possess the corresponding property of being defined over objective probability distributions. However, there is extensive evidence that when individuals have to estimate or revise probabilities for themselves they will make systematic mistakes in doing so.

The psychological literature on the processing of probabilistic information is much too large even to summarize here. However, it is worth noting that experimenters have uncovered several "heuristics" used by subjects which can lead to predictable errors in the formation and ma-

29. E.g. Milne (1981). For an application of the theory of induced preferences to choice under uncertainty, see Machina (1984).

nipulation of subjective probabilities. Kahneman and Tversky (1973), Bar-Hillel (1974) and Grether (1980), for example, have found that probability updating systematically departs from Bayes Law in the direction of underweighting prior information and overweighting the "representativeness" of the current sample. In a related phenomenon termed the "law of small numbers," Tversky and Kahneman (1971) found that individuals overestimated the probability of drawing a perfectly representative sample out of a heterogeneous population. Finally, Bar-Hillel (1973), Tversky and Kahneman (1983) and others have found systematic biases in the formation of the probabilities of conjunctions of both independent and nonindependent events. For surveys, discussions and examples of the psychological literature on the formation and handling of probabilities see Edwards, Lindman, and Savage (1963), Slovic and Lichtenstein (1971), Tversky and Kahneman (1974) and the collections in *Acta Psychologica* (December 1970), Kahneman, Slovic, and Tversky (1982), and Arkes and Hammond (1986). For examples of how economists have responded to some of these issues see Arrow (1982), Viscusi (1985) and the references cited there.

## The Existence of Subjective Probabilities

The evidence referred to above indicates that when individuals are asked to formulate probabilities they do not do it correctly. However, these findings may be rendered moot by evidence which suggests that when individuals making decisions under uncertainty are not explicitly asked to form subjective probabilities, they might not do it (or even act as if doing it) at all.

In one of a class of examples due to Ellsberg (1961), subjects were presented with a pair of urns, the first containing 50 red balls and 50 black balls and the second also containing 100 red and black balls but in an unknown proportion. When faced with the choice of staking a prize on: $(R_1)$ drawing a red ball from the first urn, $(R_2)$ drawing a red ball from the second urn, $(B_1)$ drawing a black ball from the first urn, or $(B_2)$ drawing a black ball from the second urn, a majority of subjects strictly preferred $(R_1)$ over $(R_2)$ and strictly preferred $(B_1)$ over $(B_2)$. It is clear that there can exist no subjectively assigned probabilities $p: (1 - p)$ of drawing a red vs. black ball from the second urn, even ½:½, which can simultaneously generate both of these strict preferences. Similar behavior in this and related problems has been observed by Raiffa (1961), Becker and Brownson (1964), Slovic and Tversky (1974), and MacCrimmon and Larsson (1979).

## Life (and Economic Analysis) Without Probabilities

One response to this type of phenomenon has been to suppose that individuals "slant" whatever subjective probabilities they might otherwise form in a manner which reflects the amount of confidence/ambiguity associated with them (Fellner 1961; Becker and Brownson 1964; Fishburn 1986; Hogarth and Kunreuther 1986). In the case of the complete ignorance regarding probabilities, Arrow and Hurwicz (1972), Maskin (1979) and others have presented axioms which imply principles such as ranking options solely on the basis of their worst and/or best outcomes (for example, maximin, maximax), the unweighted average of their outcomes ("principle of insufficient reason"), or similar criteria.[30] Finally, generalizations of expected utility theory which drop the standard additivity and/or compounding laws of probability theory have been developed by Schmeidler (1989) and Segal (1987).

Although the above models may well capture aspects of actual decision processes, the analytically most useful approach to choice in the presence of uncertainty but the absence of probabilities is the so-called *state-preference* model of Arrow (1953/1964), Debreu (1959) and Hirshleifer (1966). In this model uncertainty is represented by a set of mutually exclusive and exhaustive *states of nature* $S = \{s_i\}$. This partition of all possible unfoldings of the future could be either very coarse, such as the pair of states {it rains here tomorrow, it doesn't rain here tomorrow} or else very fine, so that the definition of a state might read "it rains here tomorrow *and* the temperature at Gibraltar is 75° at noon *and* the price of gold in New York is below $700.00/ounce." Note that it is neither feasible nor desirable to capture all conceivable sources of uncertainty when specifying the set of states for a given problem: it is not feasible since no mater how finely the states are defined there will always be some other random criterion on which to further divide them, and not desirable since such criteria may affect neither individuals' preferences nor their opportunities. Rather, the key requirements are that the states be mutually exclusive and exhaustive so that exactly one will be realized, and (for purposes of the present discussion) that the individual cannot influence which state will actually occur.

Given a fixed (and say finite) set of states, the objects of choice in this framework consist of alternative *state-payoff bundles,* each of which specifies the outcome the individual will receive in every possible state.

30. For an excellent discussion of the history, nature, and limitations of such approaches, see Arrow (1951).

When the outcomes are monetary payoffs, for example, state-payoff bundles take the form $(c_1, \ldots, c_n)$ , where $c_i$ denotes the payoff the individual would receive should state $s_i$ occur. In the case of exactly two states of nature we could represent this set by the points in the $(c_1, c_2)$ plane. Since bundles of the form $(c, c)$ represent prospects which yield the same payoff in each state of nature, the 45° line in this plane is known as the *certainty line*.

Now if the individual did happen to assign probabilities $\{p_i\}$ to the states $\{s_i\}$, each bundle $(c_1, \ldots, c_n)$ would imply a specific probability distribution over wealth, and we could infer his or her preferences (that is, indifference curves) over state-payoff bundles. However, since these bundles are defined directly over the respective states and without reference to any probabilities, it is also possible to speak of preferences over these bundles without making any assumptions regarding the coherency, or even existence, of such probabilistic beliefs. Researchers such as the ones cited above as well as Yaari (1969), Diamond and Yaari (1972) and Mishan (1976) have shown how this indifference curve-based approach can be used to derive results from individual demand behavior through general equilibrium in a context which requires neither the expected utility hypothesis nor the existence or commonality of subjective probabilities. In other words, life without probabilities does not imply life without economic analysis.

## Final Thoughts

*Welfare Implications.* Although the theme of this paper has been the descriptive theory of choice under uncertainty, another important issue is the implications of these developments for normative economics. Can welfare analysis be conducted in the type of world implied by the above models?

The answer to this question depends upon the model. Fanning-out behavior and the nonexpected utility models used to characterize it, as well as the state-payoff approach of the previous section, are completely consistent with the assumption of well-defined, transitive individual preference orderings, and thence with traditional welfare analysis along the lines of Pareto, Bergson and Samuelson (such as Samuelson 1947/1983, chap. 8). For example, the proof of Pareto-efficiency of a system of complete contingent-commodity markets (Arrow 1953/1964; Debreu 1959, chap. 7) requires neither the expected utility hypothesis nor the assumption of well-defined probabilistic beliefs. On the other hand, it is clear that the preference reversal phenomenon and framing effects, and at least some of the nontransitive and/or noneconomic models used to address them, will prove much more difficult to reconcile with welfare analysis, at least as currently practiced.

*A Unified Model?* Another issue is the lack of a unified model capable of simultaneously handling all of the phenomena described in this paper: fanning-out, the preference reversal phenomenon, framing effects, probability biases and the Ellsberg paradox. After all, it is presumably the same ("typical") individuals who are exhibiting each of these phenomena—shouldn't there be a single model out there capable of generating them all?

Although I am doubtful of our present ability to do this, I am also doubtful about the need to establish a unified model as a prerequisite for continued progress. The aspects of behavior considered in this paper are very diverse, and if (like the wave versus particle properties of light) they cannot be currently unified, this does not mean that we cannot continue to learn by studying and modelling them separately.

*An Essential Criterion.* The evidence and theories reported in this paper have taken us a long way from the classical expected utility approach presented at the outset. To what extent will these new models be incorporated into mainstream economic thought and practice? I believe the answer will depend upon a single factor: the extent to which they can address the important issues in the economics of uncertainty, such as search, investment, bargaining or auctions, to which the expected utility model has been so usefully applied.

## REFERENCES

Akerlof, George A. "The Market for 'Lemons': Quality Uncertainty and the Market Mechanism." *Quarterly Journal of Economics.* August 1970. 84: 488–500.

Allais, Maurice. "Le Comportement de l'Homme Rationel devant le Risque, Critique des Postulates et Axiomes de l'École Americaine." *Econometrica.* October 1953. 21: 503–46.

———. "The Foundations of a Positive Theory of Choice Involving Risk and a Criticism of the Postulates and Axioms of the American School." In Allais and Hagen (1979).

Allais, Maurice, and Ole Hagen, eds. *Expected Utility Hypotheses and the Allais Paradox.* Dordrecht, Holland: D. Reidel, 1979.

Allen, Beth. "Smooth Preferences and the Local Expected Utility Hypothesis." *Journal of Economic Theory.* 1987. 41:340–55.

Arkes, Hal R., and Kenneth R. Hammond, eds. *Judgement and Decision Making: An Interdisciplinary Reader.* Cambridge: Cambridge University Press, 1986.

Arrow, Kenneth J. "Alternative Approaches to the Theory of Choice in Risk-Taking Situations." *Econometrica*. October 1951. 19: 404–37. Reprinted in Arrow (1965).

———. "Le Role des Valeurs Boursières pour la Répartition le meilleure des risques." *Économetrie*. Colloques Internationaux du Centre National de la Recherche Scientifique, Paris, 1953. 40: 41–47. English translation: *Review of Economic Studies*, April 1964; 31: 91–96.

———. *Aspects of the Theory of Risk-Bearing*. Helsinki: Yrjo Jahnsson Saatio, 1965.

———. "Risk Perception in Psychology and Economics." *Economic Inquiry*. January 1982. 20: 1–9.

Arrow, Kenneth J., and Leonid Hurwicz. "An Optimality Criterion for Decision-Making under Ignorance." In Carter, C. F., and J. L. Ford, eds., *Uncertainty and Expectations in Economics*. Oxford: Basil Blackwell, 1972.

Bar-Hillel, Maya. "On the Subjective Probability of Compound Events." *Organizational Behavior and Human Performance*. June 1973. 9: 396–406.

———. "Similarity and Probability." *Organizational Behavior and Human Performance*. April 1974. 11: 277–82.

Battalio, Raymond C., John H. Kagel and Don N. MacDonald. "Animals' Choices over Uncertain Outcomes." *American Economic Review*. September 1985. 75: 597–613.

Becker, Gordon M., Morris H. DeGroot and Jacob Marschak. "Measuring Utility by a Single-Response Sequential Method." *Behavioral Science*. July 1964. 9: 226–32.

Becker, Selwyn W., and Fred O. Brownson. "What Price Ambiguity? Or the Role of Ambiguity in Decision-Making." *Journal of Political Economy*. February 1964. 72: 62–73.

Bell, David E. "Regret in Decision Making Under Uncertainty." *Operations Research*. September–October 1982. 30: 961–81.

———. "Disappointment in Decision Making Under Uncertainty." *Operations Research*. January–February 1985. 33: 1–27.

Berg, Joyce E., John W. Dickhaut and John R. O'Brien. "Preference Reversal and Arbitrage." Manuscript. University of Minnesota, September 1983.

Bernoulli, Daniel. "Specimen Theoriae Novae de Mensura Sortis." *Commentarii Academiae Scientiarum Imperialis Petropolitanae*, 1738. 5: 175–92. English translation: *Econometrica*, January 1954; 22: 23–36.

Blyth, Colin R. "Some Probability Paradoxes in Choice from Among Random Alternatives." *Journal of the American Statistical Association*. June 1972. 67: 366–73.

Chew Soo Hong. "A Generalization of the Quasilinear Mean With Applications to the Measurement of Income Inequality and Decision Theory Resolving The Allais Paradox." *Econometrica*. July 1983. 51: 1065–92.

Chew Soo Hong, Edi Karni and Zvi Sfra. "Risk Aversion in the Theory of Expected Utility with Rank Dependent Probabilities." *Journal of Economic Theory*. 1987. 42: 370–81.

Chew Soo Hong and William Waller. "Empirical Tests of Weighted Utility Theory." *Journal of Mathematical Psychology*. March 1986. 30: 55–72.

Debreu, Gerard. *Theory of Value: An Axiomatic Analysis of General Equilibrium*. New Haven: Yale University Press, 1959.

Diamond, Peter A., and Menahem Yaari. "Implications of the Theory of Rationing for Consumer Choice Under Uncertainty." *American Economic Review.* June 1972. 62: 333–43.

Edwards, Ward. "The Theory of Decision Making." *Psychological Bulletin.* July 1954. 51: 380–417.

———. "The Prediction of Decisions Among Bets." *Journal of Experimental Psychology.* September 1955. 50: 201–14.

Edwards, Ward, Harold Lindman and Leonard J. Savage. "Bayesian Statistical Inference for Psychological Research." *Psychological Review.* May 1963. 70: 193–242.

Ellsberg, Daniel. "Risk, Ambiguity and the Savage Axioms." *Quarterly Journal of Economics.* November 1961. 75: 643–69.

Epstein, Larry. "Decreasing Risk Aversion and Mean-Variance Analysis." *Econometrica.* 1985. 53: 945–61.

Fellner, William. "Distortion of Subjective Probabilities as a Reaction to Uncertainty." *Quarterly Journal of Economics.* November 1961. 75: 670–89.

Fischhoff, Baruch. "Predicting Frames." *Journal of Experimental Psychology: Learning, Memory and Cognition.* January 1983. 9: 103–16.

Fishburn, Peter C. "Nontransitive Measurable Utility." *Journal of Mathematical Psychology.* August 1982. 26: 31–67.

———. "Transitive Measurable Utility." *Journal of Economic Theory.* December 1983. 31: 293–317.

———. "SSB Utility Theory: An Economic Perspective." *Mathematical Social Sciences.* 1984. 8: 63–94.

———. 'A New Model for Decisions Under Uncertainty." *Economics Letters.* 1986. 21: 127–30.

Friedman, Milton, and Leonard J. Savage. "The Utility Analysis of Choices Involving Risk." *Journal of Political Economy.* August 1948. 56: 279–304.

Grether, David M. "Bayes Rule as a Descriptive Model: The Representativeness Heuristic." *Quarterly Journal of Economics.* November 1980. 95: 537–57.

Grether, David M., and Charles R. Plott. "Economic Theory of Choice and the Preference Reversal Phenomenon." *American Economic Review.* September 1979. 69: 623–38.

Hagen, Ole. "Towards a Positive Theory of Preferences Under Risk." In Allais and Hagen (1979).

Hershey, John C., and Paul J. H. Schoemaker. "Risk-Taking and Problem Context in the Domain of Losses—An Expected Utility Analysis." *Journal of Risk and Insurance.* March 1980. 47: 111–32.

Hershey, John C., and Paul J. H. Schoemaker. "Probability Versus Certainty Equivalence Methods in Utility Measurement: Are They Equivalent?" *Management Science.* October 1985. 31: 1213–31.

Hirshleifer, Jack. "Investment Decision Under Uncertainty: Applications of the State-Preference Approach." *Quarterly Journal of Economics.* May 1966. 80: 252–77.

Hogarth, Robin. "Cognitive Processes and the Assessment of Subjective Probability Distributions." *Journal of the American Statistical Association.* June 1975. 70: 271–89.

Hogarth, Robin, and Howard Kunreuther. "Decision Making Under Ambiguity." *Journal of Business.* October 1986, prt. 2. 4: 225–50.

Holt, Charles A. "Preference Reversals and the Independence Axiom." *American Economic Review.* June 1986. 76: 508–15.

Kahneman, Daniel, Paul Slovic and Amos Tversky, eds. *Judgement Under Uncertainty: Heuristics and Biases.* Cambridge: Cambridge University Press, 1982.

Kahneman, Daniel, and Amos Tversky. "On the Psychology of Prediction." *Psychological Review.* July 1973. 80: 237–51.

———. "Prospect Theory: An Analysis of Decision Under Risk." *Econometrica.* March 1979. 47: 263–91.

Karmarkar, Uday S. "The Effect of Probabilities on the Subjective Evaluation of Lotteries." Massachusetts Institute of Technology Sloan School of Business Working Paper, 1974.

———. "Subjectively Weighted Utility: A Descriptive Extension of the Expected Utility Model." *Organizational Behavior and Human Performance.* February 1978. 21: 61–72.

Karni, Edi, and Zvi Safra. "'Preference Reversal' and the Observability of Preferences by Experimental Methods." *Econometrica.* 1987. 55: 675–85.

Keller, L. Robin. "The Effects of Decision Problem Representation on Utility Conformance." Manuscript. University of California, Irvine. 1982.

Knetsch, Jack L., and J. A. Sinden. "Willingness to Pay and Compensation Demanded: Experimental Evidence of an Unexpected Disparity in Measures of Value." *Quarterly Journal of Economics.* August 1984. 99: 507–21.

Knez, Marc, and Vernon L. Smith. "Hypothetical Valuations and Preference Reversals in the Context of Asset Trading." Manuscript. University of Arizona. 1986.

Lichtenstein, Sarah, and Paul Slovic. "Reversals of Preferences Between Bids and Choices in Gambling Decisions." *Journal of Experimental Psychology.* July 1971. 89: 46–55.

———. "Response-Induced Reversals of Preference in Gambling: An Extended Replication in Las Vegas." *Journal of Experimental Psychology.* November 1973. 101: 16–20.

Lindman, Harold. "Inconsistent Preferences Among Gambles." *Journal of Experimental Psychology.* May 1971. 89: 390–97.

Loomes, Graham, and Robert Sugden. "Regret Theory: An Alternative Theory of Rational Choice Under Uncertainty." *Economic Journal.* December 1982. 92: 805–24.

MacCrimmon, Kenneth R. "Descriptive and Normative Implications of the Decision-Theory Postulates." In Borch, Karl H., and Jan Mossin, eds., *Risk and Uncertainty: Proceedings of a Conference Held by the International Economic Association.* London: Macmillan. 1968.

MacCrimmon, Kenneth R., and Stig Larsson. "Utility Theory: Axioms Versus 'Paradoxes.'" In Allais and Hagen (1979).

MacCrimmon, Kenneth R., and Donald A. Wehrung. *Taking Risks: The Management of Uncertainty.* New York: The Free Press, 1986.

Machina, Mark J. "'Expected Utility' Analysis Without the Independence Axiom." *Econometrica.* March 1982. 50: 277–323.

———. "The Economic Theory of Individual Behavior Toward Risk: Theory, Evidence and New Directions." Stanford University Institute for Mathematical Studies in the Social Sciences Technical Report. 1983a.

———. "Generalized Expected Utility Analysis and the Nature of Observed Violations of the Independence Axiom." 1983b. In Stigum and Wenstøp (1983).

———. "Temporal Risk and the Nature of Induced Preferences." *Journal of Economic Theory.* August 1984. 33:199–231.

Markowitz, Harry. "The Utility of Wealth." *Journal of Political Economy.* April 1952. 60: 151–58.

Marschak, Jacob. "Rational Behavior, Uncertain Prospects, and Measurable Utility." *Econometrica.* April 1950. 18: 111–41. "Errata." *Econometrica.* July 1950. 18: 312.

Mas-Colell, Andreu. "An Equilibrium Existence Theorem Without Complete or Transitive Preference." *Journal of Mathematical Economics.* December 1974. 3: 237–46.

Maskin, Eric. "Decision Making Under Ignorance with Implications for Social Choice." *Theory and Decision.* September 1979. 11: 319–37.

May, Kenneth O. "Intransitivity, Utility, and the Aggregation of Preference Patterns." *Econometrica.* January 1954. 22: 1–13.

McCord, Marc, and Richard de Neufville. "Empirical Demonstration that Expected Utility Analysis Is Not Operational." In Stigum and Wenstøp (1983).

———. "Utility Dependence on Probability: An Empirical Demonstration." *Large Scale Systems.* February 1984. 6: 91–103.

McNeil, Barbara J., Stephen G. Pauker, Harold C. Sox, Jr. and Amos Tversky. "On the Elicitation of Preferences for Alternative Therapies." *New England Journal of Medicine.* May 1982. 306: 1259–62.

Milne, Frank. "Induced Preferences and the Theory of the Consumer." *Journal of Economic Theory.* April 1981. 24: 205–17.

Mishan, E. J. "Choices Involving Risk: Simple Steps Toward an Ordinalist Analysis." *Economic Journal.* December 1976. 86:759–77.

Morrison, Donald G. "On the Consistency of Preferences in Allais' Paradox." *Behavioral Science.* September 1967. 12: 373–83.

Moskowitz, Herbert. "Effects of Problem Representation and Feedback on Rational Behavior in Allais and Morlat-Type Problems." *Decision Sciences.* 1974. 5: 225–42.

Mowen, John C., and James W. Gentry. "Investigation of the Preference-Reversal Phenomenon in a New Product Introduction Task." *Journal of Applied Psychology.* December 1980. 65: 715–22.

Payne, John W., and Myron L. Braunstein. "Preferences Among Gambles with Equal Underlying Distributions." *Journal of Experimental Psychology.* January 1971. 87: 13–18.

Pommerehne, Werner W., Friedrich Schneider and Peter Zweifel. "Economic Theory of Choice and the Preference Reversal Phenomenon: A Reexamination." *American Economic Review.* June 1982. 72: 569–74.

Pratt, John W. "Risk Aversion in the Small and in the Large." *Econometrica.* January/April 1964. 32: 122–36.

Quiggin, John. "A Theory of Anticipated Utility." *Journal of Economic Behavior and Organization.* December 1982. 3: 323–43.

Raiffa, Howard. "Risk, Ambiguity, and the Savage Axioms." *Quarterly Journal of Economics.* November 1961. 75: 690–94.

——— *Decision Analysis: Introductory Lectures on Choice Under Uncertainty.* Reading, Mass.: Addison-Wesley, 1968.

Reilly, Robert J. "Preference Reversal: Further Evidence and Some Suggested

Modifications of Experimental Design." *American Economic Review.* June 1982. 72: 576–84.

Rothschild, Michael, and Joseph E. Stiglitz. "Increasing Risk: I. A Definition." *Journal of Economic Theory.* September 1970. 2: 225–43.

Russo, J. Edward. "The Value of Unit Price Information." *Journal of Marketing Research.* May 1977. 14: 193–201.

Russo, J. Edward, Gene Krieser and Sally Miyashita. "An Effective Display of Unit Price Information." *Journal of Marketing.* April 1975. 39: 11–19.

Samuelson, Paul A. *Foundations of Economic Analysis.* Cambridge, Mass.: Harvard University Press, 1947. Enlarged edition, 1983.

Savage, Leonard J. *The Foundations of Statistics.* New York: Wiley, 1954. Revised and enlarged edition, New York: Dover, 1972.

Schmeidler, David. "Subjective Probability and Expected Utility Without Additivity." *Econometrica.* 1989. 57: 571–87.

Schoemaker, Paul J. H., and Howard Kunreuther. "An Experimental Study of Insurance Decisions." *Journal of Risk and Insurance.* December 1979. 46: 603–18.

Segal, Uzi. "Nonlinear Decision Weights with the Independence Axiom." Manuscript. University of California, Los Angeles. November 1984.

———. "The Ellsberg Paradox and Risk Aversion: An Anticipated Utility Approach." *International Economic Review.* 1987. *International Economic Review.* 28: 175–202.

Shafer, Wayne J. "The Nontransitive Consumer." *Econometrica.* September 1974. 42: 913–19.

Slovic, Paul. "Manipulating the Attractiveness of a Gamble Without Changing its Expected Value." *Journal of Experimental Psychology.* January 1969. 79: 139–45.

———. "Choice Between Equally Valued Alternatives." *Journal of Experimental Psychology: Human Perception and Performance.* August 1975. 1: 280–87.

Slovic, Paul, Baruch Fischhoff, and Sarah Lichtenstein. "Response Mode, Framing, and Information Processing Effects in Risk Assessment." In Hogarth, Robin, ed., *New Directions for Methodology of Social and Behavioral Science: Question Framing and Response Consistency.* San Francisco: Jossey-Bass, 1982.

———. "Relative Importance of Probabilities and Payoffs in Risk Taking." *Journal of Experimental Psychology.* November 1968, prt. 2. 78: 1–18.

———. "Comparison of Bayesian and Regression Approaches to the Study of Information Processing in Judgment." *Organizational Behavior and Human Performance.* November 1971. 6: 649–744.

———. "Preference Reversals: A Broader Perspective." *American Economic Review.* September 1983. 73: 596–605.

Slovic, Paul, and Amos Tversky. "Who Accepts Savage's Axiom?" *Behavioral Science.* November 1974. 19: 368–73.

Sonnenschein, Hugo F. "Demand Theory Without Transitive Preferences, With Applications to the Theory of Competitive Equilibrium." In Chipman, John S., Leonid Hurwicz, Marcel K. Richter, and Hugo F. Sonnenschein, eds., *Preferences, Utility and Demand.* New York: Harcourt Brace Jovanovich, 1971.

Spence, A. Michael, and Richard J. Zeckhauser. "Insurance, Information and

Individual Action." *American Economic Review Papers and Proceedings.*
May 1971. 61: 380–87.

Stigum, Bernt, and Fred Wenstøp. *Foundations of Utility and Risk Theory with Applications.* Dordrecht, Holland: D. Reidel, 1983.

Sugden, Robert. "New Developments in the Theory of Choice Under Uncertainty." *Bulletin of Economic Research.* January 1986. 38: 1–24.

Thaler, Richard. "Toward a Positive Theory of Consumer Choice." *Journal of Economic Behavior and Organization.* March 1980. 1: 39–60.

Tversky, Amos. "Intransitivity of Preferences." *Psychological Review.* January 1969. 76: 31–48.

———. "A Critique of Expected Utility Theory: Descriptive and Normative Considerations." *Erkenntnis.* 1975. 9: 163–73.

Tversky, Amos, and Daniel Kahneman. "Belief in the Law of Small Numbers." *Psychological Bulletin.* July 1971. 2: 105–10.

———. "Judgement under Uncertainty: Heuristics and Biases." *Science.* September 1974. 185: 1124–31.

———. "The Framing of Decisions and the Psychology of Choice." *Science.* January 1981. 211: 453–58.

———. "Extensional vs. Intuitive Reasoning: The Conjunction Fallacy in Probability Judgment." *Psychological Review.* October 1983. 90: 293–315.

———. "Rational Choice and the Framing of Decisions." *Journal of Business.* October 1986, prt. 2. 4: 251–78.

Viscusi, W. Kip. "Are Individuals Bayesian Decision Makers?" *American Economic Review Papers and Proceedings.* May 1985. 75: 381–85.

von Neumann, John, and Oskar Morgenstern. *Theory of Games and Economic Behavior.* Princeton: Princeton University Press, 1944. 2d ed., 1947. 3d ed., 1953.

Yaari, Menahem. "Some Remarks on Measures of Risk Aversion and On their Uses." *Journal of Economic Theory.* October 1969. 1: 315–29.

———. "The Dual Theory of Choice Under Risk." *Econometrica.* January 1987. 55: 95–115.

COMMENT: *Should a Rational Agent Maximize Expected Utility?*
John Broome

### TWO TYPES OF EXPECTED UTILITY THEORY

Daniel Bernoulli—as Mark Machina reminds us—said that a rational person, in making choices, should maximize the expectation of her utility. At least, *Econometrica*'s translation of his famous paper says that (Bernoulli 1954). Bernoulli himself spoke of *emolumentum* rather than utility. The translator ought not to have used such an ambiguous piece of economists' jargon. My dictionary translates "*emolumentum*" as "profit, benefit, or advantage." Evidently Bernoulli thought you should evaluate a prospect by assessing how good (or beneficial or advantageous) would be the various outcomes it might lead to, and then taking the expectation of this good. A better prospect is one with a greater expectation of good. You should be an expected good maximizer.

This view persisted for a long time. Alfred Marshall (1920, 843) accepted it. So, I think, did Frank Ramsey[1] (1978). It is still common today (e.g., Harsanyi 1975, 600). But there are two obvious grounds for doubting it. One is that it assumes good to be an arithmetical quantity; you cannot calculate the expectation of good if it is not. (More precisely, it assumes good to be measurable up to positive linear transformations.) But the notion of good may seem too imprecise for that. Perhaps one can talk about which prospects are better or worse, so they can be ordered, but perhaps not about how much better or worse. The second ground for doubt is that even if good is an arithmetical quantity, there seems to be no reason why you should maximize particularly its *expectation*. That implies you should be risk-neutral about good. If, say, you had a choice between getting ten units of good for certain or else a gamble at equal odds of five or fifteen units, you should be indifferent. But it seems perfectly reasonable for you to be risk-averse and prefer the certain ten units.

For these reasons, the Bernoullian expected utility theory was losing its popularity amongst economists by the 1940s. Gerhard Tintner (1942) was a pioneer in using objective functions that were more general than expectations. But Ramsey's work, and following it John von Neumann and Oskar Morgenstern's (1953), provided the basis for a new way of interpreting expected utility theory. These authors founded the theory on axioms. The axioms are imposed on the structure of a person's preferences amongst prospects. So long as the preferences satisfy the axioms, then a utility function can be defined for the person in such a way that she can be construed as an expected utility maximizer. A preferred prospect will have a higher expected utility. So her preferences come first, and utility is constructed out of them. It is constructed to *represent* the pref-

---

1. Ramsey (1978, 85) says that his theory "is based throughout on the idea of mathematical expectation; the dissatisfaction often felt with this idea is due mainly to the inaccurate measurement of goods. Clearly mathematical expectations, in terms of money, are not proper guides to conduct. It should be remembered, in judging my system, that in it value is actually defined by means of mathematical expectation in the case of beliefs of degree ½, . . ." Ramsey speaks of measurement and one can only measure something that already exists. So I think his idea was that people maximize the expectation of good, and one can use this fact to measure their good. This is the impression given in most of his paper. The remark that value is *defined* by means of mathematical expectation could point in the opposite direction. In the axiomatic theory, which I am coming to, utility is defined within the theory; it is not a previously existing quantity that is measured using the theory.

erences. Nothing in the theory says that a person's utility stands for good. The theory makes a person an expected utility maximizer, but it does not require her to be an expected good maximizer. It requires less: only that her preferences conform to the axioms. Of course, if she does happen to be an expected good maximizer, she will fit the theory; her preferences will conform. But if she is risk-averse about good, she may still fit the theory. And she may fit it even if good is not an arithmetical quantity.

Utility, then, is defined in the axiomatic theory to represent preferences. In this it is just like "the ordinal utility function of standard consumer theory" (Machina, p. 92 of this volume). Standard consumer theory and Neumann-Morgenstern theory are similar in structure. They both impose axioms on preferences. Then, if the axioms are satisfied, they show that a utility function can be defined to represent the preferences. The Neumann-Morgenstern theory constrains the function more tightly, so that it comes out cardinal in a sense, rather than ordinal. But this difference between the two utility theories is much less significant than their similarities. Most important is that neither makes any reference to the reasons why a person has the preferences she has. Neither is worried about whether she maximizes her good or anything else. To be sure, she maximizes her utility or the expectation of her utility, but this is simply because her utility is defined as what she maximizes or what she maximizes the expectation of. There need be no connection between utility and good. Life would be much easier if the term "utility" was only ever used in this sense, for a quantity defined so as to represent preferences. Economists also use it to stand vaguely for a person's good, and this causes immense confusion.

## RATIONALITY

Expected utility theory may be taken either as a theory about people's actual preferences, or as a theory of rationality, a theory about what a person's preferences would be like if she were rational. The axiomatic theory, considered as a theory of rationality, claims that a rational person will satisfy the axioms. This, I have been explaining, is less than Bernoulli's claim that a rational person maximizes her expectation of good. But is it true? The work of psychologists, including especially Daniel Kahneman and Amos Tversky, shows that, in practice, people's preferences very often conflict with the axioms. Does this mean that people are very often irrational?

Tversky and Kahneman (chapter 2 of this volume) say it does. I do not think they would defend all the axioms as requirements of rationality, but they defend at least some of them. On the other hand, they suggest that many of the authors of alternative decision theories—theories that do not require the maximizing of expected utility—treat them as theories of rationality. These authors, they say, think it is rational not to be an expected utility maximizer. But that is not my impression. I find many of these authors noncommittal about rationality. There are exceptions. Maurice Allais (1979) is the most notable. He unequivocally claims that a rational person need not be an expected utility maximizer; in particular she may violate the independence axiom. Partly this is because Allais still mistakenly supposes that maximizing expected utility implies maximizing expected good (Broome 1985), but Allais also has solid objections to the axioms. I shall come to one of them later.

Machina, on the other hand, the author of another alternative decision theory, is more reticent about rationality. In chapter 3 of this volume, he outlines the common violations of the standard axioms and discusses how expected utility theory might be altered to cope with them. He does not tell us whether or not he thinks these violations are irrational. He does not seem interested in the rationality of preferences. The one place I know where he addresses the question is in a review entitled " 'Rational' Decision Making versus 'Rational' Decision Modelling?" (Machina 1981). The scare quotes on "rational" suggest he is skeptical about the whole notion of rationality. And that is my impression about many of the economists working on decision theory. They are looking for a theory that fits behavior. They find the question of rationality uninteresting and perhaps empty.

So why should we be interested in it? Tversky and Kahneman discuss one reason. For a long time the prevailing mode of explanation in economics has been the rationalist one. People's behavior has been explained by describing the reasons that motivate them to act as they do. And these reasons have been supposed to fit a particular pattern: the person is supposed to choose the best means toward her ends. This has been a pretty successful technique in economics. If we are now to abandon it and build our theories around behavior that is not rational, that is a serious step. It may, of course, be one we have to take.

But I do not think this is the main reason for being interested in rationality. The main reason is that people expect decision theory to tell them, not just how they act, but also how they should act. To say that a person is acting irrationally is a criticism of her action; it is saying that she should not act that way. But it is easy to be skeptical here because the force of this "should" is difficult to pin down. The question "Why should I act rationally?" cannot be usefully answered. The question asks for a reason. But a person who needs to ask the question is precisely someone who does not understand the point of reasons, who does not understand how reasons motivate actions. No reason can be given for acting on reasons.

I doubt, though, that many economists are such thoroughgoing skeptics about rationality as that. Most, I think, understand how reasons motivate, and most accept that rationality requires one to adopt the best means toward one's ends. A person should, then, adopt the best means toward her ends. So here is one use of the rational "should." That is a start.

A useful heuristic device for the skeptic is to think about the preferences a person might have on behalf of someone else. Suppose you are managing some investments on behalf of a child. Then you will certainly be concerned to know what is the rational way of dealing with the uncertainty inherent in the investments. That is because you have a moral responsibility for the child. It is harder in practice to be skeptical about the rational "should" when it can be backed by a moral "should," paradoxical though this may seem. Suppose it was your own investments that were in question, and you asked "Why should I manage them rationally?" The best answer might be: "It best promotes your ends." But then the rejoinder, "Why should I promote my ends?," is hard to answer. In practice, it is easier to find answers to "Why should I promote this child's interest?" This is no more than a heuristic device, however, because moral reasons are no more than reasons and can have force only for a person who is moved by reasons—who is rational, that is. You cannot be moral if you are not already rational. The moral "should" presupposes the rational one.

But in practice some of the most interesting questions about rationality in decision theory have a moral dimension. I am thinking particularly about welfare economics and "social preferences" (however that notion may be understood [see Broome 1989]). Should social preferences conform to the axioms of expected-utility theory? Should a government be an expected-utility maximizer? These are pressing questions because the commonest approach to the welfare economics of uncertainty—the so-called *ex ante* approach—leads to social preferences that do not normally conform to the axioms.[2] A start toward answering them is to consider whether rationality requires an *individual's* preferences to conform. The next step is to consider whether the same requirements of rationality apply to social preferences as well. It is often argued that they do not (e.g., Diamond 1967). I believe, though, that the arguments about rationality apply to any agent, whether an individual or a government, if it is an agent. The only question is whether a government should act as an agent in its own right at all (see Broome 1989). Certainly the issue of rationality is an important first step. This by itself is a good reason to be concerned with the merits of expected utility theory as a theory of rationality.

When it comes to welfare economics, I find Machina (p. 125) too complacent. Uncertainty poses new problems for welfare economics. But Machina seems to believe it does not make much difference, unless framing effects and preference reversal are prevalent. He refers to the standard theorems connecting competitive equilibrium and Pareto efficiency. These theorems remain true when the standard model of general equilibrium is extended in the standard way to accommodate uncertainty. (This standard extension simply takes the goods that are traded to be "contingent commodities.") But extending the model weakens the meaning of "Pareto efficiency" so disastrously that the theorems lose most of their significance. When the economy is Pareto-efficient in this weakened sense, it is not generally true that no other feasible allocation of goods would make one person better off without making someone else worse off. Suppose, for instance, that everyone expects a fine summer and stocks up on sailboards and camping gear. Competition moves resources into producing these things, and this is Pareto-efficient. But in fact it rains every day. Resources would have been better employed on making board games and umbrellas. That might, indeed, have made everyone better off. Pareto efficiency in the weakened sense means simply that no one's prospect, as she herself chooses to assess it, can be improved without damaging someone else's as she assesses it. But a person's welfare is a matter of how well the world goes for her, not of her assessment of how well it might go. The damage done to the standard theorems by recognizing this point is, I think, well understood by now (see Hammond 1981).

2. The normal *ex ante* approach requires social preferences to be Paretian in an *ex ante* sense. If everyone prefers one prospect to another, that is to say, it should be socially preferred. A well-known theorem (e.g., Hammond 1981) shows that Paretian social preferences will fit the axioms of expected-utility theory only in exceptional circumstances.

Let us come to the question, then: does rationality require an agent to conform to the axioms of expected utility theory? What basis can we have for answering a question like this? There is no point in trying to convince a thoroughgoing skeptic. We shall have to take some part of rationality for granted. I have already said that most economists will accept that rationality requires a person to adopt the best means toward her ends. This would give us a start. By itself it has sometimes been thought to justify expected utility theory directly (and moreover in Bernoulli's strong version). The argument is this: if, on every occasion, you adopt the action that maximizes the expectation of your good, that will give you the greatest total of good in the long run; so the rule of maximizing expected good best promotes your good; therefore you should adopt it. This argument, however, fails on many counts. One is this. Whatever rule you adopt for your life, it will determine some expectation of good for you. The rule of maximizing the expectation of good on every occasion will, in some circumstances (see Marschak 1951), give you the greatest expectation of good in all. But it only follows that rationality requires you to adopt this rule if rationality already says you should aim for the greatest expectation of good in all. And that is exactly what is in question.

I suggest we argue, not from this means-ends principle, but in a different way. We can look at the internal structure of reasons, to see how they hold together. I have laid out elsewhere (Broome, 1990a, 1990b) an example of the sort of argument I mean. The argument concludes that, if rationality requires anything of preferences, it requires them to conform to the axioms of transitivity and independence (the main consistency axioms). This relies on one part of rationality to support another. So it will not convince the total skeptic. But it should convince anyone else. I cannot repeat the argument here. But I shall try to give an outline of it in the next two sections.

## INDIVIDUATING OUTCOMES

Start out from Tversky and Kahneman's "principle of invariance" (above, p. 62). This principle says that a prospect can occupy only one position in a person's preference relation. One prospect cannot occupy two different positions. Take a prospect that is specified in one way and compare it with one specified in a different way. (For instance: "200 people will be saved" and "400 people will die" in Kahneman and Tversky's example where 600 people will die unless something is done.) Before the principle of invariance can be applied, we evidently have to know whether these prospects are the same or different. We have to *individuate* prospects. Since prospects are probability distributions over outcomes, this means we have to individuate outcomes. Individuating outcomes is one of the very first steps in decision theory. Laying down axioms comes later.

How should the individuation be done? To illustrate the problem, I shall take an example from another article of Kahneman and Tversky's (1984). You can get a jacket and a calculator for $140 (*A*); one costs $15 and the other $125. Or you can drive twenty minutes and get the two articles for $135 (*B*); in one version of the example, the $15 article is reduced to $10 ($B_1$), in another the $125 article is reduced to $120 ($B_2$). (In this example there is no uncertainty, so each prospect consists of a certain single outcome.) It seems that many of us prefer $B_1$ to *A* and *A* to $B_2$. Is this irrational? Kahneman and Tversky are noncommittal. It depends, they say, on whether $B_1$ and $B_2$ are really the same outcome or different. If they are different, then a person may rationally allow them to occupy different places in her preference relation. But if they are the same, she may not. This is what the principle of invariance says.

$B_1$ and $B_2$ do, of course, differ. They are, if you like, different "possible worlds." But we generally take outcomes to be, not individual possible worlds, but classes of possible worlds taken together. The individuation of outcomes is, in fact, a matter of classification. The critical question here is whether $B_1$ and $B_2$ should be classed as the same outcome or as different ones. Is the difference between them enough to justify a different classification? How should we decide this? Well, look at the effects of our classification. If we decide they are the same outcome, the effect of this is that it will be irrational for them to occupy different places in a person's preference relation. If we decide they are different, this will not be irrational. So we had better make sure, in classifying the outcomes, that the effects are as they should be. We had better classify $B_1$ and $B_2$ as the same outcome if and only if it would be irrational for them to occupy different places in a person's preference relation.

Kahneman and Tversky mention one difference there may be between $B_1$ and $B_2$: $B_1$ may lead to a more pleasurable feeling because the price reduction is a larger fraction of the price of the article. Then they say that their principle of invariance is not violated by the preferences I have described "if such secondary consequences [e.g., the feeling] are considered legitimate" (Kahneman and Tversky 1984, 348). What they mean, I think, is: their principle of invariance is not violated if such a secondary consequence is enough to justify a person in giving the alternatives different places in her preference relation. That is what I have been saying too.

So the procedure I recommend for individuating outcomes is this. Alternatives that it is rational to have a preference between should be classified as different outcomes. Alternatives that it is irrational to have a preference between should be classified as the same outcome.

This procedure puts principles of rationality to work at a very early stage in decision theory. They are needed in fixing the set of alternative prospects that preferences can then be defined upon. The principles in question might be called "rational principles of indifference." They determine when rationality requires a person to be indifferent between two possible worlds, so that they must occupy the same place in her preference relation. These principles are unlike the principles of rationality that are supposedly expressed in the axioms. The latter—transitivity for instance—are formal; they make no reference to the particular content of the prospects. But the rational principles of indifference are substantive. For instance, such a principle might say that it is irrational to prefer one way of saving $5 to another way, when both involve you in exactly the same effort.

Many people think there can be no principles of rationality apart from the formal ones. This goes along with the common view that rationality can only be instrumental, that it can only be about means, not ends. Ends are not subject to rational assessment. Rationality, in fact, comes down to the one principle I mentioned earlier, that you ought to choose the best means to achieve your ends. According to this view, there can be no rational principles of indifference because these principles are, in a sense, trying to assess ends.

If you take this view, you will be forced to individuate outcomes in the finest possible way. If two worlds differ in any respect whatever, you will have to class them as different outcomes. Treating them together as the same outcome would prevent a person from rationally having a preference between them, and that is just what you do not want to prevent.

But using this finest individuation leads to trouble. It prevents you from ruling out *any* pattern of preferences as irrational, even one that, on the face of it, violates a formal principle such as transitivity. To see this, take the example of preference reversal, which is nicely described by Machina. Given a choice between two gambles A and B, a person would prefer A. But she assigns A a lower monetary value than B. So there is an amount of money, M, such that the person would prefer B to M, if she had the choice, and would prefer M to A, if she had the choice.

This looks like a case of intransitivity. But against the charge of intransitivity the person has a defense. If she had a choice between A and B and chose A, then the result would be that she would end up with whatever outcome emerges from the gamble A, and she would also have rejected B. But if she had a choice between A and M and chose A she would end up with whatever outcome emerges from the gamble A, but she would not have rejected B. Whether or not she has rejected B is a difference between these two results. If we acknowledge no rational principles of indifference, then—so we have to adopt the finest scheme of individuation—these must be treated as different outcomes. Therefore A, as it appears in the two choices, must be treated as two different prospects. And if there are two different prospects here, there is no intransitivity.

A move like this could be made by anyone who seems to be violating one of the consistency axioms. What seems like one prospect or one outcome could always be split into two on the basis of some small difference. Only rational principles of indifference can block such a move. The consequence is that if you acknowledge only formal principles of rationality, and deny that there are any rational principles of indifference, you will find yourself without any principles of rationality at all. A total skeptic about rationality will be happy with this conclusion. But anyone who believes at all in rationality will have to acknowledge some substantive principles: some rational principles of indifference. They are required as preconditions for the formal principles.

I think this may come as a surprise to many decision theorists. But I am pleased to say that Tversky, in another article, presents an argument that is, if I understand it, similar to mine. And he reaches the conclusion: "I believe that an adequate analysis of rational choice cannot accept the evaluation of consequences as given, and examine only the consistency of preferences" (Tversky 1975, 172). Exactly.

## TRANSITIVITY AND INDEPENDENCE

What about the person who shows preference reversal, then? Is she irrational or not? We can see now what that depends on. It depends on whether the differences between A having rejected B and A not having rejected B is enough to justify her in giving them different places in her preference relation. If it is, then her preferences are not irrational. Nor, provided we adopt my procedure for individuating outcomes, are they intransitive. My procedure will treat these as different prospects. If, on the other hand, the difference is not enough to justify the person in giving them different places, her preferences are irrational and they are also intransitive according to my procedure.

Provided prospects are individuated in the right way, then, transitivity is a requirement of rationality. Preferences that are apparently intransitive will either be irrational or turn out to be transitive on a closer inspection. And the same goes for the independence axiom. I believe that rationality requires a person to conform to this axiom. But that is only provided the right principle is adopted for individuating outcomes. The full argument for this is spelt out elsewhere (Broome, 1990a, 1990b); I can say only a little about it here.

Traditionally in the arguments about expected utility theory, outcomes have been individuated coarsely, generally by monetary prizes only. Alternatives with the same monetary prizes have been counted as the same outcome. With this scheme of individuation, people's preferences very often conflict with the independence axiom. For instance, many people fall for the Allais paradox, which Machina describes in chapter 3 (p. 98). And it is sometimes claimed that these preferences are rational.[3] Allais (1979), for instance, claims that. But the proferred explanations of why they are supposed to be rational invariably point to a feature of the outcomes that differs even when the monetary prizes are the same. Look, for instance, at the prospect Machina labels "$a_2$" (p. 98). If you had this prospect but had the bad luck to win nothing, you might be bitterly disappointed. You had a 99 percent chance of becoming rich, but it did not come off. On the other hand, if you had the prospect $a_4$ and won nothing, you would not be very disappointed because you did not have much chance of winning anyway. So the monetary prize of nothing in $a_2$ is accompanied by a much worse feeling than the same prize in $a_4$. Because of this you might prefer $a_1$ to $a_2$ on the one hand and $a_4$ to $a_3$ on the other. The difference in feelings might be enough to make such preferences rational, even though on the face of it they violate the independence axiom. But this explanation of why they are rational also shows that classifying outcomes by monetary prizes alone is not good enough. The different feelings that accompany the prizes are enough to justify a difference in preference. Therefore we must, following my scheme, classify the outcomes as different. And if we do that, there is actually no violation of the independence axiom.

This argument defends the independence axiom as a condition of rationality by refining the individuation of outcomes. I think it has been

3. Machina's own "intuitive" explanation of the paradox in chapter 3 (p. 101) is not, I think, intended to justify the preferences as rational.

recognized for a long time that the axiom can be defended by fine individuation. But there is a danger in such a defense. The finer the individuation, the less demanding the axiom becomes. I said earlier, in fact, that if the individuation is the very finest, the axiom will make no demands at all. It will become empty, because any preferences at all can be made consistent with it. That, I think, is why this way of defending the axiom has not been taken very seriously (see, e.g., Machina 1981, 173). But I have recommended a scheme of individuation that is just as fine as it should be, and no finer. Rational principles of indifference prevent it from collapsing to the finest. It gives the independence axiom just the force it should have. It is exactly as demanding as it can be without ceasing to be a condition of rationality.

I think, then, that a rational person ought to conform to the axioms of transitivity and independence. But these axioms need to be understood within a proper scheme for individuating outcomes. This scheme relies on the existence of substantive principles of rationality, of a sort that decision theory has not traditionally recognized.

## CONCLUSION

Mark Machina's work, and Amos Tversky and Daniel Kahneman's too, has been aimed at developing an alternative to expected utility theory that fits people's behavior more closely. This is an important scientific project.

Setting up the theory requires, first, specifying a collection of prospects on which preferences are defined and then specifying some assumptions or axioms about the preferences. For the scientific project, the aim should be to produce a practically convenient theory that fits behavior accurately. Machina, for instance, works almost exclusively with monetary gambles and individuates prospects by monetary prizes only. I am sure this is the right approach to the practical economic problems that interest him. And, with prospects individuated this way, expected utility theory does not fit people's behavior at all well. So Machina is right to modify it. Tversky and Kahneman demonstrate that far more radical modifications than Machina's will be needed to accommodate all the behavior people show in practice.

But besides the scientific project, it is also important to know what rationality requires. We need to know how to manage our affairs and how a government should manage its affairs. The discussion of rationality has been relatively neglected. One difficulty about it is to know what to argue *from*, what is the basis of rationality. But I think we can find a way of proceeding, and I have tried to give an example. I have argued that to understand rationality, we have to be careful about individuating outcomes. To individuate by monetary prizes is certainly too crude. And with a finer individuation, expected utility theory fares better. Some of the violations of the axioms that occur in practice may disappear with finer individuation. The Allais paradox, for instance, may cease to be a violation if our individuation takes account of feelings as well as monetary prizes. But in any case, people's actual behavior is not what is in question. We are concerned with rationality, and Tversky and Kahneman make it clear that people often behave irrationally. I believe that, with a proper individuation, the most important consistency axioms of expected utility theory can be shown to be requirements of rationality. I am more doubtful about one of the other axioms. I doubt that rationality requires a person's preferences to be complete (Broome 1990b). But I think, all the same, that, taken as a theory of rationality, expected utility theory deserves more credit than economists and psychologists have given it in recent years.

## REFERENCES

Allais, Maurice. 1979. "The Foundations of a Positive Theory of Choice Involving Risk and a Criticism of the Postulates and Axioms of the American School." In *Expected Utility Hypothesis and the Allais Paradox*, 27–145, edited by Maurice Allais and Ole Hagen. Reidel.

Bernoulli, Daniel. 1954. "Exposition of a New Theory on the Measurement of Risk." *Econometrica* 22: 23–36. Translated by Louise Sommer from "Specimen theoriae novae de mensura sortis," *Commentarii Academiae Scientiarum Imperialis Petropolitanae* 5 (1738).

Broome, John. 1985. "A Mistaken Argument Against the Expected-Utility Theory of Rationality." *Theory and Decision* 18: 313–18.

———. 1989. "Should Social Preferences Be Consistent?" *Economics and Philosophy* 5: 7–17.

———. 1990a. "Rationality and the Sure-Thing Principle." In *Rationality, Self-Interest and Benevolence*, edited by Gay Meeks. Cambridge: Cambridge University Press.

———. 1990b. *Weighing Goods*. Oxford: Blackwell.

Diamond, Peter A. 1967. "Cardinal Welfare, Individualistic Ethics, and Interpersonal Comparisons of Utility: Comment." *Journal of Political Economy* 75: 765–66.

Hammond, P. J. 1981. "Ex-ante and Ex-post Welfare Optimality under Uncertainty." *Economica* 48: 235–50.

Harsanyi, John C. 1975. "Can the Maximin Principle Serve as a Basis for Morality? A Critique of John Rawls's Theory." *American Political Science Review* 69: 594–606.

Kahneman, Daniel, and Amos Tversky. 1984. "Choices, Values and Frames." *American Psychologist* 39: 341–50.

Machina, Mark J. 1981. "'Rational' Decision Making versus 'Rational' Decision Modelling?" *Journal of Mathematical Psychology* 24: 163–75.

Marschak, J. 1951. "Why 'Should' Statisticians and Businessmen Maximize 'Moral Expectations'?" In *Proceedings of the Second Berkeley Symposium on Mathematical Statistics and Probability,* 493–506, edited by Jerzy Neyman. University of California Press.

Marshall, Alfred. 1920. *Principles of Economics,* eighth ed. London: Macmillan.

Neumann, John von, and Oskar Morgenstern. 1953. *Theory of Games and Economic Behavior.* Princeton, NJ: Princeton University Press.

Ramsey, F. P. 1978. "Truth and Probability." In his *Foundations,* 58–100. Edited by D. H. Mellor. London: Routledge & Kegan Paul.

Tintner, Gerhard. 1942. "A Contribution to the Non-static Theory of Choice." *Quarterly Journal of Economics* 56 (1942): 274–306.

Tversky, Amos. 1975. "A Critique of Expected-Utility Theory: Descriptive and Normative Considerations." *Erkenntnis* 9: 163–73.

# 4

# Rational Choice in Experimental Markets

## CHARLES R. PLOTT

The theory of rational individual choice has many different uses in experimental economics. The uses must be considered in any realistic evaluation of the theory. This paper is organized around that perspective.

If the only question posed is, "Rational choice, true or false?" then the answer is clearly false. Many critics of economics have claimed that the discipline is built on untestable foundations. Economists are indebted to psychologists for debunking such critics and demonstrating that the theory can indeed be tested. However, the gratitude can go only so far. During the process of demonstrating testability, the psychologists disconfirmed the theory. Preference transitivity experiments (Tversky 1969) and preference reversal experiments (Grether and Plott 1979) both demonstrate that the weakest forms of the classical preference hypothesis[1] are systematically at odds with facts.

It follows that theories of markets for which rational individual choice is a necessary component are either disconfirmed by the same evidence or cannot be applied because the preconditions for application are not present. The logic is compelling, and an awareness of its existence has colored how experimental economists pose questions, how they do experiments, and what they conclude. If one wants only to "test" a theory in the sense of rejection, then one should examine its most suspect predictions. If, as part of its formulation of market behavior, a theory predicts acyclic individual choice behavior—as is the case with almost all

Reprinted from *Journal of Business* 59, no. 4, pt. 2: 301–27. ©1986 by The University of Chicago. All rights reserved. Financial support from the National Science Foundation and from the Caltech Program of Enterprise and Public Policy is gratefully acknowledged. I wish to thank Kemal Guler for his help in processing the data used in section III. I also wish to thank Barry Weingast and Harvey Reed for their collaboration on the ideas and background data processing that form that section.

1. The classical hypothesis is taken to be that attitudes of preference can be represented by total, reflexive, negatively acyclic binary relations. For generalizations and alternatives to this hypothesis, see Aizerman (1985).

economics models—then one seeking a disconfirmation of the theory knows exactly where to look and how to proceed. Existing experiments on individual choice behavior provide ample machinery.

The rejection of a theory of markets on the terms described above is not an especially challenging research objective. Those who study experimental markets tend to pose the questions in different ways. Rather than inquire whether a theory is true or false, they ask if the magnitude of error in the predictions of market phenomena is acceptable; or, if no concept of degree of acceptability is readily available, the question becomes which of several competing models is the most accurate, fully realizing that the best model might still be "poor." When confronted with data that suggest the existence of erratic or irrational individual behavior, the implications are immediately evaluated in terms of the possible implications for a market level of analysis. Of course, when unusual market behavior is observed, one might then turn to models of irrational individual behavior to see if they contain the seeds of an explanation.

In brief it is almost impossible to assess the importance of any problem with rationality postulates as found in experimental market studies without assessing the performance of the market models based on such postulates. In section I, I will discuss hypotheses about rational behavior that are built directly into the foundations of laboratory market procedures. In section II, three examples of laboratory experiments will be discussed. The accuracy of the models and the rationality postulates that form the structure of the models will be covered. Section III will demonstrate how ideas of rationality can be used to explain otherwise very confusing market behavior. Section IV will examine unusual phenomena that models of rational behavior suggest might exist, and section V will discuss some pending problems for concepts of rationality as they are currently used.

## I. Laboratory Market Procedures and Rationality

For the most part, laboratory markets are created as a challenge to theory. One research objective is to construct simple markets that are special cases of the complicated phenomena to which the models are ordinarily applied. The relative accuracies of models are assessed. The models are changed in light of the data from the special case. It is hoped, as a result, that the revised models will be more useful when applied to the complex. While other research strategies can be identified (Plott 1982, esp. pp. 1519–23), this particular strategy is frequently used.

The above objective demands that laboratory economics procedures permit some reasonably direct correspondence between parameters of models and what is controlled in an experiment. The important variables of almost all economic models are preferences (as opposed to sources of motivation), beliefs, resources, market organization (institutions), technology, commodities, prices, allocations, and incomes. If a model is to be evaluated, all these variables need to be observed and sometimes controlled. If a variable cannot be observed directly, then it is always suspected of having gone awry when the model itself does not fit the data. Of course, in this context, the preferences and beliefs are key because (a) they can be used to explain almost any pattern of the other variables (Ledyard 1986) and (b) they cannot be observed directly.

Laboratory techniques control preferences or, in a sense, allow them to be observed indirectly. The basic insight is that preferences are parameters to economic models, but the source of preferences is not a parameter. The key idea is to use monetary incentives to induce preferences for abstract commodities that exist only for the purpose of the experiment. Consider the following axioms, which are a combination of the precepts used by Smith (1976) and the axioms used by Plott (1979). If the following axioms are accepted, then preferences can be induced and controlled for purposes of experimentation.

　　1. More reward medium (money) is preferred to less, other things being equal (salience and nonsatiation).

　　2. Individuals place no independent value on experimental outcomes other than that provided by the reward medium (neutrality).

　　3. Individuals optimize.

Suppose, for example, that a commodity is the set of nonnegative integers, which are called units of the commodity $X$. Another commodity, $Y$, is simply U.S. currency. An individual, $i$, is assigned a function, $R^i(x)$, indicating the reward (dollar amount) he will receive from the experimenter should he acquire $x$ units of commodity $X$. If postulates 1–3 are satisfied, then we can take as a parameter in a model, defined over $X \cdot Y$ where the operation $\cdot$ is a Cartesian product and the binary relation $P_i$, is defined by $(x, y)P^i(x', y') \Leftrightarrow R^i(x) + y > R^i(x') + y'$. The relation $P_i$ is the preference relation of $i$. If the axioms are satisfied, then $P_i$ is in fact the individual's preference relation in the same sense that it will reflect actual individual choices from the pairs in $X \cdot Y$. Since the experimenter controls the functional form of $R^i(\cdot)$, the preference relation of each individual can be controlled as desired.

Carrying the example further, we could view $R^i(x) - R^i(x - 1)$ as the willingness to pay for additional units of $X$. In some circumstances the difference would be interpreted as an (inverse) demand function. That is, suppose $p$ is a constant price that a subject must pay for units of $X$. An optimizing subject would want to maximize $R^i(x) - px$. The optimum occurs (ignoring the problem caused by the discrete formulation) at the point $\hat{x}$ such that $R^i(\hat{x}) - R^i(\hat{x} - 1) = p$. Solving the equation for $\hat{x}$, we obtain a function, $\hat{x} = D_i(p)$, which can be interpreted as an individual demand function for $X$.

Notice that, if any of the conditions, 1, 2, or 3, is not satisfied, then a key parameter is misspecified. When asked to choose over $X \cdot Y$, the subject's choices would not be those predicted by $P_i$. If this occurs, and if the experimenter is not aware of the problem, a model might be discarded as inaccurate when in fact the experiment was not properly controlled. The point to be emphasized is that a theory of rationality is basic to experimental procedures and to the interpretation of the results. If rationality is not reliable behaviorally, then one would expect economic models to be poor predictors of experimental market behavior because the basic parameters of the economic models would not be controllable.

The nature of the argument just outlined suggests a first line of defense that can be used by anyone whose pet theory has been abused by experimental data. Were the payoffs of a sort that assures that postulate 1 is satisfied? For the most part economists have used money in amounts that will accumulate to amounts comparable to wage rates (for equivalent time) of employed members of the subject pools. Typically, this amount is between \$8.00 and \$20 per hour. A failure to provide adequate incentives is known to affect results at a group level of performance in ways that do not disappear with large samples.[2] Results regarding the importance of incentives when studying individual choices have been mixed. For example, Grether and Plott (1979) found no incentive effects. The most recent study is by Grether (1981), who demonstrated that the instances of seemingly confused behavior go up when incentives go down.

The second postulate substantially differentiates those who study markets from those who study individuals. Psychologists frequently use rich descriptions of situations to elicit responses. From an economist's point

2. Only two examples exist. Once problems were detected along this line, subsequent experiments used more incentives. The committee experiments studied by Fiorina and Plott (1978) used incentives as a control. Means and variances were affected substantially. Plott and Smith (1978) demonstrate that traders tend not to trade units for which positive profits will be made. Just breaking even is not enough.

of view, this practice is one that is to be viewed with suspicion.[3] Data that lead to a model's rejection can always be explained away by hypotheses that take advantage of any ambiguity that might exist over what preferences "really" existed in the experiment.

The final condition, 3, depends not only on human nature but also on whether the subject understands the relation $R^i(\cdot)$. This function is seldom simply verbally communicated to the subject. If the function involves random elements, they are made operational with real random devices (the word "probability" is not used). Subjects are given experience with the properties of $R^i(\cdot)$ and tested on their understanding of it. Sometimes the instructions of a complicated market experiment involve exercises in which subjects choose over $X \cdot Y$ or its equivalent as a check on conditions 1–3. While these precautions are taken as a defense against disgruntled theorists who might dismiss results on the (self-serving) claim that the preferences were not controlled, they also comment on implicit assumptions about the nature of rationality: intelligence is important; verbal communication is suspect; analytical and cognitive abilities are not dependable over experience. So the experiment proceeds, allowing for the possibility that individuals might be satisficers in the Simon (1979) sense and fail to explore the nature of $R^i(x)$ if left to their own devices.

Acknowledged problems with the concept of rational choice have shaped experimental market procedures in still a third way that was mentioned in the opening paragraphs. Almost all economic models postulate the existence (on an "as if" basis) of a transitive preference over lotteries. Thus transitive choice over lotteries can be viewed as a prediction made by the models. We know from Tversky's (1969) work on transitivity and from preference reversal experiments (Grether and Plott 1979) that those particular predictions of the models will be disconfirmed; that is, we know that models of this type make predictions that are wrong. Logic thus compels us to realize that a determination of the "truth" of such models is not necessarily the only goal of the research effort because we already have the answer to that question. Instead the

---

3. I am aware of one documented example of a problem caused by the descriptions of the alternatives. In Cohen, Levine, and Plott (1978) subjects were involved in a voting experiment. The objects of choice (letters of the alphabet) were labeled in humorous ways. Traditional financial incentives were also operative. The group-choice model, which had worked well in other experiments, was not working well, so subjects were asked to explain the reasons for their votes. The recorded votes and the reasons given by subjects indicated that subjects neglected the financial incentives and chose in ways they imagined reasonable in light of the humorous description of the options.

research question becomes the degree to which one model is better than another at capturing market behavior. Experiments should be designed to make comparisons among models whenever such comparisons are possible. Which model throws light on market behavior? Which model is true is a different question.

## II. PERFORMANCE OF MARKET MODELS

If rationality assumptions are totally unreliable, then one would expect market models based on them to be similarly unreliable. Preferences for outcomes might be induced by the procedures outlined above, but it does not follow that the market supply and demand functions can be constructed from those preferences. An uncontrolled aspect of rationality is required to go from preferences to market demand; or demands and supplies might have been controlled, but laboratory markets are complicated and involve expectations formation, strategy, and so forth. The demand and supply model itself might not work as a predictor of price; or events in the market could override the incentives used. People simply might not be able to cope or might become irritated or frustrated so easily that no market model would work. If people are erratic and/or irrational, the induced preferences will not guarantee the accuracy of economic models.

Three different examples of market experiments are now summarized. Each relies on different features of human capacities. All are "success stories" in the sense that a mathematical model based on principles of rational choice seems to capture much of what is observed. The replications of these experiments have occurred in enough similar situations that the inferences drawn from the examples probably reliably reflect the facts as opposed to outlying or fortuitous observations.

### Middlemen

The first example comes from a paper by Plott and Uhl (1981). The concern was with middlemen. Each of a group of suppliers was given a marginal cost function by application of induced preferences theory. If price was constant and each followed the competitive optimizing response, the market supply curve would be as shown in figure 4.1. Similarly, final buyers each had a derived demand. Should final buyers have responded in an optimizing fashion to a fixed price, the market demand would have been as shown in the figure. Each agent was assigned a different number to use as a name during the experiment. The numbers on the market demand and supply functions refer to the agent who had the limit value at the indicated level.

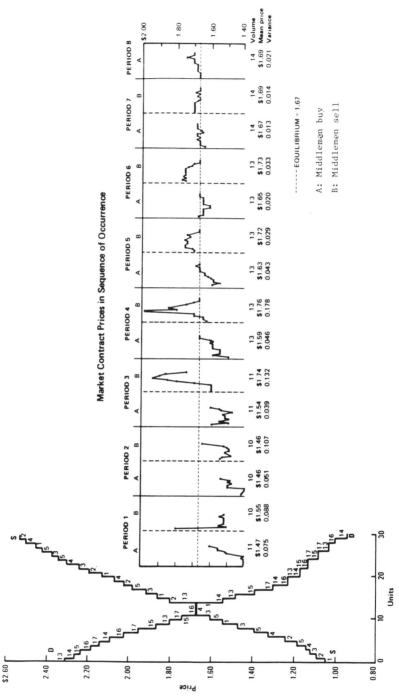

FIGURE 4.1 Market Parameters and Price Time Series; A = Middlemen Buy, and B = Middlemen Sell

Final buyers and suppliers were in different rooms and could neither trade nor communicate. A group of four middlemen (speculators) were allowed first to visit the suppliers' room, at which time a market, A, was opened. Having acquired inventories, the middlemen were then taken to the final buyers' room, where they were able to sell in market B what they had previously purchased in market A. After market B was closed, the middlemen returned to market A to start a new period (of two markets). Inventories could not be carried forward to succeeding periods. Everything acquired in A had to be sold in B or forgotten. Both markets were organized in a manner similar to oral double auctions.

If the individuals serving the middleman function were optimizers and correctly assessed the probability of sales in market B, then the prices in markets A and B should have approached equality. The level of price should have been at the demand and supply intersection. Profits of middlemen should have approached zero. The volume in both markets should have been fourteen units. If would be as if demanders and suppliers were in the same market and middlemen did not exist.

As shown in figure 4.1, the predictions of the model are approximately correct, and there is a time series of all contract prices in the order in which they occurred. With time and replication of periods the prices in both markets converged to the predicted equilibrium price of $1.67. The predicted carryforward of fourteen units was close to the actual volume. Profits of middlemen dissipated to near zero as predicted.

From a practical perspective the competitive model works rather well when applied to the middleman markets. No model of which I am aware, based on principles other than some form of rationality, does as well as does the competitive model. Indeed, in this simple example there are many chances for things to go wrong. First, notice that the theory of derived demand is working twice removed. Derived demand theory was used to postulate the market demand of final consumers as induced by the experimenter. Derived demand for a factor of production was used by middlemen when they purchased a "resource" from the sellers in room A and transformed it into a product for sale in room B. Notice that this transformation took place under conditions of extreme uncertainty. The middlemen did not know the demand function, prices, or any other aspect of the market (or market theory). Somehow they assessed the consequences of their actions with reasonable accuracy. Once having acquired inventories, the middlemen showed no evidence of falling prey to the sunk-cost fallacy. When mistakes appeared to have been made, that is, when middlemen seem to have carried too much forward, the middlemen readily sold at a loss and recovered as much as possible. (In the first period, one unit was carried forward and not sold, but in subsequent periods this problem never occurred.) Notice also that we have some confirmation of the "free riding" or "prisoner's dilemma" model as applied to public goods. Middlemen had a common interest in keeping prices low in market A and high in market B. Outbidding a fellow middleman and gaining the associated personal profits is the market analogue of free riding. These participants were not characterized by such a concern for fellow middlemen that they would forgo advantages of individual gain in order that the profits of all might be higher. Not only is there support here for a "rational" perspective, but there is support for the additional proposition that these people in this setting were not naturally concerned about others; or, if they were so concerned, it was not apparent in their collective actions.

While the middleman type of market experiment suggests that elements of the rational agent model can capture much of the actual human behavior, we cannot assume that this is the end of the story. Even this simple market exhibits behavior that at best is not predicted by the model and at worst is wholly inconsistent with the model. Notice first that the model becomes accurate only after a process of convergence. The model says nothing about that. Notice that the adjustment process contains events that are hard to reconcile with rationality. In the A market, prices existed that were substantially below those observed in the previous A market, and prices tended to move up during a period. Why did sellers simply not wait and capture the higher prices? Why in period 7 did the buyer pay $2.31 when such high prices had never been necessary before? Notice that in market B of periods 1–2 an excess demand existed but that prices were below equilibrium. The model predicts equilibrium, and in periods 1–2 this did not occur.

## Auctions

Some of the most extensive use of the precision afforded by rationality postulates is found in the auction literature. This example is of special importance because it is the only example of which I am aware that the full implications of rationality axioms have been deduced in operational terms in a form that can be examined by an experimenter. Put another way, this is the only example in all of economics where a reasonably complete theory about rational behavior in markets exists.

Compare two types of sealed-bid auctions in which a single item is to be sold. Each bidder tenders a single bid in private that is collected and examined (privately) by the market (auctioneer). The object will be awarded to the highest bidder. If the auction is a first-price auction, the winning bidder will pay the amount of his own bid. If the auction is a second-price auction, the winner will pay the amount of the second-highest bid.

The scientific challenge is to compare the bids tendered in each type of market and, more ambitiously, to predict the bids tendered. Suppose that $N$ agents are participating and that all participants know that $v_i$, the value of the object to each bidder $i$, is drawn from a probability distribution with support on the interval $[\underline{V}, \overline{V}]$. Notice three aspects of the challenge. First, the institution can be viewed as a treatment variable, so, even if the theory fails to predict individual agent behavior, it still might add insight about market behavior. When dealing with economics, the role of the market as an aspect of inquiry should always be kept in focus. Second, it is the actions taken by agents and not their thoughts, thought processes, feelings, or attitudes that are to be studied. Finally, the concepts of value and probability that are frequently a cause for concern by critics of economics are built into the theory at the outset.

An experimental approach to the problem was first developed by Coppinger, Smith, and Titus (1980) and has since expanded dramatically. To appreciate the role of rationality in this investigation we will consider only a simple case. The values $v_i$ are independently drawn from a constant density on $[0, 1]$, so, by expressing bids as a fraction of the largest possible value, any interval can be considered. Each agent knows his own value before bidding but not the value of others. The above facts are public knowledge and can be controlled for experimental purposes; that is, auctions can actually be created that objectively have the requisite properties.

How might one go about developing a model of the situation? The auction theory literature suggests that the system will behave as if the following are true. (a) Agents choose in accord with the expected utility hypothesis. To obtain a model that can be solved we will assume each player has a utility function of wealth, $U_i(y) = y^r$, where $r$ is distributed across the population by a publicly known probability distribution, $\phi$, on $[0, 1]$. The constant $r$ is a risk-aversion factor. This assumption will be treated as a maintained hypothesis for purposes of analyzing the data and testing the theory. (b) At the time of choice each agent, $i$, knows $(v_i, r_i)$, his own value and risk parameter, but knows only the probability distribution from which those of others were drawn. (*c*) Each individual follows Bayes's law in forming expectations. (*d*) Each individual will choose a Nash equilibrium bidding function. (*e*) There are N agents.

Under all the above assumptions the symmetric Nash equilibrium bidding functions are

$$b_i = \begin{cases} v_i, \text{ for all } i \text{ if the second-price auction is used;} \\ \dfrac{(N-1)v_i}{N-1+r_i}, \text{ for all } i \text{ if the first-price auction is used.} \end{cases}$$

The comparative institutional prediction is that the expected price under the first-price auction is greater than the expected price under the second-price auction. Table 4.1 reproduces the results of some of Smith's experiments. The range of the support function $[0, \overline{V}]$ was varied with N to keep expected profits, as calculated by the model, the same as N increased. First, notice that the model is very accurate when applied to the second-price auction for $N > 3$. For example, if $N = 6$, the model predicts a mean price of 12.1, and the actual price averaged 11.21. The predicted variances are also close to those observed. As predicted by the model, people tend to bid their value when they participate in the second-price auction. Second, notice that the prediction about the market treatment variable is also correct. The average price for the second-price auctions is below the average price of the first-price auctions for every value of N. The first-price auction generates more revenue as predicted.

The risk-neutral model ($r = 1$) tends to develop inaccuracies when applied to the magnitude of first-price auction bids. Of course the risk neutrality parameter was not controlled in these experiments. In any case, prices in the first-price auction are higher than those predicted by the model if we assume that $r = 1$. If the data are tested for every value of N against the risk-averse model, which predicts that observed prices will be above the risk-neutral prediction, the model cannot be rejected for $N > 3$.

The support for the Nash-equilibrium-based models has continued as research has expanded to a study of the multiple units case, although the model has encountered difficulties for some values of N. For the single-unit case, however, the full Nash equilibrium model with all its implicit and explicit rationality assumptions is the most accurate model that exists. To the extent that the model places restrictions on data it is consistent with the facts in an absolute sense.

**Table 4.1** Theoretical Predictions and Means and Variances Pooled over $N$ Markets

| Number and Statistics | First-Price Auction | | Second-Price Auction | |
|---|---|---|---|---|
| | Observed Price | Risk Neutral Theoretical ($r \equiv 1$) | Observed Price | Theoretical |
| 3:* | | | | |
| Mean | 2.44 | 2.5 | 1.97 | 2.5 |
| Variance | .589 | .384 | .759 | .96 |
| 4:† | | | | |
| Mean | 5.64 | 4.9 | ... | ... |
| Variance | 1.80 | .96 | ... | ... |
| 5:† | | | | |
| Mean | 9.14 | 8.1 | ... | ... |
| Variance | 1.37 | 1.83 | ... | ... |
| 6:† | | | | |
| Mean | 13.22 | 12.1 | 11.21 | 12.1 |
| Variance | 4.31 | 3.0 | 8.20 | 6.4 |
| 9:‡ | | | | |
| Mean | 31.02 | 28.9 | 27.02 | 28.9 |
| Variance | 4.91 | 8.38 | 18.66 | 18.85 |

SOURCE: Cox, Roberson, and Smith (1982).
* $N = 70$.
† $N = 60$.
‡ $N = 30$.

## Signaling

The third example is a demonstration that the equilibrium notions motivated by concepts of optimizing behavior can capture the essence of very complicated and interdependent phenomena. The model itself was originally motivated by a cynical view of education (Spence 1974). Imagine a world in which education has no intrinsic value but is very costly in terms of time and effort to all but the smartest people. By paying an appropriate premium for educated employees, employers can make education a profitable investment for smart people but not for others. Thus the employers can hire just the people they wish (smart) by paying a premium for an attribute they do not value (education). Theoretically, the employers can do this even though the intelligence level of the prospective employee prior to employment can be observed by no one other than the employee himself; and, when asked, a prospective employee has an incentive to lie.

The point of the experimental exercise is not to explore the appropriateness of the reasoning when applied to investments in education.

The purpose is to explore the nature of equilibrium when such asymmetric information exists in markets. We inquire about the appropriateness of equilibrating principles that are asserted to be operative and the ability of mathematical statements to capture them.

The educational interpretation is intended only to help one understand the laboratory market that was created. In the laboratory market several sellers have two units each of a commodity than can be sold. The units have two characteristics: grade, which can be either Regular (R) or Super (S), and quality, which initially is zero but can be added by the seller. Grade is like a {dumb, smart} variable, and quality is like education that can be added at cost. A seller's two units are either both R or both S. Half the sellers have R's, and the other half have S's, as determined randomly and secretly before any trading begins. Before purchase, N buyers can observe quality added, but the underlying grade is discovered only after purchase and after the market period is closed.

Buyers like Supers better than Regulars, and buyers place some value on any additional quality added by sellers (i.e., education has some value). In particular, for each unit purchased buyers have the following value (determined by the experimenter by using the techniques of induced preference described in the introduction):

$$V(g, q) = G(g) + Q(q),$$

where

$g \in \{R, S\} \equiv \{\text{Regular, Super}\};$
$q \in (0, \infty) = \text{quality added by seller};$
$$G(g) = \begin{cases} \$2.50 & \text{if } g = S, \\ \$.50 & \text{if } g = R; \end{cases}$$
$$Q(q) = \begin{cases} \$.205q - \$.005q^2 & \text{if } q \leq 20, \\ \$[(.205)(20) - (.005)(20^2)] + \$.01q & \text{if } q > 20. \end{cases}$$

Sellers face costs of adding quality of $\$.15q$ and $\$.02q$ if the units are Regulars or Supers, respectively. It costs less to add $q$ (get educated) if the unit is a Super (smart).

The most efficient signaling equilibrium is a fascinating concept when considered from a rationality perspective. The equilibrium is defined by the following equations:

> all Regulars will be produced at the same quality, $q_R$, and will sell at the same price, $P_R$;
> all Supers will be produced at the same quality, $q_S$, and will sell at the same price, $P_S$. (1)

The two conditions in (1) follow from an underlying axiom requiring that no arbitrage exists. If different prices and qualities existed within grades, then profit opportunities would exist, and rational agents would take advantage of them.

$$V(R, q_R) = P_R;$$
$$V(S, q_S) = P_S. \qquad (2)$$

The equations in (2) pick up two aspects of behavior. First, having observed the quality level, $q_R$ or $q_S$, the buyer can infer the grade, $R$ or $S$, with certainty. Quality and grade are perfectly correlated. Second, once this is known the demand and supply model under certainty becomes applicable. For any unit with characteristics $(g, q)$ a horizontal demand exists. Recall that the values of consumers were defined per unit, so, without budget constraints and with prices below value and no uncertainty, the buyer would want an infinite quantity of all possible commodities. The limited supply (vertical supply curve) and horizontal demand curve drive prices to the maximum, that is, the demand price.

$$P_R - .15q_R \geq P_S - .15q_S;$$
$$P_S - .02q_S \geq P_R - .02q_R. \qquad (3)$$

The two conditions in (3) require that truthful revelation is incentive compatible. Regular sellers maximize profits by selling units at the quality level recognized by buyers as Regulars. Super sellers maximize profits by selling units at quality levels recognized by buyers as Supers.

$$\max\{[V(R, q_R) - .15q_R] + [V(S, q_S) - .02q_S]\}. \qquad (4)$$

Condition (4) captures a type of "market rationality." It says that profits of the system will be maximized subject to the behavioral constraints defined in (1)-(3).

In less opaque terms, the final condition (4) can be interpreted as another type of demand and supply condition. The $q_S$ and $q_R$ will be adjusted to reflect gains from exchange. The maximization formulation captures the idea that this adjustment in the quality levels of the commodity will continue until further adjustments would negate the signaling value implicit in (1). The idea is explained geometrically in figure 4.2.

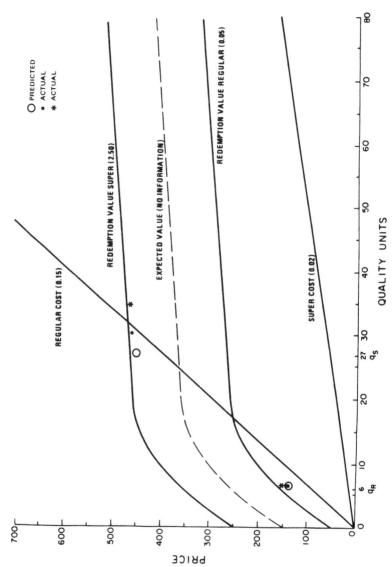

FIGURE 4.2 Model Parameters and Predictions Displayed with Actual Experimental Outcomes

The value functions for a single buyer are drawn from Regulars and Supers. The increases in value with additional quality are as shown. Equation (2) says that the price of an $S$ will be along the top curve and that the price of an $R$ will be along the bottom curve. The qualities, $q_R$ and $q_S$, must be such that they are not equal and thereby signal to the buyer the underlying grade. The qualities should also be located such that sellers of $R$'s have no interest in marketing their units at $(P_s, q_s)$, and so forth, as demanded by (2). Finally, $q_R$ should be located to maximize system profits, and $q_s$ should be the minimum possible level consistent with (2). A check of the equations will demonstrate that $(q_R, q_S) = (6, 27)$, as shown in the figure, have the requisite properties.

Twelve markets with the above (and related) parameters were reported in Miller and Plott (1985). The results were mixed in the sense that other variations of the model outlined above were more accurate than was that particular model. However, the interesting thing from the perspective of this paper is that the mode! captured any of the market data at all; yet in two of the 11 markets this complicated model that is filled with rationality postulates is very accurate. The data points are shown in figure 4.2 near the predicted equilibrium. The quality of Regulars, $q_R$, is correct, and the quality of supers, $q_s$, is a little too high. Variances in qualities and prices are very low. Prices are slightly below the predicted level, reflecting a frequently observed property of markets that agents will not trade for zero reward. Behavior of the type described in this model is certainly not beyond human or market capabilities.

### III. Ex Post Rationalization (Reparameterization)

When markets perform in unusual or unexpected ways, the rationality postulates suggest hypotheses to explain why. The econometrics and field studies literature are filled with ex post rationalization techniques, but very little has been said about them in laboratory economics papers.

The idea of reparameterization is important in a second way. Rationality at a market level of analysis can be separated from rationality at the individual level. Suppose that the market model works well given the individual agent's personal decision rules. So, from observed market behavior we can make some reasonable inferences about what actual individual decision rules must have been. Suppose further that from induced preference theory we obtain an independent theoretical idea about what a rational individual's decision rule would have been in the experiment. By comparing the inferred actual with the theoretical rational we can perhaps develop a methodology for testing the latter as they are relevant for economics.

To demonstrate how rationality principles can be used in this capacity, the data from four experiments are analyzed. These are experiments that would have been discarded because of (allegedly) poor experimental control. These experiments were done in the mid-1960s and early 1970s before some of the experimental techniques currently used had been developed. They are all oral auction markets that differed in various ways from the oral double auction now in use. Each trader had two units and could tender an all-or-none offer. Offers remain open until canceled or taken. The instructions were not administered carefully. No tests on procedures or practice rounds were allowed. The accounting was not checked for confused or cheating participants, and so on. In essence the current operational procedures for making certain that subjects understand the reward medium and the market technology were not followed—or so we would like to believe.

The nature of the markets was to induce simple demand and supply functions different from those that had previously been examined. Also present were multiple units, which, at the time of the experiments, had not been studied. The question posed was whether the observed prices and volume would converge to the equilibrium predictions of the model.

The answer was a rather resounding "no." The initial parameters are shown as the solid-line demand and supply functions in figures 4.3 and 4.4. For the most part the data are well removed from the predictions of the model.

Whenever data are trashed, a danger exists that the problem is the principles that guided the models, not the lack of parametric control. However, when examining subjects' decisions, many seemed to violate the intuitive notions of rationality stemming from confusion or a willingness to violate the rules of the market.

An exercise was undertaken to "reparameterize" the experiments. We wished to provide a method of adjusting individual preference parameters in light of their choices and determine the extent to which the revised market model fits the data. The rules used were as follows. (a) If a buyer (seller) buys (sells) a unit for more (less) than the redemption value (cost) of the unit, then the limit price is adjusted to the transaction price. (b) If an agent never bid or traded during the entire experiment and passed up profitable opportunities (suitably defined), then the parameters are adjusted as if the agent were not present. (c) If an agent failed to trade for two consecutive periods and passed up profitable opportunities (suitably

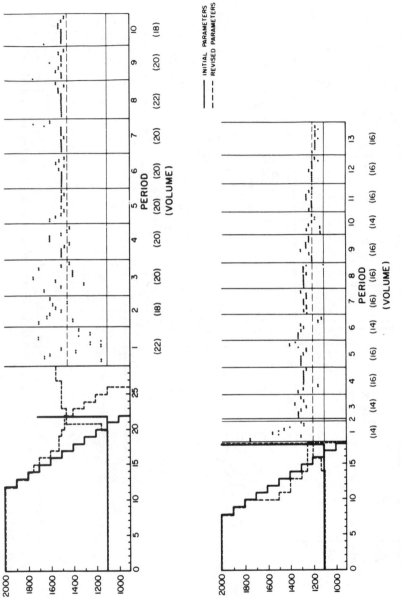

FIGURE 4.3 Parameters of Initial and Revised Models, Predictions, and Price-Time Series of Two Experimental Markets

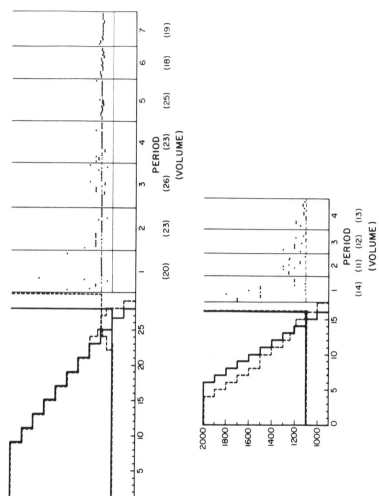

FIGURE 4.4 Parameters of Initial and Revised Models, Predictions, and Price-Time Series of Two Experimental Markets—Solid Line Represents Initial Parameters and Broken Line Represents Revised Parameters

defined), then the limit prices are revised to equal the highest (lowest) bid to buy (offer to sell) that the agent tendered or accepted for that unit in any period throughout the experiment. ($d$) If an agent transacts for more units than the maximum permitted, then the units are adjusted to the maximum number of such extra units traded in any period, and the limit prices are the highest (lowest) price paid (received) for those units during the entire experiment.

The revised demand and supplies are the dotted curves in figures 4.3 and 4.4. The price predictions of the revised model fit much better than they do in the original in three of the four cases, and in the fourth case the price predictions are identical. The volume figures are worse after reparameterization because in all cases the actual volume was low relative to the original model and because the revised parameters predicted even lower volume.

The exercise demonstrates two properties of rationality-based theories. First, the adjustment of parameters need not induce circularity in the reasoning. Ex post theories based on rationality can certainly be rejected. For example, the observed volume can be used to reject the revised model. Second, in view of subsequent experimentation, the decision to discard the data was probably correct. If these subjects are "equivalent" to those used in subsequent experiments, and if the market organization had no special effects, then the actual preferences used by the subjects were not those the experimenter attempted to induce. If preferences are stable, we know now that under the double oral auction prices converge to the competitive equilibrium. Thus subsequent experiments tell us that the markets in the figures above had adjusted to the actual preferences. Even if participants are confused and "irrational" from certain perspectives, the market model can still be applied.

The only other attempt to revise parameters of a market model based on decisions made during the experiment is the ongoing work by Knez, Smith, and Williams (1985). They have attempted to measure individual attitudes during a market, and to use those parameters for prediction they tested a market model based on measured parameters against the model with parameters as specified a priori by the experimenter. The markets themselves are for lotteries in which subjects stated their limit prices—maximum (minimum) willingness to pay (sell)—prior to the opening of each market period. Their conclusions are ($a$) that the act of measurement does not appear to affect the market; ($b$) that the market model drawn from the measured parameters is more accurate than is the model constructed from induced preferences; and ($c$) that many subjects (in the 40 percent range) exhibited a willingness to violate their own stated limit prices. Knez et al. suggest that the elicited parameters are analogous to guesses about how subjects will trade or, perhaps, are similar to wishes as opposed to true limit prices. Nevertheless, the measured parameters improve predictions about market prices.

## IV. New Institutions

The rationality postulates have been useful in suggesting new institutional arrangements that have never before existed. The research on public goods provision mechanisms is a good example. Other examples include the work by Grether, Isaac, and Plott (1981) on the allocation of landing rights by auction or the work by Rassanti, Smith, and Bulfin (1982) on a combinatorial auction to solve the same problem. Experimental methods have been the only source of data about how these new institutions might perform.

An interesting example, with possibly limited social usefulness, is the unstable dollar auction.[4] The idea is to create processes that applications of rationality theory suggest will have bizarre properties. In this case the objective is to attempt to sell a dollar to perfectly informed people for much more than a dollar. Intuitively, it seems that rational consumers would never do such a thing, but intuition is not always a reliable scientific tool.

Subjects, after having attended an economics experiment, are frequently in a room calculating their earnings. Having calculated their earnings and having not yet been paid, a dollar auction is announced. Subjects are carefully told that an English auction will be used. The market will stop if forty-five seconds elapse after a bid with no intervening bid. The dollar will be given to the highest bidder, but the second-highest bidder must pay the amount of his own bid; that is, high bidder gets the dollar, but the second-highest bidder pays for it. Bids cannot exceed the amount earned in the previous experiment, and no talking is allowed.

The game is not well understood from a game-theoretic perspective. The version with unlimited budgets and unlimited time has no solution except infinite bids. With limitations on endowments, under no circum-

---

4. This auction process first appears in print in Shubik (1971). In conversation Shubik tells me that he hesitates to take full credit for having invented the process because many unusual processes were proposed in conversation among game theorists at Princeton in the early 1950s. The theorists were using game theory to invent processes in which rational behavior by individuals would lead to surprising behavior.

stances can nonparticipation by everyone be a Nash equilibrium. Models of the situation exist in which a solution involves participation from everyone and in which everyone should be prepared to bid their endowment.[5] The point is that models based on concepts of rationality suggest that rational people might produce intuitively impossible, or perhaps irrational, results (i.e., selling a dollar for much more than a dollar).

The data from five such auctions are in figure 4.5. The dots are the actual bids in dollars as they occurred in sequence. As can be seen, the dollar always sold for much more than a dollar. In auction 1, for example, the dollar went to a bid of $27, and the price actually paid by the second-highest bidder was $20. Some of the relevant data are in table 4.2. Participants are indexed according to the size of their budget, with the person with the largest budget called person number 1. In auction 1 the person with the largest endowment had $40. The auction winner had the sixth-largest endowment at $27.54. The person who paid $20 had an endowment of $20.70. These were the only two bidders after the fourteenth bid of $8.00. Frequently, the auction stopped only after a bidder hit a constraint. The individual who acquired the dollar tended to have an above-average endowment. On the average, people lost a great deal of money.

The phenomenon suggested by the models actually exists. The data contain three interesting lessons. First, models of rational choice help us

5. A complete game-theoretic treatment of the auction is not available. Kim Border and Joel Sobel (private correspondence) have produced the following model. The insight of the model is to treat the auction like a sealed-bid auction. The sealed-bid is interpreted as a reservation price above which the subject will not go during the actual English auction bidding process. Consider only the two-person case for exposition purposes with the following rules: (i) high bidder receives $1.00 and pays nothing; (ii) second-highest bidder receives zero and pays his bid; (iii) bids must be nonnegative and no more than wealth; and (iv) common knowledge is that wealth is independently and identically distributed from cumulative density function $F(\cdot)$, is supported on $[0,A]$, and has continuous density $f(\cdot)$. Let $V(x) = (1 + x)F(x) - x$; $M(W) = \max[x \leq W: x$ max's $V$ on $[0,W]$]; and $b(W) = W - (V[M(W)] - V(W))/[1 - F(W)]$, using the convention that, if $F(W) = 1$, then $(V[M(W)] - V(W)/[1 - F(W)] = 0$. The bidding function, $b(W)$, is the equilibrium strategy of a symmetric Bayesian Nash equilibrium with risk-neutral players. Generalization to $N$ bidders is straightforward. As an example consider the two-person case in which $F(\cdot)$ is uniform over $(0, A)$. The optimum bidding function is:

$$b(W) = \begin{cases} W, & \text{if } W \geq A - 1; \\ \dfrac{W}{A - W}, & \text{if } W < A - 1. \end{cases}$$

In this case the equilibrium strategy is to be prepared to bid all your wealth if your wealth is one less than the maximum possible wealth. Border has also produced an example in which the optimal strategy is for all bidders to always bid all their wealth.

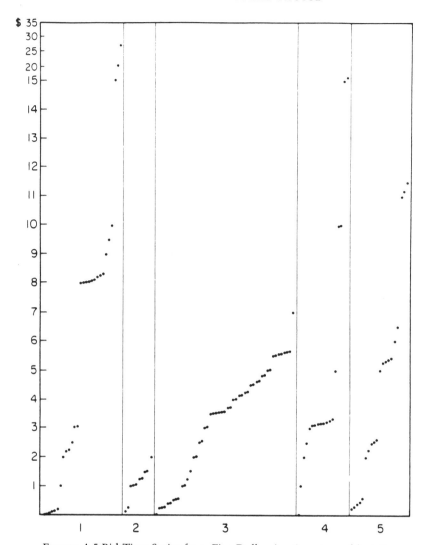

FIGURE 4.5 Bid-Time Series from Five-Dollar Auctions (see table 4.2)

look beyond the market organizations that have evolved through history to find institutions that might be capable of performing some specific task. One might imagine nobler tasks than to sell a dollar for more than a dollar, but that is not the issue. Second, the existence of intuitively "irrational" market behavior is not conclusive evidence that models based on concepts of individual rationality are inappropriate or ill-equipped to be useful in applications. Finally, the example demonstrates

**Table 4.2** Parameters for Five-Dollar Auctions, Bids That Inititate Two-Person Sequences, and the Number of People Bidding

| Auction 1:<br>PCC | Auction 2:<br>PCC | Auction 3:<br>PCC | Auction 4:<br>CIT | Auction 5:<br>CGS |
|---|---|---|---|---|
| Fourteen Participants | Fourteen Participants | Five Participants | Fourteen Participants | Eleven Participants |
| $L_1 = \$40.00$ | $L_1 = \$30.87$ | $L_1 = \$31.68$ | $L_1 = \$41.70$ | $L_1 = \$14.70$ |
| $L_w = L_6 = \$27.56$ | $L_w = L_{13} = \$23.07$ | $L_w = L_1 = \$31.68$ | $L_w = L_5 = \$21.30$ | $L_w = L_3 = \$11.90$ |
| $L_L = L_{16} = \$20.70$ | $L_L = L_6 = \$25.44$ | $L_L = L_5 = \$11.28$ | $L_L = L_{11} = \$15.05$ | $L_L = L_6 = \$11.20$ |
| $B_w = \$27.00$ | $B_w = \$2.00$ | $B_w = \$7.00$ | $B_w = \$16.00$ | $B_w = \$11.50$ |
| $B_L = \$20.00$ | $B_L = \$1.51$ | $B_L = \$5.63$ | $B_L = \$15.00$ | $B_L = \$11.20$ |
| Only traders 6 and 16, beginning with $B$ = $8.00 (fourteenth bid) | Only traders 6 and 13, beginning with $B$ = $1.02 (fifth bid) | Only traders 1 and 5, beginning with $B$ = $.52 (ninth bid) | Only traders 5 and 11, beginning with $B$ = $2.00 (third bid) | Only traders 3 and 6, beginning with $B$ = $11.20 (nineteenth bid) |
| Eight people bid at least once | Five people bid at least once | Three people bid at least once | Four people bid at least once | Five people bid at least once |

NOTE: PCC = Pasadena City College, CIT = California Institute of Technology, and CGS = Claremont Graduate School. $L_i$ = limit price of the person with the $i$th highest limit price, $L_w$ = limit price of the auction winner, $B_w$ = bid of auction winner, and $B\pounds$ = bid of auction loser—the person who paid.

that models based on optimization principles are filled with subtleties often unappreciated by critics of rationality. As far as I am aware, the game described above has never been solved with any degree of generality. We do not know some of the major properties of the Nash equilibrium strategies should they exist. Given the current development of theory, the data cannot be used either to confirm or to reject a theory.

## V. Pending Problems

The review above contains no examples of the failure of an economic model to confront the data successfully. I do not want to leave the reader with the impression that such examples do not exist. This section is intended to disabuse anyone of the notion that our models are in perfect shape and that the rationality foundation needs neither examination nor modification. Many problems and paradoxes exist. This paper was not organized around the failure of the models because the reasons for the failures are not clear. Arguments like those in section III that show differences of procedures and incentives as explanations for unexpected market behavior are very much in contention with arguments that would change entirely the way we think about economics.

The potential problems with rational choice models that have been identified by psychologists and that might be manifest in market behavior have not been systematically explored. This lack of study reflects a resource constraint and not a lack of interest or enthusiasm. Two exceptions to the general rule exist currently, and I understand that more attempts to study markets for evidence of "heuristics" are under way.

In an experimental study by Plott and Wilde (1982) the "representativeness" heuristic (Tversky and Kahneman 1974) was given an opportunity to work. Subjects had valuations for commodity units that were contingent on an underlying state of nature. Prior probabilities were generated by a bingo cage. Once a state of nature was chosen (one for each buyer), a clue to the state was generated by a draw from a second bingo cage. The distribution governing the draws from the second cage was contingent on the state determined by the first draw. After receiving their personal clue, buyers would participate in a market in which the units were being sold. After this process was repeated for several periods (during which the market equilibrated in the usual fashion), the market supply was shifted. The representativeness heuristic predicted no change in volume due to the lowered price. In reality, slight increases occurred as would be anticipated from risk-averse expected utility behavior with Bayesian agents.

A more direct examination of the base-rate fallacy has been conducted by Duh and Sunder (1985). The experiment was similar to the Plott and Wilde experiment, but the supply was completed inelastic, thereby letting price serve as a measure of valuation, and the markets were organized differently. The experiments also varied the base rate to see if the markets responded appropriately. A model based on the principle that base rates would be ignored was rejected in favor of a model based on the principle that people would follow Bayes's law.

The present lack of support in experimental markets for the psychology-based ideas is not going to be the end of the story. Many properties of markets have been observed that are not explicable in terms of current models. Posted prices have an independent effect on market prices (Plott and Smith 1978); nonbinding price ceilings affect market convergence (Isaac and Plott 1981; Smith and Williams 1981); and bubbles can be observed in asset markets (Plott and Sunder 1983; Camerer 1984; Smith, Suchanek, and Williams 1986). The dynamics of the convergence process in equilibrating markets is not theoretically understood at all (Davis and Williams, 1986). In fact we have only begun to develop a theory based on individual strategic decisions about why equilibrium is attained in any experimental markets where equilibrium has been observed (Wilson 1982; Friedman 1984; Easley and Ledyard 1986). The Dutch auction behaves differently from the first-price auction even though they are supposed to be behaviorally isomorphic (Coppinger et al. 1980). The signaling experiments discussed above contain events that suggest that some of the markets studied failed to incorporate information that was clearly present in a statistical sense. The markets appeared to adjust appropriately only after a change in experimental procedure drew attention to the statistical regularity. The questions that now exist about the need for economists to consider the decision process used by individuals in addition to observed choices are likely to occur with increasing frequency.

The role of morality, altruism, and ethical predispositions in forming choice is another area of potential discoveries. Needless to say, there has been no way of separating theories of altruistically based behavior and moralistic behavior from preference theory or rational choice theories. Furthermore, since preference theory requires no theory about the source of preferences, no overriding need for a separate theory of moral behavior has been solidly demonstrated. The fact that preferences might include or reflect moral considerations does not, on the surface, contradict a theory of rational choice or maximizing behavior. Moral considerations might influence the shape and form of preferences, but that does not contradict the existence of preferences or choices based on them. One can argue that the existence of morally based behavior provides evidence of rational choice. Experimental markets with externalities, public goods decision processes, and related commons dilemma experiments have not shown the domination of moral considerations over financial motivation (Dawes 1980). Thus no review of procedures and theories has been forced on experimentalists. Nevertheless, evidence of morally based decisions does exist (Palfrey and Rosenthal 1985). In committee experiments the evidence is pronounced especially when as few as three participants are involved (Isaac and Plott 1978; Eavey and Miller 1984). Furthermore, a methodology for investigating experimentally the phenomena and related theories of moral choices is being explored. Hoffman and Spitzer (1985) formulate a strong case that it is possible to formulate in operational terms competing theories about moral attitudes and that it is possible to use experimental techniques to assess their relative accuracy. How our models of rational choice become modified to include the technical features of moral attitudes (consistent? myopic? stable? sensitivity and responsiveness of choice to evidence?), if such exist, remains an open question.

## VI. Closing Remarks

The tone of this paper is defensive. Claims about the irrelevance of models of rational choice and the consequent irrelevance of economics are not uncommon topics of conversation. Even economists sometimes engage in disparaging remarks about the discipline because of doubts about either the testability or the validity of the optimization hypothesis. If one looks at experimental markets for evidence, the pessimism is not justified. Market models based on rational choice principles (including the subspecies of satisficing) do a pretty good job of capturing the essence of very complicated phenomena.

On the other hand, the evidence presented here should provide no one with a feeling of overconfidence. Referees who summarize experimental papers by saying. "The results are obvious because they follow immediately from rational choice," have not looked very closely at the theory and the data. While the theory of rational choice provides a very useful set of general principles, it is a mistake to elevate the theory to the status of irrefutable law that always reliably operates and need not be challenged.

# REFERENCES

Aizerman, M. A. 1985. "New Problems in the General Choice Theory: Review of a Research Trend." *Social Choice and Welfare* 2 (December): 235–82.

Camerer, Colin. 1984. "Speculative Price Bubbles in Asset Markets: A Theoretical Survey and Experimental Design. Unpublished manuscript. Philadelphia: University of Pennsylvania, Wharton School.

Cohen, Linda, Michael E. Levine, and Charles R. Plott. 1978. "Communication and Agenda Influence: The Chocolate Pizza Design." In H. Sauermann (ed.), *Coalition Forming Behavior: Contributions to Experimental Economics*. Vol. 8. Tübingen: Mohr (Siebeck).

Coppinger, Vicki M., Vernon L. Smith, and Jon A. Titus. 1980. "Incentives and Behavior in English, Dutch and Sealed-bid Auctions." *Economic Inquiry* 18 (January): 1–22.

Cox, James C., Bruce Roberson, and Vernon L. Smith. 1982. "Theory and Behavior of Single Object Auctions." In V. L. Smith (ed.), *Research in Experimental Economics*. Vol. 2. Greenwich, Conn.: JAI.

Davis, Douglas D., and Arlington W., Williams. 1986. "The Effects of Rent Asymmetries in Posted Offer Markets." *Journal of Economic Behavior and Organization*. 7 (September): 303–16.

Dawes, Robyn M. 1980. "Social Dilemmas." *Annual Review of Psychology* 31:169–93.

Duh, Rong Ruey, and Shyam, Sunder. 1985. "Incentives, Learning and Processing of Information in a Market Environment: An Examination of the Base Rate Fallacy." Department of Accounting Working Paper 1985–5. Minneapolis: University of Minnesota at Minneapolis–St. Paul.

Easley, David, and John Ledyard. 1986. "Theories of Price Formation and Exchange in Double Oral Auctions." Social Science Working Paper no. 611. Pasadena: California Institute of Technology.

Eavey, Cheryl, and Gary J. Miller. 1984. "Fairness in Majority Rule Games with a Core." *American Journal of Political Science* 28 (August): 570–86.

Fiorina, Morris P., and Charles R. Plott. 1978. "Committee Decisions under Majority Rule." *American Political Science Review* 72 (June): 575–98.

Friedman, Dan. 1984. "On the Efficiency of Experimental Double Auction Markets." *American Economic Review* 74 (March): 60–72.

Grether, David M. 1981. "Financial Incentive Effects and Individual Decision Making." Social Science Working Paper no. 401. Pasadena: California Institute of Technology.

Grether, David M., R. Mark Isaac, and Charles R. Plott. 1981. "The Allocation of Landing Rights by Unanimity among Competitors." *American Economic Review* 71 (May): 166–71.

Grether, David M., and Charles R. Plott. 1979. "Economic Theory of Choice and the Preference Reversal Phenomenon." *American Economic Review* 69 (September): 623–38.

Hoffman, Elizabeth, and Matthew L. Spitzer. 1985. "Entitlements, Rights, and Fairness: Some Experimental Results." *Journal of Legal Studies* 14 (June): 259–98.

Isaac, R. Mark, and Charles R. Plott. 1978. "Cooperative Game Models of the Influence of the Closed Rule in Three Person, Majority Rule Committees: Theory and Experiments." In P. C. Ordeshook (ed.), *Game Theory and Political Science*. New York: New York University Press.

———. 1981. "Price Controls and the Behavior of Auction Markets: An Experimental Examination. *American Economic Review* 71 (June): 448–59.

Knez, P., Vernon L. Smith, and A. Williams. 1985. "Individual Rationality, Market Rationality and Value Estimation." *American Economic Review* 75 (May): 397–402.

Ledyard, John O. 1986. "The Scope of the Hypothesis of Bayesian Equilibrium." *Journal of Economic Theory.* 39 (June) 59–82.

Miller, Ross M., and Charles R. Plott. 1985. "Product Quality Signaling in Experimental Markets." *Econometrica* 53 (July): 837–71.

Palfrey, Thomas R., and Howard Rosenthal. 1985. "Altruism and Participation in Social Dilemmas." Graduate School of Industrial Administration Working Paper no. 35–84–85. Pittsburgh: Carnegie-Mellon University.

Plott, Charles R. 1979. "The Application of Laboratory Experimental Methods to Public Choice." In C. S. Russell (ed.), *Collective Decision Making: Applications from Public Choice Theory.* Baltimore: Johns Hopkins University Press.

———. 1982. "Industrial Organization Theory and Experimental Economics." *Journal of Economic Literature* 20 (December): 1485–1527.

Plott, Charles R., and Vernon L. Smith. 1978. "An Experimental Examination of Two Exchange Institutions." *Review of Economic Studies* 45 (February): 133–53.

Plott, Charles R., and Shyam Sunder. 1983. "Rational Expectations and the Aggregation of Diverse Information in Laboratory Security Markets." Social Science Working Paper no. 363. Pasadena: California Institute of Technology.

Plott, Charles R., and Jonathan T. Uhl. 1981. "Competitive Equilibrium with Middlemen: An Empirical Study." *Southern Economic Journal* 47 (April): 1063–71.

Plott, Charles R., and Louis L. Wilde. 1982. "Professional Diagnosis versus Self-diagnosis: An Experimental Examination of Some Special Features of Markets with Uncertainty." In V. L. Smith (ed.), *Research in Experimental Economics.* Vol. 2. Greenwich, Conn.: JAI.

Rassenti, S., Vernon Smith, and R. Bulfin. 1982. "A Combinatorial Auction for Airport Time Slot Allocation." *Bell Journal of Economics* 13 (Autumn): 402–17.

Shubik, Martin. 1971. "The Dollar Auction Game." *Journal of Conflict Resolution* 15 (Fall): 109–11.

Simon, H. A. 1979. "Rational Decision Making in Business Organizations." *American Economic Review* 69 (September): 493–514.

Smith, Vernon L. 1976. "Experimental Economics: Induced Value Theory." *American Economic Review* 66 (May): 274–79.

Smith, Vernon L., Gerry L. Suchanek, and Arlington W. Williams. 1986. "Bubbles, Crashes and Endogenous Expectations in Experimental Asset Markets." Working Paper no. 86–2. Tucson: University of Arizona, Department of Economics.

Smith, Vernon L., and Arlington W. Williams. 1981. "On Nonbinding Price Controls in a Competitive Market." *American Economic Review* 71 (June): 467–74.

Spence, M. A. 1974. *Market Signaling: Informational Transfer in Hiring and Related Screening Processes.* Cambridge, Mass.: Harvard University Press.

Tversky, Amos. 1969. "Intransitivity of Preferences." *Psychological Review* 76 (January): 31–48.
Tversky, A., and D. Kahneman. 1974. "Judgment under Uncertainty: Heuristics and Biases." *Science* 185:1124–31.
Wilson, Robert. 1982. "Double auctions." Technical Report 391. Stanford, Calif.: Stanford University, Institute for Mathematical Studies in the Social Sciences, October. Reprinted in T. Groves, R. Radner, and S. Reiter (eds.), *Information Incentives and Economic Mechanisms: Essays in Honor of Leonid Hurwicz*. Minneapolis: University of Minnesota Press, 1987.

COMMENT: *Individual Decision Making versus Market-Level Predictions: The Applicability of Rational Choice Theory*
Karen S. Cook and Jodi A. O'Brien

As sketched by Elster in this section of the book, the fundamental tenets of the "standard" theory of rational choice may be summarized in four propositions: (i) Actions must be optimal with respect to given beliefs and desires; (ii) the beliefs and desires must be internally consistent; (iii) the beliefs must be optimal with respect to the given evidence; (iv) the evidence collected must be optimal with respect to beliefs and desires. The theory attempts to derive and predict, or normatively prescribe, people's behavior from given conditions together with a simple optimizing postulate. The essential question posed in this section concerns the theoretical and empirical limits of rational choice theory. The response depends on the task the theory is asked to perform. As the contributions to this volume indicate, social scientists have different expectations regarding the theory's applications and its potential as a general explanatory framework.

Elster's essay is an attempt to specify and illustrate two ways in which rational choice theory can fail: "It can fail to predict or people can fail to conform to its predictions." He constructs a set of scope conditions for rational choice theory by identifying situations in which the theory does and does not fail. As Elster indicates, rational choice theory can be evaluated as an "explanatory concept" or viewed from a "normative angle." As an explanatory/descriptive framework, Elster argues rational choice theory has limited utility because under a large array of circumstances it fails to make unique predictions. In his words, "A theory which does not make unique predictions is incomplete." However, he continues, "it may still be vastly superior to having no theory at all." Elster then

175

describes, primarily by example, the many circumstances in which rational choice theory fails to make unique predictions (covering the well-established problems with multiple optima, noncooperative games, incompleteness of preferences, strategic interaction, etc.). The classification of situations by "size of problem" and "number of agents" grants success to rational choice theory only in cases where problems are medium range, e.g., involve decisions in the intermediate range, and there is either one agent, e.g., a central planner, or many, e.g., a market). Many social scientists dismiss the explanatory utility of rational choice theory entirely, claiming that the theory is too "elastic" or too "malleable" (that is, that the propositions generated are true by definition). For this reason alone Elster's attempt to limit and to specify the scope of the theory is a useful and necessary enterprise. However, without even considering the additional problems and issues raised in this section of the book, Elster has restricted the scope of the rational choice framework enormously.

Brennan counters that Elster has adopted the wrong focus. "Whether and in what sense rational choice theory can be said to fail depends critically," he argues, "on the work one expects the theory to do." For Elster "the work in question is to predict individual actions." Brennan argues that rationality in this standard version and in most plausible nonstandard versions (see Machina for a catalog of these variants), cannot do the predictive work Elster demands of it. Prediction, Brennan claims, requires knowledge of the agent's ends or purposes and not just the assumption that the agent is rational. It fails as a predictive "device," he argues, "long before we get to the conceptual complications that Elster raises." For rational choice theory to provide an adequate description of individual-choice behavior, the content of the actor's utility function must first be specified independently. Broome refers to this same issue as "individuating outcomes." According to Brennan, it is not just the case that the theory is incomplete as a descriptive/predictive theory or that it is underdetermined; it is that "there is no action that rational choice theory rules out. That is, for virtually any action there exists some purpose for which that action is best" (p. 49 of this volume).

Given this limitation, it has been suggested that the real purpose of rational choice theory is to provide a normative basis for social choice theory and modern welfare economics. Even Elster views rational choice theory as "first and foremost a normative theory." Both Brennan and Broome are strong proponents of this role for the theory. For Broome, "Some of the most interesting questions about rationality in decision theory have a moral dimension" (p. 136 of this volume). Brennan is not so much advocating rational choice as a moral basis as he is pointing out that the theory is often used in this way—as a defense for "liberal" institutions. While his argument concerning the logical limitations of rational choice as a predictive theory of behavior are compelling, his case for its normative application is less well-formulated. Broome presents a strong argument in favor of the merits of rational choice as the basis for social choice, though he avoids discussing the complexities surrounding the issue of "social preferences." In fact, the same fundamental limitations apply to social preferences: preferences vary across individuals, hence social welfare does not necessarily equal aggregate individual welfare. (See part III for further discussion).

The force of the theory, Brennan argues, is not as a descriptive model of choice, but rather in the normative function it serves—lending the actions that actors perform in society a certain "normative authority." In other words, "it serves to establish a connection between action and individual well-being that vests agent action with a normative authority it would otherwise lack" (p. 54 of this volume). Such a claim, he notes, is central to modern welfare economics. For example, it is critical, he argues, for the "standard welfare economics argument for market arrangements in provision of private goods" (p. 55). It is in this arena, according to Brennan, that rationality assumptions do their most "formidable work."

While proponents of the normative role of rational choice theory may be less interested in how people actually do make choices and in how the process relates to action, for many social scientists these remain fundamental questions. Elster is attempting not only to promote rational choice theory as a starting point for building a more complete understanding of individual decision making, but to extend our knowledge of the theory's overall applicability (including its limits) to human behavior. Despite its limitations, rational choice theory still has more explanatory and predictive value than many other theoretical frameworks in the social sciences. The broad applicability of the theory has been demonstrated, for example, in the analyses of friendships, marriages, and the family (for example, Becker 1981), as well as in labor markets and economic markets. That rational choice theory can and does predict outcomes with more than a modest degree of accuracy in certain arenas is uncontestable. The interesting theoretical question that remains is whether it is individually rational behavior that produces predictable outcomes at the aggregate level. If so, then can it also be concluded that individuals behave rationally? Not necessarily; in fact, as Kahneman and

Tversky have demonstrated empirically, it appears that individual-level decision making frequently violates the basic assumptions of rational choice theory. As one sympathetic observer of this theoretical dilemma notes: "The importance of rationality models is clearly revealed in various attempts to account for institutions and social practices and ethics. Yet, ironically, no one can identify the real human actor who would make the choice to set up sensible institutions and fair practices . . . many have thought and continue to think that the only entity with enough power and intelligence and foresight and impartiality to make such choices is some hypothetical rational actor called God" (Shweder 1986, 353)

Most social scientists would be loathe to accept Shweder's notion that it is "some powerful, hypothetical rational actor" that transforms the rationality-violating behavior of individuals into perfect market outcomes. Yet, this notion is not too far removed from the concept of the invisible hand of the market place. The continued success and applicability of rational choice theory demands that we specify the nature of the mechanisms whereby individual choices are transformed into aggregate outcomes. The implicit assumption made by many economists and rational choice theorists is that market conditions of scarcity and competition serve a selective function analogous to the "survival of the fittest"—the "fittest" in this case being those who act rationally. The tautology of this line of reasoning is not only obvious but, as Elster (1985) has noted, it is the inevitable downfall of functionalist reasoning in the social sciences, which lacks an underlying causal explanation for the functionalist "shorthand" that applies in the natural sciences. Positing scarcity and competition as the underlying conditions that force this selective hand is not an adequate explanation for the market arrangements that exist. Furthermore, empirical evidence suggests that competition and scarcity are not as directly responsible for market outcomes as standard economic analyses would lead us to believe. For the most recent efforts to elaborate the theory of natural selection in economic markets, see the work of Nelson and Winter (1982).

Psychologists and other decision theorists are engaged in attempts to produce an empirically based theory of individual decision-making processes. Many of these researchers begin with some variant of rational choice theory, such as Kahneman and Tversky (1984) and Beach and Mitchell (1987). Economists such as Plott employ experimental markets to address the very timely and pertinent question of "determining whether individual behavior that appears to violate rational choice principles will be corrected by market activity" (Kunreuther 1986, 333). The remaining contributions to this part deal with these considerations; they characterize an ongoing debate between psychologists and economists. On the surface, the argument concerns the applicability of assumptions of rationality to individual decision making with economists countering that they are not primarily interested in individual processes, rather they are concerned with market-level predictions, and rational choice theory, they argue, works remarkably well at this level. The deeper issue concerns whether or not psychologists really have anything to offer economists: are they actually tearing down the micro-foundations of economic theory? Do economists require an accurate descriptive theory of behavior in order to continue to produce accurate market-level predictions? The question can be rephrased as an issue of prediction versus explanation. Rational choice theory holds considerable predictive power in certain economic analyses. The question is, to what extent does it offer an adequate explanation of individual-level decision-making processes.

Kahneman and Tversky distinguish what Schumpeter called the "logic of choice" from the "psychology of value" and argue that the normative model of "thin" rationality derived from neoclassical economics (and the general theory of decision making under risk) is not a good descriptive model of the behavior of real people in real decision-making situations. Their thesis is that the "logic of choice" does not provide an adequate foundation for a descriptive theory of decision making." Why not? Because the theory fails to accurately predict people's actual behavior and the deviations from the model are too systematic and "too fundamental to be accommodated by relaxing the normative system," which is the tack Machina takes in his endeavors to resolve the dilemmas created by the mounting experimental evidence of widespread "violations" of the assumptions of the standard model.

The prospect theory, outlined only briefly by Kahneman and Tversky (see Kahneman and Tversky 1984 for elaboration), is a two-stage theory requiring a phase of cognitive framing and then an evaluation phase, in which choices are made on the basis of dominance or comparative value. As an alternative to rational choice theory it is designed to explain preferences and choices, "whether or not they can be rationalized." They conclude their essay by arguing that an adequate account of choice "cannot ignore the effects of framing and context, even if they are normatively distasteful and mathematically intractable." But as they make so evident in their analysis, "the introduction of psychological considerations both enriches and complicates the analysis of choice." It enriches the descriptive theory of choice because it incorporates into the theory variables that appear to be important determinants of actual choice (such as, whether or not the probability assessments are transparent or not), but it complicates the analysis of choice in that it reduces the power and simplicity of the expected-utility model.

Machina addresses the issues posed by Kahneman and Tversky. He reviews the standard theory of rational choice (or, more precisely, the theory of decision making under uncertainty) and links recent developments in the field of economic theories of choice to challenges from psychologists and others regarding the robustness of the underlying assumptions of the model (namely, the preference axioms). According to Machina, "the need to analyze and respond to growing empirical challenges has led economists in the 1980s to concentrate on the behavioral restrictions implied by the expected-utility hypothesis."

Machina takes the model as a descriptive theory of choice and attempts to identify major variants of the model that "solve" the empirical problems associated with the fundamental preference axioms. He acknowledges that within economics, as in the other social sciences, "as the evidence against the model mounts, this has led to a growing tension between those who view economic analysis as the description and prediction of what they consider to be rational behavior and those who view it as the description and prediction of observed behavior" (p. 97 of this volume)—what Elster labels the normative versus descriptive angles. Machina treats the model as an explanatory model of choice.

Recent versions of the model, which deal with the observed violations of the linearity in the probabilities (in the standard expected utility model), are discussed by Machina. In particular, he examines "non-expected utility models of preference" that posit nonlinear functional forms for individual preference functions. Although, as Machina notes, these models are useful and promising responses to the phenomena of nonlinearities in the probabilities, they do not offer solutions to the more problematic empirical results offered by Kahneman and Tversky, and others. These include the problems of invariance (the framing effect), and preference reversals (e.g., Slovic and Lichtenstein 1983; Grether and Plott 1979, etc.), or intransitivity. Discussion of these issues and alternative models (such as the "expected regret" model) for choice derived from attempts to provide general solutions to these problems concludes with Machina's dictum: "when psychologists are able to hand us enough systematic evidence on how these effects operate, economists will be able to respond accordingly." Until then, he is unwilling to accept the notion that these effects may be a result of different "response modes" individuals adopt in different choice situations, the ultimate claim of the psychologists. His hope is that economic models with slight modifications can incorporate "choice of frame," for example, into the model such that firms might maximize on this aspect of the decision-making process as well by treating it as a "joint maximization problem" (that is, include it in their preference function). Or the frame can be held "constant" and the model can remain intact.

In conclusion, Machina argues that these issues also raise problems for developments in "normative economics," especially for welfare analysis, but he does not deal with this topic in detail. He also argues that the lack of a "unified" model at this juncture need not impede progress. For Machina, progress entails a fine-grained analysis of the axioms and revisions in the models in order to produce a more adequate theory of choice under uncertainty. In this sense, the task he sets for economists is identical to the task Kahneman and Tversky have set for psychologists. This is a juncture that should prove fertile for dialogue between economists and psychologists. Economists, for example, recognize the importance of transaction costs in decision making. Cognitive limitations and the scarcity of attention as a resource can be represented as information or transaction costs in their most basic form. How decision makers systematically deal with these constraints is a central concern of the current work on decision behavior in psychology.

Recent experimental research in economics on market economies, as described by Plott, attempts to assess in detail the impact of the challenges to the rational choice framework coming from psychologists and social psychologists. The admittedly "defensive" tone of Plott's chapter suggests that it is not easy for economists to set aside these particular challenges to the fundamental premises of rational choice theory, especially the issues raised by psychologists such as Kahneman and Tversky. This confrontation between economists and psychologists may be based on less substantial grounds than initially implied by a cursory look at the contradictory "evidence." A key problem, mentioned in the introduction to this part, is that rational choice theory is used in distinctly different ways in each discipline. The theoretical problems for one discipline are often the fundamental assumptions or "givens" for another (Blau 1987). This is particularly the case for work based on the rational-choice paradigm in economics and psychology.

Economists, as Plott's chapter exemplifies, take preferences as given, or to be experimentally induced. In other words, the source of these preferences is treated as an *exogenous* factor. Furthermore, these "given" preferences are assumed to obey certain "laws" or rules (for example, the rule of transitivity: if $x$ is preferred over $y$, and $y$ over $z$, then $x$ must be preferred to $z$). Within economics such individual-level preferences are more often assumed than examined empirically, though there are some exceptions (see, for example, the work on "preference reversals" by Grether and Plott 1979). Psychologists, however, have taken the fundamental assumptions of rational choice theory as problematic and as specifying only one possible model of decision making.

What does this evidence really suggest? Several possible conclusions can be drawn: (1) that individuals ("subjects") are sometimes irrational; (2) that individuals' choice behavior under certain conditions violates specific assumptions of rational choice theory; (3) that the basic assumptions of rational choice theory misspecify the process of individual choice; and/or (4) that individuals' choice behavior refutes rational choice theory more generally.

All of these conclusions have been reached by various authors, including some economists (such as Sen 1979) at one time or another. In the past decade, partly in response to the increase in empirical work on the topic, the evidence obtained by psychologists has been treated as a fundamental challenge to the entire framework of rational choice theory, especially the basic assumptions about preferences entailed in the individual-level predictions. For this reason, economists like Plott and others in the social sciences, whose work is based upon the rational-choice paradigm, have adopted a defensive posture. We contend, however, that this defensiveness is unnecessary, at least for economists interested in markets and perhaps for other social scientists interested primarily in macrolevel phenomena based on microlevel assumptions about rational choice behavior.

Our argument is based on two beliefs: (1) the evidence, while problematic for psychologists interested in formulating general models of decision making, does not yet present insurmountable challenges to *market* models within economics, and (2) the extent to which the research within these two camps (psychology and economics) actually addresses the same underlying issues of relevance to the standard theory of rational choice has been overdrawn. There are more differences between these research programs than have been acknowledged explicitly. A comparison of the kind of experimental work on markets described by Plott and the types of experiments conducted by Kahneman and Tversky will help to clarify the argument. These two research programs, one in economics and the other in psychology, differ not only in terms of stated purpose, but more importantly with respect to levels of analysis. This creates problems when attempts are made to establish direct links between these theoretical research programs.

For Plott the *primary* task of experimental economic inquiry is to compare various market models based on rational-choice assumptions to determine which models work best under specified sets of conditions. According to Plott, "Rather than inquire whether a theory is true or false, they (those who study experimental markets) ask if the magnitude of error in the predictions of market phenomena is acceptable . . . Or, . . . the question becomes which of several competing models is the most adequate, fully realizing that the best model might still be 'poor.' "

The explicandum for economists is typically some aspect of the functioning of a market (or markets), not the specific choices of individual actors. The data that are obtained and analyzed are most frequently prices (or some other market parameter), calculated at the aggregate level. Usually the primary questions include what is the "equilibrium" market price and is the observed equilibrium price consistent with (or within an acceptable range of) the predicted value.

These market models can predict *market-level* outcomes quite well, based on simplistic rational choice assumptions about individual-level behavior (for example, individuals prefer more of the reward medium to less of the reward medium). Plott's chapter demonstrates this. In his words (p. 172), "Market models based on rational choice principles (including the subspecies of satisficing) do a pretty good job of capturing the essence of very complicated phenomena." The models are not always perfectly consistent with the obtained data (see especially the well-known "dollar-auction" experiments discussed by Plott), but the deviations from prediction are relatively infrequent and often inconsequential. It is important to understand the role of individual-level assumptions concerning rational decision making within the context of experimental tests of market models. As Plott points out, the theory of rationality forms the basis for market-level predictions; it is fundamental to experimental procedures as well as the interpretation of results. "If rationality is not reliable behaviorally, then one would expect economic models to be poor predictors of experimental market behavior." But this seems not to be the case at least for the "subspecies" of experimental studies conducted on markets. An excellent example cited by Plott is the research on double oral auctions, which demonstrates that prices do converge to the competitive equilibrium, "if preferences are stable."

In the attempt to link microlevel theories with macrolevel events, it is critical, as Plott argues in his chapter, to distinguish levels of analysis. In the case of rational choice theory, the rationality of markets must be distinguished from the rationality of individuals. It is not a simple matter to link theories of rationality across levels of analysis. Evidence suggesting that assumptions of rationality are sometimes violated when individuals make economic decisions does not necessarily imply that *market-level* predictions based on assumptions of individual-level rationality will be erroneous. Two fundamental issues are often ignored in discussions of this type: (1) levels of analysis, as noted above, and (2) the scope or range of applicability of the theoretical formulations. Economic and psychological experiments on rational choice make predictions at different levels of analysis: markets for economists, and individual decisions for psychologists. Furthermore, the theoretical formulations being developed in economics and psychology appear to have quite different scope conditions, though these have not yet been fully delineated.

The primary significance of the experimental research on markets (e.g., Plott, chap. 4 of this volume; Smith 1982; etc.) is that it relates aggregate-level "market" phenomena with explicit theoretical assumptions concerning the individual-level processes involved and the nature of the specific institutional arrangements entailed in markets to yield determinate empirical predictions. Market theory is thus rendered fully testable (or competing market models are rendered empirically testable). In Plott's words, "Some of the most extensive use of the precision afforded by rationality postulates is found in the auction literature . . . this is the only example in all of economics where a reasonably complete theory about rational behavior in markets exists." Though this work is limited in scope, it is exemplary precisely because it makes direct connections between microlevel assumptions about rational choice and the macrolevel phenomena presumed to be the aggregate consequences of the individual-level choice processes. The microlevel assumptions can be relatively simplistic, as they are in the case of rational choice principles, yet sufficient to capture the essence of the choice process as it relates to macrolevel predictions.

Note that in Plott's experimental work he is able to derive predictions about market parameters from three fairly simple assumptions about individual preferences and choice behavior (which also dictate experimental operationalizations).[1] A more complete model of the individual-level process is not essential and would probably not substantially improve the precision of the theory with respect to market-level predictions.

Another important feature of the experimental work in economics is that it allows the evaluation of alternative "institutional" arrangements; and, in some cases, the identification of new institutional arrangements. The example Plott gives of the latter is the experimental work on the provision of public goods. Markets can be viewed as one class or category of institutional arrangements. For that class of institutional arrangements the experimental work on alternative market models suggests that the "standard" theory of rational choice is sufficient for deriving fairly accurate predictions concerning *market* parameters. This assessment applies to this general program of research and is not limited to only the "success" stories discussed by Plott in his review of the experimental work on markets. Economists, however, are not as a result exonerated from further consideration of the current troubles that have befallen rational choice theory. They must articulate more clearly the scope of their market models, recognizing that many of the interesting theoretical problems in economics lie outside the domain of market structures. Monetized markets, as MacNeil (1986) argues, represent only a subset of economic exchange relations, a subset that assumes heavily discrete transactions, a "relative rarity even in the most market-oriented economies" (MacNeil 1986). Plott himself remarks that often journal referees in economics have a tendency to dismiss the findings of experimental work saying "the results are obvious because they follow immediately from rational choice" (p. 172). Such comments obscure the very point that the principles of rational choice theory do require some degree of empirical validation to establish scope conditions. As Plott concludes, "it is a mistake to elevate the theory to the status of irrefutable law that always reliably operates and need not be challenged."

Most of the current debate that surrounds the use of rational choice theory is really about the overall scope and applicability of the theoretical principles. The general importance of work in experimental economics is the attempt to demonstrate precisely what it is that occurs between

---

1. The three axioms include: "(1) More reward medium (money) is preferred to less, other things being equal (salience and nonsatiation); (2) individuals place no independent value on experimental outcomes other than that provided by the reward medium (neutrality); (3) individuals optimize" (Plott, p. 148 of this volume).

the level of individual action and market-level outcomes. The purpose is to assess whether rational choice principles are operative at this intermediate level. Psychologists pick up the thread at the level of individual behavior.

The issue for psychologists is not how do markets function (based on the aggregate effects of individual actors' decisions), but on what basis do individuals make decisions: on the basis of simple rationality considerations, behavioral consistency, habit, ritual, tradition, or some other set of principles? Psychologists' efforts are not aimed at producing more accurate or more reliable models of market phenomena. The explicandum for psychologists is individual-level decision making or choice behavior. The implications of microlevel assumptions about choice behavior for macrolevel phenomena are rarely, if ever, discussed by psychologists.

The major impact of Tversky and Kahneman's work in the social sciences is testimony to the dominance of the rational choice paradigm in the field of decision making. But the importance of their work is not that it provides a challenge to the underpinnings of neoclassical market models in economics, but that it raises significant questions about the limits of rational choice theory as a general theory of decision making. Few economists would insist that most, if not all, human decisions are guided principally by rational choice considerations. (Becker is a notable exception.) The "framing effect" (c.f., Kahneman and Tversky 1984) clearly indicates that individuals, under certain conditions, may not be capable of making decisions that are consistent with rational choice predictions. The work by Tversky and Kahneman and others on this topic has begun to explicate the nature of choice processes and individual decision making under various conditions. This research may lead not only to an explicit (and narrower) specification of the scope conditions of rational choice theory, but also to alternative theories of decision making under different circumstances.

Neither psychologists nor economists are particularly dedicated to the model Sen (1979) refers to as the model of "rational fools." Broome states that it is his impression that many economists find the "question of rationality" uninteresting and perhaps empty. Kahneman and Tversky, as well as Plott, however, recognize the general utility of the "standard" theory of rational choice because in both research programs it provides the basis for making predictions. For Plott, these are predictions about markets; for Kahneman and Tversky, they are predictions about "nonrational" decision processes. While psychological theories about decision making have been affected in significant ways by Tversky and Kahneman's results, economic theories about markets have not, for reasons made evident in Plott's chapter. As Broome (this volume) notes: "For a long time the prevailing mode of explanation in economics has been the rational one. This has been a pretty successful technique in economics. If we are now to abandon it and build our theories around behavior that is not rational, that is a serious step. It may, of course, be one we have to take."

Both research programs are important in the social sciences precisely because they force those in each discipline to be more explicit about the scope of their theoretical formulations and about the linkages between microlevel processes and macrostructures. Markets of the type experimental economists tend to study are a limited set of institutional arrangements in which economic transactions occur. Thus while economics may not need a highly complex model of individual-level decision making, it may well need an expanded set of notions about how different institutional arrangements affect and are affected by individual decision making. What is called for is a more comprehensive theory of institutional arrangements (linked to individual-level assumptions about rational choice) in which markets are but one subspecies. (The contributions in part III of this book address this major issue.) In contrast, psychologists do need a more complete model of individual-level decision making (or set of models) and explicit consideration of the range of applicability of such a model(s).

In conclusion, we note that rational choice theory is still the most robust and reliable model for describing and predicting aggregate-level outcomes that are the result of individual-level decisions. This is particularly the case in situations, such as monetary markets, where information regarding preferences is readily available. The power of the theory to explain the mechanisms whereby individual actions are translated into aggregate outcomes remains to be seen. This problem, usually referred to as the micro-macro question, is itself a major point of debate. At this time, however, rational choice theory provides the only model capable of representing these "bridging questions" as testable propositions (Wippler and Lindenberg 1987). Finally, it is at the level of individual decision making that rational choice principles have come under the greatest attack. That rational choice propositions can be rejected at this level of analysis is evident. Again, however, we underscore the importance of a starting point (that is, a theory that generates testable propositions) in launching productive research agendas such as those embarked upon by Kahneman and Tversky, as well as Plott.

## REFERENCES

Beach, L. R., and T. R. Mitchell. 1987. "Image theory: Principles, Goals and Plans in Decision Making." *Acta Psychologica* 66: 201–20.

Becker, G. 1981. *A Treatise on the Family.* Cambridge, MA: Harvard University Press.

Blau, P. 1987. "Contrasting Theoretical Perspectives." In *The Micro-Macro Link,* edited by J. Alexander, et al. Berkeley: University of California Press.

Elster, J. 1985. *Explaining Technical Change.* Cambridge: Cambridge University Press.

Grether, D. M., and C. R. Plott. 1979. "Economic Theory of Choice and the Preference Reversal Phenomenon." *American Economic Review* 69: 623–38.

Kahneman, D., and A. Tversky. 1984. "Choices, Values and Frames." *American Psychologist* 39: 341–50.

Kunreuther, H. 1986. "Comments on Plott and on Kahneman, Knetsch, and Thaler." *Journal of Business* 59: 329–35.

MacNeil, I. 1986. "Exchange Revisited: Individual Utility and Social Solidarity." *Ethics* 96: 567–93.

Nelson, R., and S. Winter. 1982. *An Evolutionary Theory of Economic Change.* Cambridge, MA: Belknap.

Sen, A. 1979. "Rational Fools." In *Philosophy and Economic Theory,* edited by M. Hollis and F. Hahn. Oxford: Oxford University Press.

Shweder, R. 1986. "Comments on Plott and on Kahneman, Knetsch, and Thaler." *Journal of Business* 59: 345–54.

Slovic, P., and S. Lichtenstein. 1983. "Preference Reversals: A Broader Perspective." *American Economic Review* 72: 596–605.

Smith, V. 1982. "Microeconomic Systems as Experimental Science." *American Economic Review* 72: 923–55.

Wippler, R., and S. Lindenberg. 1987. "Collective Phenomena and Rational Choice." *The Micro-Macro Link,* edited by J. Alexander, et al. Berkeley: University of California Press.

# PART TWO

# Preference Formation
# and the Role of Norms

# De Gustibus Non Est Disputandum

## George J. Stigler and Gary S. Becker

The venerable admonition not to quarrel over tastes is commonly interpreted as advice to terminate a dispute when it has been resolved into a difference of tastes, presumably because there is no further room for rational persuasion. Tastes are the unchallengeable axioms of a man's behavior: he may properly (usefully) be criticized for inefficiency in satisfying his desires, but the desires themselves are *data*. Deplorable tastes—say, for arson—may be countered by coercive and punitive action, but these deplorable tastes, at least when held by an adult, are not capable of being changed by persuasion.

Our title seems to us to be capable of another and preferable interpretation: that tastes neither change capriciously nor differ importantly between people. On this interpretation one does not argue over tastes for the same reason that one does not argue over the Rocky Mountains—both are there, will be there next year, too, and are the same to all men.

The difference between these two viewpoints of tastes is fundamental. On the traditional view, an explanation of economic phenomena that reaches a difference in tastes between people or times is the terminus of the argument: the problem is abandoned *at this point* to whoever studies and explains tastes (psychologists? anthropologists? phrenologists? sociobiologists?). On our preferred interpretation, one never reaches this impasse: the economist continues to search for differences in prices or incomes to explain any differences or changes in behavior.

The choice between these two views of the role of tastes in economic theory must ultimately be made on the basis of their comparative analytical productivities. On the conventional view of inscrutable, often capricious tastes, one drops the discussion as soon as the behavior of tastes

Reprinted from *The American Economic Review* 67, no. 2 (March 1977): 76–90. The authors had helpful comments from Michael Bozdarich, Gilbert Ghez, James Heckman, Peter Pashigian, Sam Peltzman, Donald Wittman, and participants in the Workshop on Industrial Organization.

becomes important—and turns his energies to other problems. On our view, one searches, often long and frustratingly, for the subtle forms that prices and incomes take in explaining differences among men and periods. If the latter approach yields more useful results, it is the proper choice. The establishment of the proposition that one may usefully treat tastes as stable over time and similar among people is the central task of this essay.

The ambitiousness of our agenda deserves emphasis: we are proposing the hypothesis that widespread and/or persistent human behavior can be explained by a generalized calculus of utility-maximizing behavior, without introducing the qualification "tastes remaining the same." It is a thesis that does not permit of direct proof because it is an assertion about the world, not a proposition in logic. Moreover, it is possible almost at random to throw up examples of phenomena that presently defy explanation by this hypothesis: Why do we have inflation? Why are there few Jews in farming?[1] Why are societies with polygynous families so rare in the modern era? Why aren't blood banks responsible for the quality of their product? If we could answer these questions to your satisfaction, you would quickly produce a dozen more.

What we assert is not that we are clever enough to make illuminating applications of utility-maximizing theory to all important phenomena— not even our entire generation of economists is clever enough to do that. Rather, we assert that this traditional approach of the economist offers guidance in tackling these problems—and that no other approach of remotely comparable generality and power is available.

To support our thesis we could offer samples of phenomena we believe to be usefully explained on the assumption of stable, well-behaved preference functions. Ultimately, this is indeed the only persuasive method of supporting the assumption, and it is legitimate to cite in support all of the existing corpus of successful economic theory. Here we shall undertake to give this proof by accomplishment a special and limited interpretation. We take categories of behavior commonly held to demonstrate changes in tastes or to be explicable only in terms of such changes and show both that they are reconcilable with our assumption of stable preferences and that the reformulation is illuminating.

---

1. Our lamented friend Reuben Kressel offered an attractive explanation: since Jews have been persecuted so often and forced to flee to other countries, they have not invested in immobile land, but in mobile human capital—business skills, education, etc.—that would automatically go with them. Of course, someone might counter with the more basic query: but why are they Jews, and not Christians or Moslems?

## I. The New Theory of Consumer Choice

The power of stable preferences and utility maximization in explaining a wide range of behavior has been significantly enhanced by a recent reformulation of consumer theory.[2] This reformulation transforms the family from a passive maximizer of the utility from market purchases into an active maximizer also engaged in extensive production and investment activities. In the traditional theory, households maximize a utility function of the goods and services bought in the marketplace, whereas in the reformulation they maximize a utility function of objects of choice, called commodities, that they produce with market goods, their own time, their skills, training and other human capital, and other inputs. Stated formally, a household seeks to maximize

$$U = U(Z_1, \ldots Z_m) \qquad (1)$$

with

$$Z_i = f_i(X_{1i}, \ldots X_{ki}, t_{1i}, \ldots t_{\lambda i}, S_1, \ldots S_\lambda, Y_i), i = 1 \ldots m \qquad (2)$$

where $Z_i$ are the commodity objects of choice entering the utility function, $f_i$ is the production function for the $i$th commodity, $X_{ji}$ is the quantity of the $j$th market good or service used in the production of the $i$th commodity, $t_{ji}$ is the $j$th person's own time input, $S_j$ the $j$th person's human capital, and $Y_i$ represents all other inputs.

The $Z_i$ have no market prices since they are not purchased or sold, but do have "shadow" prices determined by their costs of production. If $f_i$ were homogeneous of the first degree in the $X_{ji}$ and $t_{ji}$, marginal and average costs would be the same and the shadow prize of $Z_i$ would be

$$\pi_i = \sum_{j=1}^k \alpha_{ji}\left(\frac{p}{w_1}, \frac{w}{w_1}, S, Y_i\right)p_j + \sum_{j=1}^l \beta_{ji}\left(\frac{p}{w_1}, \frac{w}{w_1}, S, Y_i\right)w_j \qquad (3)$$

where $p_j$ is the cost of $X_j$, $w_j$ is the cost of $t_j$, and $\alpha_{ji}$ and $\beta_{ji}$ are input-output coefficients that depend on the (relative) set of $p$ and w, S, and $Y_i$. The numerous and varied determinants of these shadow prices give concrete expression to our earlier statement about the subtle forms that prices take in explaining differences among men and periods.

2. An exposition of this reformulation can be found in Robert Michael and Gary Becker (1973). This exposition emphasizes the capacity of the reformulation to generate many implications about behavior that are consistent with stable tastes.

The real income of a household does not simply equal its money income deflated by an index of the prices of market goods, but equals its full income (which includes the value of "time" to the household)[3] deflated by an index of the prices, $\pi_i$, of the produced commodities. Since full income and commodity prices depend on a variety of factors, incomes also take subtle forms. Our task in this paper is to spell out some of the forms prices and full income take.

## II. Stability of Tastes and "Addiction"

Tastes are frequently said to change as a result of consuming certain "addictive" goods. For example, smoking of cigarettes, drinking of alcohol, injection of heroin, or close contact with some persons over an appreciable period of time, often increases the desire (creates a craving) for these goods or persons, and thereby cause their consumption to grow over time. In utility language, their marginal utility is said to rise over time because tastes shift in their favor. This argument has been clearly stated by Alfred Marshall (1923) when discussing the taste for "good" music:

> There is however an implicit condition in this law [of diminishing marginal utility] which should be made clear. It is that we do not suppose time to be allowed for any alteration in the character or tastes of the man himself. It is therefore no exception to the law that the more good music a man hears, the stronger is his taste for it likely to become . . . (p. 94)

We believe that the phenomenon Marshall is trying to explain, namely that exposure to good music increases the subsequent demand for good music (for some persons!), can be explained with some gain in insight by assuming constant tastes, whereas to assume a change in tastes has been an unilluminating "explanation." The essence of our explanation lies in the accumulation of what might be termed "consumption capital" by the consumer, and we distinguish "beneficial" addiction like Marshall's good music from "harmful" addiction like heroin.

Consider first beneficial addiction and an unchanging utility function that depends on two produced commodities:

---

3. Full income is the maximum money income that a household could achieve by an appropriate allocation of its time and other resources.

$$U = U(M, Z) \tag{4}$$

where $M$ measures the amount of music "appreciation" produced and consumed and $Z$ the production and consumption of other commodities. Music appreciation is produced by a function that depends on the time allocated to music $(t_m)$, and the training and other human capital conducive to music appreciation $(S_m)$ (other inputs are ignored):

$$M = M_m (t_m, S_m). \tag{5}$$

We assume that

$$\frac{\partial M_m}{\partial t_m} > 0, \frac{\partial M_m}{\partial s_m} > 0$$

and also that

$$\frac{\partial^2 M_m}{\partial t_m \partial S_m} > 0.$$

An increase in this music capital increases the productivity of time spent listening to or devoted in other ways to music.

In order to analyze the consequences for its consumption of "the more good music a man hears," the production and consumption of music appreciation has to be dated. The amount of appreciation produced at any moment $j$, $M_j$, would depend on the time allocated to music and the music human capital at $j$: $t_{mj}$ and $S_{mj}$, respectively. The latter in turn is produced partly through "on-the-job" training or "learning by doing" by accumulating the effects of earlier music appreciation:

$$S_{mj} = h (M_{j-1}, M_{j-2} \ldots, E_j). \tag{6}$$

By definition, the addiction is beneficial if

$$\frac{\partial s_{mj}}{\partial M_{j-v}} > 0, \text{ all } v \text{ in (6).}$$

The term $E_j$ measures the effect of education and other human capital on music appreciation skill, where

$$\frac{\partial s_{mj}}{\partial E_j} > 0$$

and probably

$$\frac{\partial^2 S_{mj}}{\partial M_{j-v} \partial E_j} > 0.$$

We assume for simplicity a utility function that is a discounted sum of functions like the one in equation (4), where the $M$ and $Z$ commodities are dated, and the discount rate determined by time preference.[4] The optimal allocation of consumption is determined from the equality between the ratio of their marginal utilities and the ratio of their shadow prices:

$$\frac{MU_{mj}}{MU_{zj}} = \frac{\partial U}{\partial M_j} \bigg/ \frac{\partial U}{\partial Z_j} = \frac{\pi_{mj}}{\pi_{zj}}. \tag{7}$$

The shadow price equals the marginal cost of adding a unit of commodity output. The marginal cost is complicated for music appreciation $M$ by the positive effect on subsequent music human capital of the production of music appreciation at any moment $j$. This effect on subsequent capital is an investment return from producing appreciation at $j$ that reduces the cost of production at $j$. It can be shown that the marginal cost at $j$ equals[5]

4. A consistent application of the assumption of stable preferences implies that the discount rate is zero; that is, the absence of time preference (see the brief discussion in section VI.)

5. The utility function

$$V = \sum_{j=1}^{n} a^j U(M_j, Z_j)$$

is maximized subject to the constraints

$$M_j = M(t_{mj}, S_{mj}); \; Z_j = Z(x_j, t_{zj})$$
$$S_{mj} = h(M_{j-1}, M_{j-2}, \ldots, E_j)$$
$$\sum \frac{px_j}{(1+r)^j} = \sum \frac{wt_{wj} + b_j}{(i+r)^j}$$

196

$$\pi_{mj} = \frac{w\partial t_{mj}}{\partial M_j} - w\sum_{i=1}^{n-j}\frac{\partial M_{j+i}}{\partial S_{mj+i}}\bigg/\frac{\partial M_{j+i}}{\partial t_{mj+i}}\cdot\frac{dS_{mj+i}rb}{dM_j}$$

$$\cdot\frac{1}{(i+r)^i} = \frac{w\partial t_{mj}}{\partial M_j} - A_j = \frac{w}{MP_{tmj}} - A_j, \quad (8)$$

where $w$ is the wage rate (assumed to be the same at all ages), $r$ the interest rate, $n$ the length of life, and $A_j$ the effect of addiction, measures the value of the saving in future time inputs from the effect of the production of $M$ in $j$ on subsequent music capital.

With no addiction, $A_j = 0$ and equation (8) reduces to the familiar marginal cost formula. Moreover, $A_j$ is positive as long as music is beneficially addictive, and tends to decline as $j$ increases, approaching zero as $j$ approaches $n$. The term $w/MP_{tm}$ declines with age for a given time

———————

and $t_{wj} + t_{mj} + t_{zj} = t$,

where $t_{wj}$ is hours worked in the $j$th period, and $b_j$ is property income in that period. By substitution one derives the full wealth constraint:

$$\sum\frac{px_j + w(t_{mj} + t_{zj})}{(1+r)^j} = \sum\frac{wt + b_j}{(1+r)^j} = W.$$

Maximization of $V$ with respect to $M_j$ and $Z_j$ subject to the production functions and the full wealth constraint gives the first-order conditions

$$a^j\frac{\partial U}{\partial Z_j} = \frac{\lambda}{(1+r)^j}\left(\frac{pdx_j}{dZ_j} + \frac{wdt_{zj}}{dZ_j}\right) = \frac{\lambda}{(1+r)^j}\pi_{zj}$$

$$a^j\frac{\partial U}{\partial M_j} = \frac{\lambda}{(1+r)^j}\cdot\left(\frac{wdt_{mj}}{\partial M_j} + \sum_{i=1}^{n-j}\frac{wdt_{mj+i}}{dM_j}\cdot\frac{1}{(1+r)^i}\right) = \frac{\lambda}{(1+r)^j}\pi_{mj}.$$

Since, however,

$$\frac{dM_{j+i}}{dM_j} = 0 = \frac{\partial M_{j+i}}{\partial S_{mj+i}}\frac{dS_{mj+i}}{dM_j} + \frac{\partial M_{j+i}}{\partial t_{mj+i}}\frac{dt_{mj+i}}{dM_j}$$

then

$$\frac{dt_{mj+i}}{dM_j} = -\frac{\partial M_{j+i}}{\partial S_{mj+i}}\bigg/\frac{\partial M_{j+i}}{\partial t_{mj+i}}\cdot\frac{dS_{mj+i}}{dM_j}.$$

By substitution into the definition of $\pi_{mj}$, equation (8) follows immediately.

input as long as music capital grows with age. The term $A_j$ may not change so much with age at young ages because the percentage decline in the number of remaining years is small at these ages. Therefore, $\pi_m$ would tend to decline with age at young ages because the effect on the marginal product of the time input would tend to dominate the effect on $A$. Although $\pi_m$ might not always decline at other ages, for the present we assume that $\pi_m$ declines continuously with age.

If $\pi_z$ does not depend on age, the relative price of music appreciation would decline with age; then by equation (7), the relative consumption of music appreciation would rise with age. On this interpretation, the (relative) consumption of music appreciation rises with exposure not because tastes shift in favor of music, but because its shadow price falls as skill and experience in the appreciation of music are acquired with exposure.

An alternative way to state the same analysis is that the marginal utility of time allocated to music is increased by an increase in the stock of music capital.[6] Then the consumption of music appreciation could be said to rise with exposure because the marginal utility of the time spent on music rose with exposure, even though tastes were unchanged.

The effect of exposure on the accumulation of music capital might well depend on the level of education and other human capital, as indicated by equation (6). This would explain why educated persons consume more "good" music (i.e., music that educated people like!) than other persons do.

Addiction lowers the price of music appreciation at younger ages without any comparable effect on the productivity of the time spent on music at these ages. Therefore, addiction would increase the time spent on music at younger ages: some of the time would be considered an investment that increases future music capital. Although the price of music tends to fall with age, and the consumption of music tends to rise, the time spent on music need not rise with age because the growth in music capital means that the consumption of music could rise even when the time spent fell with age. The time spent would be more likely to rise, the more elastic the demand curve for music appreciation. We can express this result in a form that will strike many readers as surprising; namely, that the time (or other inputs) spent on music appreciation is more likely to be

6. The marginal utility of time allocated to music at $j$ includes the utility from the increase in the future stock of music capital that results from an increase in the time allocated at $j$. An argument similar to the one developed for the price of music appreciation shows that the marginal utility of time would tend to rise with age, at least at younger ages.

addictive—that is, to rise with exposure to music—the more, not less, elastic is the demand curve for music appreciation.

The stock of music capital might fall and the price of music appreciation rise at older ages because the incentive to invest in future capital would decline as the number of remaining years declined, whereas the investment required simply to maintain the capital stock intact would increase as the stock increased. If the price rose, the time spent on music would fall if the demand curve for music were elastic. Consequently, our analysis indicates that the observed addiction to music may be stronger at younger than at older ages.

These results for music also apply to other commodities that are beneficially addictive. Their prices fall at younger ages and their consumption rises because consumption capital is accumulated with exposure and age. The time and goods used to produce an addictive commodity need not rise with exposure, even though consumption of the commodity does; they are more likely to rise with exposure, the more elastic is the demand curve for the commodity. Even if they rose at younger ages, they might decline eventually as the stock of consumption capital fell at older ages.

Using the same arguments developed for beneficial addiction, we can show that all the results are reversed for harmful addiction,[7] which is defined by a negative sign of the derivatives in equation (6):

$$\frac{\partial S_j}{\partial H_{j-v}} < 0, \text{ all } v \text{ in } (6) \qquad (9)$$

where $H$ is a harmfully addictive commodity. An increase in consumption at any age reduces the stock of consumption capital available subsequently, and this raises the shadow price at all ages.[8] The shadow price would rise with age and exposure, at least at younger ages, which would induce consumption to fall with age and exposure. The inputs of goods and time need not fall with exposure, however, because consumption

7. In some ways, our analysis of beneficial and harmful addiction is a special case of the analysis of beneficial and detrimental joint production in Michael Grossman (1971).

8. Instead of equation (8), one has

$$\pi_{h_j} = \frac{w}{MP_{t_j}} + A_j$$

where $A_j \geq 0$.

capital falls with exposure; indeed, the inputs are likely to rise with exposure if the commodity's demand curve were inelastic.

To illustrate these conclusions, consider the commodity "euphoria" produced with input of heroin (or alcohol or amphetamines). An increase in the consumption of current euphoria raises the cost of producing euphoria in the future by reducing the future stock of "euphoric capital." The effect of exposure to euphoria on the cost of producing future euphoria reduces the consumption of euphoria as exposure continues. If the demand curve for euphoria were sufficiently inelastic, however, the use of heroin would grow with exposure at the same time that euphoria fell.

Note that the amount of heroin used at younger ages would be reduced because of the negative effect on later euphoric capital. Indeed, no heroin at all might be used only because the harmfully addictive effects are anticipated and discourage any use. Note further that if heroin were used even though the subsequent adverse consequences were accurately anticipated, the utility of the user would be greater than it would be if he were prevented from using heroin. Of course, his utility would be still greater if technologies developed (methadone?) to reduce the harmfully addictive effects of euphoria.[9]

Most interestingly, note that the use of heroin would grow with exposure at the same time that the amount of euphoria fell, if the demand curve for euphoria and thus for heroin were sufficiently inelastic. That is, addiction to heroin—a growth in use with exposure—is the *result* of an inelastic demand for heroin, *not,* as commonly argued, the *cause* of an inelastic demand. In the same way, listening to music or playing tennis would be addictive if the demand curves for music or tennis appreciation were sufficiently elastic; the addiction again is the result, not the cause, of the particular elasticity. Put differently, if addiction were surmised (partly because the input of goods or time rose with age), but if it were not clear whether the addiction were harmful or beneficial, the elasticity of demand could be used to distinguish between them: a high elasticity suggests beneficial and a low elasticity suggests harmful addiction.[10]

9. That is, if new technology reduced and perhaps even changed the sign of the derivatives in equation (9). We should state explicitly, to avoid any misunderstanding, that "harmful" means only that the derivatives in (9) are negative and not that the addiction harms others, nor, as we have just indicated, that it is unwise for addicts to consume such commodities.

10. The elasticity of demand can be estimated from the effects of changes in the prices of inputs. For example, if a commodity's production function were homogenous of degree one, and if all its future as well as present input prices rose by the same known percentage,

We do not have to assume that exposure to euphoria changes tastes in order to understand why the use of heroin grows with exposure, or why the amount used is insensitive to changes in its price. Even with constant tastes, the amount used would grow with exposure, and heroin is addictive precisely *because* of the insensitivity to price changes.

An exogenous rise in the price of addictive goods or time, perhaps due to an excise tax, such as the tax on cigarettes and alcohol, or to restrictions on their sale, such as the imprisonment of dealers in heroin, would have a relatively small effect on their use by addicts if these are harmfully addictive goods and a relatively large effect if they are beneficially addictive. That is, excise taxes and imprisonment mainly transfer resources away from addicts if the goods are harmfully addictive and mainly reduce the consumption of addicts if the goods are beneficially addictive.

The extension of the capital concept to investment in the capacity to consume more efficiently has numerous other potential applications. For example, there is a fertile field in consumption capital for the application of the theory of division of labor among family members.

## III. Stability of Tastes and Custom and Tradition

A "traditional" qualification to the scope of economic theory is the alleged powerful hold over human behavior of custom and tradition. An excellent statement in the context of the behavior of rulers is that of John Stuart Mill (1972):

> It is not true that the actions even of average rulers are wholly, or anything approaching to wholly, determined by their personal interest, or even by their own opinion of their personal interest. . . . I insist only on what is true of all rulers, viz., that the character and course of their actions is largely influenced (independently of personal calculations) by the habitual sentiments and feelings, the general modes of thinking and acting, which prevail throughout the community of which they are members; as well as by the feelings, habits, and modes of thought which characterize the particular class in that community to which they themselves belong. . . . They are also much influenced by the maxims and traditions which

---

the elasticity of demand for the commodity could be estimated from the decline in the inputs. Therefore the distinction between beneficial and harmful addiction is operational: these independently estimated commodity elasticities could be used, as in the text, to determine whether an addiction was harmful or beneficial.

have descended to them from other rulers, their predecessors; which maxims and traditions have been known to retain an ascendancy during long periods, even in opposition to the private interests of the rulers for the time being. (p. 484)

The specific political behavior that contradicts "personal interest" theories is not clear from Mill's statement, nor is it much clearer in similar statements by others applied to firms or households. Obviously, stable behavior by (say) households faced with stable prices and incomes—or more generally a stable environment—is no contradiction since stability then is implied as much by personal interest theories as by custom and tradition. On the other hand, stable behavior in the face of changing prices and incomes might contradict the approach taken in this essay that assumes utility maximizing with stable tastes.

Nevertheless, we believe that our approach better explains when behavior is stable than do approaches based on custom and tradition and can at the same time explain how and when behavior does change. Mill's "habits and modes of thought," or his "maxims and traditions which have descended," in our analysis result from investment of time and other resources in the accumulation of knowledge about the environment, and of skills with which to cope with it.

The making of decisions is costly and not simply because it is an activity which some people find unpleasant. In order to make a decision one requires information, and the information must be analyzed. The costs of searching for information and of applying the information to a new situation are such that habit is often a more efficient way to deal with moderate or temporary changes in the environment than would be a full, apparently utility-maximizing decision. This is precisely the avoidance of what J. M. Clark termed the irrational passion for dispassionate rationality.

A simple example of economizing on information by the habitual purchase from one source will illustrate the logic. A consumer buys one unit of commodity $X$ in each unit of time. He pays a price $p_t$ at a time t. The choices he faces are:

1. To search at the time of an act of purchase to obtain the lowest possible price $\hat{p}_t$ consistent with the cost of search. Then $\hat{p}_t$ is a function of the amount of search $s$ (assumed to be the same at each act of purchase):

$$\hat{p}_t = f(s), f'(s) < 0 \qquad (10)$$

where the total cost of $s$ is $C(s)$.

2. To search less frequently (but usually more intensively), relying between searches upon the outcome of the previous search in choosing a supplier. Then the price $p_t$ will be higher (relative to the average market price), the longer the period since the previous search (at time $t_o$),

$$p_t = g(t - t_o), g' > 0$$

Ignoring interest, the latter method of purchase will have a total cost over period T determined by: (1) $K$ searches (all of equal intensity) at cost $K$ $C(s)$; (2) Each search lasts for a period $T/K$, within which $r = T/K$ purchases are made, at cost $r\,\bar{p}$, where $\bar{p}$ is the average price. Assume that the results of search "depreciate" (prices appreciate) at rate $\delta$. A consumer minimizes his combined cost of the commodity and search over the total time period; the minimizing condition is[11]

11. The price of the $i$th purchase within one of the $K$ search periods is $p_i = \hat{p}(1 + \delta)^{i-1}$. Hence

$$\bar{p} = \frac{1}{r} \sum_{i=1}^{r} \hat{p}(1 + \delta)^{i-1} = \hat{p} \frac{(1 + \delta)^r - 1}{r\delta}.$$

The total cost to be minimized is

$$TC = Kr\bar{p} + KC(s) = K\hat{p}\frac{(1 + \delta)^r - 1}{\delta} + KC.$$

By taking a second-order approximation to $(1 + \delta)^r$, we get

$$TC = T\left\{\hat{p}\left[1 + \frac{(r - 1)\delta}{2}\right] + \frac{C}{r}\right\}.$$

Minimizing with respect to $r$ gives

$$\frac{\partial TC}{\partial r} = 0 = T\left(\frac{\hat{p}\delta}{2} - \frac{C}{r^2}\right)$$

or

$$r = \sqrt{\frac{2C}{\delta\hat{p}}}.$$

$$r = \sqrt{\frac{2C}{\delta \hat{p}}}.$$

In this simple model with $r$ purchases between successive searches, $r$ is larger the larger the amount spent on search per dollar spent on the commodity $(C/\hat{p})$, and the lower the rate of appreciation of prices $(\delta)$. If there were full search on each individual act of purchase, the total cost could not be less than the cost when the optimal frequency of search was chosen and might be much greater.

When a temporary change takes place in the environment, perhaps in prices or income, it generally would not pay to disinvest the capital embodied in knowledge or skills, or to accumulate different types of capital. As a result, behavior will be relatively stable in the face of temporary changes.

A related situation arises when an unexpected change in the environment does not induce a major response immediately because time is required to accumulate the appropriate knowledge and skills. Therefore, stable preferences combined with investment in "specific" knowledge and skills can explain the small or "inelastic" responses that figure so prominently in short-run demand and supply curves.

A permanent change in the environment, perhaps due to economic development, usually causes a greater change in the behavior of young than of old persons. The common interpretation is that young persons are more readily seduced away from their customs and traditions by the glitter of the new (Western?) environment. On our interpretation, young and old persons respond differently, even if they have the same preferences and motivation. To change their behavior drastically, older persons have to either disinvest their capital that was attuned to the old environment or invest in capital attuned to the new environment. Their incentive to do so may be quite weak, however, because relatively few years remain for them to collect the returns on new investments, and much human capital can only be disinvested slowly.

Young persons, on the other hand, are not so encumbered by accumulations of capital attuned to the old environment. Consequently, they need not have different preferences or motivation or be intrinsically more flexible in order to be more affected by a change in the environment: they simply have greater incentive to invest in knowledge and skills attuned to the new environment.

Note that this analysis is similar to that used in the previous section to explain addictive behavior: utility maximization with stable preferences, conditioned by the accumulation of specific knowledge and skills. One does not need one kind of theory to explain addictive behavior and another kind to explain habitual or customary behavior. The same theory based on stable preferences can explain both types of behavior and can accommodate both habitual behavior and the departures therefrom.

## IV. STABILITY OF TASTES AND ADVERTISING

Perhaps the most important class of cases in which "change of tastes" is invoked as an explanation for economic phenomena is that involving advertising. The advertiser "persuades" the consumer to prefer his product, and often a distinction is drawn between "persuasive" and "informative" advertising.[12] John Kenneth Galbraith (1958) is the most famous of the economists who argue that advertising molds consumer tastes:

> These [institutions of modern advertising and salesmanship] cannot be reconciled with the notion of independently determined desires for their central function is to create desires—to bring into being wants that previously did not exist. This is accomplished by the producer of the goods or at his behest.—Outlays for the manufacturing of a product are not more important in the strategy of modern business enterprise than outlays for the manufacturing of demand for the product. (pp. 155–56)

We shall argue, in direct opposition to this view, that it is neither necessary nor useful to attribute to advertising the function of changing tastes.

A consumer may indirectly receive utility from a market good, yet the utility depends not only on the quantity of the good but also the consumer's knowledge of its true or alleged properties. If he does not know whether the berries are poisonous, they are not food; if he does not know that they contain vitamin C, they are not consumed to prevent scurvy. The quantity of information is a complex notion: its degree of accuracy, its multidimensional properties, its variable obsolescence with time are all qualities that make direct measurement of information extremely difficult.

---

12. The distinction, if in fact one exists, between persuasive and informative advertising must be one of purpose or effect, not of content. A simple, accurately stated fact ("I offer you this genuine $1 bill for 10 cents") can be highly persuasive; the most bizarre claim ("If Napoleon could have bought our machine gun, he would have defeated Wellington") contains some information (machine guns were not available in 1814).

How can this elusive variable be incorporated into the theory of demand while preserving the stability of tastes? Our approach is to continue to assume, as in the previous sections, that the ultimate objects of choice are commodities produced by each household with market goods, own time, *knowledge,* and perhaps other inputs. We now assume, in addition, that the knowledge, whether real or fancied, is produced by the advertising of producers and perhaps also the own search of households.

Our approach can be presented through a detailed analysis of the simple case where the output $x$ of a particular firm and its advertising $A$ are the inputs into a commodity produced and consumed by households; for a given household:

$$Z = f(x, A, E, y) \tag{12}$$

where $\partial Z/\partial x > 0$, $\partial Z/\partial A > 0$, $E$ is the human capital of the household that affects these marginal products, and $y$ are other variables, possibly including advertising by other firms. Still more simply,

$$Z = g(A, E, y)x \tag{13}$$

where $\partial g/\partial A = g' > 0$ and $\partial^2 g/\partial A^2 < 0$. With $A$, $E$, and $y$ held constant, the amount of the commodity produced and consumed by any household is assumed to be proportional to the amount of the firm's output used by that household.[13] If the advertising reaching any household were independent of its behavior, the shadow price of $Z$, the marginal cost of $x$, would simply be the expenditure on $x$ required to change $Z$ by one unit. From equation (13), that equals

$$\pi_z = \frac{p_x}{g} \tag{14}$$

where $p_x$ is the price of $x$.

An increase in advertising may lower the commodity price to the household (by raising $g$), and thereby increase its demand for the commodity and change its demand for the firm's output, because the household is made to believe—correctly or incorrectly—that it gets a greater output of the commodity from a given input of the advertised product. Consequently, advertising affects consumption in this formulation not by

13. Stated differently, $Z$ is homogenous of the first degree in $x$ alone.

changing tastes, but by changing prices. That is, a movement along a stable demand curve for commodities is seen as generating the apparently unstable demand curves of market goods and other inputs.

More than a simple change in language is involved: our formulation has quite different implications from the conventional ones. To develop these implications, consider a firm that is determining its optimal advertising along with its optimal output. We assume initially that the commodity indirectly produced by this firm (equation (12)) is a perfect substitute to consumers for commodities indirectly produced by many other firms. Therefore, the firm is perfectly competitive in the commodity market, and could (indirectly) sell an unlimited amount of this commodity at a fixed commodity price. Observe that a firm can have many perfect substitutes in the commodity market even though few other firms produce the same physical product. For example, a firm may be the sole designer of jewelry that contributes to the social prestige of consumers and yet compete fully with many other products that also contribute to prestige: large automobiles, expensive furs, fashionable clothing, elaborate parties, a respected occupation, etc.

If the level of advertising were fixed, there would be a one-to-one correspondence between the price of the commodity and the price of the firm's output (see equation (14)). If $\pi_z$ were given by the competitive market, $p_x$ would then also be given, and the firm would find its optimal output in the conventional way by equating marginal cost to the given product price. There is no longer such a one-to-one correspondence between $\pi_z$ and $p_x$, however, when the level of advertising is also a variable, and even a firm faced with a fixed commodity price in a perfectly competitive commodity market could sell its product at different prices by varying the level of advertising. Since an increase in advertising would increase the commodity output that consumers receive from a given amount of this firm's product, the price of its product would then be increased relative to the fixed commodity price.

The optimal advertising, product price, and output of the firm can be found by maximizing its income

$$I = p_x X - TC(X) - Ap_a \qquad (15)$$

where $X$ is the firm's total output, $TC$ its costs of production other than advertising, and $p_a$ the (constant) cost of a unit of advertising. By substituting from equation (14), $I$ can be written as

$$I = \pi_z^o g(A)X - TC(X) - Ap_a \qquad (15')$$

where $\pi_z^o$ is the given market commodity price, the advertising-effectiveness function $(g)$ is assumed to be the same for all consumers,[14] and the variables $E$ and $y$ in $g$ are suppressed. The first-order maximum conditions with respect to $X$ and $A$ are

$$p_x = \pi_z^o g = MC(X) \qquad (16)$$

$$\frac{\partial p_x}{\partial A}X = \pi_z^o Xg' = p_a. \qquad (17)$$

Equation (16) is the usual equality between price and marginal cost for a competitive firm, which continues to hold when advertising exists and is a decision variable. Not surprisingly, equation (17) says that marginal revenue and marginal cost of advertising are equal, where marginal revenue is determined by the level of output and the increase in product price "induced" by an increase in advertising. Although the commodity price is fixed, an increase in advertising increases the firm's product price by an amount that is proportional to the increased capacity (measured by $g'$) of its product to contribute (at least in the minds of consumers) to commodity output.

In the conventional analysis, firms in perfectly competitive markets gain nothing from advertising and thus have no incentive to advertise because they are assumed to be unable to differentiate their products to consumers who have perfect knowledge. In our analysis, on the other hand, consumers have imperfect information, including misinformation, and a skilled advertiser might well be able to differentiate his product from other apparently similar products. Put differently, advertisers could increase the value of their output to consumers without increasing to the same extent the value of the output even of perfect competitors in the

14. Therefore,

$$p_x X = \pi_z^0 g \sum_{i=1}^{n} x_i$$

where $n$ is the number of households.

208

*commodity* market. To simplify, we assume that the value of competitors' output is unaffected, in the sense that the commodity price (more generally, the commodity demand curve) to any firm is not affected by its advertising. Note that when firms in perfectly competitive commodity markets differentiate their products by advertising, they still preserve the perfect competition in these markets. Note moreover, that if different firms were producing the same physical product in the same competitive commodity market, and had the same marginal cost and advertising-effectiveness functions, they would produce the same output, charge the same product price, and advertise at the same rate. If, however, either their marginal costs or advertising-effectiveness differed, they would charge different product prices, advertise at different rates, and yet still be perfect competitors (although not of one another)!

Not only can firms in perfectly competitive commodity markets—that is, firms faced with infinitely elastic commodity demand curves—have an incentive to advertise, but the incentive may actually be greater, the more competitive the commodity market is. Let us consider the case of a finite commodity demand elasticity.

The necessary conditions to maximize income given by equation (15'), if $\pi_z$ varies as a function of $Z$, are

$$\frac{\partial I}{\partial X} = \pi_z g + X \frac{\partial \pi_z}{\partial Z} \frac{\partial Z}{\partial X} g - MC(X) = 0, \qquad (18)$$

or since $Z = gX$, and $\partial Z / \partial X = g$,

$$\pi_z g \left( 1 + \frac{1}{\epsilon_{\pi z}} \right) = p_x \left( 1 + \frac{1}{\epsilon_{\pi z}} \right) = MC(X) \qquad (18')$$

where $\epsilon_{\pi z}$ is the elasticity of the firm's commodity demand curve. Also

$$\frac{\partial I}{\partial A} = X \frac{\partial p_x}{\partial A} - p_a = \pi_z \frac{\partial Z}{\partial A} + \frac{\partial \pi_z}{\partial Z} \cdot \frac{\partial Z}{\partial A} \cdot Z - p_a = 0 \qquad (19)$$

or

$$X \frac{\partial p_x}{\partial A} = \pi_z g' X \left( 1 + \frac{1}{\epsilon_{\pi z}} \right) = p_a. \qquad (19')$$

Equation (18') is simply the usual maximizing condition for a monopolist that continues to hold when there is advertising.[15] Equation (19') clearly shows that, given $\pi_z g'X$, the marginal revenue from additional advertising is greater, the greater is the elasticity of the commodity demand curve; therefore, the optimal level of advertising would be positively related to the commodity elasticity.

This important result can be made intuitive by considering figure 5.1. The curve $DD$ gives the firm's commodity demand curve, where $\pi_z$ is measured along the vertical and commodity output $Z$ along the horizontal axis. The firm's production of $X$ is held fixed so that $Z$ varies only because of variations in the level of advertising. At point $e^o$, the level of advertising is $A_o$, the product price is $p_x^o$, and commodity output and price are $Z_o$ and $\pi_z^o$, respectively. An increase in advertising to $A_1$ would increase $Z$ to $Z_1$ (the increase in $Z$ is determined by the given $g'$ function). The decline in $\pi_z$ induced by the increase in $Z$ would be negatively related to the elasticity of the commodity demand curve: it would be less, for example, if the demand curve were $D'D'$ rather than $DD$. Since the increase in $p_x$ is negatively related to the decline in $\pi_y$,[16] the increase in $p_x$, and thus the marginal revenue from the increase in $A$, is directly related to the elasticity of the commodity demand curve.[17]

The same result is illustrated with a more conventional diagram in figure 5.2: the firm's product output and price are shown along the horizontal and vertical axes. The demand curve for its product with a given level of advertising is given by $dd$. We proved earlier (fn. 15) that with

15. If the level of advertising is held constant, $Z$ is proportional to $X$, so

$$\epsilon_{\pi_z} = \frac{dZ}{Z} \bigg/ \frac{d\pi_z}{\pi_z} = \epsilon_{p_z} = \frac{dX}{X} \bigg/ \frac{dp_z}{p_x}.$$

16. Since $\pi_z g = p_x$,

$$\frac{\partial p_z}{\partial A} = \pi_z g' + g\frac{\partial \pi_z}{\partial A} > 0.$$

The first term on the right is positive and the second term is negative. If $g$, $g'$, and $\pi_z$ are given, $\partial p_z/\partial A$ is linearly and negatively related to $\partial \pi_z/\partial A$.

17. Recall again our assumption, however, that even firms in perfectly competitive markets can fully differentiate their products. If the capacity of a firm to differentiate itself were inversely related to the elasticity of its commodity demand curve, that is, to the amount of competition in the commodity market, the increase in its product price generated by its advertising might not be directly related to the elasticity of its commodity demand curve.

210

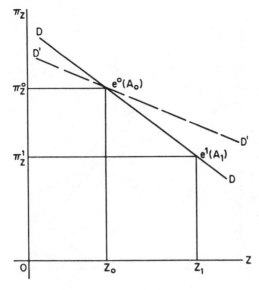

FIGURE 5.1

advertising constant, the elasticity of the product demand curve is the same as the elasticity of its commodity demand curve. An increase in advertising "shifts" the product demand curve upward to $d'd'$, and the marginal revenue from additional advertising is directly related to the size of the shift; that is, to the increase in product price for any given product output. Our basic result is that the shift is itself directly related to the elasticity of the demand curve. For example, with the same increase in advertising, the shift is larger from $dd$ to $d'd'$ than from $ee$ to $e'e'$ because $dd$ is more elastic than $ee$.

This role of information in consumer demand is capable of extension in various directions. For example, the demand for knowledge is affected by the formal education of a person, so systematic variations of demand for advertisements with formal education can be explored. The stock of information possessed by the individual is a function of his age, period of residence in a community, and other variables, so systematic patterns of purchase of heavily and lightly advertised goods are implied by the theory.

## V. FASHIONS AND FADS

The existence of fashions and fads (short episodes or cycles in the consumption habits of people) seems an especially striking contradiction of

211

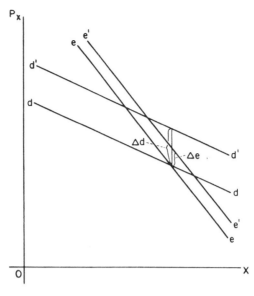

FIGURE 5.2

our thesis of the stability of tastes. We find fashions in dress, food, automobiles, furniture, books, and even scientific doctrines.[18] Some are modest in amplitude, or few in their followers, but others are of violent amplitude: who now buys an ouija board, or a bustle? The rise and fall of fashions is often attributed to the fickleness of people's tastes. Herbert Blumer (1968), the distinguished sociologist, gave a characteristic expression of this view:

> Tastes are themselves a product of experience, they usually develop from an initial state of vagueness to a state of refinement and stability, but once formed they may decay and disintegrate. . . .
>
> The fashion process involves both a formation and an expression of collective taste in the given area of fashion. The taste is initially a loose fusion of vague inclinations and dissatisfactions that are aroused by new experience in the field of fashion and in the larger surrounding world. In this initial state, collective taste is amorphous, inarticulate, and awaiting specific direction. Through models and proposals, fashion in-

18. "Fashion" indeed, does not necessarily refer only to the shorter-term preferences. Adam Smith says that the influence of fashion "over dress and furniture is not more absolute than over architecture, poetry, and music" (p. 283).

212

novators sketch possible lines along which the incipient taste
may gain objective expression and take definite form. (p. 344)

The obvious method of reconciling fashion with our thesis is to resort
again to the now familiar argument that people consume commodities
and only indirectly do they consume market goods, so fashions in market
goods are compatible with stability in the utility function of commodities. The task here, as elsewhere, is to show that this formulation helps
to illuminate our understanding of the phenomena under discussion; we
have some tentative comments in this direction.

The commodity apparently produced by fashion goods is social distinction: the demonstration of alert leadership, or at least not lethargy,
in recognizing and adopting that which will in due time be widely approved. This commodity—it might be termed *style*—sounds somewhat
circular, because new things appear to be chosen simply because they are
new. Such circularity is no more peculiar than that which is literally displayed in a race—the runners obviously do not run around a track in
order to reach a new destination. Moreover, it is a commendation of a
style good that it be superior to previous goods, and style will not be
sought intentionally through less functional goods. Indeed, if the stylish
soon becomes inferior to the unstylish, it would lose its attractiveness.

Style, moreover, is not achieved simply by change: the newness must
be of a special sort that requires a subtle prediction of what will be approved novelty, and a trained person can make better predictions than
an untrained person. Style is social rivalry, and it is, like all rivalry, both
an incentive to individuality and a source of conformity.

The areas in which the rivalry of fashion takes place are characterized
by public exposure and reasonably short life. An unexposed good (automobile pistons) cannot be judged as to its fashionableness, and fashions in a good whose efficient life is long would be expensive. Hence
fashion generally concentrates on the cheaper classes of garments and
reading matter, and there is more fashion in furniture than in housing.

Fashion can be pursued with the purse or with the expenditure of time.
A person may be well-read (i.e., have read the recent books generally
believed to be important), but if his time is valuable in the market place,
it is much more likely that his spouse will be the well-read member of
the family. (So the ratio of the literacy of wife to that of husband is
positively related to the husband's earning power and inversely related
to her earning power.)

The demand for fashion can be formalized by assuming that the distinction available to any person depends on his social environment and his own efforts: he can be fashionable, give to approved charities, choose prestigious occupations, and do other things that affect his distinction. Following recent work on social interactions, we can write the social distinction of the $i$th person as

$$R_i = D_i + h_i \qquad (20)$$

where $D_i$ is the contribution to his distinction of his social environment, and $h_i$ is his own contribution. Each person maximizes a utility function of $R$ and other commodities subject to a budget constraint that depends on his own income and the exogenously given social environment.[19] A number of general results have been developed with this approach (see Becker), and a few are mentioned here to indicate that the demand for fashion (and other determinants of social distinction) can be systematically analyzed without assuming that tastes shift.

An increase in $i$'s own income, prices held constant, would increase his demand for social distinction and other commodities. If his social environment were unchanged, the whole increase in his distinction would be produced by an increase in his own contributions to fashion and other distinction-producing goods. Therefore, even an average income elasticity of demand for distinction would imply a high income elasticity of demand for fashion (and these other distinction-producing) goods, which is consistent with the common judgment that fashion is a luxury good.[20]

If other persons increase their contributions to their own distinction, this may lower $i$'s distinction by reducing his social environment. For distinction is scarce and is to a large extent simply redistributed among persons: an increase in one person's distinction generally requires a reduction in that of other persons. This is why people are often "forced" to conform to new fashions. When some gain distinction by paying attention to (say) new fashions, they lower the social environment of others. The latter are induced to increase their own efforts to achieve

19. The budget constraint for $i$ can be written as

$$\Pi_{R_i} R + \Pi_z Z = I_i + \Pi_{R_i} D_i = S_i$$

where $Z$ are other commodities, $\Pi_{zi}$ is his marginal cost of changing $R$, $I$, is his own full income, and $S_i$ is his "social income."

20. Marshall believed that the desire for distinction was the most powerful of passions and a major source of the demand for luxury expenditures (see 1923, 87–88, 106).

distinction, including a demand for these new fashions, because an exogenous decline in their social environment induces them to increase their own contributions to their distinction.

Therefore, an increase in all incomes induces an even greater increase in $i$'s contribution to his distinction than does an increase in his own income alone. For an increase in the income of others lowers $i$'s social environment because they spend more on their own distinction; the reduction in his environment induces a further increase in $i$'s contribution to his distinction. Consequently, we expect wealthy countries like the United States to pay more attention to fashion than poor countries like India, even if tastes were the same in wealthy and poor countries.

## VI. Conclusion

We have surveyed four classes of phenomena widely believed to be inconsistent with the stability of tastes: addiction, habitual behavior, advertising, and fashions, and in each case offered an alternative explanation. That alternative explanation did not simply reconcile the phenomena in question with the stability of tastes, but also sought to show that the hypothesis of stable tastes yielded more useful predictions about observable behavior.

Of course, this short list of categories is far from comprehensive: for example, we have not entered into the literature of risk aversion and risk preference, one of the richest sources of *ad hoc* assumptions concerning tastes. Nor have we considered the extensive literature on time preference, which often alleges that people "systematically undervalue . . . future wants."[21] The taste for consumption in say 1984 is alleged to continue to shift upward as 1984 gets closer to the present. In spite of the importance frequently attached to time preference, we do not know of any significant behavior that has been illuminated by this assumption. Indeed, given additional space, we would argue that the assumption of time preference impedes the explanation of life cycle variations in the

---

21. This quote is taken from the following longer passage in Böhm-Bawerk (1959):

We must now consider a *second* phenomenon of human experience—one that is heavily fraught with consequence. That is the fact that we feel less concerned about future sensations of joy and sorrow simply because they do lie in the future, and the lessening of our concern is in proportion to the remoteness of that future. Consequently we accord to goods which are intended to serve future ends a value which falls short of the true intensity of their future marginal utility. *We systematically undervalue our future wants and also the means which serve to satisfy them.* (p. 268).

allocation of resources, the secular growth in real incomes, and other phenomena.

Moreover, we have not considered systematic differences in tastes by wealth or other classifications. We also claim, however, that no significant behavior has been illuminated by assumptions of differences in tastes. Instead, they, along with assumptions of unstable tastes, have been a convenient crutch to lean on when the analysis has bogged down. They give the appearance of considered judgment, yet really have only been *ad hoc* arguments that disguise analytical failures.

We have partly translated "unstable tastes" into variables in the household production functions for commodities. The great advantage, however, of relying only on changes in the arguments entering household production functions is that *all* changes in behavior are explained by changes in prices and incomes, precisely the variables that organize and give power to economic analysis. Addiction, advertising, etc. affect not tastes with the endless degrees of freedom they provide, but prices and incomes, and are subject therefore to the constraints imposed by the theorem on negatively inclined demand curves, and other results. Needless to say, we would welcome explanations of why some people become addicted to alcohol and others to Mozart, whether the explanation was a development of our approach or a contribution from some other behavioral discipline.

As we remarked at the outset, no conceivable expenditure of effort on our part could begin to exhaust the possible tests of the hypothesis of stable and uniform preferences. Our task has been oddly two-sided. Our hypothesis is trivial, for it merely asserts that we should apply standard economic logic as extensively as possible. But the self-same hypothesis is also a demanding challenge, for it urges us not to abandon opaque and complicated problems with the easy suggestion that the further explanation will perhaps someday be produced by one of our sister behavioral sciences.

## References

Becker, G. S. 1974. "A Theory of Social Interaction." *Journal of Political Economy* 82 (November/December): 1063–93.

Blumer, H. C. 1968. "Fashion." In vol. 5 of *International Encyclopedia of Social Sciences*. New York.

Böhm-Bawerk, Eugen von. 1959. *Capital and Interest*, vol. 2. South Holland, IL.

Galbraith, John K. 1958. *The Affluent Society*. Boston.

Grossman, M. 1971. "The Economics of Joint Production in the Household." Reprint 7145. University of Chicago: Center for Mathematical Studies in Business Economics.

Marshall, Alfred. 1923. *Principles of Economics,* 8th edition. London.
Michael, R. T., and G. S. Becker. 1973. "On the New Theory of Consumer Behavior." *Swedish Journal of Economics* 75 (December): 378–96.
Mill, John S. 1972. *A System of Logic,* 8th edition. London.
Smith, Adam. 1969. *Theory of Moral Sentiments.* New Rochelle.

## COMMENT: *De Gustibus Non Est Explanandum*
## Robert E. Goodin

The ordinary economic calculus proceeds, via rationality postulates, from statements of people's preferences to predictions of their actions. Preferences themselves are taken as given, presumably being determined by something outside the model. Stigler and Becker challenge that presumption. They say that the economist should "continue to search for differences in prices or incomes to explain any differences or changes in behavior"; they go on to say that "one may usefully treat tastes as stable over time and similar among people" and explain apparently differing preferences between people as deriving from their differing stocks of "consumption capital." This varies, less interestingly, with people's differing stocks of information about the goods: that is what drives the Stigler-Becker theses about habit and advertising. It varies, much more interestingly, with the differing quantities of the goods that people have consumed in the past: that is what drives Stigler and Becker's analysis of addiction. For purposes of this brief comment, the latter, more novel claim can serve as our portmanteau.

### I

Notice, first, that differences in tastes cannot *wholly* be explained in these ways. Stigler and Becker concede as much, remarking in passing at one point in their conclusion that "we have *partly* translated 'unstable tastes' into variables in the household production functions for commodities" (emphasis added). That brief and grudging concession deserves amplification.

It is clear enough, on the Stigler-Becker model of addiction, how once people begin consuming different goods in different quantities they might then come to acquire different tastes over those goods. What is not explicable in these taste-based terms is how they start consuming different goods in different quantities in the first place. (Saying that they merely had different feasible sets simply shifts us out of taste-based talk, of course.) Supposing that everyone has the same basic tastes, and that the only thing that distinguishes between them is the history of their consumption acts, then *ex ante* of those differentiating consumption acts there is nothing to distinguish between them. How they set off down these different, self-reinforcing consumption paths remains a mystery that must be solved outside the Stigler-Becker model of addiction.[1] And they face strictly analogous problems, within their model, in explaining how in the very first instance habits or traditions got going at all.

Furthermore, not all preferences necessarily manifest the Stigler-Becker pattern. It is not at all clear that all goods require "consumption capital" of the sort they are talking about for their enjoyment; or, if they do, that that consumption capital always necessarily varies with information or previous experience; or, if it does, that it varies in any very interesting fashion. (With most ordinary consumer staples, for example, our stock of consumption capital seems to top out pretty early and does not increase appreciably with subsequent inputs of information or consumption experiences.) Fancy goods might be an "acquired taste," but standard sorts of food, shelter, clothing, autos, etc. are not: few of us find that we need to make much effort to "learn to like" hamburgers or Hondas. Neither, once we have certain minimal information about their attributes, do we find our subsequent choices all that much influenced by further facts. There are, of course, substantial variations and shifts in tastes for precisely such ordinary consumer staples. But those variations and shifts cannot credibly be attributed to preferences being altered by any subtle shifts in consumption capital, as Stigler and Becker would wish.

## II

In the Stigler-Becker model of addiction, past consumption might affect present enjoyment of goods either positively or negatively. "Beneficial addiction" refers to the former case, "harmful addiction" to the latter. Let us consider these two cases in turn.

The sort of "consumption capital" that is involved in Stigler and Becker's "beneficial addiction" is a very queer kind of capital. Usually, at any given moment, capital investment and current consumption constitute two *competing* claims on our resources. The more we do of one, the less

1. This may be what Stigler and Becker mean when, in their conclusion, they grudgingly allow that "we would welcome explanations of why some people become addicted to alcohol and others to Mozart, whether the explanation was a development of our approach or a contribution from some other behavioral discipline." But if so, then the explanation must necessarily lie more decisively outside their model than they there admit.

we can do of the other. In the case of beneficial addiction, as Stigler and Becker see it, that is not the case. There, consumption and capital formation are complementary: we build up our stock of music-appreciation capital by the very act of consuming music.

The argument from queerness, in and of itself, merely reinforces my earlier comment about the limited range of goods to which the Stigler-Becker model might apply. Building on this observed peculiarity of the capital involved in "beneficial addiction" as that model analyzes it, however, we can mount yet another more telling objection.

The crux of the matter, bluntly stated, is this: if Stigler and Becker are right about this curious property of consumption capital, then why should anyone ever invest in capital of any other sort? Beneficial addictions, thus construed, present unique opportunities for having your cake and eating it too—for enjoying consumption in the present at the same time as you are enhancing consumption in the future. This is an economic analogue to the fast breeder reactor. The more you use, the more you have to use. The offer looks irresistible.

My point here is not that if Stigler and Becker are right, then everyone ought necessarily to take all their consumption in forms that are beneficially addictive. That would be to say that people ought necessarily value investments in future consumption, whereas it is ordinarily thought best to leave open questions of why people ever want to invest in the future at all and how much they value future satisfactions relative to present ones. My point is merely that, however much one does value the future, one ought to prefer investing in beneficially addictive consumption capital to investing in any other form of capital, *ceteris paribus*. That is simply because beneficially addictive consumption capital yields present payoffs in addition to future ones, whereas any other sort yields the latter alone.[2]

Neither is that necessarily to say that everyone ought necessarily to make all their investments in the form of beneficially addictive consumption capital. The *ceteris paribus* condition might not be met. Other forms of capital investment might yield a higher rate of return, so that even

2. Analogously, assuming that the production values of both were the same, Stigler and Becker should predict that we would always prefer watching commercials to watching features on television. The former necessarily enhance consumption capital in a way that the latter do not (or, anyway, do not necessarily). Since much more money is spent, minute-for-minute, to produce commercials than features, we can safely assume that their production values are, if anything, higher. Despite that fact, I know of no one who uses the video recorder's fast-forward to zap out features and to search for commercials to watch.

with its present payoffs added in the beneficially addictive consumption capital is less lucrative overall. Or, since capital is not all homogenous, it may turn out that you have to have certain other sorts of capital to take fullest advantage of your beneficially addictive consumption capital. But the point remains, even after all these qualifications have been taken into account, that capital investment should be heavily biased in favor of beneficially addictive consumption capital, if Stigler and Becker are right about it.

Casual empiricism suggests, first, that that is not the way that people do invest. The bulk of our society's investments, and the bulk of any individual's investments, are decidedly not of the beneficially addictive sort. And that is not, I think, just because the opportunities for investment of that sort are lacking.[3]

III

Harmful addictions point to the negative effects of past consumption on present enjoyment. The model here is heroin addiction: the more heroin you have consumed in the past, the less of a buzz any given quantity of the drug provides you at present; so to get the same buzz, you have to take more heroin than ever.

This, again, can be translated into the language of "consumption capital" by saying that consumption of the good in any one period has a negative effect on (that is, reduces) the consumption capital that will be available in subsequent periods. Rewriting the double negative as a positive, "avoiding reductions in consumption capital" becomes "investing in consumption capital." Then here, just as in standard economic theory, current consumption and capital investment are at odds with one another. The queer complementary relation, found in the case of beneficial addictions, has here disappeared.

But with it has gone much of the novelty of the model's claims. Harmfully addictive behavior becomes just a special case of someone with short time horizons trading present pleasure for future suffering. The pattern is perfectly familiar from standard economic theory and is per-

---

3. One possible reply is that there are complementaries between goods, such that good A is subject to the positive development of consumption capital only if co-consumed with good B, which is subject to negative capital formation. Another is that goods that are initially positively addictive, beyond some point, become negatively addictive; something along those lines is implicit in Tibor Scitovsky's *Joyless Economy* (Oxford: Oxford University Press, 1976). I am grateful to Hugh Ward for these suggestions.

fectly well modelled by it. The only contribution Stigler and Becker add is to emphasize that that shifting pattern of consumption (e.g., ever larger intake of heroin by addicts) should not be analyzed in terms of changing tastes, but rather in terms of changing prices. An addict's subjective taste for the buzz remains constant; all that has altered, the more heroin the addict has consumed, is the quantity of the drug required to produce the same objective physiological state. But it is unclear that many economists thought otherwise, or that their error in this peripheral matter seriously infected their broader economic theory.

What is singularly in need of explanation, in the heroin addiction case, is why addicts should demand exactly the same buzz, in the face of constantly increasing prices. It may not be strictly irrational, but it nonetheless is distinctly odd, that consumers should be so utterly insensitive to such dramatic price changes. That is the oddity that must be explained, if we are to explain satisfactorily why addicts are driven to consume ever-increasing (ultimately, life-threatening) quantities of the drug.

Whether this is a peculiarity of the heroin case, or typical of all harmful addictions, is unclear. In any event, Stigler and Becker are at a loss to explain it. True, they have postulated that consumers' underlying tastes are stable; but stable preferences, in the face of shifting prices, should lead to shifting consumption patterns. True, they have explained how habit, analyzed as accumulated information, should make us slow to respond to price changes, but that merely explains a little bit of stickiness in the response function, rather than an insistent and persistent refusal to accept any less of a buzz, whatever the price; and in any case, it cannot plausibly be said to be *information* (or, anyway, not information about *relative prices*) that heroin addicts lack.

## IV

Stigler and Becker have indeed pushed back the limits to rationality, showing that some of the differences and changes in taste that we observe are amenable to analysis in ordinary economic ways. They have also left much unexplained. Analysis of the formation and reformation of tastes still remains largely outside the rationality model.

# 6

# Cooperation and Rationality: Notes on the Collective Action Problem and Its Solutions

## Michael Taylor

### What Is the Collective Action Problem?

It has been widely asserted—and is still being asserted—that individual preferences in public goods interactions and in collective action problems more generally are, or usually are, those of a Prisoners' Dilemma game. In fact, many interesting public goods interactions are better represented by quite different games. In particular, in cases where each individual can choose between just two strategies, the Assurance game and especially the Chicken game, in their standard two-person forms and in their (rarely studied) N-person generalizations, are often the appropriate models; and where, more realistically, each individual can choose to contribute a continuously variable amount within some range (or choose from a large number of discrete amounts that may be approximated by a continuous variable), the individual preferences are most unlikely to resemble those of a Prisoners' Dilemma and are more likely to be those of a Chicken-like game or an Assurance-like game or a hybrid of these two.[1] Surely, then, we shouldn't identify the problem of collective action with the Prisoners' Dilemma—even though *some* of these alternative representations of public goods interaction (the Assurance game, for example) do not seem to present "problems" in the sense which I think most people intend by use of the expression "collective action problems." So what *do* we mean by this expression?

Jon Elster gives a "strong definition" of the collective action problem, which identifies it with the Prisoners' Dilemma, and a "weak definition," which requires that (1) universal cooperation is preferred to universal noncooperation by every individual (as in the Prisoners' Dilemma) and

Previously published, in a slightly different form, as "Solutions? Unity, States, Entrepreneurs, Property Rights, and Norms," in *The Possibility of Cooperation* (Cambridge: Cambridge University Press, 1987).

1. See Michael Taylor and Hugh Ward, "Chickens, Whales, and Lumpy Goods: Alternative Models of Public-Goods Provision," *Political Studies* 30 (1982): 350–70.

(2) cooperation is individually unstable and individually inaccessible.[2] There is individual instability if each individual has an incentive to defect from universal cooperation, and there is individual inaccessibility if no individual has an incentive to move unilaterally from universal noncooperation. But then he points out that there are cases in which cooperation is either individually unstable or individually inaccessible but not both— for example Chicken and Assurance games—but which nevertheless present collective action problems (though "less serious" ones in the case of Assurance games).

The definition which I think gathers up all the cases that Elster and others are actually concerned with is that a collective action problem exists where rational individual action can lead to a strictly Pareto-inferior outcome, i.e., an outcome that is strictly less preferred by every individual than at least one other outcome. The problem with this definition—an unavoidable problem, it seems to me, if one wants to give a general definition that covers *all* the cases one intuitively thinks of as collective action problems—is that it's not clear in some situations what rationality prescribes (even if we rule out, as I'm assuming we should do here, notions of rationality not considered by game theorists). This is true of Chicken games. Any outcome of a Chicken game, including the Pareto-inferior mutual Defection outcome, can be rationalized. Hence, rational action *can* plausibly lead to a Pareto-inferior outcome, so that on my account it is a collective action problem.

Whether Assurance games are collective action problems again depends on what one takes rationality to prescribe. I shall take the view that, if a game has multiple equilibria (as the Assurance game does), but one of them is strictly preferred to all the others by everyone, then the Pareto-preferred one will be the outcome. On this view, rational action in an Assurance game does *not* lead to a Pareto-inferior outcome, so that this game is not a collective action problem.

Since preferences in some public goods interactions are those of an Assurance game, not all such interactions are collective action problems.

In the case of the (one-shot) Prisoners' Dilemma, rational action unequivocally leads to a Pareto-inferior outcome, so on my account all situations representable as Prisoners' Dilemma are collective action problems. So are many other games. Of course, not all these games (including

2. Jon Elster, "Rationality, Morality, and Collective Action," *Ethics* 96 (1985): 136–55. The weak definition, identifying collective action problems with the Prisoners' Dilemma, is adopted by Elster in "Weakness of Will and the Free-Rider Problem," *Economics and Philosophy* 1 (1985): 231–65.

the Prisoners' Dilemma and Chicken games) correspond to public goods interactions.

Elster has said that politics is "the study of ways of transcending the Prisoners' Dilemma."[3] In the light of this discussion of "the collective action problem," I think we should be a little more expansive and say that politics is the study of ways of solving collective action problems.

## SOLUTIONS TO COLLECTIVE ACTION PROBLEMS

A wide range of disparate processes and institutions—including conditional cooperation, conventions, selective incentives, the state, community, political entrepreneurs, property rights and norms—have been offered as "solutions" to the collective action problem. Are they?

In general, and very broadly speaking, there are two sorts of solutions to collective action problems, which I call "spontaneous" or "internal" solutions and "external" solutions. *Internal* solutions neither involve nor presuppose changes in the "game," that is, in the possibilities open to the individuals (which are in part determined by the transformation function, specifying how much of the public good can be produced with a given contribution), together with the individuals' *preferences* (or more generally attitudes) and their *beliefs* (including expectations). *External* solutions, on the other hand, work by changing the game, i.e., by changing people's possibilities, attitudes, or beliefs. The changes do not necessarily originate outside the group of individuals who have the collective action problem. Since individual action is the direct product of the individual's possibilities, attitudes, and beliefs, these two exhaust the possible sorts of solution.

In the case where an internal "solution" is forthcoming, it could be said that there was no "problem" there to solve. For example, if the "problem" is correctly modeled by a dynamic game, which, though it consists, let us say, of an iterated Prisoners' Dilemma, is not itself a Prisoners' Dilemma, and as a consequence the outcome produced by rational egoists (without any external assistance or other interference) would be mutual cooperation throughout the game, then it could be said that preferences (including intertemporal preferences), etc., are such that there is no collective action *problem*. This would be a perfectly reasonable use of the world problem, but I shall not adopt it here. In fact I shall take the view that the internal solution is the *basic* one, in two connected senses.

3. Jon Elster, "Some Conceptual Problems in Political Theory," in *Power and Political Theory,* edited by Brian Barry (London: Wiley, 1976), pp. 248–49.

It is, first, the only one that is complete in itself. All the external solutions presuppose the prior and/or concurrent solution of other problems, usually (always?) of collective action problems. Many of them, for example, involve the use of threats and offers of sanctions, and the creation and maintenance of the sanction system entail the prior or concurrent solution of collective action problems. (Why, for example, should the rational egoist pay his portion of the taxes that the state requires to maintain its police forces, etc., or why should the individual member of a community go to the trouble of punishing a free-rider when he could be a free-rider on the sanctioning efforts of others?) The internal solution is basic in a second sense: until we know whether a solution of this kind is possible and what form it will take, we cannot say what work, if any, remains to be done by other putative solutions. Thus, understanding the prospects for and obstacles in the way of an internal solution helps us see what sorts of external solutions are necessary and are likely to emerge in a given context.

External solutions can themselves be divided into two broad categories, which, for short, I'll call centralized and decentralized; or, better, they can be arrayed along a continuum running from perfectly centralized to perfectly decentralized. Combinations of them are possible—normal, in fact. A solution is *decentralized* to the extent that the initiative for the changes in possibilities, attitudes, or beliefs that constitute an external solution is dispersed amongst the members of the group; or, the greater the proportion of the group's members involved in solving the collective action problem (for example, applying sanctions to free-riders), the more decentralized the solution. Contrariwise, a solution is *centralized* to the extent that such involvement is concentrated in the hands of only a few members of the group.

Centralized solutions are typified, of course, by *the state,* while decentralized solutions characterize *community.* I have discussed elsewhere the ways in which a community can provide itself with public goods without the help of the state.[4] By a community I mean a group of people (1) who have beliefs and values in common, (2) whose relations are direct and many-sided, and (3) who practice generalized as well as merely balanced reciprocity. The members of such a group of people, or all of its active adult members, can wield with great effectiveness a range of positive and negative sanctions, including the sanctions of approval and disapproval—the latter especially via gossip, ridicule, and shaming. Decen-

4. *Community, Anarchy and Liberty* (Cambridge: Cambridge University Press, 1982).

tralized solutions can sometimes be effective where there is little community, but the size of the group would still have to be relatively small (as it must be in a community).

External solutions are not necessarily restricted to the use of threats and offers of positive and negative sanctions. These, it is true, work not by altering an individual's preferences among outcomes (properly defined) but by altering his expectations about the actions to be taken by others (and hence the expected utility associated with alternative courses of action). But there are other ways in which an individual's expectations about others' behavior can be altered and other ways in which he can be induced to contribute to a public good that do not involve the use of threats and offers of force, whether centralized or decentralized. These include persuasion—providing information and arguments about the alternatives, about the consequences of adopting the various courses of action, about others' attitudes and beliefs, and so on. Such methods are characteristic of the political entrepreneur, an external "solution" (relatively centralized, though usually closely combined with decentralized mechanisms) which I shall discuss after making some brief remarks on recent work on internal or "spontaneous" solutions.

## "Spontaneous" Cooperation

I said earlier that in public goods interaction the preferences at any point in time are not necessarily those of a Prisoners' Dilemma game but in many interesting cases are those of a Chicken game (especially when the good is lumpy) or, occasionally, an Assurance game. When preferences are those of an Assurance game, there is unlikely to be a problem of collective action: cooperation will occur spontaneously even in the one-shot game. In the case of Chicken, however, a cooperative outcome is not so assured.

The crucial feature of the $2 \times 2$ Chicken game is the existence of an incentive for each player to bind herself irrevocably to noncooperation (or at least to convince the other players that she is certain not to cooperate), an incentive deriving from her expectation that such a commitment will compel the other player to cooperate. I would define the *N-person Chicken* (a game which has received negligible attention) as any game having this property, or rather its generalization, namely, that each player has an incentive to precommit herself to noncooperation because she believes that this will compel *some or all* of the other players to cooperate.[5] For this to be so, of course, there must be stable profitable subgroups (at least one corresponding to each player) whose members find it in their interests to cooperate when individuals outside the group do not.

It is clear, then, that in the N-person Chicken, as in the N-person Prisoners' Dilemma, rational action can lead to the unintended consequence of a Pareto-inferior outcome. For in the rush to be among the first to make a commitment to non-cooperation (and thereby secure a free ride on the cooperation of others), the number so binding themselves may exceed the maximum number of players able to commit themselves without inducing non-provision of the public good. Nevertheless, the prospects for cooperation are a little more promising in Chicken games than they are in the Prisoners' Dilemma. In particular, it can be shown that if pre-commitment is modeled as a risky decision, in which each player puts a subjective probability on each other player committing herself to non-cooperation, then there is a range of realistic conditions under which some cooperation will be forthcoming in a one-shot, N-person, two-strategy Chicken game,[6] which is more than can be said for the one-shot Prisoners' Dilemma. The same general conclusion can be shown to follow when strategy sets are continuous, in those (arguably common) cases when the game is Assurance-like or Chicken-like or a hybrid of these.[7] In all these cases, if the game is played only once, *some* cooperation is more likely to be forthcoming than in the cases for which the Prisoners' Dilemma is the appropriate model.

But, of course, public goods interactions and collective action problems are not realistically modeled by one-shot games, and we should therefore be more interested in the analysis of dynamic or repeated games. Of the dynamics of behavior in iterated Chicken games almost nothing is known.[8] As for iterated Prisoners' Dilemma, about which

5. As it stands this definition does not fully determine the permissible preference structures. For a fuller account, see Taylor and Ward, "Chicken, Whales, and Lumpy Goods" or Taylor, *The Possibility of Cooperation*, chapter 2.

6. See Taylor and Ward. The same analysis can also be found in Amnon Rapoport, "Provision of Public Goods and the MCS Paradigm," *American Political Science Review,* 79 (1985): 148–55.

7. See *The Possibility of Cooperation*, chapter 2.

8. Bart Lipman has applied Axelrod's approach to the iterated two-person Chicken game; but this work suffers from the same limitations as Axelrod's work, to be discussed below. See "Cooperation among Egoists in Prisoner's Dilemma and Chicken Games," *Public Choice,* 51 (1986): 315–31. Hugh Ward has made a promising start on the dynamics of

much more is known, there have been a number of different approaches, and I want to comment briefly on some of these.

I take it, first of all, that if the problem is to be modeled as an iterated game at all, the appropriate model for most public goods interactions and other processes giving rise to collective action problems is that of a supergame of indefinite length (which can be interpreted either as being composed of a countably infinite number of constituent games or as having a known and fixed probability of terminating in any time period), in which the players discount future payoffs exponentially. This is, I think, the view of most economists; nevertheless a number of recently published mathematical studies consider finite supergames and infinite supergames with no discounting. Whether or not one thinks the future *should* be discounted, the idea that rational egoists playing supergames of indefinite length would actually place as much value on a payoff to be received in the distant future as on the same payoff to be received immediately is quite implausible. In the case of the supergame with only a finite number of constituent games, it has been shown that the well-known result that noncooperation in every constituent game is the only undominated strategy no longer holds if a small amount of uncertainty is introduced into the game: if players are not quite certain about each other's motivations, options, or payoffs, the standard backwards induction argument cannot be applied.[9]

Returning, then, to infinite supergames with discounting, the central result in the case of the two-person Prisoners' Dilemma is that mutual *conditional* cooperation ("I'll cooperate if and only if you do" or "tit-for-tat") is an equilibrium provided that each player's discount rate is sufficiently small (and under certain conditions, too messy to summarize

---

behavior in the repeated N-person Chicken in "The Risks of a Reputation for Toughness: Strategy in Public Goods Provision Problems Modelled by Chicken Supergames," *British Journal of Political Science* 17 (1987): 23–52.

9. See David M. Kreps, et al., "Rational Cooperation in the Finitely Repeated Prisoners' Dilemma," *Journal of Economic Theory* 27 (1982): 245–52; David M. Kreps and Robert Wilson, "Reputation and Imperfect Information," *Journal of Economic Theory* 27 (1982): 253–79; and Kreps and Wilson, "Sequential equilibria," *Econometrica* 50 (1982): 863–94. On infinite games without discounting, see especially A. Rubinstein, "Equilibrium in Supergames with the Overtaking Criterion," *Journal of Economic Theory* 21 (1979): 1–9; Steve Smale, "The Prisoners' Dilemma and Dynamical Systems Associated to Noncooperative Games," *Econometrica* 48 (1980): 1617–34; and Robert J. Aumann, "Survey of Repeated Games," pp. 11–42, in R. J. Aumann et al., *Essays in Game Theory and Mathematical Economics in Honor of Oskar Morgenstern* (Mannheim/Wien/Zurich: Bibliographisches Institut, 1981).

here, this equilibrium will be the outcome).[10] A generalization of this result holds in the $N$-person case: cooperation by every player throughout the supergame, sustained by the use of the generalized tit-for-tat strategy, in which each player cooperates on the condition that every other player does, is an equilibrium provided that every player's discount rate is not too great. Moreover, it can be shown that even when some of the players insist on unconditional noncooperation throughout the supergame, cooperation may still be rational for the rest—provided that there are *some* players who cooperate conditionally on the cooperation of *all* the other cooperators, both conditional and unconditional, and that all the cooperators' discount rates are not too great.

This last possibility gives rise to an interesting problem. It may very well be that *several* of the strategy vectors in which some players (*m* of them, say) cooperate conditionally while the rest unconditionally defect throughout the supergame are equilibria. (In the special case of a symmetrical game—in which the players have identical payoff functions—if one such strategy vector is an equilibrium, then all the $(N/m)$ possible such vectors are equilibria, $(N/m)$ being the number of subsets of size $m$ that can be drawn from the $N$ players). In this case, an individual is indifferent between all the equilibria *if* he is going to cooperate *or* if he is going to defect. And each player would prefer to cooperate conditionally *if* otherwise there would be no cooperation (that is, if his cooperation is critical to the success of the "compact" between the conditional cooperators). But if one of the equilibria is going to be the outcome, then *he would rather it was one in which he defected unconditionally than one in which he cooperated.* Every player has this preference. If the public good is going to be provided by a *sub*group, he'd rather it was a subgroup that did not include him.

Each player, then, has an incentive in this situation to *pre-commit* or *bind* himself to noncooperation, in the expectation that others will have to cooperate and he will be a free-rider on their efforts. The existence of an incentive of this kind is precisely the defining characteristic of the $N$-person *Chicken* game (or so I have argued).[11] We have, then, a Chicken nesting in the Prisoners' Dilemma supergame.

10. See Michael Taylor, *Anarchy and Cooperation* (London: Wiley, 1976), chapter 3, where, however, only the necessity part of this condition is proved. For a clearer presentation of the analysis, including the sufficiency part of the proof, see *The Possibility of Cooperation*, chapter 3.

11. Several readers of *Anarchy and Cooperation* pointed out this problem but did not recognize that it gave rise to a Chicken game and did not provide any analysis of it. See

In this situation, it has been suggested, there would be a "chaotic" scramble in which each individual tries to ensure that he is not left behind in a subgroup whose members are obliged (by their own preferences) to provide the public good and there is no reason to expect a subgroup of the right size to emerge from this "stampede." [12] But it must be emphasized that there is no warrant (either in the model being discussed here or in any alternative model offered by the proponents of this view) for this conclusion: conclusive arguments of this kind could only be made if pre-commitment behavior were explicitly incorporated into the model. In fact, a subgroup of conditional cooperators *might* emerge if enough players are sufficiently risk-averse—but arguments of this sort too must await a richer specification of the model. [13]

A theorem similar to the simple two-person result referred to earlier is at the center of Axelrod's argument in *The Evolution of Cooperation*. Actually his theorem concerns, not the (Nash) equilibrium of the strategy pair in which both players use tit-for-tat (call this strategy $B$), but the "collective stability" of $B$. The notion of collective stability derives from the concept of an "evolutionarily stable strategy" introduced into biology by Maynard Smith and is defined in a model that supposes there is a population of individuals all using a certain strategy ($S$, say) and asks whether it can be "invaded" by a single mutant individual using some other strategy ($S'$). The mutant strategy is said to *invade* the native strategy if it can do better playing repeatedly against a native than a native can do against another native. Then, a strategy is said to be *collectively stable* if no strategy can invade it.

Thus, a collectively stable strategy is, as Axelrod puts it, "in Nash equilibrium with itself," that is, if $S$ is a collectively stable strategy then ($S,S$) is an equilibrium. But of course an equilibrium need not consist of a pair (or a population) of identical strategies. Nash equilibrium, then, is not the same thing as collective stability (and Axelrod's Characteriza-

---

Michael Laver, "Political Solutions to the Collective Action Problem," *Political Studies* 28 (1980): 195–209; Iain McLean, "The Social Contract and the Prisoner's Dilemma Supergame," *Political Studies* 29 (1981): 339–51; and Russell Hardin, "Individual Sanctions, Collective Benefits," in *Paradoxes of Rationality and Cooperation: Prisoners' Dilemma and Newcomb's Problem,* edited by Richmond Campbell and Lanning Sowden. (Vancouver: University of British Columbia Press, 1985).

12. See the articles by Laver and McLean cited in the previous footnote.

13. Early indications from simple computer simulation exercises with one such model (in unpublished work by Hugh Ward) suggest that a precommitment "scramble" could occur that would level out and stabilize at the desired subgroup size.

tion Theorem is not very helpful in carrying out a full equilibrium analysis).

Axelrod, in fact, confines his attention to *tournaments,* in which individuals play in *pairs.* (This is true both of his theoretical analysis, which is based, as we have seen, on the notion of a collectively stable strategy, and of the round-robin computer tournament he conducted, which in both its versions was won by tit-for-tat).

Axelrod comes to the same *general* conclusion that had been reached by the equilibrium analysis of the two-person supergame, namely that "the two key requisites for cooperation to thrive are that the cooperation be based on reciprocity, and that the shadow of the future is important enough to make this reciprocity stable." [14] But is his approach, based on the idea of the tournament and the concept of a collectively stable strategy, to be preferred to an analysis using the notion of a (Nash) equilibrium? I think not. Pairwise interaction may be characteristic of non-human populations (though even this is doubted by Maynard Smith himself), but it certainly does not characterize most human interactions that give rise to collective action problems. These of course generally involve more than two individuals and, especially where the provision of public goods is at stake, an individual's behavior typically depends on the whole aggregate pattern of behaviors of the rest of the group. For example, his decision whether or not to cooperate in the provision of a public good would generally be contingent on there being *enough others* cooperating. Situations of this kind cannot be characterized in terms of pairwise interactions. Even where, in the real world, interactions are truly pairwise, they are most unlikely to take the strange form assumed by Axelrod: his analysis hinges on the assumption that an individual will play out the whole of an infinite supergame with one other player, or each player in turn, rather than, say, ranging through the population, or part of it, playing against different players at different times in the supergame (possibly playing against each of them a random number of times). [15]

Returning to the equilibrium analysis of the two-person Prisoners' Dilemma supergame, let us note that *if* (B, B) is an equilibrium, it is also a *coordination equilibrium.* A coordination equilibrium is a strategy pair such that either player is made no better off not only if she herself uni-

14. Robert Axelrod, *The Evolution of Cooperation* (New York: Basic Books, 1984), p. 173.

15. This last point is made by Norman Schofield in "Anarchy, Altruism and Cooperation," *Social Choice and Welfare* 2 (1985): 207–19.

laterally changes strategy but also if the *other* player does. Consider (B, B). If, for example, the other player defects to unconditional noncooperation, the effect on the nondefecting player is the same as if *she* had defected, except in the first constituent game, where she gets even less than she would have done had she defected; so that if her own defection makes her no better off, the other's defection certainly won't. Similar remarks apply to changes to other strategies. Thus, if (B, B) is an equilibrium, it is a coordination equilibrium. This is not true, of course, of the strategy pair in which both players choose unconditional noncooperation, which is always an equilibrium but never a coordination equilibrium.

Russell Hardin believes that the fact that (B, B) and other strategy vectors are *coordination* equilibria makes an important difference to the explanation of behavior in Prisoners' Dilemma games. A coordination equilibrium, he says, is even more likely to be the outcome than a mere equilibrium because it is "supported by a double incentive to each player," for each player has an interest in herself "conforming" *and* an interest in the other player conforming as well.[16]

Actually, in the Prisoners' Dilemma supergame with discounting, (B, B) need not even be an equilibrium. But we have to assume that Hardin has in mind an indefinitely iterated Prisoners' Dilemma *with no discounting,* since, strangely, he nowhere mentions discounting, and that each player's supergame payoffs are long-run averages of the constituent game payoffs. In my view, these games are of little importance in the analysis of social life. They are also much simpler analytically, since they involve none of the complex trade-offs between payoffs in different time periods that are possible in supergames with discounting. In these no-discount games, (B, B) is in fact always an equilibrium and also a coordination equilibrium.

But even if (B, B), or any other strategy vector, is a coordination equilibrium, this fact does not provide any player with a "double incentive" to conform to it. That *I* want the *other* player to conform is of no relevance to her, for we have assumed that she, like me, is a rational egoist: *my* interest in her conforming has no effect on her actions, just as my actions are unaffected by her desire that I should conform. The possibility that my interest in her actions would lead me to do something to ensure that she acts in the right way is not one that can be considered

---

16. Russell Hardin, *Collective Action* (Baltimore: Johns Hopkins University Press, 1982), p. 171.

within Hardin's framework (or that of the ordinary equilibrium analysis of the supergame discussed above). "My interest in your conforming means that, if there is a way to do so at little or no net cost to me, I will want to give you further incentive to conform," says Hardin,[17] but options in *this* cost-benefit comparison are not in the model to begin with and, as always, should not be wheeled in *ad hoc*. Bringing options of this general sort into the model from the start would in some cases yield not a double rationalization of the outcome (*B, B*) but a rationalization of a different outcome altogether.

## EXTERNAL SOLUTIONS TO COLLECTIVE ACTION PROBLEMS

Turning finally to external solutions, I want to comment briefly, first, on the role of the political entrepreneur in the solution of collective action problems and, second, on the claims made by a number of writers that certain collective action problems can be solved by establishing private property rights and by norms.

### Political Entrepreneurs

In what sense do political entrepreneurs or leaders "solve" collective action problems? In general, to solve or remove a collective action problem he or she must of course change individual preferences (or more generally attitudes), or change beliefs (including expectations), or inject resources (very probably knowledge, or new technology, like guns) into the group so as to make its members' efforts more productive.

Merely offering his services (working to obtain the public good) in exchange for support (subscriptions, food and shelter, or whatever) does not in itself constitute a distinctive solution to the problem. For, in the first place, the entrepreneur's services are themselves a public good, so that supporting him also gives rise to a collective action problem. This includes the case of the politician who in seeking electoral support offers his constituents legislative or other changes they favor. The collective action problem his potential supporters had in obtaining the public goods such changes would have brought them is replaced by the collective action problem of getting him elected. And, second, if the entrepreneur gains support by offering selective incentives, as well as by promising to work for the public good, then the solution is precisely the one proposed by Olson himself, in his "by-product" theory.[18]

17. *Collective Action*, p. 171.
18. The two points in this paragraph were first made by Brian Barry in *Sociologists, Economists and Democracy* (London: Collier-Macmillan, 1970), pp. 27–39.

In many interesting cases the political entrepreneur may require little or no support from the members of the group whose collective action problem is at issue, because he is supported by (that is, brings resources from) some external source. He might, for example, in his efforts to solve a *local* collective action problem, be supported by a pre-existing organization (the Communist Party, say, or the Catholic Church). This makes it easier to explain why the local problem is solved (for the members of the local group don't have to produce a "surplus" to pay or feed the entrepreneur), but it leaves unexplained (1) the production of the resources brought in by the political entrepreneur, which will usually entail that a prior collective action problem—for example the creation and maintenance of an organization—has been solved; and (2) how, even though the (local) group does not have to support the entrepreneur, it now manages to solve a collective action problem that it couldn't solve without him. If the only difference the entrepreneur makes is the addition of selective incentives to their benefits, then, once again, we don't have a distinctive solution.

But the political entrepreneur is not just "an innovator with selective incentives,"[19] or someone who simply concentrates or centralizes resources. What is perhaps more characteristic of political entrepreneurship is its role in changing beliefs—beliefs about the public good itself, about what others have done and are likely to do, and about others' beliefs. Above all, we must remember that most collective action must involve some form of conditional cooperation, for at a minimum an individual would not cooperate if *nobody* else did. Conditional cooperation, however, is a very precarious business. It requires amongst other things that the conditional cooperators have information about others' behavior. The required monitoring can be done by the political entrepreneur.

The entrepreneur can also try to persuade people that their contributions make a big enough difference, either directly or indirectly through their effect on others' behavior. The second of these might be achieved by persuading people that others' efforts are contingent on theirs.

An organization whose aim is to provide public goods for a very large group might be able to expand its membership and achieve its aims by having its cadres work to solve, through any or all of these entrepreneurial methods, smaller scale collective action problems for much smaller

19. Mancur Olson, *The Logic of Collective Action* (Cambridge: Harvard University Press, 1971 edition), Appendix, p. 177.

subgroups. A nationwide movement, for example, may be built upon the success of its cadres in solving local collective action problems and bringing tangible benefits quickly. Samuel Popkin has given an excellent account of activities of this sort in Vietnam, showing how four politico-religious movements (the Catholic Church, the Cao Dai, the Hoa Hao and the Communist Party) won support by having their cadres help the villages, both by providing selective incentives and by facilitating cooperation in the provision of public goods.[20] These private and public goods—with varying degrees of indivisibility and excludability—included the provision of educational opportunities; the creation of insurance and welfare systems; agricultural improvements; establishing stock-farm cooperatives; improvements in water storage and irrigation facilities; the creation of local courts to arbitrate disputes; and protection against French courts, marauding notables, and local landlords.

## Property Rights

Many economists, and nearly all those of the "property rights" school, believe that the solution to free-rider problems in public goods provision, and in particular those which would lead to the overexploitation of a "common property resource," lies in the establishment of private property rights. Without such rights, the argument goes, every individual has an incentive to intensify his use of the resource because although, with each increment in use, every unit of his (and everybody else's) input becomes slightly less productive, this is (up to a point) outweighed by the marginal return from the increased input. Intensifying use of the resource is continued up to the point where all the "rent" (income or other return) from the resource has been dissipated. Likewise, the benefits arising from any improvement or renewal or other investment he might make in the resource would be shared by all the users while the costs would be borne by the individual alone. There will therefore be overuse and underinvestment. With the establishment of private property rights, however, the external effects of each individual's actions are "internalized": *all* the costs of an increase in use of the resource are borne by the individual, as are all the benefits of investing in its conservation or improvement.

The argument that the "tragedy of the commons" is the fate of common property resources, and that overuse or underinvestment will be avoided only if common property rights are displaced by private prop-

20. Samuel L. Popkin, "Political Entrepreneurs and Peasant Movements in Vietnam," in *Rationality and Revolution*, edited by Michael Taylor (Cambridge: Cambridge University Press, 1987).

erty rights, seems to be positively mocked by the facts. The commons of the European open-field system, far from being tragically degraded, were generally maintained in good health during the whole of their lifetimes of many hundreds of years. There is a detailed study of a Swiss alpine village (not, of course, operating an open-field system) whose members have for more than five hundred years possessed and used in common various resources, including mountainside pastures, side by side with privately owned land and other resources, and during all this time the productivity of the common land has been maintained and much effort has been invested in its improvement.[21] Contrast with this the treatment, especially in recent decades, of much privately owned land by its very owners: the destruction of vast tracts of rain forest for the sake of a few profitable years of ranching; or the set of practices that are causing the loss of topsoil from cultivated land through wind and water erosion on such a scale that, according to a recent report, there will be a third less topsoil per person by the end of the century.[22] In parts of Africa, and elsewhere in the world, overexploitation of grazing lands has been caused not by common property arrangements *per se* but by their destruction or disruption.[23] There are, of course, perfectly good reasons why the rational private owner or user of a resource might knowingly destroy it; in particular, he might place a very low value on benefits to the derived from the resource in the distant as opposed to the immediate future.

Where do the property rights economists go wrong?[24] In the first place, many of them do not distinguish common property in a resource from *open access* to it. "Communal rights," say Alchian and Demsetz, ". . . means that the use of a scarce resource is determined on a first-come, first-serve basis and persists for as long as a person continues to use the

21. Robert McC. Netting, *Balancing on an Alp: Ecological Change in a Swiss Mountain Community* (Cambridge: Cambridge University Press, 1981), especially chapter 3.

22. Lester Brown and Edward Wolf, *Soil Erosion: Quiet Crisis in the World Economy* (Washington, D.C.: Worldwatch Institute, 1984). According to this report, U.S. farms are losing topsoil at the rate of 1.7 billion tonnes a year. *The New York Times* (December 10, 1985) reports that the U.S. Congress looks set to vote to pay farmers to stop farming up to 40 million acres of the worst affected land.

23. See, for example, Michael H. Glantz, ed., *Desertification: Environmental Degradation In and Around Arid Lands* (Boulder, Colorado: Westview Press, 1977).

24. The following comments, which are critical of the property rights school's treatment of the "tragedy of the commons," do not imply a wholesale rejection on my part of the property rights approach.

resource." [25] This is wrong, or at least an abuse of language. If there is open access, then nobody is excluded from using the resource and there is no regulation of the activities of those who do use it. But if there is common ownership or collective control of the resource, then the members of the collectivity, whatever it is, can regulate its use. This is what happened in the European open-field system, where the villagers rigorously excluded outsiders from use of the various commons they owned or possessed collectively and carefully regulated insiders' use, typically by allotting to individuals "stints" in proportion to their (privately owned) arable holdings and punishing people for infringements. The alpine community described by Netting similarly practiced strict external and internal regulation of its commons. So too have countless "primitive" collectivities and peasant villages all over the world.

It is to resources with open access, not to "common property resources," that the property rights economists' argument about overexploitation and underinvestment applies. It is not a matter of establishing the right sort of property rights, of moving from collective to private property rights. It is rather a matter (at this stage of the argument at least) of establishing property rights where there were none; for property entails exclusion, so that where there is open access to a resource, there is no property in it. [26]

The property rights economists tend to see only two or three possibilities: open access and private property, to which is sometimes added state ownership. But almost any group of individuals can own or possess property collectively. Historical and contemporary examples are: a family; a wider kin group, such as a matrilineage; all those in a village who also possess land privately; a band; an ethnic group. Where the property rights economists do notice common property rights, they then argue that the costs of negotiating agreements regulating use and, if agreements are forthcoming, the costs of policing them, will be very great, and in this respect, common property rights compare unfavorably with private property rights. [27] But there is no necessary reason why transaction costs of all kinds should in total be greater in the case of common property

25. A. A. Alchian and Harold Demsetz, "The Property Rights Paradigm," *Journal of Economic History* 33 (1973): 16–27.

26. See S. V. Ciriacy-Wantrup and Richard C. Bishop, "'Common property' as a Concept in Natural Resources Policy," *Natural Resources Journal* 15 (1975): 713–27.

27. See, for example, Harold Demsetz, "Toward a Theory of Property Rights," *American Economic Review* (Papers and Proceedings) 57 (1967): 347–59.

rights than in the case of private property rights—and in the case of the open-field system it was in fact the other way round, essentially because of economies of scale in pastoral production.[28]

Finally, the property rights economists, having generally failed to notice common property (as opposed to open access) and to study how individual rights in it are guaranteed, tend to assume that property rights must be enforced by the state.[29] But there can also be decentralized enforcement or maintenance of property rights—both private and common. (The sense of "decentralized" intended here is the same as that used in the general remarks made earlier on the solution of collective action problems.) If a collectivity itself is to enforce its members' private property rights or their rights to use the common property, then it must of course be able to wield effective sanctions—unless the property rights are respected as a result of "spontaneous" conditional cooperation. If the collectivity is a community, then, as we have seen, conditions are conducive to conditional cooperation, and if this fails the community's members have at their disposal a range of effective sanctions. The joint owners of the commons in European open-field villages, for example, were communities in the required sense.

Enough has now been said, I think, to show that, insofar as the solution of collective action problems is concerned, nothing new is added by the introduction of property rights *per se*. An individual has property in something only if others forbear from using it, and the forbearance is the result of the threat or offer of *sanctions*, centralized or decentralized (or of conditional cooperation—unless this be reckoned also to involve threats and offers). It is the threats and offers of sanctions (and/or conditional cooperation) that is solving the collective action problem, if it is solved at all. Furthermore, as I remarked in an earlier section, the use of some of these sanctions presupposes the solution to prior collective action problems (for example, the formation and maintenance of a state!).

## Norms

There is, finally, the suggestion that norms solve collective action problems. I'll comment on this very briefly, for my reaction to it is similar to my view of the suggestion that the introduction of private property rights

28. Carl J. Dahlman, *The Open Field System and Beyond* (Cambridge: Cambridge University Press, 1980).

29. See, for example, Eirik G. Furobotn and Svetozar Pejovich, "Property Rights and Economic Theory: A Survey of Recent Literature," *Journal of Economic Literature* 10 (1972): 1137–62.

solves collective action problems, and both follow from the general remarks about solutions to these problems made in an earlier section (though I shall not argue, as some have done, that property rights *are* norms). The view that norms solve collective action problems—or more precisely that they solve, amongst other things, the problems inherent in "generalized PD-structured situations" and coordination problems—has been expounded by Edna Ullman-Margalit.[30] I shall take it that a norm is generally conformed to and is such that nonconformity, when observed, is generally punished. It's unclear whether this is what Ullman-Margalit means by a norm, but in any case it is fairly clear from her discussion of "PD norms" that it is only "a norm, *backed by sanctions*" or "a norm . . . *supported by sufficiently severe sanctions*" that is capable of solving Prisoners' Dilemma problems.[31] So norms alone—mere prescriptions for action that people generally conform to—do *not* solve these problems.

If a norm is generally observed simply because it pays the individual to do so (in the absence of sanctions), then there is no (collective action or other) "problem" to be solved in the first place. This would be the case if the norm had been "internalized." I take this expression to indicate that conformity to the norm does not require the application of external sanctions, inducements or any other considerations; as a result of the norm's being internalized, the individual *prefers* to conform (without the threat of punishment) or at least has some sort of motivational disposition to do so. But then, as I say, we wouldn't say that there was a Prisoners' Dilemma or collective action "problem" to be solved: the individual preferences would not be those of a Prisoners' Dilemma or would not be such as to lead to a collective action problem. Of course, we might nevertheless wish to explain how the norm came to be internalized or how people came to have such preferences.

If, on the other hand, a norm is generally observed because nonconformity, when noticed, is generally punished, then it's the sanctions that are doing the real work of solving the Prisoners' Dilemma or collective action problem. The sanction system can of course be centralized or de-

---

30. Edna Ullman-Margalit, *The Emergence of Norms* (Oxford: Clarendon Press, 1977). A "generalized PD-structured situation . . . is one in which the dilemma faced by the . . . participants is recurrent, or even continuous" (p. 24); but Ullman-Margalit gives no analysis of iterated games nor takes any account of their distinctive problems (so, amongst other things, does not see that cooperation in these situations can occur *without* norms enforced by sanctions). Incidentally, very little of this book actually deals with the emergence of norms; it is mainly taken up with generally informal discussion of some very simple games.

31. *The Emergence of Norms*, pp. 22 and 28; my emphasis.

centralized, in the way discussed in an earlier section. And again, it remains to be explained how the system of sanctions itself came into being and is maintained. To this problem, the general point made earlier about sanction systems applies: the maintenance of a system of sanctions itself constitutes or presupposes the solution of another collective action problem. Punishing someone who does not conform to a norm—punishing someone for being a free-rider on the efforts of others to provide a public good, for example—is itself a public good for the group in question, and everyone would prefer others to do this unpleasant job. Thus, the "solution" of collective action problems by norms presupposes the prior or concurrent solution of another collective action problem. And as my earlier remarks make clear, this would still be the case if the sanctions were wielded by the state or by a political entrepreneur.[32]

COMMENT: *On the Inadequacy of Game Theory for the Solution of Real-World Collective Action Problems*[1]
## Michael Hechter

Collective action problems exist whenever rational individual action can lead to a strictly Pareto-inefficient outcome. Michael Taylor argues that there are two types of solutions to these problems. The first of these, which he terms the internal solution, emerges spontaneously and endogenously among the parties to interaction. It is sustained by the action of each player. The second, external, solution is sustained by the force of formal third-party controls that provide mechanisms for monitoring and sanctioning. This third party, in turn, can vary from a single centralized ruler (such as an absolute monarch) at one extreme all the way to the members of a group or community at the other.

For Taylor, the basic solution to collective action problems is the internal one. It owes its pride of place to the fact that it is the only kind of solution that is endogenous, namely, complete in and of itself. This is in marked contrast to the external solutions, which presuppose the prior and/or concurrent solution of second-order collective action problems. Since (by definition) internal solutions depend upon fewer assumptions than external ones, they are always to be preferred. I have no quarrel with his argument on this point. Yet the real message of his paper lies elsewhere. Taylor implies that an acceptable internal solution to collec-

32. I have neglected here the role of normative *beliefs* in solving collective action problems. This complex subject deserves a separate treatment. I hope to publish one soon.
1. I am grateful to Debra Friedman, Edgar Kiser, and Werner Raub for their comments.

tive action problems already exists and that this solution derives from his version of the theory of repeated games. About this conclusion I remain skeptical.

Those writers, like Taylor, who see a solution to real-world collective action problems in the application of repeated game theory usually base their optimism on analyses of the Prisoners' Dilemma supergame.[2] To my mind, however, the theory of repeated games has as yet yielded precious *little* in the way of solutions to such collective action problems. The inadequacy of repeated game theory, in this respect, is due to the existence of multiple equilibria in the supergame, on the one hand, and to the assumption that players are endowed with perfect information, on the other. I will try to indicate that neither of these difficulties has been satisfactorily resolved in the theory of repeated games. Finally, I will suggest that a better understanding of the solution of collective action problems may be found in an entirely different direction.

## Problems in Repeated Game Theory

Consider the original structure of the Prisoners' Dilemma supergame. This takes $G$ to be an $N$-person game in strategic form. Two strong assumptions then are made: the games are *infinitely repeated* and the players have *perfect information*. What is meant by infinite repetition? If $G$ is one play of the supergame $G^*$, then $G^*$ consists of an infinite sequence of plays of $G$. What is meant by perfect information? At the end of each stage (that is, a particular play of $G$ in the sequence of $G^*$), each player is informed of the strategy chosen by all other players at this stage. Thus the information available to a player when choosing her strategy for a particular stage consists of the strategies used by all players at all previous stages. Under these particular conditions, the following result, known as the Folk Theorem of repeated game theory, obtains: "*The Folk Theorem:* The payoff vectors to Nash equilibrium points in the supergame $G^*$ are the feasible individual rational payoffs in the game $G$" (Aumann 1985, 210–11).[3] One of these Nash equilibria occurs when the players engage in the strategy of conditional cooperation, or tit-for-tat. Since the repetition itself, with its possibilities for retaliation, is the en-

---

2. To be sure, this is not the only relevant game, as Taylor indicates. Games with different structures—like Chicken and the Assurance game—provide different outcomes than the Prisoners' Dilemma. There is, of course, a sense in which the very structure of the game is an equilibrium that requires explanation in its own right.

3. The words *feasible* and *individually rational* have technical definitions that need not detain us here. For elaboration, see Aumann (1985).

dogenous enforcement mechanism, the players have no need to rely upon any third-party controls.

Is this the internal solution to the collective action problem for which we have all been searching? Not at all. The enthusiasm with which some have greeted this result must be severely tempered for two reasons.

## MULTIPLE EQUILIBRIA

Under the strong assumptions that yield the Folk Theorem, it so happens that there is "a bewildering wealth" (Aumann 1985, 214) of equilibrium payoffs. Since some of these equilibria are Pareto-inefficient, it is obvious that these do *not* resolve the collective action problem. How do we know when a Pareto-efficient equilibrium will be realized as against an inefficient one? There is no good answer to this question. Yet even if there were, and we could, on this account, thereby confine our attention solely to the set of multiple efficient equilibria, this too would not suffice to resolve the collective action problem. There would still be a problem because the preferences of the players with respect to these efficient equilibria might not coincide, and, consequently, they would face a noncooperative bargaining problem (Harsanyi 1977, 128–30). The Folk Theorem, therefore, has a most significant implication. Whereas solutions to collective action problems *can* emerge from such repeated games, it is by no means clear that they *will* emerge.

Many of the recent developments in the theory of repeated games are attempts to reduce the vast indeterminacy produced by the Folk Theorem. One way in which the indeterminacy of the Folk Theorem can be narrowed is by altering one of the initial assumptions about the supergame structure: that which requires each player to engage in infinitely repeated games. Although this assumption appeared necessary in order to avoid spiraling terminal effects, it seems highly unrealistic. Why would rational players in the real world always commit themselves to participate in any given interaction indefinitely?

The assumption of infinite replay can be replaced by the introduction of a discount rate. If the players' decisions to stay in the game are solely a function of the expected value of all future payoffs, then the higher this discount rate is, the less the expected value of future payoffs. Hence the discount rate may be interpreted as a stop probability, a measure of impatience, or both. The higher the discount rate, then, the higher the probability of leaving the game. Thus Taylor asserts that at *some* (not too large) positive discount rate in repeated games of indefinite length, there will be a unique efficient equilibrium (p. 228).

Even if fiddling with the discount rate does reduce the probability of attaining inefficient equilibria, however, there is something questionable about the procedure. How do we know what discount rate to select for our supergame? It is, of course, sometimes possible to select exactly that rate which yields a unique efficient equilibrium (when such a rate exists). Yet the game theorist's assumption of *any* specific, positive discount rate is alarmingly ad hoc in these analyses.[4] This move is strikingly akin to the economists' arbitrary selection of some attitude toward risk in their models when they readily admit to having no theory of risk-preference. In what way can an internal solution to the collective action problem rely upon such a gratuitously *exogenous* assumption?

Whereas all theories are built on the basis of some assumptions, there is little point in making the kinds of assumptions that foreordain the desired outcome—in this case a unique Pareto-efficient equilibrium. This results in a pretty thin performance, rather, as Brian Barry (1977, 279) once put it in a different context, "like a conjurer putting a rabbit in a hat, taking it out again and expecting a round of applause."

Although the assumption of discounting eliminates some inefficiency in the set of equilibria, it fails to eliminate the ultimate inefficient outcome—the payoffs to a strategy of mutual defection (Aumann 1985, 217–18). Manipulating the rate of discount, then, does not do away with the indeterminacy resulting from the Folk Theorem—the existence of multiple equilibria (both inefficient and efficient) in the supergame.

## THE PROBLEM OF IMPERFECT INFORMATION

Yet the assumption of perfect information raises an issue that is more damaging by far. Were this assumption realistic, then real-world participants in collective action dilemmas would have *zero monitoring costs*. Whereas the introduction of discount rates into supergames increases the likelihood of attaining Pareto-efficient equilibria, the opposite occurs when the assumption of perfect information is relaxed. If the players have zero monitoring costs, then there is a much greater chance that they can reach a cooperative equilibrium. By the same token, to the degree

---

4. Whereas the assumption of a positive discount and rate happens to be consistent with the bulk of quantitative behavioral research on the diminution of the efficacy of rewards with delay, this same evidence suggests, however, that the size of this positive discount rate is extremely *high*, rather than low (Renner 1964). The findings in this behavioral research, which seldom appear in the game-theoretic literature, therefore cast further doubt on the repeated game approach to collective action.

that monitoring costs are positive, the probability of attaining a cooperative equilibrium decreases significantly.

To engage rationally in conditional cooperation, or tit-for-tat, one must be confident in one's estimate of the other party's future intentions. Past behavior is as good an indication of this as any, but information about past behavior can only come from previous monitoring activity. Intuitively, it is easy to appreciate that the larger the number of players, the more costly this monitoring will be. It is one thing to argue that A can trust B only if A knows that he will have an opportunity to punish B whenever his expectation that B will cooperate proves unfounded. For this kind of logic to account for cooperation in large groups, every member of the group must have this kind of detailed information about every other member.[5] But, except in the case of the smallest groups, it is impossible for each member to have direct knowledge about the past behavior of every other member, or even about a group of players who might be capable of forming a conditionally cooperative coalition (Schofield 1985). This intuitive reasoning is also supported by mathematical analysis (Bendor and Mookherjee 1987; Boyd and Richerson 1988).

Further, it turns out that the consequences of imperfect monitoring appear to be significant *even in the case of two-person games*. In so-called principal-agent games—games with one-sided imperfect monitoring—efficient outcomes can be closely approximated by equilibria for low discount rates. But one can also design games that more closely resemble real-world collective action problems, such as repeated partnership games with two-sided imperfect monitoring and with positive discount rates. What kinds of equilibria are produced in these more realistic games? The answer is disconcerting: here too there are multiple equilibria, and at least in the case of one such game *all of these equilibria are inefficient* (Radner, Myerson, and Maskin 1986). What this indicates is that the more that game theorists attempt to model real-world collective action problems (where monitoring costs tend to be very high indeed), the less adequate the internal solutions to these problems appear to be.

Due to the problems of multiple equilibria and of imperfect information, therefore, repeated game theorists have not yet been able to provide

5. Of course, the monitoring problem would be less severe if players adopted a rule such as, "cooperate as long as all others cooperate. If someone defects, defect yourself on all later stages." Whereas the adoption of this rule would imply less severe monitoring costs in large groups, it would also make collective action a less probable outcome.

a robust basis for the solution of collective action problems.[6] Whether they will ever be able to do so must be regarded as an open question at this juncture. The record of the last decade's research efforts in this regard does not inspire much optimism. At any rate, this record certainly does not seem to warrant Taylor's main conclusion.

## A Modest Proposal

How, then, shall we proceed? If, as I have argued, the pure internal solution is unavailable, perhaps we should consider the alternative. External, or contractarian, solutions—those that depend upon some planned enforcement mechanism—may deserve greater emphasis, but only if we are able to account for their evolution on the basis of rational choice premises. It is undeniable that collective action problems sometimes *do* get solved by real-world agents. How can these individuals manage to arrive at Pareto-efficient equilibrium solutions to their collective dilemmas? Insight into this process can only come from the observation of people's actual behavior in the field.

Before proceeding down this admittedly untidy trail, however, we must be careful not to take too much social structure for granted in our explanations. There can be no justification for assuming, as Taylor (1982) has done, the existence of something like "community," which can conveniently serve as a *deus ex machina*—that is, the very third-party enforcer of Pareto-efficient equilibria that we are setting out to explain. For insofar as this kind of community maintains social order by providing *formal controls* (that is, by monitoring and sanctioning potential free-riders and deviants), it represents a solution to a second-order collective action problem and, as such, requires explanation on rational choice grounds.

Instead, we must look into how such formal controls can arise in the absence of pre-existing social structures that have already solved a large part of the collective action problem. In other words, *the task is to find a path from internal solutions of the collective action problem to external ones.* (This is exactly what Hobbes had set out to do in *Leviathan,* but his ignorance of the free-rider dilemma condemned him to failure.)

Individuals (or, more realistically, individual nuclear families) in a state of nature are wont to contemplate collective action in order to provide

---

6. Note that the likelihood of attaining efficient equilibria in the theory of dynamic games is surely lower than it is in the theory of *repeated* games.

themselves with jointly produced goods (hereafter, joint goods) that either cannot be supplied at all by their individual efforts or cannot efficiently be supplied by this means. Production and distribution of the joint good, however, requires the enactment of rules, and the attainment of compliance with these rules requires the establishment of formal controls.

Yet since controls are themselves a collective good, their establishment has been difficult to explain from choice-theoretic premises. It is possible, however, to devise an endogenous explanation for the rise of such controls from rational choice premises given that production and distribution of the joint good occur with high *visibility* (see Hechter 1989). Their establishment may be seen as a series of solutions to a three-tier free-rider problem involving (1) the formulation of a plan to procure and distribute some demanded joint good, (2) the establishment of an initial group constitution that permits these agents to reach collective decisions, and (3) the implementation of the agreed-upon plan of action.

For a good to be maximally excludable, the individual's role in both its production and its distribution must be highly visible. In the absence of visibility, neither free-riding (a production problem) nor overconsumption (a distribution problem) can be precluded. Production visibility is at a maximum when individual effort can be well measured by output assessment. Distribution visibility, however, is at a maximum when individuals must draw measurable shares of a joint good publically from some central store or repository.

Most of the positive externalities of groups that promote cooperative welfare rest on the advantages of pooling individual assets so that a common central store, or bank, is thereby established. The individual depositor expects to draw some net private benefit from this central store. Thus, in rotating credit associations (Ardener 1962; Geertz 1962), individuals pool a given amount of money for the right to draw upon the common store of money to increase their purchasing power. In this way the monetary contributions of individual participants generate a credit line, access to which is highly visible to all other participants (Hechter 1987, chapter 6).

Once individual assets are pooled in a central place, however, another free-rider problem occurs: how is it possible to stop a depositor from taking more than her fair share or from consuming the entire fund? This is a question that faces all rational investors—would you be likely to deposit your paycheck in a bank that you believe soon will be robbed? Presumably, only if you had some assurance that your deposit is secure.

*Hence it is rational for individuals to establish formal controls in cooperative institutions so as to preserve the integrity of their investment* (which, after all, is a quintessentially private good). By establishing these controls, individuals inadvertently provide themselves with a collective good—namely, security of the common fund.

The driving force in this explanation of the origin of formal controls lies in the individual's desire to consume goods that can only be produced jointly and, therefore, that induce these individuals to enter into cooperative social relations. No doubt, the character of the social context plays an important role in determining the demand for these particular goods. The inhabitants of territories where security is problematic are likely to desire security; those who live through drastic fluctuations in climatic conditions are likely to desire insurance, those who live in capital-poor environments demand credit, and so forth.

The demand for these joint goods enables otherwise unconnected individuals to identify a course of action that their expectations of each other can converge on. Linked by their common interest in consuming some joint good, these individuals are, however, reluctant to invest their own time and other assets in cooperative efforts in the absence of an agreed-upon enforcement mechanism, for they want to be assured that their investment will yield a positive return. This assurance can only be provided if it is expected that free-riding will be deterred. Hence, in order to consume these joint goods, individuals must create their own controls.

The essential determinant of the rise of controls lies in conditions allowing for visibility in both the production and consumption of given joint goods. In relatively noninstitutionalized environments, this visibility will be at a maximum when joint goods are collected and dispersed from some central place.

The decision to abscond with the central fund is akin to defection in the game setting, and, as such, it must be regarded as the dominant strategy. The contractarian solution to this problem is the establishment of some agreed-upon enforcement mechanism—that is, formal controls. Does this explanation not assume some iteration of the game setting? And, if so, then how does it differ from one that is based *entirely* on repeated game theory? The principal differences are these.

In the first place, entry into and exit from iterated games—or into social structures that guarantee iterations, like village communities—are decisions that must be treated endogenously in any complete explanation of collective action. The great bulk of ethnographic evidence about simple horticultural societies suggests that, while resources are plentiful, nuclear families prefer to reside in isolation rather than subjecting themselves to the controls that are inherent in small communities (Johnson and Earle 1987). Invoking iteration as a given in collective action is the repeated game theorists' version of the economists' infamous "assume the can opener" ploy—it works, but it takes too much pre-existing social structure for granted. In my example, the players will not even consent to *enter* the game (that is, contribute their private resources for the production of a joint good)—let alone subject themselves to repeated plays of the game—in the absence of the assurance provided them by the establishment of formal controls.

In the second place, iteration may be necessary, but it is also insufficient to ensure collective action. Even in an iterative social context, such as the traditional village community, people seek to raise the costs of defection, and they institute formal controls as a means of doing so. Only by establishing formal controls can the small numbers of problems of game-theoretic solutions be overcome.

There is no necessary conflict between internal and external explanations of collective action. These two types of solutions should be regarded as complements rather than substitutes. As James Buchanan (1988,342) notes,

> viable social order depends on both those institutions that embody reciprocally cooperative behavior on the parts of interacting individuals and those institutions that reflect constructed constraints that effectively prevent noncooperating deviants from exploiting those who do adhere to the social norms, and beyond that on the constructed constraints that come about even before the norms of reciprocity emerge in the beginning.

We must not forget what is at stake in the problem of collective action: issues of vital concern in human history and in social science, including the formation of social institutions and the dynamics of revolution and nationalism. The chasm between these substantive issues and game-theoretic analyses seems no less wide today, after a long period of intense research effort, than it was more than a decade ago. The utility of game theory, in this respect, must not be judged solely by the mathematical elegance of its solutions, but by its capacity to shed light on these real-world collective action problems.

# REFERENCES

Ardener, Shirley. 1962. "The Comparative Study of Rotating Credit Associations," *Journal of the Royal Anthropological Institute of Great Britain and Ireland* 94 (2): 201–29.

Aumann, Robert J. 1985. "Repeated Games." In *Issues in Contemporary Microeconomics and Welfare,* edited by George R. Feiwel, 209–42. Albany, NY: State University of New York Press.

Barry, Brian. 1977. "Justice Between Generations." In *Law, Morality and Society,* edited by P. M. S. Hacker and J. Raz, 268–84. Oxford: Clarendon Press.

Bendor, Jonathan, and Dilip Mookherjee. 1987. "Institutional Structure and the Logic of Ongoing Collective Action." *American Political Science Review* 81 (1): 129–54.

Boyd, Robert, and Peter J. Richerson. 1988. "The Evolution of Reciprocity in Sizable Groups." *Journal of Theoretical Biology* 132: 337–56.

Buchanan, James M. 1988. "Review of R. Sugden's *The Economics of Rights, Cooperation and Welfare.*" *Economics and Philosophy* 4: 341–42.

Geertz, Clifford. 1962. "The Rotating Credit Association: A 'Middle Ring' in Development." *Economic Development and Cultural Change* 10 (3): 243–63.

Harsanyi, John C. 1977. *Rational Behavior and Bargaining Equilibrium in Games and Social Situations.* New York: Cambridge University Press.

Hechter, Michael. 1989. "The Emergence of Cooperative Social Institutions." In *Social Institutions: Their Emergence, Maintenance and Effects,* edited by Michael Hechter, Karl-Dieter Opp, and Reinhard Wippler. New York: Aldine de Gruyter.

———. 1987. *Principles of Group Solidarity.* Berkeley and London: University of California Press.

Johnson, Allen W., and Timothy Earle. 1987. *The Evolution of Human Societies: From Foraging Group to Agrarian State.* Stanford, CA: Stanford University Press.

Radner, Roy, Roger Myerson, and Eric Maskin. 1986. "An Example of a Repeated Partnership Game with Discounting and with Uniformly Inefficient Equilibria." *Review of Economic Studies* 53: 59–69.

Renner, K. E. 1964. "Delay of Reinforcement: A Historical Review." *Psychological Bulletin* 61: 341–61.

Schofield, Norman. 1985. "Anarchy, Altruism, and Cooperation." *Social Choice and Welfare* 2 (3): 207–19.

Taylor, Michael. 1982. *Community, Anarchy, and Liberty.* Cambridge: Cambridge University Press.

# 7

# Norm-Generating Structures

## James S. Coleman

Recent work involving populations of strategic actors in interaction provides a tool for examining the conditions for emergence of norms in a social system. In this paper, I use this tool to examine the effects of variations in social structure on the emergence of behavior patterns that could be said to obey a norm.

I will begin with some clarifying definitions. By the term *norm* I will mean only a circumscribed portion of what is ordinarily referred to by this term. I will mean the prescription or proscription of an action—with the prescription or proscription agreed upon by members of a social system—when the action that is prescribed is not in the interests of the actor to carry out, or the action that is proscribed is in the interests of the actor to carry out. That is, the norm opposes the actor's own interests, either directing him toward doing something he would not otherwise want to do or toward not doing something he would otherwise want to do. The action that is subject to the norm I will call the *focal* action.

Although norms may be imposed either by internal sanctions or by external sanctions or both, I will not address here the processes internal to the individual that impose sanctions on his own actions in the absence of any expectation of external sanctions. The examination in this paper will be limited to external sanctions.

One class of norms consists of those that are imposed on one set of persons (the *beneficiaries* of the norm) by another set (the *targets* of the norm), such as norms held by parents for the behavior of children. Another class consists of norms in which the set of persons who impose the norm, the beneficiaries, is the same as the set of persons to whose action the norm is directed, the targets. The norm of honesty held by members of a social system for one another exemplifies such a norm. The set of beneficiaries coincides with the set of targets.

A final element in the definition of what I will examine here is a terminological convention. Although I will use both the term "norm" and the term "sanction," I will mean by "norm" nothing more than the set of sanctions that act to direct the behavior in question. I will use the term "sanction" to refer to a single instance of this, that is an action which, if effective, guides the focal action.

Without justification, I will state some general points concerning the conditions for the emergence of norms. (Justification can be found in Coleman 1990.) These conditions can be usefully divided into the conditions under which there is a demand for the norm by a set of potential beneficiaries of the norm and the conditions under which the demand is supplied by effective sanctions.

The demand for a norm will arise when an action by one actor imposes externalities on other actors. When the externalities are positive, the demand is for a prescriptive norm, to encourage or induce the focal action. When the externalities are negative, the demand is for a proscriptive norm, to discourage the focal action.[1] If there are only two alternative choices for the actor who would be the target of the norm, then the distinction between a prescriptive norm and a proscriptive norm vanishes. In that case, the same norm which encourages one action must discourage the other. In the work to be reported here, I will treat this case. The set of potential holders of the norm, identical to the set of potential sanctioners, consists of all those actors who experience the externalities imposed by the focal action.

The conditions under which the demand for a norm will be met by effective sanctions concern the expected costs and benefits to the potential sanctioner or sanctioners of applying an effective sanction. The benefits of a sanction lie in its effect on future actions of the target of the sanction. The future actions depend on his expectation that the interaction will be with an individual by whom he has already been sanctioned. This expectation in turn depends upon the social structure of interaction, which I assume here to be exogenous. I assume that a focal action cannot be sanctioned in the current interaction, but can be sanctioned in a subsequent interaction.

With this as the general background, I want to examine in this paper the effect of variations in social structure on the effectiveness of sanctions in guiding a focal action. This examination is based on work involving populations of strategic actors in interaction.

---

1. A special case is that in which the same action imposes positive externalities on one set of actors and negative externalities on another set. Then two conflicting norms for the same target action may arise. I will not deal with that case here.

## Populations of Strategic Actors in Interaction

A biologist, John Maynard Smith, has observed the nondestructive actions used in intraspecies animal conflict and has attempted to show how such nondestructive strategies would have survival value in an evolutionary sense, even though they had a greater than even chance of losing in confrontation with a more destructive strategy. Maynard Smith developed the concept of "evolutionarily stable strategy," a strategy such that, if it is in use in a population of individuals, the population cannot be successfully invaded by a mutant using a different strategy. Maynard Smith and Price (1973) showed that in a particular setting there was an evolutionarily stable strategy that was neither the most submissive nor the most destructive. Certain submissive strategies could be successfully invaded (that is, killed off) by mutants with a destructive strategy, but as those mutants multiplied, they would in turn kill each other off and because of their low level of survival, could be successfully invaded by mutants with a strategy which could defend fairly successfully against the destructive strategy but in interaction with one another had a higher survival rate. This last strategy could not, in turn, be successfully invaded by any other strategies among those specified by Maynard Smith and Price. Robert Axelrod (1984) added to the concept of evolutionary stability the concepts of viability (the ability of a strategy to invade a population in which another strategy is in use) and robustness (the ability to maintain itself in a variegated population consisting of several different strategies).

Axelrod employed an innovative device for exploring the success of various strategies by carrying out two computer-assisted tournaments in which each of a number of strategies for an iterated prisoner's dilemma submitted by various game theorists, computer scientists, and social scientists were pitted against each other. Axelrod (1984) used the results of the computer tournaments and the notions of evolutionary stability to study the problem of how cooperation could evolve in a game structure (the iterated prisoner's dilemma) that allowed cooperative behavior, but provided greater rewards for exploitative behavior so long as the exploitation did not bring about retaliation.

In the prisoner's dilemma, there are two players, each with two alternative actions, which can be termed "cooperate" and "defect." If both cooperate, both receive a medium level of reward that is higher for each than if both defect. But if player 1 cooperates and player 2 defects, player 2 receives an even higher reward than for cooperation (he is "exploiting"

**Table 7.1** Prisoner's Dilemma Payoff Matrix

|  |  | Player 2 | | Player 2 | |
|  |  | Cooperate | Defect | Cooperate | Defect |
|---|---|---|---|---|---|
|  | Cooperate | 0, 0 | −2, 1 | $p_1, r_1$ | $p_2, r_3$ |
| Player |  |  |  |  |  |
|  | Defect | 1, −2 | −1, −1 | $p_3, r_2$ | $p_4, r_4$ |
|  |  | (a) | | (b) | |

the other), while player 1 receives a reward (sometimes termed the "sucker's payoff") even lower than that in which both defect.

A game matrix which fits the above description is given in table 7.1, where the first number in each cell is the reward to player 1 and the second is the reward to player 2. The left-hand matrix shows numbers and the right-hand matrix shows the general payoff structure, where $p_3 > p_1 > p_4 > p_2$ and $r_3 > r_1 > r_4 > r_2$. Inspection of the reward structure shows that whatever player 2 does, cooperate or defect, player 1 is better off defecting. Because the game is symmetric, this is true for player 2 as well. Whatever player 1 does, player 2 is better off defecting. For both players the defect action can be said to *dominate* the cooperate action, since it is superior to cooperation, independently of the other's action.

For this reason, the only rational action on the part of the two players is to defect, leading to the outcome (defect, defect). This has been regarded as paradoxical, for both players would prefer a (cooperate, cooperate) outcome. Yet it is clear that for a single play of the prisoner's dilemma (defect, defect) is the only outcome consistent with individual rationality.

The matter is different when the same players play more than once in an iterated prisoner's dilemma. For if either player can induce the other to make his action contingent on his own, then it may be rational to make his own action contingent on that of the other.[2] It is this which makes the iterated prisoner's dilemma a different game than the single-play prisoner's dilemma. And it is this which allows the emergence of

2. The Nash equilibrum in a predetermined number of plays is always to defect. Following Luce and Raiffa (1957), if the iterated prisoner's dilemma has a predetermined number of plays, it is rational to defect on all iterations, since on the last play the only rational action is to defect, and if this is so, it implies that the same is true for the next-to-last play, and so on back to the beginning. However, Kreps et al. (1982) have introduced the concept of sequential equilibrium, which depends upon each player no longer assuming with certainty that the other is playing the Nash strategy. Kreps et al. show that this incomplete information can lead rational players to engage in substantial cooperation.

strategies other than the defect strategy that is dominant in the single-play game.[3]

## THE EMERGENCE OF NORMS WITH SANCTIONS

The body of work described above, involving populations of strategic actors in interaction over time, with the particular reward structure provided by an iterated prisoner's dilemma, can be extended to examine the conditions under which effective norms (enforced by sanctions) will emerge. Axelrod (1984) discusses the importance of repeated interactions with the same individual in the emergence of cooperation: "The basic idea is that an individual must not be able to get away with defecting without the other individuals being able to retaliate effectively. The response requires that the defecting individual not be lost in a sea of anonymous others. Higher organisms avoid this problem by their well-developed ability to recognize many different individuals of their species. The other important requirement is that the probability, $w$, of the same two individuals meeting again must be sufficiently high" (p. 100).

It is this "social structure of interaction" that is of interest for the emergence of effective norms. In particular, certain structures of interaction bring an individual face to face with the same individual over a whole sequence of interactions, while in others, there is a very low probability that one will interact with the same individual in the near future.

The first step in using the iterated prisoner's dilemma for exploring the conditions under which effective norms arise is to examine how well the actions taken in the prisoner's dilemma fit the criteria specified earlier for the demand for norms. Does taking one or the other action impose an externality on the other?

The answer is that it does. In the reward structure of part (a) of table 7.1, a cooperative action on the part of actor 1 rather than a defect action

3. In the iterated prisoner's dilemma the payoffs must be such that $p_2 + p_3 < 2p_1$, and $r_2 + r_3 < 2r_1$, if the (cooperate, cooperate) outcome is to be better for both players than an alternation of (cooperate, defect) and (defect, cooperate). If evolution of strategies is assumed (or learning), then if these inequalities do not hold, the joint alternating strategies can be assumed to emerge. This would not allow evolution of strategies which attempt to induce cooperation from the other, but hold the threat of retaliation if the other defects instead. Perhaps the simplest such strategy is a tit-for-tat strategy (the strategy that gave the highest total scores in both of Axelrod's computer tournaments), which cooperates until the other defects, but follows each defection of the other with a defection. The major reason for the success of this simple strategy compared to more complex strategies probably lies in the minimal level of communication possible in the iterated prisoner's dilemma, which restricts the information that can be extracted from the other's play.

improves actor 2's rewards by two points (at a cost of one point to himself), and actor's 2's action does the same for actor 1. Thus each has an incentive to induce a cooperative action on the part of the other.

The prisoner's dilemma fits the normative structure in which the set of beneficiaries of the norm coincides with the set of targets of the norm. Defection in the prisoner's dilemma game is equivalent to disobeying a norm, while cooperation is equivalent to obeying the norm. Each of the two players is a beneficiary of the norm, for each would benefit by inducing the other to obey the norm (that is, act cooperatively), and each is a target of the norm, for each carries out the focal action.

There are, however, three special properties of the iterated prisoner's dilemma that narrow the class of norm-generating structures that it can simulate. The most serious limitation is that in a prisoner's dilemma, each player's action imposes externalities only on one other, since these are two-person interactions. Thus it cannot mirror situations in which the focal action imposes externalities on a number of others, but benefits the actor sufficiently that an effective sanction is too costly for any one potential norm beneficiary, though not too costly for each if all the potential beneficiaries shared the cost. This brings about what has been called a "second-order" free-rider problem, since no potential beneficiary is motivated to apply an effective sanction.

This limitation makes the iterated prisoner's dilemma irrelevant for a large class of actions for which norms sometimes arise. In the final section I will discuss an extension of the prisoner's dilemma to the study of norm emergence in these multi-person situations.

There are two other special properties of the iterated prisoner's dilemma, both of which impose constraints on communication that may not be present in real-life norm-generating situations. One is the property that the two players act simultaneously, each having knowledge of the other's previous actions, but neither having knowledge of the other's action on this round. The result can be a lack of coordination, in a form that Axelrod calls an "echo" between certain pairs of strategies (1984, 37). There are, however, real-life situations corresponding to the unmodified prisoner's dilemma. For example, each of two persons who regularly meet can either arrive on time ("cooperation") or late ("defection"). If one person comes late for one meeting, and if each responds to the other's previous action by retaliation, then they will not be able to coordinate from that meeting onward, but will alternate being late.

A second special property of an iterated prisoner's dilemma which narrows the class of norm-generating structures that it can simulate by restricting communication is the fact that the same action must serve as the sanctioning action and the focal action. Thus if on round $n$, player 1 defects following a defection of player 2 on round $n - 1$, player 2 does not know whether player 1 is sanctioning 2's defection to signal that a defection will be met with retaliation or is merely defecting without regard for player 2's previous action. If it is the former, then player 2 would be well advised to obey the sanction and cooperate on round $n + 1$. If the latter, then player 2 would be well advised to retaliate with a sanction of his own, a defection.

Here again, there are certain social structures with limited communication that correspond to this structure. In an argument, a conflict, or an arms race, a hostile action on one player's part can lead to retaliation, which in turn leads to further retaliation, and so on. But again, a wider class of norm-generating structures consists of those in which the sanction is a different action from the focal action. Often the sanction is an expression of disapproval, or as a more serious sanction, ostracism or shunning, for a wide variety of focal actions (or in the case of a positive sanction, admiration or expressions of approval).

Despite these limitations of the iterated prisoner's dilemma for mirroring a norm-generating structure, it will serve as a useful starting point—in part because of the prior work with this game and because of its extension in the work of Maynard Smith, Axelrod, and others to populations of interacting strategies.

## STRATEGIES AND STRUCTURES

My principal aim will be to examine the effect of interaction structure in leading or failing to lead to cooperative actions. I will examine this effect first under the condition that strategies are fixed so that the only changes over time are in actions, not in strategies. Then I will examine the effect of interaction structure on the evolution of strategies themselves. In all simulations, the payoff structure of part (a) of table 7.1 is used. As expressed in the Axelrod statement quoted earlier, a requirement for the growth of cooperation (equivalent to the emergence of an effective sanctioning system) is that a defecting individual "not be lost in a sea of anonymous others." This involves two elements: the frequency of repeated interactions with the same individuals and the memory of both the identity and actions of individuals with whom one has had previous interactions. That is, sanctioning, and a cooperative response in anticipation of a sanction, can occur only if individuals meet those with whom they have interacted previously and if they remember those individuals and their actions in the prior interactions. In the computer tournaments carried out by Axelrod, the same two individuals interacted on each round of a given match. Strategies were devised with the knowledge that the partner on the next round would be the same individual as on the last. In this paper I will examine a structure in which this condition does not hold.

If we consider a social system consisting of one hundred persons, then substructuring of this system can be represented by divisions of the total system into subgroups within which interaction occurs and between which none occurs. The structure can range from fifty subgroups of two members each (so that each interaction is with the same partner, as in the Axelrod case), to a single group of one hundred members, with each interaction randomly selected from all the possible relations between the one hundred members. I will examine the effect of this substructuring upon the mix between cooperative and defecting actions. I will call this substructuring of the system into closed, randomly interacting subgroups the degree of *closure* of the interaction. If interaction is limited to a small group, there is a high degree of closure; if it is equally likely to occur with any member of a large group, then there is a low degree of closure.[4]

I will assume that each remembers the identity of the current interaction partner if he was among the last $m$ interaction partners and remembers the partner's action in the *last* interaction with that partner, as well as his own in the interaction preceding that one (if that interaction is among the last $m$). Thus suppose the system is substructured into groups of three members, and each individual remembers the identity of his last two interaction partners. Within one subgroup, consider an interaction sequence of (1, 2), (1, 2), (1, 3), (1, 3). If the next interaction is between 1 and 2, then 2 would remember 1's previous action toward him and his own action preceding that, but 1 would not remember interaction with 2, because two interactions with 3 intervened. Thus 1 would regard 2 as a stranger, while 2 would regard 1 as an acquaintance. If strategies are different toward strangers and acquaintances, then 2 would use the "acquaintance" strategy, and 1 would use the "stranger" strategy. If memory of the last two interactions leads to an "old acquaintance" strategy and

---

4. Closure may also vary more continuously, without having closed groups of varying sizes, but with a gradient in the probability of interaction with persons according to their "social distance." Variations in the gradient would constitute variations in the degree of closure. How different the norm-emergence would be in such a structure from that in the structure used here remains to be studied.

memory of only one leads to a "new acquaintance" strategy, 2 will use the "old acquaintance" strategy.

In this simulation, it is assumed that a player employs one strategy toward strangers, another toward new acquaintances, and a third toward old acquaintances.

In the first simulation, the strategy toward strangers is always to defect. The rationale behind this is that of the single-play prisoner's dilemma: assuming a single interaction (as would be assumed with strangers), the defect strategy dominates the cooperate strategy, for it is better independently of what the other does.

Toward an old acquaintance (an individual with whom one was engaged in at least two of his last $m$ interactions, where $m$ is the limit of his memory), the strategy involves paying attention to the action of the other in their last previous interaction and one's own action in the last interaction between the two preceding that one. The general idea is this: one will respond to an acquaintance's cooperative action with a cooperative action and to an acquaintance's defection with a defection (that is, a tit-for-tat strategy in interaction with acquaintances), with one exception. If the other's defection itself follows a defection of one's own on the interaction preceding that one, then one regards this as a negative sanction for one's own defection and cooperates on the next move.[5]

Altogether, the strategies toward strangers, new acquaintances, and old acquaintances can be described as in table 7.2, where $D$ refers to defect, $C$ to cooperate, and the subscript $e$ is for ego, subscript $a$ for alter.

Note that this strategy is more forgiving than a blind retaliatory strategy: Ego responds not merely to alter's prior action, but to his own action prior to that as well, to which alter may have been responding.

Viewed as a system of action involving focal actions and sanctioning, ego's defection in pattern 1 can be regarded as an exploitative target action, while ego's defections in patterns 3 and 5 of table 7.2 can be regarded as negative sanctions. The cooperation in pattern 7 can be regarded as a compliant focal action following a sanction ($D_a$ on round $n - 1$). The cooperation in patterns 4 and 6 can be regarded either as a positive sanction, a reward to the other for cooperation, or as a compliant focal action designed to elicit a positive sanction from the other. The ambiguity in these interpretations illustrates the fact mentioned ear-

---

5. A weakness of the pure tit-for-tat strategy is that it has no way of recovering from defections unless the other is more forgiving than oneself. If a defection occurs for any reason whatsoever, and the other uses a strategy which is as retaliatory as tit-for-tat, then a defection will echo back and forth from that point onward.

**Table 7.2** Strategy in Simulation 1 toward Strangers, New Acquaintances, and Old Acquaintances

|  | Round | | | Pattern |
|  | $n-2$ | $n-1$ | $n$ | |
|---|---|---|---|---|
| Stranger | — | — | $\rightarrow$ | $D_e$ | 1 |
| New Acquaintance | — | $C_a$ | $\rightarrow$ | $C_e$ | 2 |
| | — | $D_a$ | $\rightarrow$ | $D_e$ | 3 |
| Old Acquaintance | $C_e$ | $C_a$ | $\rightarrow$ | $C_e$ | 4 |
| | $C_e$ | $D_a$ | $\rightarrow$ | $D_e$ | 5 |
| | $D_e$ | $C_a$ | $\rightarrow$ | $C_e$ | 6 |
| | $D_e$ | $D_a$ | $\rightarrow$ | $C_e$ | 7 |

lier that in the prisoner's dilemma, unlike many settings in which norms may emerge, the same action must serve as focal action and sanction. A consequence of this, of course, is that communication is more difficult to establish and an effective set of sanctions more difficult to institute.

## CHANGES IN ACTIONS WITH FIXED STRATEGIES

In this simulation, there is no evolution of strategies, either by a learning process through which a strategy changes to fit the environment or by the birth of new strategies and the selective survival of existing ones. Thus the important question of what mix of strategies (or single strategy) may exist at equilibrium is not investigated in this simulation. The simulation does not show how sanctions modify behavior *strategies;* it shows only how sanctions modify the behavior itself when the strategy remains intact.

What can be examined here is the effect of closure in the structure of interactions, given a particular strategy, under the condition of different lengths of memory. In the study of norms, the sole question that is being investigated here is how, in a situation where each individual's action imposes an externality upon the person with whom he interacts (thus creating a setting in which a demand for norms arises), the effectiveness of sanctions varies with the degree of closure of the structure of interaction.[6]

6. It should be pointed out that Axelrod's simulation of an evolutionary system is unclear and perhaps incorrect on exactly the question that is examined here. In that simulation, a large number of individuals, with a variety of strategies, interact, the more successful strategies having a higher rate of reproduction than the less successful ones. What is unclear is whether the interactions are repeated interactions with the same individual. Axelrod states that "each [individual] can recognize individuals it has already interacted with, and can

Effectiveness of a sanction in such a population requires that the waiting time until the next interaction with an individual in a position to sanction be sufficiently short that exploitation or defection does not pay. This can be achieved in either of two ways: by limiting the size of the interacting group (or increasing the closure of networks), or by changing the structure of interaction following a defection, that is pursuit of the defector. Only the first of these is examined here.

## RESULTS OF SIMULATION 1: FIXED SINGLE STRATEGY

Figure 7.1 shows the rate at which proportion of defections approaches equilibrium when memory is only of the last two time periods (the minimum necessary to have less than total defection), and the total system has different degrees of closure, that is, groups of 3, 4, 6, 8, 10. The rate of approach to equilibrium is rather straightforward and could be calculated analytically, for equilibrium is reached when the number of interactions between each pair of partners reaches the limit of memory, so that the probability of meeting an individual regarded as a stranger stabilizes. Figures 7.2 and 7.3 show how this approach to equilibrium is slowed as the length of memory increases. In these figures, the scale on the time axis is fixed so that the number of interactions per person per unit time is independent of the group size. The total number of interactions in a unit of time within a subgroup of size $2n$ is twice that within a subgroup of size $n$.

As figures 7.1, 7.2, and 7.3 show, the approach to equilibrium is similar in groups of all sizes. However, the defection rate at equilibrium increases as the group size increases. If a larger system is structured into subgroups, for example, figure 7.3 shows that a memory of the last ten interactions will generate defection less than ten percent of the time if the groups are of size 3; for a system divided into groups of size 6 with memories of the same length, there will be defection nearly half the time.

As these figures show, long memories compensate for less structural closure in social interaction. There is, in this simulation, a trade-off between size of the interaction set and length of memory, such that a population of individuals with memories of the last six interactions, struc-

---

remember salient aspects of their interaction, such as whether the other has usually cooperated" (p. 49). But this is insufficient. So long as the expected time to the next interaction with a particular other is far into the future (as it will be in a large population of the sort Axelrod envisions), and so long as there is discounting of future payoffs, a defect strategy will escape sanctions and will dominate all others.

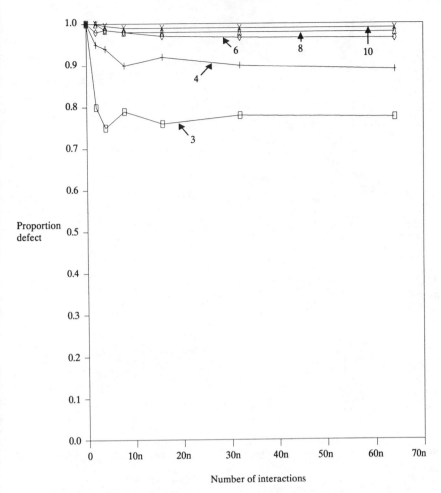

FIGURE 7.1 Proportion defections, in an iterated prisoner's dilemma in freely interacting groups of size 3, 4, 6, 8, and 10, with a strategy of exploiting strangers. Memory is of last two interactions.

tured into groups of size 4, shows approximately the same defection rate as one in which memories are of the last ten interactions and is structured into groups of size 6.[7]

7. This trade-off between group size and memory length depends on the fact that this strategy does not discount future payoffs. If there is discounting with a discount rate of $d$ per interaction, the present value of a future sanction which will occur with probability $p$ on any interaction, with a discount rate of $d$ is

$$S[p(1 - d) + (1 - p)\, p(1 - d)^2 + (1 - p)^2 p(1 - d)^3 + \ldots] =$$
$$Sp(1 - d)/[1 - (1 - d)\,(1 - p)].$$

261

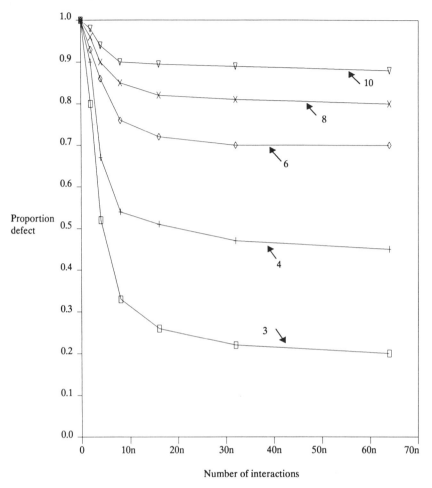

FIGURE 7.2 Proportion defections, in an iterated prisoner's dilemma in freely interacting groups of size 3, 4, 6, 8, and 10, with a strategy of exploiting strangers. Memory is of last six interactions

RESULTS OF SIMULATION 2: STRANGERS NOT ALWAYS EXPLOITED

In the above simulation, strangers were always exploited. In the second simulation, the strategy differs in one respect: each individual has a prob-

---

If ego takes into account that sanction only, then this is the total present value of the cost of an exploitative action. If ego assumes a comparable cost on every future interaction with that individual, the total cost would be $S[Q + Q^2 + Q^3 + \ldots]$, where $Q = p(1 - d)/[1 - (1-d)(1-p)]$. This reduces to a simple quantity, $Sp(1 - d)/d$.

If there is communication among individuals with whom ego interacts, then the cost of

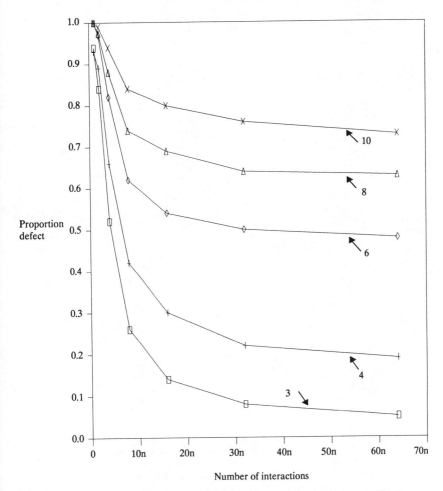

FIGURE 7.3 Proportion defections, in an iterated prisoner's dilemma in freely interacting groups of size 3, 4, 6, 8, and 10, with a strategy of exploiting strangers. Memory is of last ten interactions.

ability of cooperating with strangers, rectangularly distributed between zero and one. This means that there will be defection against strangers about half the time.

---

exploitation can be much greater, for it can lead to sanctions not only from that individual, but from others. Gossip and the creation of reputations certainly in part originate through the benefits they provide to potential interaction partners of exploitative individuals. But gossip and reputation depend on dense communication within a group or population, and that is lacking when there is random mixing or open networks in large populations.

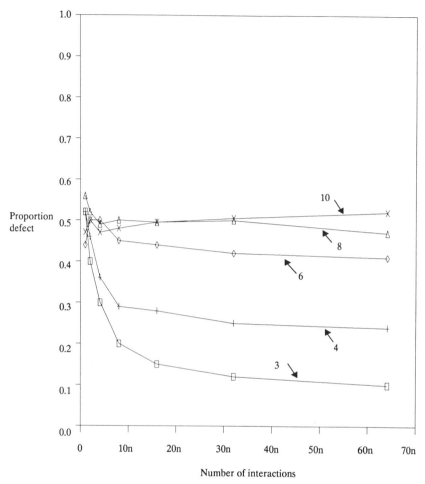

FIGURE 7.4 Proportion defections, in an iterated prisoner's dilemma in freely interacting groups of size 3, 4, 6, 8, and 10, with half the strategies exploiting strangers and half not. Memory is of last six interactions.

In this simulation, there will obviously be more cooperation, because only about half the acquaintanceships begin with exploitation by one of the parties. (About one-fourth begin with both exploiting, and about one-fourth with both cooperating.) Individuals only sometimes exploit strangers, not always; and that can lead to a more cooperative string of future relations.

Figure 7.4 shows the proportion of defections over time for groups of different sizes, with memory of the last six interactions. Comparing this with figure 7.2 shows that the proportion of defections is much lower; reducing the defection against strangers from always to about half the time leads to a much lower probability of defecting in early periods, and this greater cooperativeness leads to a much lower defection at equilibrium.

In both the simulations discussed above, there was no evolution of strategy; the changes shown in the graphs reflected only changes in actions as the proportion of encounters with strangers, new acquaintances, and old acquaintances reached equilibrium. Both length of memory and size of group affected these equilibria and thus affected the proportion of defections at equilibrium. But the absence of evolution of strategy precluded asking an important question: Does the structure of interaction affect the mix of strategies that will evolve?

To answer this question, I will begin with two strategies, from which evolution proceeds. The first is the strategy of simulation 1, a strategy of always exploiting strangers. The second is a strategy of never exploiting strangers. Initially, each strategy occurs with a probability of 0.5. The result is a mixture of actions toward strangers like that of simulation 2, in which each person played these two actions about half the time.

Evolution occurs as follows: after each interaction, each of the two parties to it has a probability of death equal to the negative of its score, discounted over past time, divided by the total number of trials. If the group members have been cooperative, there is a low probability of death for all; if one individual has been particularly unsuccessful (others frequently defecting against him), he has a high probability of death. Thus there is selective retention of strategies, depending on their success.

A new individual is born to take the place of each that dies, with a strategy that is the opposite of the strategy held by the individual who died. (This can be conceived as an evolution of strategies, with an unsuccessful strategy discarded for its opposite.) Thus any evolution that occurs takes place both through selective retention, that is different chances of survival for different individuals, and through birth rates differing in the direction opposite to that of the death rates. It is not clear at this point whether the more cooperative individuals or the more exploitative will have higher survival rates, since one's score (on which survival depends) is better the more cooperative one's interaction partners (which depends partly on one's own cooperation), but it is also better the more one is able to successfully exploit others.

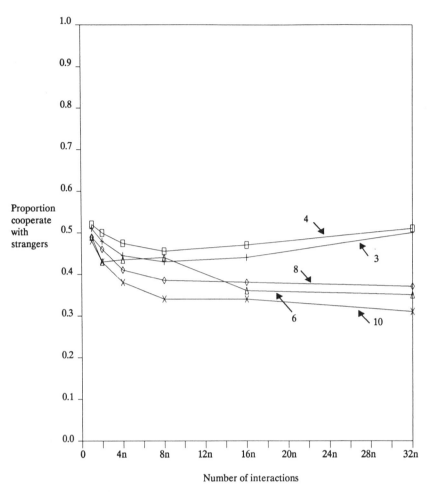

FIGURE 7.5 Proportion of strategies that cooperate with strangers, in groups of differenct sizes. The evolutionary process involves selective retention of strategies that are successful. Memory is of last six interactions.

For this simulation, I will examine only one memory length, memory of the past six interactions. What is of interest here is how the proportion of the two types of individuals in the population changes when the population is divided into closed groups of sizes 3, 4, 6, 8, and 10. Figure 7.5 shows, for the first $32N$ interactions, the proportion of "cooperators" in each of these populations. Shown in the figure are averages for ten groups of each size. Although some random variation remains, it is clear that by the $32Nth$ trial (when the average individual in each size group will have had 32 interactions), the proportion of cooperators in the population declines as the size of the interacting group increases. For a population structured into groups of size 3, the proportion is about .5, as at the outset, while for a population structured into groups of size 10, only about .3 are cooperators. Because of the random variability remaining in the results, more precise inferences, such as the initial decline in proportion of cooperators for groups of size 3 and 4, cannot be made with assurance. Nor is it clear from figure 7.5 how near equilibrium these populations are.

It is possible to examine these systems somewhat more analytically by comparing payoffs to ego for cooperation and for defection with a stranger under different assumptions about the subsequent memory of these actions by ego and alter. (The subsequent memory is determined by length of memory and number of intervening interactions with others.) In particular, we can ask whether either cooperation with or exploitation of strangers dominates the other, in an extension of the concept of domination: if ego assumes the other employs his own strategy toward new and old acquaintances, then cooperation dominates defection if, whichever action alter takes on the first interaction (i.e., with a stranger), cooperation by ego leads to a higher payoff to ego in the subsequent sequence. For example, if memories and intervening interactions are such that both ego and alter remember the last preceding interaction with the other (but not the last two), then each will henceforth treat the other as a new acquaintance. If alter begins by defecting, or by cooperating, then the subsequent sequence of play between these two if ego defects and if ego cooperates is given by:

| *If alter defects:* | | | | | | | *Payoff to Ego* |
|---|---|---|---|---|---|---|---|
| Ego cooperates | Alter | D | C | D | C | payoff after 4 trials | −2 |
| | Ego | C | D | C | D | payoff after 5 trials | −4 |
| Ego defects | Alter | D | D | D | D | payoff after 4 trials | −4 |
| | Ego | D | D | D | D | payoff after 5 trials | −5 |
| *If alter cooperates:* | | | | | | | |
| Ego cooperates | Alter | C | C | C | C | payoff after 3 trials | 0 |
| | Ego | C | C | C | C | payoff after 4 trials | 0 |
| Ego defects | Alter | C | D | C | D | payoff after 3 trials | 0 |
| | Ego | D | C | D | C | payoff after 4 trials | −2 |

As the sequences and the corresponding payoffs show, cooperate dominates defect for ego, if both ego and alter remember exactly one interaction in the past, on each subsequent interaction. Similar examinations can be made for each combination of memories of ego and alter to determine if either strategy toward strangers dominates for that combination of memories. Since memories may differ in each interaction due to intervening interactions with others, the examination of combinations of memories as if they were fixed does not exhaust the possibilities. It shows, however, conditions under which each of the actions toward a stranger dominates, given the payoff matrix of table 7.3. Part (a) of table 7.3 shows which action dominates for ego when ego and alter have memories at each subsequent interaction of 0, 1, or 2 previous interactions with the other (thus treating the other as a stranger, new acquaintance, or old acquaintance).

The question, then, of which type of individual will in the long run predominate, and by how much, in a particular social structure with a particular memory length depends on how likely an interaction is to be of each of these types in that social structure and memory length. Part (b) of table 7.3 shows the probability that a given interaction in a group of size 4 with memories of length 2 will be of each of these types. Applying these probabilities to part (a) of table 7.3 shows that the probability of being in a configuration in which cooperation dominates is .5, the probability of being in a configuration in which defection dominates is .28, and the probability of being in a configuration in which neither dominates is .22.[8] This indicates that a population structured into groups of size 4 with memories of length 2 would evolve in the direction of cooperation with strangers.

Altogether, these results show that given strategies in an iterated prisoner's dilemma like those used here (both modifications of a tit-for-tat strategy), the degree of closure of social structure can affect greatly the actions in a fixed population and can affect even more greatly the mix of individuals between those who cooperate with strangers and those who exploit strangers.

It is interesting to take note of an empirical instance of differing behavior in differing social structures in a situation in which there are norms and in which sanctions might be expected. The situation is the interview situation in a wave of a national panel survey, the behavior is the reporting of drug use by the respondent, and the interviews are tabulated according to the number of previous contacts with this interviewer

8. The application of the probabilities of table 7.3(a) to 7.3(b) is only approximately correct, since Table 7.3(a) shows only the configurations on a single interaction. To be correct, it would be necessary to determine domination for sequences of interactions in which memories might differ on each interaction and to apply probabilities for each of these sequences.

**Table 7.3** Dominating actions toward a stranger for ego, when ego and alter each remember 0, 1, or 2 previous interactions, on subsequent meetings; and (b) probabilities for each combination of memories in a group of size 4 with memory of length 2.

|  |  | Alter Memory | | | Alter Memory | | |
|---|---|---|---|---|---|---|---|
|  |  | 2 | 1 | 0 | 2 | 1 | 0 |
| | 2 | C | C | D | 1/9 | 2/9 | 1/81 |
| Ego Memory | 1 | neither | C | D | 2/9 | 1/9 | 3/54 |
| | 0 | D | C | D | 1/81 | 3/54 | 16/18 |
| | | (a) | | | (b) | | |

**Table 7.4** Reported Lifetime Prevalence of Marijuana and Cocaine by Number of Times Responded to the Same Interviewer as in 1984

| Number of previous contacts with same interviewer or with 1984 interviewer | Ever Used Marijuana | | | | Ever Used Cocaine | | | |
|---|---|---|---|---|---|---|---|---|
| | Male | | Female | | Male | | Female | |
| | % | N | % | N | % | N | % | N |
| Never same interviewer | 71 | (873) | 68 | (720) | 30 | (873) | 19 | (720) |
| Never '84 interviewer | 71 | (1,550) | 58 | (1,718) | 23 | (1,556) | 14 | (1,743) |
| '84 interviewer once before | 69 | (1,106) | 61 | (1,001) | 22 | (1,109) | 14 | (1,001) |
| '84 intereviewer twice before | 69 | (889) | 60 | (884) | 20 | (889) | 14 | (884) |
| '84 interviewer three times before | 64 | (1,317) | 56 | (1,350) | 17 | (1,318) | 11 | (1,348) |

('84 interviewer) or whether the respondent has ever had the same interviewer twice. Table 7.4, from Kandel and Mensch (1986) shows that the more often the respondent has seen the same interviewers, the lower the frequency of drug use reported, that is, the lower the frequency of an admission that might lead to disapproval by the interviewer.

## EXTENSION OF THE PRISONER'S DILEMMA TO SECOND-ORDER FREE-RIDER PROBLEMS

As indicated earlier, in many situations in which there is a demand for a norm, this demand cannot be met by a single person except at a net loss, though it might be met by more than one sharing the cost of sanctioning. The problem of sharing the cost of sanctioning is the problem described as the second-order free-rider problem. The prisoner's dilemma is not suited for such a problem. It is possible, however, to extend the prisoner's dilemma so that this problem may be treated. In this section, I will show the character of the simplest form of this extension, involving three individuals.

First, however, an intuitive sense of the problem can be given. Suppose there is a project which will benefit three persons, with benefits equally divided. Each must decide whether to pay his portion of the project or to be a free-rider who benefits without paying the cost. If one does not pay, then he may be sanctioned by either of the others; but the cost of a sanction which makes it no longer profitable for the free-rider to fail to pay is more than either of the others would gain by sanctioning, though not more than they would gain if both sanctioned.

A 2 × 4 matrix showing a set of payoffs in the initial game which fit the criteria for a three-person (symmetric) prisoner's dilemma is shown in part (a) of table 7.5. Part (b) of table 7.5 shows the constraints that must be met for the first stage of the three-person symmetric two-stage prisoner's dilemma. A scenario that describes part (a) of table 7.5 is this:

> 1. Each of the three players has the following choice:
> C: Put in $9
> D: Put in $0
> 2. Payoff: $1 is added to the pot for every $3 in it, and the pot is divided equally among the three players.

The second stage of the game is described by table 7.6, with part (a) showing a typical set of payoffs and part (b) showing the general relations necessary among the payoffs. A scenario that describes the second, or sanctioning, stage of the game is the following:

> 1. In stage 1, each player's choices are expanded to three:
> CS: Put in $9 at stage 1, $3 at stage 2
> CN: Put in $9 at stage 1, $0 at stage 2
> D: Put in $0 at stage 1
> 2. Payoff: Payoffs in stage 1 are as indicated earlier. Stage 2 is played only if the outcome of stage 1 is 2C, 1D. In stage 2, $4 is taken from the stage 1 defector for every $3 in the sanctioning pot. The money contributed to the sanctioning pot is lost (the cost of sanctioning), but the $4 is divided equally between the stage 1 contributors, that is, between the players of the stage 2 game.

As part (a) of table 7.6 shows, if both players in the sanctioning game play N (no sanction), the payoffs remain as in the stage 1 outcome. If both play S, it costs each $3. From player 3, $8 is taken and divided between players 1 and 2. The resulting payoffs are as if all three defected in stage 1. If only one plays S, that player is worse off than if he had not sanctioned, while the nonsanctioner is better off than if neither or both had sanctioned. For the two players, the sanctioning game is a prisoner's

**Table 7.5** Payoff Matrix for the First Step of a Three-Person Two-Stage Symmetric Prisoner's Dilemma

| | | Player 3 | | | | | |
|---|---|---|---|---|---|---|---|
| | | C | | | D | | |
| | | Player 2 | | | Player 2 | | |
| | | C | D | | C | D | |
| Player 1 | C | 3, 3, 3 | −1,8,−1 | | −1,−1,8 | −5,4,4 | |
| | D | 8,−1,−1 | 4,4,−5 | | 4,−5,4 | 0,0,0 | |

(a)

| | | Player 3 | | | | | |
|---|---|---|---|---|---|---|---|
| | | C | | | D | | |
| | | Player 2 | | | Player 2 | | |
| | | C | D | | C | D | |
| Player 1 | C | e,e,e | b,a,b | | b,b,a | d,c,c | |
| | D | a,b,b | c,c,d | | c,d,c | 0,0,0 | |

(b)

Constraints: $a > c > e > 0 > b > d$
$3e > a + 2b, 3e > d + 2c$

dilemma; for the stage 1 defector, it is a game in which sanctions progressively reduce his gains from defection.

I will not attempt to analyze this two-stage game here, but a few points are worth mentioning. The tabulation below shows the payoff to each strategy under each combination of others' actions.

| Own Action | Other's Actions | | | | | |
|---|---|---|---|---|---|---|
| | CS,CS | CS,CN | CN,CN | CS,D | CN,D | D,D |
| D | 0 | 4 | 8 | 4 | 4 | 0 |
| CN | 3 | 3 | 3 | 1 | −1 | −5 |
| CS | 3 | 3 | 3 | 0 | −2 | −5 |

As this tabulation shows, no choice dominates both other strategies. But CN dominates CS. By usual game theoretic analysis, this eliminates the combinations of others' strategies that include CS, leading to the following reduced set of payoffs.

| | CN,CN | CN,D | D,D |
|---|---|---|---|
| D | 8 | 4 | 0 |
| CN | 3 | −1 | −5 |

Here, D dominates CN. Thus the elimination of the CS strategy by CN has resulted in CN's itself being dominated. But any player that cooper-

**Table 7.6** Payoff Matrix for the Second (Sanctioning) Stage of a Three-Person, Two-Stage Symmetric Prisoner's Dilemma, Where Player 3 Has Chosen $D$ in Stage 1, and Players 1 and 2 Have Chosen $C$

|  |  | Player 2 | | Player 2 | |
|---|---|---|---|---|---|
|  |  | $S$ | $N$ | $S$ | $N$ |
| Player 1 | $S$ | 0,  0,0 | $-2$,  1,4 | $f,f,g$ | $i,h,j$ |
|  | $N$ | 1,$-2$,4 | $-1,-1,8$ | $h,i,j$ | $k,k,m$ |
|  |  | (a) | | (b) | |

Constraints: $h > f > k > i$
$2f > h + i$
$m > j > g, e > g$

ates at stage 1 has an interest in the other player's playing $CS$ in the sanctioning stage, precisely because it is the other's $CS$ play which makes possible a combination which keeps $D$ from dominating $C$.

What may be described as "solving the second-order free-rider problem," or "solving the sanctioning problem," consists in this context of devising a procedure of play for this game such that a rational player will play $CS$.

## CONCLUSION

The work reported here constitutes a beginning toward examination of the conditions under which effective norms arise to constrain individuals from acting in immediate self-interest. Here, the effect of restricted interactions within small groups was investigated, and the effect of group size is striking indeed: the larger the group, the more difficult it is for sanctioning to effectively restrain exploitative behavior. Indeed, as was pointed out earlier, this implies that the results of an iterated prisoner's dilemma (with the same two persons interacting over a large number of interactions) cannot be extended to a population of freely interacting individuals. The effects of increasing the number of different other persons with whom each individual interacts are strong ones, as the results show.

Two effects were shown, one an effect on actions, given a fixed population of strategies (figures 7.1–7.4), and the other an effect on the population of strategies, given a birth-death process with selective retention of successful strategies (figure 7.5).

The work presented does not address the second-order free-rider problem when there are multiple potential holders of a norm, no one of which finds it to his interest to sanction alone. A device for exploring this was introduced as a three-person prisoner's dilemma with a second sanctioning stage following the first stage.

## REFERENCES

Axelrod, Robert. 1984. *The Evolution of Cooperation.* New York: Basic Books, Inc.

Coleman, James. 1990. *Foundations of Social Theory.* Cambridge, MA: Harvard University Press.

Kandel, Denise, and Barbara Mensch. 1988. "Underreporting of Drug Behavior in a National Longitudinal Youth Cohort." *The Public Opinion Quarterly* 52: 100–124.

Kreps, David, Paul Milgram, John Roberts, and Robert Wilson. 1982. "Rational Cooperation in the Finitely Repeated Prisoner's Dilemma." *Journal of Economic Theory* 27: 245–52.

Luce, R. Duncan, and Howard Raiffa. 1957. *Games and Decisions.* New York: Wiley.

Maynard Smith, John, and G. R. Price. 1973. "The Logic of Animal Conflicts." *Nature* 246: 15–18.

Rapoport, Anatol, and Albert M. Chammah. 1965. *Prisoner's Dilemma.* Ann Arbor: University of Michigan Press.

COMMENT: *An Alternative Approach to the Generation and Maintenance of Norms*

## Stephen J. Majeski

James Coleman's contribution to this volume, "Norm-Generating Structures," is an example of the renewed interest in *norms* among scholars concerned with individual and collective choice. Coleman focuses on "the effects of variation in social structures on the emergence of behavior patterns said to obey a norm" (p. 250). He takes a decidedly *behavioral* approach to norms by explicitly equating norms with a form of behavior. Specifically, a norm is a set of sanctions that act to direct the behavior in question where a sanction is a single instance of the norm.[1] While aspects of this definition are very narrow, defining norms in behavioral terms is quite typical of recent trends. For example, Axelrod (1986) also opts for a behavioral definition over alternatives based on expectations or values. Axelrod suggests that "a norm exists in a given social setting to the extent that individuals usually act in a certain way and are often punished when seen not to be acting in this way" (1986, 1097). Axelrod makes the linkage between action and norms more explicit when he goes on to

---

1. Coleman also delimits his analysis further by considering only norms that are strictly negative. They either prescribe an action not in the actor's interest or proscribe an action in the actor's interest. Thus, Coleman fails to consider norms that advocate behavior consistent with the actor's interests (tastes, preference orderings, goals). Finally, Coleman also rules out norms that are imposed by processes internal to the individual.

say that "the extent to which a given type of action is a norm depends on just how often the action is taken . . ." (1986, 1097).

Let us consider for a moment the implications of a behavioral approach to norms. Without reference to values, expectations or processes internal to the individual (the messy cognitive side), norms are either conflated with behavior or remain unobservable phenomena the traces of which are observed in patterned behavior. While such an approach is cleaner and easier, since we need not know what individuals are thinking (that is, what values they hold, the expectations they have of others' behavior, and the arguments and justifications for their own actions such as appeals to norms), it does not come without costs.

The costs of conflating norms and behavior appear to be particularly steep. Typically, and certainly within the rational choice game theoretic perspective, choices are assumed to be a function of some individual decision rules that reflect a strategy based upon the classical rational choice decision model. Choice is explained by reference to the assumptions of the rational actor model. Certainly we would not equate these assumptions, which represent individual rules for decision making, with the choice or action. To do so would be to conflate the premises or assumptions of the decision model with the conclusions (behavior). The result is a loss in the explanatory power of the model and the associated decision rules. To conflate norms with behavior produces the same result. Norms, which are assumed to guide decision and choice, lose their explanatory power when equated with the behavior that is to be predicted and explained.

For Coleman, a norm is a set of sanctions, where a sanction is "an action which, if effective, guides the target action" (p. 251). Thus, while Coleman equates norms with actions, he does not fall into the trap described above because the norms, as sanctions, are not designed to explain the behavior of the sanctioner. They are designed to explain the behavior of the individual who is the target of the sanction. However, the nature of the sequential prisoner's dilemma (SPD) game creates problems. As Coleman notes, the same action (cooperation or defection) must serve as both the sanctioning action and the target action. By examining behavior, it is unclear whether the action is a function of a sanction, a sanction itself, a combination of the two, or simply the product of the assumed rational choice strategy for playing the game. Under the circumstances, it seems to be difficult to determine the presence or absence of norms much less assess their effect on choice as distinct from the individual decision rules of the rational choice model.

Axelrod (1986) moves slightly away from directly equating norms with some observable form of behavior. He talks about the existence of a norm being *reflected* by the extent to which individuals usually act in certain ways. Instead of linking norms directly to actions as Axelrod goes on to do, let us for the moment consider norms as having the same status as individual decision rules. Individuals usually defect in a one-shot prisoner's dilemma game because we assume they are rational actors and make utility-maximizing choices. Thus the defection choice is a product of a set of rules (rational choice model) invoked by the individual. Similarly, rather than equating a norm with an action, we link the instantiation of a norm with the action. The action is a product of the invoked norm. It is consistent with the application of a norm that advocates such action. Thus, the instantiation of the norm provides an explanation of the behavior just as the rational choice assumptions provide an explanation of the defection choice in the one-shot prisoner's dilemma game.[2]

Testing for the existence of a norm by determining the extent to which individuals usually act in a certain way consistent with the norm is reasonable if one invokes the "as if" argument. It seems to me, however, that an "as if" approach is inappropriate when applied to norms. The existence or application of a set of norms, unlike the assumptions of the rational choice model, is not considered to be universal. Norms, by their very nature, are perceived to be context specific. Their existence or degree of existence is determined by and is a function of the social setting. Thus the existence of and specific form of a norm for any given time and social setting is an *empirical question*. Under these conditions, it seems not only unreasonable but dangerous to make arguments on "as if" grounds. Explanations of behavior that include norms must provide some direct empirical evidence of their existence and application. Without such evidence there is no reason to believe that behavior is in fact a function of norms rather than a set of other plausible factors.

What separates a norm from a specific unique individual decision rule is the very social, cultural nature of norms. Norms are social rules that have been internalized by individuals. They are norms because they have social standing. Norms are rules that achieve the status of objective knowledge, like facts or lessons learned, because they are socially accepted. For example, post–World War II western (particularly U.S.) na-

---

2. This view of norms is consistent with the more traditional view of norms. For example, Parsons (1968) defined a norm as "a verbal description of the concrete course of action thus regarded as desirable, combined with an injunction to make certain future actions conform to this course."

tional security policymakers use the decision rule "do not appease aggressors," which is generated partially by a shared image of an historical narrative—"the lesson of Munich." It is a norm not only because it is used (internalized) almost universally by the specific relevant social group, but because it is accepted by that group and appealed to both to justify and to explain behavior.

The first time a rule that eventually becomes a norm is invoked by an individual in the group it is *not* a norm. It is an individual contextually generated decision rule. The first national security policymaker to employ the Munich case and the "do-not-appease-aggressors" rule was not following a norm. Neither is the first player to "sanction" a defector in an SPD game nor the first to apply the "metanorm" to punish a player who fails to punish another defector in Axelrod's norms game. An individual rule becomes a norm when the application of the rule by other members of the social group is justified by appeal to the precedent application, or when the application is justified by the individual as the expected and/or appropriate behavior of a member of the group. Also, an individual rule becomes a norm when the rule is so established in the group that individuals perceive it to be the only plausible alternative. When the precedent-setting case and the associated rule and appropriate action is the same for most, if not all, of the policymakers in the relevant social group, then the social rule or norm becomes a convention. If maintained long enough, the norm will be applied by individuals who have no personal knowledge or even historical knowledge of the precedent-setting case. Thus, a rule becomes a norm because its formation and maintenance is not simply an individual cognitive process but also a *social process* (see Anderson 1984; Majeski 1987).

If norm construction and maintenance requires a social process, then Coleman's simulations, which are a series of *n* two-person games, may not be a very useful approach to analyze norms. Because there is no communication among individuals (no labeling of defectors, no signaling to others to punish a defector, no ability of other players to witness other games played and observe defection), punishing defectors is strictly a function of *individual* behavior.[3] It has no *social component*. Given the

---

3. It is not surprising that cooperation does not emerge unless the group size is quite small and memory is long. Cooperative outcomes depend on the ability of individual players to sanction defectors. As the likelihood of interacting with the same player decreases, the number of players increases and memory is shortened, then the likelihood of punishing defectors decreases and cooperative outcomes decline. Cooperation is simply a function of interaction opportunities. If a player does not *expect* to be able to punish another player

*asocial* construction of the simulations, similar individual rules, but not norms, are constructed and applied by individuals. Axelrod (1986) generates a social context by constructing an $n$-person norms game where players have a certain probability of witnessing other players' defections and immediately punishing them. A social component could be infused in Coleman's analysis by labeling defecting players and allowing other players to detect the label with some probability.

If norms are conceived of as *cognitively and socially constructed decision rules* people either voluntarily or coercively internalize and employ, then we want to know "how norms arise, how norms are maintained, how one norm displaces another" (Axelrod 1986, 1096), and how norms affect choice and behavior. There are several ways to study the emergence, maintenance, effects, and replacement of norms. Coleman's analysis represents a rational choice approach. He is concerned with assessing the effects of different settings or structures on strategies (incorporating sanctions) employed by rational actors. As Axelrod suggests, "deductions about what fully rational actors will do are valuable for their own sake" (Axelrod 1986, 1097). However, empirical examples of norm usage suggest *real people* make decisions based on principles other than the rational choice model (Axelrod 1986, 1097). Based upon the empirical observation that people are more likely to use trial and error behavior than detailed calculations based on accurate beliefs about the future, he advocates an alternative evolutionary approach based on the principle that more effective strategies are more likely to be retained than ineffective strategies (Axelrod 1986).[4]

Unfortunately Axelrod's work fails to include any actual mechanism or computational way in which effective strategies are identified, compared, or constructed. He does suggest three mechanisms which he argues are compatible with the evolutionary principle: (1) the biological notion that individuals employing more effective strategies are likely to survive and reproduce, (2) effective strategies are the product of learning through trial and error, and (3) players observe each other and imitate the strategies that are doing better (Axelrod 1986, 1097–98). Most empirical work, Coleman's included, of the evolution of strategies rests on

---

who unilaterally defects because she is not likely to play that particular player again, then there is no logic in taking the short-term gamble to cooperate.

4. In effect Axelrod's evolutionary principle (see Axelrod 1984) is quite consistent with bounded rationality models such as Steinbruner's (1974) and Simon's (1985) notion of "procedural rationality."

a biological birth-death mechanism. This is not surprising since it is the only approach that can be formalized and tested without developing a model of individual cognition. It is, however, the least persuasive approach for explaining the effects of norms on social behavior. Norms often behave in quite nonevolutionary ways. Norms can arise and also be destroyed very quickly in a given social context, and their creation and destruction can occur without the replacement of individuals. More importantly, there is no explanation for why individuals come to hold certain norms originally other than by chance.

A rejection of a biological perspective leaves only approaches that have some form of human cognition. Axelrod offers two simple but plausible alternatives noted earlier, but recent empirical work on historical and natural SPD games (Alker and Hurwitz 1980; Alker and Tanaka 1981; Alker et al. 1985) and more general collective insecurity problems (Alker et al. 1980) indicate that individuals appear to be employing more complex mechanisms of recognition, interpretation, and choice. Players appear to employ precedent-based reasoning. They solve their decision problem by selecting past situations most closely resembling the present situation and apply the prescriptions of the past to the present.[5]

Human behavior is rule-following, and it appears to me that the empirically supported precedent-based approach to human reasoning provides a useful foundation for examining the generation, application, and maintenance of norms. A precedent-based approach provides a role for a socially and contextually based history in reasoning. It is historical in that individuals recall the most relevant precedent given a current decision problem. An individual does not search back over the last two or $n$ plays of the SPD game as in Coleman's simulations. Rather, individuals recall similar and prominent decisions, the precedent-setting case, and the associated lessons and rules for appropriate action.

A precedent-based approach also provides an account of learning. Individuals and groups of individuals learn from their own and others previous mistakes and successes. Precedents are packaged in the form of narratives. These narratives contain analogies that provide mechanisms for identification, action, and evaluation. Learning is constrained, and informational requirements are reduced in a number of ways. By perceiv-

5. Notions of bounded rationality (Simon 1957, 1982) and "muddling through" (Lindbloom 1959) are consistent with precedent-based reasoning. Precedent-based reasoning is prevalent in work in cognitive psychology and artificial intelligence (see, for example, Winston 1980, 1984; Schank and Abelson 1977; Newell and Simon 1972; Carbonell 1983) and foreign policy decision making (see, for example, Mefford 1986; Schrodt 1985; Anderson 1981; and Vertzberger 1986).

ing a decisional situation as similar to previous situations and by employing precedents and analogies to interpret it, individuals and groups of individuals *frame* or *prestructure* the situation. This prestructuring creates a propensity to understand and interpret in a particular way rather than other plausible ways. It reduces informational requirements, limits the view of plausible alternatives, and elevates the precedent interpretation and associated action. If the evaluation of the precedent action is positive, and the analogy and associated action is widely supported by the relevant group, then the likelihood of perceiving or generating plausible alternative actions is very low. As a precedent becomes more established in a group, it not only narrows plausible and acceptable alternatives for each individual but also narrows what appeals to the group and what can be justifiable to the group.

Precedent-based reasoning also establishes social roles and labels for the participants. Social roles and labels generated from the precedent provide shorthand descriptions of the players (competitors in an SPD game). These descriptions often include the beliefs, intentions, and expectations of behavior for the various players. These descriptions as well as appropriate actions are formalized in *plans*. Plans contain the general information, usually in the form of scripts, on how an actor achieves a goal (Schank and Abelson 1977). When a situation is frequently encountered by an individual, she usually has a script for that situation—that is, a standardized, generalized episode extracted from the individual's prior experience in the situation. Plans then are precedent-based and represent strategic reasoning. Plans contain actions designed to achieve goals. Taken into account are the likely responses of other actors to these actions. A plan also contains second-order actions, which are expected to elicit responses from the competitor that are consistent with the planners' goals.

Norm construction and maintenance are both cognitive and social processes. A precedent-based approach provides an empirically defensible and computationally tractable account of human reasoning. Precedents, as historical and contextually specific narrative accounts, invoke and constrain interpretation, understanding, and choice. The narrative quality of precedent-based reasoning is consistent with planning (strategic reasoning that requires the formation of beliefs, intentions, and normative orientations of other players) and justificatory activity in policymaking. It also accounts for the construction and maintenance of the social aspects of role identification and expectations of "appropriate" and/or likely behavior so prevalent in norms. Thus a precedent-based

279

approach provides a model of social action that can account for the generation and maintenance of norms. As an approach grounded in procedural rationality (Simon 1985), it is a nonstochastic, symbolically mediated functional account of human reasoning processes (Newell 1980) that is verbal in nature. Therefore, norm generation and maintenance are best understood in a qualitative, natural language medium and most appropriately modeled using formal computational (artificial intelligence type) approaches.

## REFERENCES

Alker, H., and R. Hurwitz. 1980. *Resolving Prisoner's Dilemmas.* Washington, D.C.: American Political Science Association.
———, J. Bennett, and D. Mefford. 1980. "Generalized Precedent Logics for Resolving Insecurity Dilemmas." *International Interactions* 7: 165–206.
———, and A. Tanaka. 1981. "Resolutional Possibilities in 'Historical' Prisoner's Dilemmas." Paper presented at the 1981 Annual Meeting of the International Studies Association, Philadelphia, March 1981.
———G. Duffy, and J. C. Mallery. 1985. "From Quality to Quality: A New Research Program on Resolving Sequential Prisoner's Dilemmas." Paper presented at the Annual Meeting of the American Political Science Association, New Orleans, August 1985.
Anderson, P. 1981. "Justification and Precedents as Constraints in Foreign Policy Decision Making." *American Journal of Political Science* 25: 738–61.
———1984. "Using Artificial Intelligence Models to Understand the Outbreak of Wars." Paper presented at the Annual Meeting of the American Political Science Association, Washington, D.C., August 1984.
Axelrod, R. 1984. *The Evolution of Cooperation.* New York: Basic Books.
———1986. "An Evolutionary Approach to Norms." *American Political Science Review* 80: 1095–111.
Carbonell, J. 1983. "Learning by Analogy: Formulating and Generalizing Plans from Past Experience." In *Machine Learning: An Artificial Intelligence Approach,* edited by R. S. Michalski, J. Carbonell, and T. Mitchell, 137–61. Palo Alto: Togia Publishing.
Lindbloom, C. 1959. "The Science of Muddling Through." *Public Administration Review* 19: 79–88.
Majeski, S. 1987. "A Recommendation Model of War Initiation: The Plausibility and Generalizability of General Cultural Rules." In *Artificial Intelligence and National Security,* edited by S. Cimbala, 61–87. Lexington, MA: Lexington Books.
Mefford, D. 1986. "Analogical Reasoning and the Definition of the Situation: Back to Snyder for Concepts and Forward to Artificial Intelligence for Method." In *New Directions in the Comparative Study of Foreign Policy,* edited by C. F. Hermann, W. Kegley, Jr. and J. N. Rosenau. New York: Allen and Unwin.
Newell, A., and H. Simon. 1972. *Human Problem Solving.* Englewood Cliffs, NJ: Prentice-Hall.
Newell, A. 1980. "Physical Symbol Systems." *Cognitive Science* 4: 135–83.

Parsons, T. 1968. *The Structure of Social Action.* New York: The Free Press, originally published in 1937.

Schank, R., and P. Abelson. 1977. *Scripts, Plans, Goals, and Understandings.* Hillsdale, NJ: L. Erlbaum.

Schrodt, P. 1985. "Precedent-Based Logic and Rational Choice: A Comparison." In *Dynamic Models of International Conflicts,* edited by M. D. Ward and U. Luterbacher. Boulder, CO: Lynne Reiner Publishing.

Simon, H. 1957. *Models of Men: Social and Rational.* New York: Wiley.

———1982. *Models of Bounded Rationality: Behavioral Economics and Business Organization.* Cambridge: MIT Press.

———1985. "Human Nature in Politics: The Dialogue of Psychology with Political Science." *American Political Science Review* 79: 293–304.

Steinbruner, J. 1974. *The Cybernetic Theory of Decision.* Princeton: Princeton University Press.

Vertzberger, Y. 1986. "Foreign Policy Decision-makers as Practical-Intuitive Historians: Applied History and Its Shortcomings." *International Studies Quarterly* 30: 223–47.

Winston, P. H. 1980. "Learning and Reasoning by Analogy." *Communications of the ACM* 23: 689–703.

———. 1984. *Artificial Intelligence.* Reading, MA: Addison-Wesley.

# PART THREE
# Institutions

# 8

# Reason and Rationality

## Arthur L. Stinchcombe

### Introduction

The central dependent variable in this paper is a specified ideal long-run relationship between what Max Weber called "substantive rationality" and what he called "formal rationality." By formal rationality he meant standardized methods of calculation on which routines can be based, such as "a bachelor's degree should involve passing 120 semester hours of courses," or "profits are maximized when marginal costs are equated with marginal revenue," or "iterated proportional fitting of a cross tabulation approaches the maximum likelihood estimates of the cell frequencies under loglinear models with any of several sampling schemes," or "contracts in which one of the parties receives no 'consideration,' no benefit from the transaction, cannot be enforced."

By substantive rationality we mean going behind such formal methods to the substance of the matter, as in the process by which instruction received in England or France is translated into American semester hours by rough theories of international equivalency, or by which the back list of a publisher, the inventory of books, is judged to represent a certain flow of marginal revenue based on the experience of the industry, or even more basically that money returns are a good approximation to marginal revenue, or by the principles of asymptotic efficiency which make maximum likelihood estimates of appropriate statistics a good thing, or by

Reprinted with revisions by the author from *Sociological Theory* 4 (Fall 1986): 151–66.

Andrew Abbott and Kim Scheppele provided me with detailed and astringent critiques of a previous version of this paper. I have not changed the essential argument in response to their astringency, but I believe I have removed a large number of unclear patches from it, sometimes so as to sharpen the disagreements between us. I measure the quality of comments on drafts by the number and importance of changes induced in the paper (this "quality" is of course a joint product of my receptivity and the inherent quality of the critiques). By that measure these critiques were intelligent and relevant, and I greatly appreciate them. This paper was presented in Paris at the Maison des Sciences de l'Homme in a conference organized by Jon Elster and Pierre Bourdieu on rationality and norms.

the hypothesis in legal reasoning that if a contract lays costs on one of the parties but gives them no benefits it is likely to be based on coercion, fraud, or illegal trading and that contracts so based are a bad thing.

The basic reason we are interested in the relationship between these two things is that for reliable social organization of calculation, one needs routines and procedures that can be judged quickly by external features, can be taught to ordinary men and women, and the like. The social extension of modes of reasoning by institutions depends on the formality of reasoning. But in general formal reasoning is vulnerable to variations in the situation—for example, social surveys are never carried out by any of the sampling schemes that justify iterative proportional fitting, so loglinear parameters do not ever have the standard errors estimated for them in sociology—and to variations in the objectives, so that few of us value the production of our books as exactly equal to the discounted stream of sales, because it still gives us a thrill to see them checked out of a library twenty years after they are out of print. So formal rationality is only as good as its grounding in substantive rationality. Only if semester hours are in fact equal (which we teachers all know they are not from differences between our own courses and differences of students within them) is a bachelor's degree a reliable measure of educated competence.

So what we want of our institutions of reason is a proper balance between efficient formal approximations that can have a reliable social effect, and substantive good sense to know their limits and to improve them. I should emphasize that substantive rationality is vulnerable, and often inferior to formal rational rationality, as in the example of "clinical judgment" in medical investigations.

The big predictor in whether a medical procedure appears in the literature as a success or as a failure is whether or not there was a control group (Gilbert, Light, and Mosteller 1975; Gilbert, McPeek, and Mosteller 1977). By basing their medical results on clinical substantive judgment rather than on a formal experimental control, physicians regularly deceive themselves.

Anyhow, what one wants to preserve from a policy point of view is a correct relation between socially instituted formal methods of calculation and substantive good sense. This can be seen as an argument about what that dependent variable looks like in reality, how one recognizes high values of it in social life, and about what its main causes are. The ideal type of a rationalized institution, that is the outcome of the first half of this essay, is a combination of an analysis of what the variable looks like in social life, and an analysis of its causes. For example, when I argue (following Parsons 1939) that no serious institution of reason can do without protections from its judges' rationality, it is on the one hand an indicator of where in society we may have found a system that balances the institutional efficiency of formal rationality with substantive good sense. On the other hand it is, of course, an analysis of the causes of disinterested reasoning, of that socially precarious pattern of preferring the right answer over the wrong one merely because it is right. One of the causes of that precarious pattern is socially instituted protections of decision processes from corruption by passions or interests. It is a sign by which we can recognize normative elements in the use of reasoning in social life, and a cause of the solidity of norms that lead us to prefer good reasoning to bad.

The remainder of the essay after the development of the ideal type is about the variety of relations that the normative use of rational faculties have with the theory of utility maximization that we have lately come to understand as rationality. One part of the argument here is that normative behavior can very often be analyzed in terms of what has come to be called the theory of agency in economics, but with more of less fictional, socially established, utilities of the principals. The central contribution to this extension of the theory of agency is an unpublished paper by Carol Heimer (1986). It involves an analysis of what we mean by "taking responsibility," as in the sentence, "I'll take responsibility for the seminar series this year."

Another part of the argument is that the definition of the improvement of bodies of reason is a derivative of the proper balance of substantive and formal rationality. Only if a body of reasoning is routinized is it self-reproducing. Only if grounded in new conquests of substantive understanding of reality is it improving. So if we get the causes of the dependent variable of the paper, the balance of formal and substantive rationality, we will also have the causes of the evolution of bodies of reason, namely the causes of reliable reproduction and those of the preservation of favorable changes.

Another bit of the argument is that formal reasoning would not in general be socially viable, would not produce the social advantages of reliability and calculability that Weber emphasized so much, unless it were truly better. Unless the law of contract in fact allows people to enforce their voluntary agreements but is not easily available for coerced or fraudulent agreements, it will not provide the calculability needed for capitalism because people will avoid it. So the formal rule about consideration has to be applied with some discretion, so that it achieves the ends of the law of contract, or people will try to invent other ways of making voluntary agreements work, and to exclude coerced and fraudulent agreements. Similarly the formal rationality of an American university registrar is only socially viable if there are very few ways to get a semester hour's credit without reading a book. A theory of why people go through ritual motions of reasoning—a theory of what social incentives there are to get a semester hour of credit regardless of the substance of the course, for example—will not suffice to explain why education has come to be a central institution in the American labor market and marriage market. Only by noting that there is some rational substance in most of those semester hours of credit can we understand the economic and social functions of semester hours of credit.

I would add as a preliminary caveat that there are many forms of substantive rationality that are not embedded in formal structures for getting an authoritative rational answer. There are other ways of getting authority for an answer than reason.

Bargaining is one. What makes a bargain authoritative is its being agreed to by the parties. People bargaining give many reasons, but the reasons are to persuade, not to give authority. For example in April of 1986 there was a lot of bargaining about the limits of the right to strike or to lockout in public employment in Norway. It took the form of applying for "dispensations" from the effects of the strike or the lockout. The public airline might apply for a dispensation from a strike of a union which includes controllers at airports, and whether or not that dispensation is granted is a bargain over whether *that* degree of damage to the public is part of the right to strike. Both the labor union and the management bargainers have to agree to a dispensation. People gave many arguments, as well as threats of binding arbitration if the dispensation were not granted, consultations of public opinion polls, offers to restrict the work in such a way as to minimize the revenues of the other party to the strike, and so on. Some combination of reason and perceived bargaining advantage was no doubt involved in the agreements that were reached by granting or not granting the dispensation. But what made the grant authoritative was the agreement of labor and management that the dispensation should be granted, not that the reasoning behind the application was unchallenged.

Similarly people in legislatures make arguments about legislation of very varying quality. But once the vote has been taken, the quality of the arguments does not affect the validity of the legislation. It may possibly make it more or less likely that the legislation will be reconsidered by the legislature at another time, or that it will be struck down by the Supreme Court. But although we all believe that much better legislation comes about in legislatures with quite free debate, what makes legislation authoritative is not the reasoning but the votes.

Bargaining systems and legislatures then have substantive reasoning involved in them, but not routinized formal reasoning, and are no doubt the better for it. But they are not institutions of reason in the sense of this paper and should be distinguished from institutions such as science, appellate court legal reasoning, or auditing financial accounts, which satisfy the criteria for institutions of reason developed in the first half of this essay. Not all socially significant reasoning is institutionalized so that reasons are the source of authority, and such reasoning is excluded from consideration here.

### REASONING IN NORMATIVE SYSTEMS AND IN RATIONAL ACTION

In this paper I want to use the word "reason" and its relatives to refer to *norms governing a body of thought recognized as authoritative* in a culture, so that reason is characteristic of science, of the law, or of accounting practice. I want to use the term "rationality" and its relatives to refer to *individual behavior that maximizes benefits or minimizes costs* in achieving some goals of individuals or of groups such as households or firms, so rationality is a characteristic of the ideal-typical economic man, of the person who obeys maximizing rules of strategy given in game theory, or of Machiavellian use of the law or of accounting practice for one's own ends.

Reason then is a normative concept in the sense that following the rules of, say, legal reasoning from precedent results in an authoritative judgment about what law applies to a particular case, whether following such rules maximizes anything for the individual judge or not. Rationality is normative only in the sense that one can derive a correct course of action *given* a set of goals; in some sense the normative element inheres in the set of goals, not in the derivation from them or the profit or utility maximizing course of conduct, as Parsons argued in *The Structure of Social Action* (1937).

By reason then I mean a socially established method of calculating what should be authoritative in a particular case. For example, when an appellate court in the United States makes a ruling on a particular case and explains it, this provides an authoritative paradigm for reasoning about similar cases. The paradigm may tell, for example, what "facts" must be established for there to be an "invasion of privacy," or what warnings must be given to a prisoner for police conduct to be acceptable "due process of law." The point here is that the judgment of the appellate court is stated in general form, in the written opinion by the court itself, rather than just being an administrative decision about a particular case. But the ultimate purpose of this formal reasoning is in general to increase the capacity of legal reasoning to produce substantive justice. This general form of the reasoning given allows other lawyers, including in particular lower court judges, to apply the paradigm laid down as authoritative in deciding whether some other particular breach of good taste by a newspaper is an invasion of privacy in the eyes of the law. A city attorney can use it in deciding, for example, what routine procedures should be instituted in police departments so that their convictions will stand up in court.

Such a standard method of calculation of authoritative normative judgments then is the application of "legal reasoning," and the development of such paradigms, and the social systems for creating and interpreting paradigms, constitutes the "rationalization" of law.

Similarly when a referee of an academic paper makes a recommendation against publication, he or she is ordinarily required to give reasons why it is unacceptable (see generally on referees Zuckerman and Merton 1971). These reasons must be couched in terms acceptable in the discipline, so that the availability of reagents of standard purity from chemical supply houses rules out challenges that the authors did not specify purification procedures, or the asymptotic efficiency of maximum likelihood estimates makes such estimates routinely acceptable in disciplines that usually use large samples, challengeable in disciplines that often work with small samples. But these "terms acceptable in the discipline" form a more or less coherent set of principles of reasoning, so that a referee's report recommending rejection will ordinarily contain a rationale of why the scientific results reported in *this* particular paper may be faulty, given the standards of evidence and reasoning accepted as authoritative in the discipline. That is, the referee is applying a standard method of calculation, a paradigm of reasoning, in coming to his or her judgment, and any sign that that judgment is "rational" from the point of view of the individual interests of the referee is ordinarily taken as a mark against it.

When scientific procedures in a laboratory for testing drugs fall below a minimum professional level (the minimum here seems to be pretty low), the FDA can inform drug manufacturers that reports from that laboratory will be examined with special care, and drive the laboratory out of business (Braithwaite 1984, 86). The willingness to apply sanctions of such severity shows that the methods of calculation involved are authoritative (e.g., that one should not substitute new animals for those that died after being administered the drug, and try again for a better result) and can be used to specify delicts.

Similarly the rules of accounting practice specify how inventories should be evaluated. In the book industry much of the inventory will never be sold for the current market price: some convention must be adopted that does not count capital value as accruing at the nominal price when the books are produced, and there is some dispute between the tax authorities and the industry about what that convention should be (Coser, Kadushin, and Powell 1982, 370–71). But when an auditor comes into a firm he or she is supposed to apply a convention that will protect potential investors or creditors as well as satisfy the tax authorities. The reasoning of the auditor is normative in the sense that one looks askance at auditors who provide reports on corporations based on their own self interest, or the self interest of the present officers of the corporation.

It may be useful to contrast the use of "normative" in phrases like "the standards of legal reason are normative" from other uses of that word. The general meaning of normative is that some social process, which may, for example, be quite unorganized "public opinion" or quite organized "due process of law," recognizes some decisions or actions or symbolic products as better. A theory of the normative order is, so to speak, a generative grammar of judgments of "better." The simplest such grammar is perhaps the stratification grammar suggested by Bourdieu (1984), perhaps with roots in Veblen (1899): "better" consists of those symbols by which people with more resources urge that they are more distinguished than those with less, so the dimensions of better, the dimensions of the normative, are dimensions which describe what people with more resources can do that people with less cannot. Normative judgments then are simply judgments with an invidious purpose, used to distinguish the rich, the wise, and the well born from their inferiors. The difficulty with such a theory was crisply formulated by Paul Veyne, "one is not ostentatious unless one feels superior (Veyne 1976, 232)." A symbol cannot be convincing as a sign of distinction unless it adds something, unless it makes the greater amount of resources into meaningful superiority.

A second proposal is that of Jaeger and Selznick (1964), based in part on Dewey (1958), that what is better in a cultural sense is that set of things that people actually experience as giving meaning to their lives, that bring order, that symbolize values, that turn the flow of events into memorable experiences. But it is hard to apply that criterion here to recognize a reasoned judgment as better, because while some reasoning may improve our appreciation of values and may turn the flow of events into meaningful experiences, others such as the proper valuation of inventories so that inflation of their value does not appear as profit are merely technically better for recognized human purposes.

We are arguing for a sense of "normative" which implies that the people or organizations involved have a hierarchy of standards. They recognize rules or principles by which, in particular cases, "better" judgments or outcomes can be judged. In particular, for a normative system to be a system of "reason" as we are using it here, standards that rank highly in the system must require that reasons developed according to accepted paradigms are an essential component of judging some decision as "better" than alternative decisions. People may, for example, get carried away by an elegant model of neighborhood segregation by Schelling (1971, 1978), but when reasoning shows that the model bears no sustainable relation to empirical reality (Taub, Taylor, and Dunham 1984, 142–66) the superiority of the norm of empirical reasoning in social science outweighs the aesthetic norm of elegant simplicity and the feeling of understanding the sources of evil in a good world, that we get from Schelling and that the Jaeger and Selznick theory of the normative in culture would lead us to predict should receive the judgment of "better." That is, what makes the norms of rationality normative is that when people agree that they are participating in a science, they agree that a particular set of norms of reasoning will be taken as authoritative, unless and until that body of norms of reasoning is improved by the application of more general and higher ranking principles of reasoning.

Of course reason in the sense defined above is useful to individuals trying to be rational in several ways. In the first place, some types of reason are authoritative because they are thought to give the right answer. A rational actor might want the right answer about whether, for example, a ship of a given design loaded in a particular way might have its center of buoyancy below its center of gravity and consequently turn turtle. A naval engineer working for a classification society is normatively required to be able to give the right answer to such a question, whether it is in his or her own interest or not, and so his behavior manifests institutionalized reason. But insurance companies insist on an opinion from a classification society because they want that right answer, because if ships turn turtle insurors lose money (Heimer 1985a).

Further the paradigm of rational action is itself sometimes a paradigm which is socially established as normative. For example, in deciding what to do with an inventory, a rational actor would rationally want to know what it was worth on the market, and older accounting conventions which gave systematically wrong answers in times of inflation were bad for rational action of the inventory holder. But an auditor is obliged to protect investors and creditors in part by making sure that the accounting conventions of a corporation are correctly evaluating the inventory, in the sense that in an emergency it could be sold for somewhere near what is evaluated at in the accounts. So it is the responsibility of auditors (and others who specialize in the paradigm of accounting) to propose new accounting conventions when inflation systematically gives the wrong answer about the value of inventories. The paradigm of rational action in a market then is binding on auditors in a normative sense, in the sense that a really good auditor will look for assets overevaluated by the accounting conventions of a firm.

So just as rationality may make use of socially established paradigms of reasonable calculation for achieving private ends, so some socially established paradigms of reason have sections which are adopted from the theory of rational action. The crucial difference between an auditor's use of the theory of rational action and the firm's is that the auditor is required to follow the rules in order to make an authoritative judgment of the creditworthiness (and other financial characteristics) of a particular firm, rather than to choose his or her own most rational course of action. And while a firm which overvalues its inventory and so does not sell when it should is acting irrationally, its irrationality is not by the same token socially irresponsible, a violation of institutional responsibilities to calculate correctly according to a body of norms. In fact the management of the firm is not responsible for knowing all the conventions of good accounting.

What has been implicit in the distinction above is that the explanation of the incidence of reason in social life will not, in general, be the same as the explanation of rationality. For example, the function of legal reasoning, of enabling citizens (or at least other lawyers) to predict what the courts will do in the future, to predict the terms on which violence and coercion will be available in civil society, is not the same as the functions that one might expect to be served by rationality in the application of coercion, as we have known at least since Hobbes.

The purpose of this essay taken as a whole is to point to differences in the motives of behavior, in the effectiveness of action, in the possibilities of development to higher levels of the use of the faculties of rationality, that we have when we are explaining the incidence or consequences of reason rather than the incidence of, or the systemic consequences of, rationality.

The rest of the essay has four sections. The second section after this introduction treats the preconditions of reason as an institutionalized normative order governing some subpart of social life. In some ways this is a brief explication of what Max Weber means by the "rationalization" of social institutions in Western society (for a good short definition of what he means, see the discussion of "intellectualization" in Weber 1919, 139; see also Kalberg 1980). The third section deals with the problem of the rationality of judges, and how that can interfere with the institutionalization of reason; the problem of a person being a judge in his or her own case is the core of this section. The fourth section elaborates the point made briefly above, that reason in institutions often has to take account of the rationality of individuals, so that authoritative normative reasoning about rationality is a part of what reason is. The fifth section discusses the functions of reason for rationality, in particular its sociological function of providing social predictability rather than its function of being in fact the most rational method of calculation for individuals.

## AN IDEAL TYPE OF SOCIALLY INSTITUTIONALIZED REASON

The purpose of this section is to outline the elements that we find in fully developed institutions which enjoin the use of standards of reasoning in an area of social life. If we imagine our dependent variable as the degree to which paradigms of calculation of normative results that are reproducible by the use of a cognitive process are pervasive in an area of social life, and the degree to which the different outcomes of the application of reason in that area of social life can be reduced to a few "reasoned" paradigms well understood by practitioners in that area, we can search for arrangements of social life that would produce such a social pattern. The main source for building such an ideal type of "rationalization" is Max Weber's work on the rationalization of Western culture, especially in his sociology of law (Weber 1921–22; especially 785–808), but also in his famous ideal type of bureaucracy and scattered in his treatment of rationalization of other institutions.

The first obvious requirement for such a social institution to function is that there be a supply of practitioners who know the system of reason. Weber observed (Weber 1921–22, 785–92, 802–5) that the rationalization of a body of culture depended on future practitioners being taught in schools rather than in apprenticeships. The existence of schools secures two important features of an institution of reason: that there will be teachers (and textbooks written by teachers) who will rationalize (in the sense of "systematizing," of reducing the body of practice to the fewest possible paradigms of reasoning) the body of culture, and that the learner can learn in a way dictated by the structure of the body of culture rather than in a way dictated by the flow of work or what sort of culture is necessary to complete a given task as a whole, as an apprentice necessarily learns.

The segregation of schools from work allows enough detachment to the teacher so that he or she can attend to the "impractical" matter of fitting the body of culture into paradigms, either by inductive methods as in studying cases in American law schools or by more deductive methods as in "continental" law schools. The same segregation allows students to learn the "impractical" paradigms without their work suffering because they do not yet know enough about the details to complete any job of work. Of course, as Weber points out in his discussion of rationalization in schools of theology, such rationalization can be entirely formulaic, and impractical in the sense that it could never be applied (1921–22, 809–38).

Institutions based on reason are of course often in fact created to give advantages to the practitioners of a given variety of reason, rather than to perfect the exercise of reason. Medicine and law try to create monopolies for people officially certified as practitioners of reason in their fields, and many of the people so certified are not very good at reason, nor at all interested in extending the discipline to new areas or in developing techniques that will be more effective but will make their skills archaic. Institutions of reason, like other institutions that purportedly serve higher values, depend as little as they can on the altruism of their members.

Such a temple built on a sewer will, of course, show signs of its lack of a thoroughly sacred character. Medical practitioners will keep secrets about other physicians' malpractice so that physicians will be less vulnerable to lawsuits. Lawyers will oppose no-fault divorces because these use smaller amounts of lawyers' services. Colleges devoted to teaching will hire people with research degrees because these look good to accrediting agencies, and then make no provision in teaching loads or facilities to make research possible. The politics of the professions can at most produce an institution guided by reason part of the time, because the same rational motives it "makes use of" by creating career incentives for the use of reason are also often served by the corruption of the institution.

The learning of apprentices is in general organized in a fashion that will allow them to complete simple jobs, then later to complete complex jobs. The basic principles to which practice can be reduced do not necessarily come arranged from simple to complex in the same order as the jobs that constitute a work flow are organized from simple to complex. A particular law case may, for example, embody some principles from the law of evidence, some from the law of contracts, and some from the law relating to monopoly. The paradigms of such subfields may be learned separately in law school. But the process of using the power of discovery in an anti-trust case against IBM to get evidence of the use of contracts to monopolize a market may be extremely complex, while the same mixture of bodies of law might be relatively simple, and much of the work turned over to paralegals, when one is merely trying to collect damages *after* an anti-trust finding has been established in a different proceeding.

The basic idea then is that the existence of schools that teach a large share of what needs to be known to practice in an area of social life facilitates the rationalization of the body of culture pertaining to it by producing specialists in rationalization, the teachers. It also facilitates rationalization by producing learners for whom rationalization promotes efficiency, students, rather than learners for whom rationalization distracts from mastery of enough different components of the culture to get some useful work done, apprentices. A powerful indicator of such rationalization is the appearance of textbooks designed for use in schools, rationalized into an orderly presentation; then behind these an indicator of the depth of rationalization is the appearance of technical monographs or scholarly papers which the writers of textbooks read.

In addition to having teacher rationalizers and student users of rationalized culture, the body of culture has to be inherently rationalizable. One of the difficulties with charismatic authority from this point of view is that the arbitrary will of a person endowed with the gift of grace cannot be reproduced by a paradigm (though it can perhaps be functionally replaced by the arbitrary will of a substitute). Part of the reason that succession crises tend to lead toward rationalization is that they bring up the question of reproducibility of the authority, and so can lead to the production of paradigms.

In general a principle like "the greater glory of monarch" is not as reducible to rationalized paradigms as "due process of law" or "maximum likelihood estimation." For another example, the physics of pitch and of the temporal periodicity of rhythm are rationalizable, and can form the basis of a notation for music. But the feeling of wanting to dance to certain types of music cannot easily be reduced to a paradigm or a notation, nor can the feeling of sadness induced by a dirge, nor the feeling of listening to one's own kind of music when one hears the music one heard all through childhood. Musicology is much more likely to become a scholarly profession than is virtuoso performance for that reason (this may be why Max Weber's essay on the rationalization of music is often taken as essentially irrelevant by people who like music).

The rationalizability of a body of culture depends then on having at its core principles which are inherently rationalizable; a complex subfield of culture like music which has some rationalizable and some unrationalizable elements will result only in a partially rationalized system, even under the influence of music teachers and music schools.

The most difficult conceptual job here is to distinguish rationalization which gets at the core of an area of culture (I imagine the rationalization of physics to be at the high extreme here) from rationalization which is "scholasticism," which rationalizes an irrelevant part of the culture because that is all that can be rationalized and leaves the core unrationalized (number mysticism or numerology would be an extreme of scholasticism). When one gets schools and students studying subjects which have an irrational principle (in the sense of not being reducible to a paradigm) at their core, the same process that produces reason in inherently paradigmatic bodies of culture produces scholasticism, produces mechanical prayer wheels that increase one's productivity at praying, or the fluffy critics' language to describe the experience of listening to music. It takes a great gift in writing, like George Bernard Shaw's, to make music criticism sound sensible (of course, whether or not it correctly represents the music, as well as being good reading, is a matter that we can hardly judge now).

I suppose the decisive criterion to distinguish such bodies of rationalized nonparadigmatic culture is that different experts tend not to come to the same judgments after applying their methods of calculation to produce an authoritative judgment. The reliability or reproducibility of the judgments of experts (in the mass of cases—of course there are un-rationalized areas of the law or of a science like physics as well as of aesthetic experience—the question is the correlation among experts' judgments over a large mass of cases, not whether or not there are disagreements) is a central operative criterion.

But for an area of social life to be rationalized, institutionalized reason not only has to exist—it also has to be used to resolve particular cases. Here the crucial social criterion is whether the person (or committee or whatever) who makes a judgment in an individual case can be required to give an explanation to other experts justifying that decision. Thus when a scientist announces that he or she (tentatively) believes a certain thing in a scientific paper, an explanation of the reasoning and evidence leading to that belief is required. When a referee recommends that the paper be rejected, he or she is ordinarily required to give a reason, which in its turn involves showing that in some respect the reasoning and evidence of the author were not adequate to the purpose. Similarly appellate courts give "opinions" explaining the legal reasoning behind their judgments; auditors can be required by a firm to give an explanation of their different evaluations of the state of the firm's finances than the firm itself has arrived at; a physician's diagnosis can be compared with an autopsy report or with a second opinion (though in less rationalized areas of medicine such as psychiatry the institution of a second opinion is not as well developed, and of course the autopsy report is not ordinarily a useful check on the diagnosis of a psychiatrist).

The expectation in a rationalized area of culture then is that a skilled practitioner can produce the elements of the paradigm he or she has used to make a judgment and that these elements can be judged by other skilled practitioners and used in a calculation that ought to produce the same result. The criterion of reliability or reproducibility then is socially institutionalized when an area of social life is rationalized, as well as being a criterion a sociologist can use to tell whether a bit of culture is really rationalized. This social institutionalization of reproducibility criteria provides a mechanism for ensuring discipline in the application of the paradigm. And the most sensitive indicator of whether reproducibility or reliability is socially instituted is whether or not a judge of a particular case is normally required (or can be required if there is a question) to produce his or her reasons.

The normal form of the rule about producing reasons is that they should be routinely produced whenever there would be any reason to question them. Thus the requirement is universal in scientific papers, because there would be no reason to publish the paper unless there were some question about what to believe, but explanation of the evidence is not at all universal in textbooks. The requirement to explain in rationalized legal systems applies to appellate judgments (the appeal shows that there was some uncertainty about the application of the paradigm) but not always to lower court judgments. The requirement in auditing does not ordinarily apply if the auditor approves the accounts as kept by the firm, but only if the auditor finds an error or evidence of dishonesty.

A second opinion or an autopsy may not be required in medicine when there is not much doubt about the judgment of the physician or when there is little risk if the physician is wrong: autopsy reports when these are routinized ordinarily show that physicians are wrong about the cause of death in more than a third of the cases—the reason medicine is not pervaded with the sense of uncertainty about physicians' judgments is presumably that in most cases, even if they had known the correct diagnosis, there wouldn't have been anything they could have done to prevent the death (Geller 1983, 125–27).

Reason is a weak cause of people's behavior, and can only work reliably when the strong causes, personal interests and passions or "rationality" in the now conventional sense, are segregated from institutional decisions. If therefore an institution is going to reliably produce decisions guided by principles in the paradigms embedded in the institution, it has to have arrangements not only to make the paradigm available to practitioners, but also to prevent personal interests and passions from interfering. Unless such provisions to prevent "conflicts of interest" are present, the sociologist can assume that an institution is not very serious about institutionalizing reason; unless it has protected reason from corruption by the judges' personally oriented rationality. Weber analyzes this most completely in his ideal type of bureaucracy.

When Weber specifies that "rational-legal" administration requires full time officials recruited from schools rather than from aristocratic families, having a career involving promotions in the bureaucracy and lasting until retirement, having bureaucratic property separated from their own property and the office separated from the home, he is describing a set of provisions to keep the personal and family interests of officials from interfering with the reasoned judgment of cases (Weber 1921–22, 956–89). These are extensive provisions that all tend toward a bureaucrat never being judge in his or her own case.

Similar normative arrangements try to ensure that judges in law courts withdraw when they have an interest in the case, that scholars' papers are not refereed by colleagues who have collaborated with the author (or either married or divorced the author), that physicians do not treat close relatives, especially if they are beneficiaries of the relatives' insurance policies, or that accountants employed by a firm cannot serve as auditors.

Finally, reason has to have materials to work on, a flow of evidence regularly provided by social institutions that tend to make that information accurate. Auditors are nearly helpless without accounting departments within the firm trained in accounting practice. Scientists without laboratories and papers without citations are both indications that a finding is not backed up by the routine information collecting structures that make science reliable. The trial court is a core method of establishing facts relevant to legal cases and is backed up by laws or regulations about discovery (requiring the opponent in a legal case to provide the evidence that shows legally relevant facts), about compulsory process for witnesses, about delays to prepare a defense, about availability of counsel, and so on. Weber uses the criterion that the administration keeps files about its cases in his ideal type of bureaucracy.

Social structures that make information available to decision makers and that protect the quality of information reaching those decision makers are essential to the operation of reason as a social institution.

Thus we can construct an ideal type description of institutionalized reason with the following elements:

1. People are trained as practitioners in an area in schools in which both the role of teacher and the role of student are differentiated from the roles in the practical work of the institution; in the highest development the role of teacher itself carries an obligation to contribute to the rationalization of the body of culture by writing textbooks or technical monographs and papers, and students learn the paradigms separately from practice rather than only by doing progressively more complex jobs.

2. The body of culture itself has at its core cultural principles that can be reduced to paradigms, structures of rules of rational calculation which produce a capacity of different experts to come to the same judgment in a large number of cases.

3. Judges of particular cases in the institutionalized area are required, at least in problematic cases, to give reasons which can be examined by other experts to justify their decisions. In general standardized reasoning is used to try to persuade other experts, so that concerted social action

(e.g., incorporating scholarly findings in textbooks, routinized warnings about their rights to arrestees being questioned) is ordinarily preceded by institutionalized exchanges of reasons: debates or litigation or refereed publications.

4. There are structural provisions that have the purpose of keeping the personal interests of the judge in a given case separate from the process of judgment, a set of norms of "disinterestedness" so that reason can prevail over both rationality and passion.

5. There are regular routines for information collection before judgment, in which information is protected from corruption and degradation, examined for veracity and relevance, and entered into a regular information storage system so that it will be available for the application of reason to it. This information collection is socially established rather than being at the discretion of the reasoning person. For example, a scientist cannot publish a paper without doing the experiment even if he or she knows how it will come out.

Like all ideal types, this one describes the high end of a variable: reason is the more institutionalized, the more all five characteristics given above describe practice in an area of social life.

But one can make distinctions along the dimension of "degree of institutionalization of reason" at various points. For example, the evaluation of artworks for their authenticity, aesthetic value, and economic value is more of a rationalized body of social practices than is the aesthetic response of members of the general population who might, like Dwight D. Eisenhower, say, "I don't know much about art, but I know what I like." But it is by no means as rationalized as, say, nuclear physics or pure mathematics, which show all the above five characteristics to a very high degree.

## The Rationality of Judges

It is now time to consider the implications of all the above considerations on "conflicts of interest" for the problem of the rationality of judges. It is clear that many of the same "faculties" are assumed for judges as are necessary to the model of people as rational actors: judges have to receive and assess information, to calculate according to paradigms that have a high probability of giving the right answer, to modify the paradigms when evidence or reasoning shows that the paradigm as previously used sometimes gives the wrong answer, sometimes to put oneself in the place of other rational actors (e.g. firms being audited) to see what would be rational for them, and the like. But equally obviously the institutions of reason depend on judges in courts or referees of scientific journals or auditors of firms *not* pursuing their own interests, not seeking bribes, not doing as little work as possible to make a decision, not plagiarizing papers submitted to journals, not modifying their decisions out of fear or favor.

Further the maintenance of the institutions that prevent conflicts of interest in judges themselves require an amount of rational care. Judges in law courts are themselves supposed to declare themselves unable to hear a case when their interests would lead them to be prejudiced, and judges are supposed to monitor each other to see that this norm is followed. The requirements here are very often called "professional ethics" or the "responsibilities of office." As Parsons pointed out long ago, the requirements of professional ethics are, in some sense, rational for a professional, because one's professional fate often depends on a reputation among one's colleagues as a person to be trusted (Parsons 1939).

But the principles by which the institutions are constructed which make it rational to maintain a professional reputation for ethical behavior are perhaps best summed up in Weber's phrase, the "ethic of responsibility," though it is the power of institutionalized reason rather than the power of violence of the state that has to be applied in a way balanced among ends (Weber 1921, e.g. at p. 127). By the ethic of responsibility one means roughly that one is required to use the faculties that would otherwise make one selfishly rational to adjust one's own professional response, or an institution's response, to a situation so that some value is served. To put it another way, what an ethic of responsibility means is that one should be rational on behalf of others or on behalf of a value, rather than on behalf of one's own utilities and purposes. Weber's point was especially that since political action involves coercion, all responsible choices in politics have to take account of the costs of using coercion as part of the process of choice. The use of socially institutionalized reason is coercive on people's motives and beliefs in much the way that physical force is and necessarily involves some making of choices for others that involves them in costs and opportunities forgone.

So from the point of view of the rationality of judges, the key thing we need to do is to explain what is going on in the exercise of "rationality on behalf of" people or values.

Presumably a set of values embedded in an institution, say the set of ideals that make up the notion of "justice" in the legal system, or of "financial soundness" in the accounting profession, or of "scientific creativity" in scholarship, has to be thought of as a utility function of the institution. Or rather perhaps a "stylized utility function," a set of trade-offs between objectives and principles and costs that represent approximately what the institution is all about. This institutionalized utility function is, from the point of view of the individual, an intellectual notion. It embodies such principles in the law as "in construing a contract, the central question is what the contracting parties intended, but one should not be too interested in idiosyncratic intentions of particular parties, but rather than customary understandings of intentions in the line of business of the parties," or in science such principles as "theories in a science should be compatible with the experimental results, but fundamental theoretical innovations often have this or that difficulty at first in explaining particular results and one should extend an appropriate degree of latitude to reasoning on fundamental questions."

These are not politically determined *rules* of an institution, but principles defended in collegial settings within the institution, and *sometimes manifested* in attempts to write rules on particular subjects or opinions on particular decisions. One expects that different members of the institution will have somewhat different weights for the values in trade-offs (e.g., different relative evaluations of teaching versus research in science, or of enforcing the customary practices in contracts versus codification and uniformity of the law in the legal profession). But within the range of responsible interpretations of the institutional utility function, practitioners are supposed to act in their institutional roles as rational actors trying to maximize the institutional utility function as if it were their own. (I do not mean here literally "maximize," as by taking derivatives and the like. Instead I mean the sort of behavior humans actually do, which economists and game theorists approximate by models of rational action. Since the choices we are concerned with involve several values or dimensions of utility and multiple sources of causal uncertainty [it is all this complexity that makes managing them a profession requiring training], the behavior is ordinarily quite far from the model. The model will be at most a predictor of the central tendency. In what follows "maximize" and its relatives should be read in this loose sense, as no more than what economists and game theorists mean by it when they are trying to predict or explain real behavior.)

In particular, the profit maximization of a corporation is such a conventionalized utility function. It forms the basis of a corporation-specific institution of reason, with its arrangements for giving reasons for decisions (in terms of profit maximization), protecting against the corrupt rationality of the institution's members on their own behalf by auditing practices, procedures internal to the corporation for bringing evidence to bear on decisions, and all the other features of an institutionalized rationality that we have defined as "reason."

The utility function set up in such a conventional fashion in a corporation usually is not, even in its "official" form, a simple profit maximizing rule. For example a life insurance company is supposed to have a different trade-off between income versus risk, and between capital appreciation versus maximum current return, than does a uranium prospecting company or a wildcat oil driller. All profit maximizing rules actually involve an implicit choice for the firm of the trade-off between risk and profit, and a choice of the shape of the prospective income stream over time. These choices can, of course, be controlled by portfolio methods in corporations that engage in many businesses, but even then each investment in the portfolio has to be held to its income, risk, and time stream trade-offs in order for the portfolio to have the aggregate features chosen.

This means that even the profit-maximizing rule of a corporation is actually a complex utility function involving trade-offs among at least three values. The actual utility function that shapes the reasoning about firm decisions often has other utilities in it, such as reputation (crucial for professional firms), craftsmanship, commitment to a historical industry (e.g., Ford's commitment to the American car market for a long period in which they had to spend profits earned abroad to sustain American losses), satisfying regulatory authorities, safety (for example, unless deep sea diving firms treat safety as a more or less ultimate value, they have difficulty hiring experienced divers), or developing new products (a general feature of firms in the chemical industry, for example).

The point then is not that institutions of reason never maximize the same things people do, such as profits. Instead the contrast is that institutions of reason, even when maximizing something that an individual entrepreneur might maximize, do so by controlling and limiting the rationality of their component individuals. A main implication of this essay is that, as a primitive institution of reason, a corporation will tend to look in certain respects like the institutions of justice or the institutions of science, though these maximize other conventionalized utilities than profits. In other respects, of course, corporations look quite different from the law or from science.

In particular institutions of reason will tend to have roles making important institutional decisions which are organized as *fiduciary* roles, roles whose defining features have much to do with *responsibility* for the general structure relating the institution's conventionalized utility function to the rationalized procedures that make up its formal organization. Such responsible roles are, then, in particular responsible for *creating* the formal procedures, formal job descriptions, and the like, that constitute the institution as a formal organization. Such a structure describes well the internal organization of the corporation.

Of course such "responsibility" to an institutionalized utility function may not in fact produce the utilities for individuals it is supposed to. For example, if "responsible" military reason, as exemplified in the higher staff colleges of a country's armed services and carried into reality by the generals trained there, creates a national security utility function that makes an international arms race an equilibrium outcome, every nation's security may in fact be decreased. Responsibly extending such a utility function into space may (or, of course, may not) destabilize the balance of terror that keeps the peace, and may wipe out all the people who might otherwise have had different utilities. In modern states not too many individuals find it rational in their personal best interests to go to war, but a well developed tradition of rationality built up in a staff college may make it institutionally reasonable and responsible for millions to go to war. Part of the problem here is that not all people's individual interests may get into the utility function that institutions become committed to. Part of the problem is that specialized rationalities may not be able to handle reasonably utilities outside their purview. (See Weber 1922, 171, on why pacifist movements very often fail.)

To some degree acting as a fiduciary on behalf of individuals (on behalf of beneficiaries of a trust, or on behalf of stockholders in a corporation entrusting investments to a board of directors, etc.) is much the same sort of thing. When for example an inheritance is administered by a trustee on behalf of a minor child, the trustee is supposed to create a fictional utility function for the child—"what the child would choose if he or she were an adult." Fiduciary institutions will develop rules deriving from an institutionalized notion of what such a utility function ought to look like, and courts will try to enforce vague trade-offs by a "reasonable man rule." What shows that a trustee is not acting "as an agent" on behalf of a "principal" is that the child does not get to correct the trustee when he or she does not agree with the trustee's interpretation of the utility function, while presumably a principal does.

There is then continuous variation between this notional utility function of an abstract beneficiary of a trust and the imposed utility function of principals who impart (with sanctions of their own choosing) information to an agent about what their individual utility functions actually are.

The more the rational faculty of people adapting action to a situation is governed by an institutionalized definition of what utility function ought to be maximized, the more we have to deal with "reason" rather than "rationality." And the more this is true, the more what is demanded of the actor in an institutionalized role is "responsibility," pursuing institutionalized utility functions rationally in changing situations, rather than the "rationality" that is assumed about the agent in the economic theory of the principal-agent relationship. Thus a physician may refuse to accept the wishes of the parents (who are paying) that a defective baby should not be given expensive life support (which the parents will have to pay for although they opposed it). The partiality of the institutionalization of a utility function for the clients is indicated by the fact that the physician will follow the parents wishes during the first trimester of pregnancy, and that it is only after the child is potentially viable that a fictionalized utility function of the child spends the parents' money.

The question of the definition and social supports of "responsibility" in general is beyond the scope of this essay (see Heimer 1986).

But from the point of view of this essay, what this conception of responsibility implies is that much of the substantive content of reason in the socially institutionalized sense is the same sort of calculation that is involved in the theory of rationality. Insofar as people are being responsible members of an institution embodying reason, what they are quite often doing is to behave as if they were rational individuals, but trying to maximize someone else's utility function. The function may be that which some sort of abstract someone else (an ideal system of justice, the advance of science, or a conventionalized idea of what the utility function of a minor child who was an adult would look like) is imagined to have by an institution responsible for the values. But that means they have to be prevented by the institution from being rational on their own behalf, so that they can be rational on behalf of such an institutionalized fiction.

## NORMATIVE RATIONALITY IN INSTITUTIONS OF REASON

If we now imagine the history of a body of doctrine embedded in an institution like we have just described, it will be a process of depositing precedents by a long line of people professionally concerned with trying to embody rational decision-making in a set of institutional practices. Each improvement of institutional regulations will be, at least in apparent intention, for example, a development of a more complex notion of what is needed to maximize the long run welfare of minor beneficiaries of trusts, or what is needed to maximize the long-run degree of support for scientific creativity in the structure of careers in universities, or whatnot.

We can think of such a history as an evolutionary process, in which, by and large, a more nuanced and rational way of maximizing the long run welfare of minor children or of scientific creativity will tend to win out. It will win out because the principles of reason are institutionalized over a long period of time, and people keep on applying their rational faculties to improving the rationality of that fictional child or improving the fictional utility function of the advance of science. The individuals who have, during this evolutionary process, applied their rational faculties to a particular maximization problem in a particular situation may not have been able to maximize the whole utility function over the whole set of aspects of the situation, but may have improved it somewhat for that particular situation.

What this means in its turn is that there may be an "institutional wisdom," a rationality at a deeper level than is routinely understood consciously by the practitioners, so that by following the tradition of the institution people do better, behave more rationally, than they would do with their unaided rational faculties.

Where there are subtle problems in particular kinds of contracts, such as the problem of "moral hazard" in insurance contracts, then one may find a model of what is rational in the institutions of insurance that is as good as the rational model even an expert in rationality can construct *ab novo*. An empirical investigation of how the institutions of insurance deal with varying problems of moral hazard, such as that carried out in Carol A. Heimer's *Reactive Risk and Rational Action* (1985b), may be more illuminating about what is rational from the point of view of an individual insurer than the advice the insurer might get from Kenneth Arrow (1971). Of course, then again, it may not.

The tradition of the American or English law review article is to apply this insight to the codification of law, and thereby to its improvement. The notion is that if one can find the deep structure behind the individual opinions on appellate decisions, the argument of the review article will be more reasonable as a paradigm of calculation on how to achieve the ends in view in a given area of law, and consequently will be more rational for individuals to know whenever they want to use the law for their own purposes. Similarly Paul Lazarsfeld's mode of developing the methodology of quantitative social science, by picking out pieces of quantitative analysis he thought good and trying to give a systematic account of the reasoning behind what they had done, takes advantage of the rationality of individuals in their particular situations to construct a better "model of a social scientist acting rationally."

The evolutionary drift is, in general, governed by the institutionalized utility function it is supposed to serve. After the "liberal revolution" in English law, the revolution often associated with the name of Jeremy Bentham, the evolutionary drift of master-servant law in both England and the United States was in the direction of destroying all non-market protections of workers (Kim Scheppele pointed this out in a critique of a previous version of this paper; she mentioned specifically the fellow-servant rule, which largely exempted employers from liability for industrial accidents). The time span between the big change in philosophy (marked, say, by the new poor laws or by the repeal of the statute of artificers) and the development of a thoroughly bourgeois master-servant common law should be measured in decades or half centuries, perhaps the ordinary pace of social evolutionary processes.

The tendency of British trade unions to think that all law and all formal regulation will be to the disadvantage of the working class (and the lesser version of this belief in the United States), and the lowered assent to efficiency-improving innovations that it has carried with it, may be the indirect outcome of that persistent antiproletarian evolution which rationalized Benthamite thought in nineteenth-century labor law.

The only thing that can be expected to improve over time in an institution of reason is the intellectual technology for refining and achieving institutionalized utilities or values. Those purposes tend to be refined, the trade-off between them made subtler, their adaptation to a changing world made more rapid, by being embedded in an institution of reason. This fine tuning may, of course, be quite socially irrational if, for example, creating agile institutions for destroying protections of workers intensifies class conflict. As Andrew Abbott put it in a critique of an earlier draft, "There is . . . a 'politics' of who is the client hidden behind your evolutionist view."

The prediction of evolutionary improvement of the reasonableness of institutions of reason is derived from the ideal type. One of the most common ways for the ideal type to fail to be fulfilled in reality is for individual rewards to become tied to particular actions in the institutions. The special concern of foreign language departments in universities a few years ago to preserve language requirements for scientific degrees, the drift of obstetric practice away from vaginal deliveries toward higher-fee caesarean, the careful preservation of impossibly complex land transfer procedures in English law (Andrew Abbott pointed out this example in the critique mentioned above), all show that reason often has a hard time winning out over the interests of institutional practitioners. Other people's interests may be rationalized away without much delay, as in the case of non-market protections of workers mentioned above, but solicitors' interests are very resistant to rationalization.

The same interrelationship between reason and rationality that explains evolutionary improvement in institutionalized reason means that development of the theory of rationality may itself make substantial contributions to institutional development. For example, the development of formal risk analysis in actuarial science and in economic theory has contributed to the specification of what a life insurance company should look like (specifications in turn to be embedded in regulations requiring life insurance companies to look like that). This improves the ability of buyers of insurance to cover the risks they want to insure against as much as they want to, for the premium they are willing to pay, by guaranteeing the amount of risk reduction the contract formally promises through reserve requirements imposed on insurance companies (Hansmann 1985, 133–38). In the old days before such regulations, the only way to get insurance companies to keep enough reserves so they could actually pay off was to organize a mutual—once the state figured out what an insurance company had to do to be safe, and demanded it of all insurance companies, then one could buy as good insurance from a stock company as from a mutual, and evolutionary pressures started which increased the proportion of all insurance provided by stock companies.

That is, because many of the substantive purposes of bodies of reason require the application of that reason to maximizing the welfare of clients, or maximizing an institutionalized system of trade-offs which might be called the institution's utility function, institutions have a built in interest in developments in the formal theory of rationality. For example, when new optimizing techniques are developed in statistics for unusual situations ("robust" statistics), they spread quickly in the relevant scientific community, and are demanded in situations where before other, more vulnerable, methods gave the same results. When economically more rational methods of cash management are developed, auditors start to look askance at companies that keep too large balances in too highly liquid (and hence low return) accounts. And in general the innovations of economics spread out imperially to the institutions of reason, as maximizing principles designed to explain the behavior of rational actors become institutionalized principles of how reason should be applied. This makes economics a broadly "applied" discipline, because its micro theory promptly becomes institutionalized in many places in social life.

Institutionalization of new varieties of reason of course often leads to fake rationality. People use the newest statistical procedures when they have not yet learned to manage them. For example, I recall Jöreskog (1973) using LISREL in an early example in a data set that caused him to overestimate the measurement error of a verbal test, hence overestimate its effect, and consequently to show that mathematical ability decreased achievement in science—almost any standard psychometric method of estimating the measurement error of the verbal test (including looking it up in a reference on psychometric tests) would have given better results than this "provably statistically best" technique. Computer simulations of infantry and armored tactics are usually constructed in imaginary perfectly flat fields, and so greatly underestimate the value of shovels as defensive weapons, and hence greatly overestimate the value of armor and mobile artillery (Stockfisch 1973). Cost-benefit techniques are generally alleged to underestimate the effects of a program on utilities that are hard to measure (though convincing examples are hard to come by). The general point is that fashions in rational technique can spread faster than their value justifies, and value choices can be concealed in the choice of technique not understood by the people or organizations whose utilities are supposedly being maximized by rational means.

In spite of all the reservations above, I am arguing something stronger than an evolutionary pressure on formal rationality. If reasons must be given and defended, if self-interested behavior of institutional officials is seen as a force that has to be protected against, and all the rest, then good reasons will tend to dominate in the long run over bad reasons—that is my argument. For example: the evolution of course content (as part of the substantively rational institution of science) will be faster than the evolution of the course numbering system (as a part of formal rationality); course content will evolve in the same direction in different countries, while course numbering systems will differ radically between countries; in rationalized legal systems procedural rights essential to the achievement of justice will tend to be instituted more readily (and will die out more slowly) than procedures that make people consult lawyers over simple land transfers; if the extra caesareans actually kill more mothers and babies than retaining more vaginal births would, the institution of medicine will eventually work out tighter decision principles on when caesareans are indicated, when vaginal births are indicated. In short, I am arguing for a reserved and somewhat cynical polyanna view of the institutions of reason, insofar as the institution fits the ideal type developed above. The "insofar" in the previous sentence is central to the argument of this essay.

## REASON AS A SOCIAL BASIS FOR RATIONALITY

Max Weber emphasizes the importance of the predictability of the law for capitalism (Weber 1921–22, 333–37). Capitalism involves coordinated activity, and the mechanisms of coordination are political creations like money, sales and labor contracts, penal law for thefts, organizational charters for corporations, and so on. Weber's argument is that such market coordination ("the peaceful pursuit of market advantage," in Weber's phrase) can only take place if these political instrumentalities of market exchange are available to participants in the market on predictable terms. Only if the political system is predictable (at least in respect to these central mechanisms of exchange) is the rational calculation of the meaning of contracts, charters of incorporation, and the like, possible. Weber studies the rationalization of law because, he argues, rationalization is the central process that increases predictability of the law.

Paul Starr (1982, 112–44) makes a rather similar point about medicine, that the establishment of the cultural authority of medicine involved the institutionalization of many of the features of the ideal type of reason as outlined above, and that the consequence of this was a sense among the public of the predictability of what sort of medicine one was going to get if one went to a physician. To establish the right to a monopoly over medical practice, medicine had to establish that the service one got from a certified physician was reliably better than one would get elsewhere. This required, in Magali Sarfatti Larson's wonderful phrase, "the production of standardized producers" of professional services (1977, 14–18). But that standardization in its turn required the rationalization of medicine, and in particular its rationalization as a "science" which could claim cultural authority from its method, and its rationalization as a subject for a school, which could transfer that cultural authority to practicing clinicians.

In both these cases there are actually two aspects to the use that non-practitioners make of the fact that a body of culture has been rationalized. The first has to do with the fact that any paradigm with nonrandom rules of calculation of authoritative outcomes is *predictable*. The printing of the marriage service in the Book of Common Prayer makes the content of the ceremony predictable, without presumably making it any more effective in achieving the ends of the parties to the marriage; the printed version is an authoritative paradigm without any pretence to a rationalization which might establish that this was a *better* marriage ceremony.

The second has to do with the presumption that the long-term evolution of repeated applications of reason to institutional practice will have made, for example, the standard form of the contract efficient for the usual ends of capitalist contracting parties, or will have produced the best standardized producer of medical services that could reasonably be produced with the current knowledge of bacteriology, oncology, and anesthesiology.

The first of these features of the activities of the institutions of reason ensures that the parties to various interactions know what to calculate about in maximizing their own ends. They provide secure inputs of knowledge of what will happen under this and that condition for the calculations of actors in the market, without the parties having to invent complicated structures of hostages, reserves of resources in escrow, and the like, that would otherwise be required to make contracts certain. It "reduces transaction costs" to have such paradigms institutionalized elsewhere.

In the extreme, the paradigms of reasoned action may be so thoroughly embedded in the structure of the offer the institution makes that clients need not (and sometimes cannot) calculate about it at all. For example, by offering health insurance in group plans only if all the employees of a company are required to be covered, insurance companies prevent "adverse selection," namely people buying insurance only if they know they are in bad health and likely to need it. Except when people try to buy the same insurance individually, and discover they must pay twice as much, they do not ever calculate the advantages of buying insurance with a contract that prevents adverse selection from operating. If the health insurance company does not offer individual insurance (as many do not) the client cannot calculate even from market information the advantages of a contract that prevents adverse selection.

The second feature, that institutionalized reason has been repeatedly applied to improve institutional practice, secures the quality of the service being rendered by the institution. The clients need not develop the competence to make rational choices for themselves, because lawyers', physicians', scientists', or auditors' skills will make a better choice than they could themselves. One need not worry because one knows how the courts will interpret a standard contract, but one also need not worry because the standard contract will provide for most of the contingencies that need to be provided for in ordinary business relations, without having to hire a master of contract law to advise one on constructing such a contract. One can consult standard statistics textbooks so that one's computations will give the same result as is common in one's discipline, but also do so rather than going back to read R. A. Fisher on why maximum likelihood is in general a best estimate, because one can have (more or less) faith that the writers of statistics textbooks will have examined Fisher's reasoning, and will have picked out the best statistic. One reduces computation costs for oneself by using institutionalized computations, because one has some faith that those institutionalized computations will be as good as one could do for oneself.

Of course the institution can create a situation in which "the good is the enemy of the best," because for example cookbook techniques in a scientific discipline are accepted by referees who were trained to use them, preventing especially sophisticated practitioners from using techniques more appropriate to the particular problem being addressed. One may have to write a general article justifying a method before one can use the method in a particular substantive work, because one needs a citation to show that it is part of the paradigm. I have enough examples of this that I could write a long, tedious and tendentious paragraph here on the subject.

Thus rationalized institutions, the embodiment of reason in social life, improve the rationality of individuals. They do so first by regularizing social and political life, that principal source of uncertainty in attempts to apply rationality to one's personal goals. And they do so secondly by enabling one to construct one's rationality out of pieces of reasoning which someone better at it than the client has already "suboptimized," in the sense of perfecting the reasoning in that piece so that for most purposes of most clients, there will be no better solution of a legal, medical, scientific, or auditing problem.

## CONCLUSION

The achievement of civilization could be formulated as the successful detachment of the faculties that make people rational from the limiting context of personal goals, so that they can be applied to the improvement of social life. The result of such provision of an "irrational" context for the faculties of rationality is an improvement in rationality through the institutionalization of reason. The institutionalization of reason in vari-

313

ous fields makes people individually more rational. If Weber was right, the rationalization of law makes the free market possible; at least it is clear that it makes it a lot easier, reduces transaction costs, and generally lubricates the wheels of capitalism. Rational actor models become reasonable models of individual action especially in societies in which a lot of people's rational faculties are applied to the maximization of goals not their own.

But the case is more complicated still, for much of the content of rationalized institutions, those institutions which have to be defended against corruption, against the individual rationalities of the judges, consists of models for maximization. This is perhaps most obvious if we examine who mostly uses the latest advances of economics to maximize economic goals—it is usually corporate entities run by people who are, as best we as stockholders can secure it, maximizing on behalf of someone else. Corporate policy is more shaped by the normative content of economic science than is the policy of individuals. But it is also true that judges try to set up the rules for interpreting contracts so as not to interfere with their understanding of what rational actors will be trying to achieve with the law of contracts; the science that goes into auditing (including the special branches like actuarial science that goes into auditing insurance companies) is a science of what a corporation ought to be doing in order for a rational person to want to invest in it. So the body of institutionalized reason includes as a large part of its substantive content the norms of rationality in the narrow sense, a body of doctrine about how best to maximize returns or minimize costs.

In order to embody rationality and reason in institutions protected from too much rationality of their institutional practitioners, one has to construct institutions with due care that the utilities and rationalities of the judges can be achieved without undermining reason in social life. Such protections in fact require intelligent attention by the judges themselves. This is most obvious when a judge personally has to declare that he or she is too much an interested party in a case to render an unbiased judgment and so should be disqualified. But the vigorous debates about, for example, what "academic freedom" ought to consist of, how it should be defended, which parts should be part of the contract of employment of professors as construed by the courts and which merely parts of the grievance procedure within universities, and the like, show that a good deal of intellectual effort has to go into keeping the institutions of reason in good shape. One needs judges who are not only disinterested in particular cases, but also are disinterested developers of better institutions of reason itself (cf. Oakeshott 1962, 100–106, for the argument that rationality works mainly by improving a traditional line of conduct, i.e., by improving "reason" as defined here).

Such institutions of reason render social life more predictable. Since it is in social life that most valuable things are created, this means that most sources of most valuable things will be more amenable to rational self-interested calculation in societies that are more rationalized. But the institutions of reason would not govern so much of social life unless they were seen not only as predictable, but also as better. And they will be seen as better only if people do not have the daily experience of knowing better than the institutions they have to deal with. Unless the teacher actually knows more about the subject than the student, academic authority is unstable. Unless medicine has better answers on the average than chiropractic, it will not be likely to gain a monopoly of delivery of medical services (insurance companies would presumably usually rather pay the lower fees of chiropractors, if they could convince their clients that the services were as effective—but in fact insurors generally refuse to pay chiropractic fees, because the reasoning behind their expertise does not enjoy cultural authority). And in general unless rationalized institutions give, on the average, better answers than the unaided reason of individuals, they will not prosper and grow.

The social matrix of individual rationality then is institutionalized reason, and people are more rational than they used to be because they live in a more rationalized society.

## REFERENCES

Arrow, Kenneth. 1971. *Essays in the Theory of Risk Bearing.* Chicago: Markham.
Bourdieu, Pierre. 1984. *Distinction: A Social Critique of the Judgment of Taste.* Cambridge, MA: Harvard.
Braithwaite, John. 1984. *Corporate Crime in the Pharmaceutical Industry.* London: Routledge and Kegan Paul.
Coser, Lewis A., Charles Kadushin and Walter W. Powell. 1982. *Books: The Culture and Commerce of Publishing.* New York: Basic Books.
Dewey, John. 1958. *Art as Experience.* New York: Capricorn Books.
Geller, Stephen. 1983. "Autopsy." *Science American* 248:124–136.
Gilbert, J. P., R. J. Light and F. Mosteller. 1975. "Assessing Social Innovation: An Empirical Base for Policy." In *Evaluation and Experiment,* edited by C. A. Bennett and A. A. Lumsdaine. New York: Academic Press.
Gilbert, J. P., B. McPeek and F. Mosteller, 1977. "Progress in Surgery and Anesthesia: Benefits and Risks in Innovative Therapy." In *Costs, Risks and Benefits of Surgery,* edited by J. P. Bunker, B. A. Barnes and F. Mosteller. New York: Oxford University Press.

Hansmann, Henry. 1985. "The Organization of Insurance Companies: Mutual versus Stock." *Journal of Law, Economics and Organization* 1:125–53.

Heimer, Carol A. 1985a. "Allocating Information Costs in a Negotiated Information Order: Interorganizational Constraints on Decision Making in Norwegian Oil Insurance." *Administrative Science Quarterly* 30:395–417.

———. 1985b. *Reactive Risk and Rational Action*. Berkeley: University of California Press.

———. 1986. "On Taking Responsibility." Northwestern University. Unpublished ms.

Jaeger, Gertrude, and Philip Selznick. 1964. "A Normative Theory of Culture." *American Sociological Review* 29:653–69.

Jöreskog, K. G. 1973. "A General Method for Estimating a Linear Structural Equation System." In *Structural Equation Models in the Social Sciences,* edited by Arthur S. Goldberger and Otis Dudley Duncan, 85–112. New York: Seminar Press.

Kalberg, S. 1980. "Max Weber's Types of Rationality: Cornerstones for the Analysis of Rationalization Processes in History." *American Journal of Sociology* 85:1145–79.

Larson, Magali Sarfatti. 1977. *The Rise of Professionalism: A Sociological Analysis*. Berkeley: University of California Press.

Oakeshott, Michael. 1962. "Rational Conduct." In *Rationalism in Politics and Other Essays,* by Michael Oakeshott, 80–110. London: Methuen.

Parsons, Talcott. (1937) 1949. *The Structure of Social Action*. New York: Free Press.

———. (1939) 1954. "The Professions and Social Structure." In *Essays in Sociology,* by Talcott Parsons, 34–49. New York: Free Press.

Schelling, Thomas. 1971. "Dynamic Models of Segregation." *Journal of Mathematical Sociology* 1:143–86.

———. 1978. *Micromotives and Macrobehavior*. New York: W. W. Norton.

Starr, Paul. 1982. *The Social Transformation of American Medicine*. New York: Basic Books.

Stockfisch, Jacob A. 1973. *Plowshares into Swords: Managing the American Defense Establishment*. New York: Mason and Lipscomb.

Taub, Richard P., D. Garth Taylor, and Jan D. Dunham. 1984. *Paths of Neighborhood Change: Race and Crime in Urban America*. Chicago: University of Chicago Press.

Veblen, Thorstein. (1899) 1934. *The Theory of the Leisure Class*. New York: Random House Modern Library.

Veyne, Paul. 1976. *Le pain et le cirque: Sociologie historique d'un pluralisme politique*. Paris: Editions de Seuil.

Weber, Max. (1919) 1946. "Science as a Vocation." In *From Max Weber: Essays in Sociology,* edited by Hans H. Gerth and C. Wright Mills, 129–56. New York: Oxford University Press.

———. (1921) 1946. "Politics as a Vocation." In *From Max Weber: Essays in Sociology,* edited by Hans H. Gerth and C. Wright Mills, 77–128. New York: Oxford University Press.

———. (1921–1922) 1968. *Economy and Society,* edited by Gunther Roth and Claus Wittich. New York: Bedminster Press.

———. (1922) 1946. "Structures of Power." In *From Max Weber: Essays in Sociology,* edited by Hans H. Gerth and C. Wright Mills, 159–79. New York: Oxford University Press.

Zuckerman, Harriet, and Robert K. Merton. 1971. "Patterns of Evaluations in Science: Institutionalization, Structure, and Functions of the Referee System." *Minerva* 9:66–100.

## COMMENT: *Stinchcombe's "Reason and Rationality"*
### Andrew Abbott

Stinchcombe's paper embodies the combination of rationalism and functionalism long characteristic of his theoretical work. My comments on his argument will therefore implicitly concern the more general uses of these theoretical styles. But I shall remain close to his details, hoping to avoid trading abstractions in a factual vacuum. I shall also sketch the basic structure of my own theory of the events Stinchcombe analyzes, thereby giving readers clear grounds for comparison.

Stinchcombe makes five major points. The first is that reason in the broad sense of thought governed by authoritative norms should be distinguished from reason in the narrow sense of an optimized calculus of ends and means, the latter being what we usually call rationality. I shall hereafter call these two versions reason(1) and reason(2). Stinchcombe then argues that there are institutions of reason(1) and that they share certain common properties: (1) specialists, (2) rationalizable knowledge, (3) formally defensible decisions, (4) control of practitioner interests, and (5) maintenance of regular information. Third, institutions of reason follow "institutional utility functions" analogous to those hypothesized for individuals by microeconomists. While reason(2) (calculating rationality) is one such utility function, it is not the only possibility. Fourth, reason(1) and its institutions survive, in the long run, only if they produce "good results." Moreover, over the long run they will improve their "intellectual technology for refining and achieving institutionalized utilities or values." Fifth, institutionalized reason(1) permits individuals to improve their reason(2) by insuring predictability of outcome and optimality of technique (under current conditions) over a wide range of human activities.

The definitional aspects of Stinchcombe's position may be accepted as given. Distinguishing reason and rationality (thereby returning the former to its Enlightenment sense) affords a useful premise for discussion. The five-point ideal type of institutionalized reason(1) basically repeats the picture of bureaucratic expertise familiar from Hegel and Weber. These definitional points granted, Stinchcombe's positive position rests on the assertions that institutions of reason exist in fact, that they survive through efficacy, and that they improve through practice. I will argue that these positions are empirically problematic and, moreover, that they end up hiding many of the interesting questions about "institutions of reason."

First, existence. Social structures resembling Stinchcombe's version of the Weberian ideal type clearly exist in all developed societies, most commonly taking the form of professions. The five properties Stinchcombe lists do characterize professions, although with important caveats in every case. Specialism exists in most of the professions, but civil and military service, business management, and other administrative groups are clear exceptions. Rationalizability of knowledge pervades the twentieth-century professions, although nineteenth-century professions cared little about it. Arrangements for controlling practitioners' interests are common (ethics codes, disciplinary bodies), although generally conceded to be ineffectual. Defense of judgments is central to professional beliefs, but rare in practice. The Stinchcombian ideal type is thus commonly embodied in modern societies, certainly in the legitimation claims of professions and to a lesser extent in their practice as well. But does the partial resemblance of twentieth-century professions to this ideal type guarantee that those professions *are* institutions of reason in the broader theoretical sense Stinchcombe intends?

There are several reasons why it does not, each arising from a caveat just mentioned. First, early professionalism laid much less claim to rationality than to good character and exclusive (as opposed to rational) knowledge. Stinchcombe might answer that these improve predictability, but so, after all, do train schedules. The connection of reason(1) to the early professions may in fact be adventitious. Standardized production of standardized producers in medicine, for example, considerably antedates scientific rationalization of medicine in the sense Stinchcombe means. Second, twentieth-century professions resemble institutions of reason far more in the legitimation claims of professional leaders than in actual professional practice. Perhaps claims of reason(1) simply conceal monopolistic intent. While Stinchcombe might argue that his argument doesn't promise perfection, enough doubt has been cast on it by the monopolization theory of professions that he must provide an affirmative demonstration that professions are "reasonable" in the broad sense.

Third, central to Stinchcombe's conception is the notion of an institutional utility function, a calculus of values, costs, objectives, principles, and the like, behaving rather like an individual utility function. Can we argue that such things exist in professions? More precisely, are the assumptions involved in the assertion that they exist worth the trouble they cause? Leaving aside the usual problems with the concept of individual utility functions (for example, their assumption of general commensurability), we can at least agree that an individual has a utility function and makes decisions based on it. But here *society* has the utility function and *specialists* act on it. How does that work? To answer "through institutionalization," as Stinchcombe essentially does, is to dump all the interesting questions about the history of institutions of reason into the word "institutionalization" and ignore them. Following the functional logic familiar in the Davis-Moore theory of stratification, one could argue that professionals as a group are given rewards conditional on the *overall* professional provision of service. But who judges the latter? What services are involved? Which values predominate? Who decides whether accounting rules work? Does "working" include nonviolation of general rules of equity? Does it entail maximization of public benefit, or shareholder benefit, or state benefit? Again, we require an affirmative demonstration that the admittedly pretty notion of utility functions is more than the tautology it typically becomes in imperialist economic writing.

Considering the existence of institutions of reason thus leads ineluctably to the questions of their survival and improvement. For Stinchcombe's theory is fundamentally an evolutionary theory. Like any evolutionary theory it requires variation, competition, and selection. With variation I have no problems; it is endemic in history. But consider again the problem of selection, just mentioned. How long does it take irrational or functionless professions or professional ideas to be destroyed? Who does it and how? Most important, can one show that professions themselves do not manipulate mechanisms of selection? If the answer to this last is no—and it most certainly is—we have the most damaging possible criticism of Stinchcombe's theory. For if professions themselves control the mechanisms of selection, then no feedback can dislodge them. (This is a case of the "functional historicist causation" outlined by Stinchcombe himself years ago [1967]). Yet we know that nineteenth-century medicine persuaded people that more shock meant better cures, even while homeopaths, with their mild therapies, killed fewer patients and hence performed "objectively" better services. Professions, that is, not only coopt state authority, but largely control definitions of efficacy itself. But in that case professions are nearly impregnable.

What about competition? Clearly, professions and professional ideas will be unseated only if more effective competitors emerge, something Stinchcombe has ignored. He has no explanation for where competitors come from, how they overcome direct opposition by settled practitioners, who or what provides their start-up resources, and so on. It's rather like examining a so-called competitive market without recognizing the effects of initial distributions of wealth. Even more important, there is buried in Stinchcombe's analysis an assumption that the work performed by institutions of reason is somehow "out there," to be gradually discovered by the evolutionary process of trial and error. (This assumption is parallel to the general microeconomic assumption that "the market" is there, rather than being a constructed thing.) But there is massive evidence that professions create the work they do as much as they discover it. Psychiatry with neurosis is merely the most famous case. Medicine itself has created the syllogism that "doing the function of health" is a matter of "saving the dying," when in fact most health improvements in modern society came from public health measures. The modern idea of profit—not in the vague functional sense of coming out better than before but in the specific and ultimately most important sense of showing black on the balance sheet—is largely a creation of accounting conventions. That this "works" in the sense that firms showing such "profits" survive may be due as much to self-fulfilling prophecy as to the "scientific" accuracy of accounting. The central point is that professions partially constitute what they do, thereby exercising enormous definitional control over it, control that translates into an ability to hide the evidence of failure necessary to propel Stinchcombian evolution. It is worth noting that some recent work in biology explicitly considers the ability of the organism to define its own niche (Levins and Lewontin 1985).

Moreover, Stinchcombe's evolutionary position implies convergence among experts. What "works" in America should "work" in France, Japan, etc. Yet we see enormous variation in experts worldwide. The United States has many lawyers, Japan few. Librarians and their books have dominated information systems in America, while documentalists and their databases have done so in Europe. The same kinds of differences exist in the social structures of these "institutions of reason." In America professions tend to be independent and powerful; in France, they are state-controlled and unionized. Why should massive law firms have developed in the United States when the English refused barristers the right to partnership and the French held legal firms to five principals? These are important, and many of them continuing, differences among experts, and yet Stinchcombe's evolutionary theory, with its corollary of convergence, must ignore them all. He has remembered what he taught us about functionalist causation, but forgotten what he said about historicism (Stinchcombe 1967).

My central arguments against Stinchcombe's position are thus: (1) that he assumes expert work is "there" rather than partly self-generated, (2) that he ignores the ability of "unreasonable" institutions of reason to coopt and control the selection devices governing evolution, (3) that he cannot account for either international variation or the emergence of the competitors that drive evolution, (4) that he assumes rather than demonstrates the "reasonability" of institutions of reason, and (5) that his central idea of institutional utility functions involves assumptions tenable at the individual level but impossibly obscure at the group level.

These problems are partly problems of length. In a more elaborate analysis they would be confronted more directly. But they reflect problems inherent in the functional approach. The first such problem is ahistoricity. It is of course true that efficacy affects the survival of professions and their subsegments. But notions of efficacy change, just as notions of the expertised things-to-be-done change. Yet Stinchcombe makes the implicit assumption that neither changes, that there is a given world, with given work to be done and given criteria for how well it is done, *sicut erat in principio et nunc et semper et in saecula saeculorum.*

Stinchcombe's difficulties here point to a larger issue in the current expansion of rational choice theory. To ignore the continually changing criteria of success, the partially reflexive change of tasks and products, the fluctuating cultural construction of professional work, is to impose a simple external explanatory scheme on turf unsuited for it. Many of the more esoteric applications of choice theory have the same quality; intellectually challenging and elegant, they are ultimately less effective than less abstract theories formed with more respect for the data. Thus, someone might argue that the "economic irrationality" of Middle Ages can be explained not as a matter of people not caring about the thing a modern economist calls value but as a long price freeze. I suppose one could think about medieval land law that way, but to do so ignores most of the interesting things-to-be-explained about the period. Even if such explanations produced one or two surprises, a medievalist would find them ultimately uninteresting, and rightly so. They make too many unacceptable assumptions about the uniformity of human nature, about the unimportance of context, and about the fixity of a human world in fact subject to continual, reflexive reinterpretation. If we make utility analysis broad enough to embrace such things, as economists often do today (e.g., Hirshleifer 1985), it becomes a fairy tale. We simply have to accept the empirical fact that many people have *reasonably* (sense 1) behaved in ways we consider irrational (sense 2). That means that Stinchcombe's first point—the value of distinguishing reason(1) in the broad sense from reason(2) in the narrow sense—is decisively correct. Scholars who believe that all forms of disciplined thought or activity must be isomorphic to rationality in the narrow sense are dead wrong; Stinchcombe and I agree on that. But I feel that his reason(1) still draws on the untenable assumptions that lie behind the narrow view.

Another common functionalist problem evident in Stinchcombe's argument is the ignoring of power and its place in an apparently market-driven system. The equilibrating, evolving process Stinchcombe invokes can work only if one can demonstrate that professional power is unable to subvert it. I agree that ultimately power cannot defend inefficacy against efficacy. But one must make far more allowances for power, take it far more seriously than this paper does, if one is to provide a theory that effectively accounts for the development of institutions of reason. The time required to dislodge inefficacious professional power may be fifty to a hundred years. Unimportant in the grand scheme of things, such a period still embraces several human generations; we cannot ignore professional authority that is unjustified by results but yet endures so long.

My own view of professional "institutions of reason" (Abbott 1988), like Stinchcombe's, makes broadly functional, evolutionary assumptions. At any given time there is a group of professions and a group of tasks to be done. The activity of professional work—diagnosing, treating, inferring, researching—transforms undefined tasks into fully shaped areas of professional work. It creates links between professions and these areas of work, links that I call links of jurisdiction. These cultural links have greater or lesser strength depending on efficacy of treatment as well as on dozens of other things. Jurisdictional links are then reinforced by social claims before public, workplace, and legal audiences, as well as by structural rearrangements of professions themselves. These social links may also be reinforced by various forms of power. The structure of jurisdictional links (social and cultural) at any given time makes up a tightly bound ecology of groups and niches, a system of professions. Into this system come changes from various sources. Some are internal to individual professions; shifts in demographic structure, in organization for work, in stratification, and in knowledge available to do work. Others are external, arising in the general social and cultural systems: new areas for professional work, new ways of organizing work, new audiences for professional claims, new forms of knowledge, new concepts of legitimacy, new structures for knowledge transfer and development. These external changes affect professions idiosyncratically, since the current arrangement of jurisdictions makes such changes help some professions while hurting others. Once a change falls on the system, its force is absorbed through an extensive and competitive jostling among the existing (and possibly new) professions. Since changes are common and continuous, the system is perpetually reshuffling itself.

Now this model involves plenty of rational choice. Professions can choose various jurisdictional and structural strategies, for example. But the external forces imposing changes on the system cannot be so understood. Nor can the *effects* of professional choices, for these depend not only on the ensemble of other competitors and their choices (other competitors who are not simply the faceless many of microeconomics but a highly individualized few, themselves facing complex situations on other fronts). These effects also depend on dozens of unforeseen system interconnections and on the sudden restructurings that result from global changes in legitimation patterns and other cultural forces. The game, that is, can be remade at any time, both by the actors and by the larger system. One cannot then apply a rational choice model to the system in any but the loosest way. Efficacy probably does win out, but only in the very long run. And definitions of efficacy are ultimately hegemonic, not "true."

I thus agree with Stinchcombe's fundamental project. I, too, am a "cynical pollyanna" about institutions of reason. I deeply approve of his attempt to separate broad reason from narrow rationality, which reflects, it seems to me, his normative faith in the virtue of both reason and civilization. While I think he chooses badly in taking utility functions as models for reason in the broad sense, I appreciate the elegant parsimony involved. I have preferred to think of institutions of reason as a complex ecology, to specify the variables defining relations in that ecology, and, for the rest, to emphasize the immensely accidental quality of history. I *do* think our institutions of reason are both more creative and more dangerous than Stinchcombe does. But we agree that understanding them must be one of social theory's first tasks.

## REFERENCES

Abbott, A. 1988. *The System of Professions.* Chicago: University of Chicago Press.

Hirshleifer, J. 1985. "The Expanding Domain of Economics." *American Economic Review* 75: 53–68.

Levins, R., and R. Lewontin. 1985. *The Dialectical Biologist.* Cambridge: Harvard.

Stinchcombe, A. 1967. *Constructing Social Theories.* New York: Harcourt Brace.

## 9

# Managerial Dilemmas: Political Leadership in Hierarchies

## Gary J. Miller

As long as we insist on budget-balancing [in our system of incentives] and there are externalities present, we cannot achieve efficiency. Agents can cover improper actions behind the uncertainty concerning who was at fault. Since all agents cannot be penalized sufficiently for a deviation in the outcome, some agent always has an incentive to capitalize on this control deficiency.

(Bengt Holmstrom, 1982)

From very early times in organization theory, there have been two rather distinct literatures on the topic of organizational control. One views organizational control as a mechanistic problem of designing incentive systems and sanctions so that self-interested and intrinsically unmotivated employees will find it in their own interest to work toward the organization's goal. In other words, management is seen as shaping subordinate behavior through the correct system of rewards and punishments, aligning self-interest and organizational well-being.

This literature is associated with such luminaries as Frederick Taylor, the father of scientific management, who was a devout advocate of incentive wage systems as a way of motivating subordinates. It was certainly associated with historical figures in management, such as Henry Ford, who said that men work for two reasons: "One is for wages, and one is for fear of losing their jobs" (Halberstam 1986, 93). Most recently, economics has contributed "principal-agency theory." In this theory,

This article is based upon work supported in part by the National Science Foundation under grant #SES 8218571. In addition, I am especially grateful to Thomas Hammond, Jack Knott, and Terry Moe. Many of the ideas in this paper are clearly related to ideas that were worked out in the course of co-authoring a series of papers in organization theory with these three scholars over the past five years. Randy Calvert, Bob Bates, Bill Bianco, Eric Amel, Ray Brooks, Kenneth Shepsle and Krishna Ladha provided additional helpful comments. Elizabeth Case provided editorial assistance. Errors in this version are my own responsibility.

agents are perceived as having distinct tastes (such as the desire to limit costly effort or an aversion to risk) which they pursue as rational maximizing individuals. The principal's job is to anticipate the rational responses of these agents and to design a set of incentives such that the agents find it in their own interests to take the best possible set of actions (from the principal's perspective). "The behavior of the organization is the equilibrium behavior of a complex contractual system made up of maximizing agents with diverse and conflicting objectives" (Jensen 1983, 327).

"Leadership" plays virtually no role in this approach, since the manager's goal is essentially the engineering of the best possible "equilibrium behavior" of the self-interested agents bound by a system of contracts. If the manager has engineered the correct system of incentives, then she doesn't have to "lead" or "inspire" subordinates to do the right thing; they will be led by their own self-interested behavior to that correct behavior.

This entire literature contrasts sharply with the second, more organic, view of organizations, which is primarily centered in political science, sociology, and organizational psychology. This second literature regards the manager's primary role as demonstrating leadership—that is, inspiring a willingness to cooperate, to take risks, to go beyond the level of effort that a self-interested analysis of the incentives would summon. An early example of this literature is Chester Barnard's *Functions of the Executive* (1938). Barnard regards organizations as fundamentally cooperative groups of individuals, and the executive's primary job is the facilitation of this cooperation. The manager's task, according to the heart of this definition, is to inspire "sacrifice," rather than shape self-interest. Other "abilities will not be put forth, will not even be developed, without that sense of responsibility which makes the sacrifices involved a matter of course, and which elicits the initial faith in cooperation. . . . Organizations endure, however, in proportion to the bread of the morality by which they are governed. This is only to say that foresight, long purposes, high ideals, are the basis for the persistence of cooperation" (p. 282).

The contrast is clear. Economists assume subordinates make self-interested maximizing responses to incentive systems. Barnard urges managers to inspire subordinate "sacrifice" by the "breadth of morality" used in organizational governance. Economists must regard Barnard's urgings as futile at best, dangerously counterproductive at worst. Barnard and his disciples must feel that the mechanistic designing of "opti-mal contracts" is a chokingly narrow view of the possibilities of leader-ship.

The purpose of this essay is to argue that the view of management as the mechanical manipulation of economic incentives "self-destructs" under close examination, even under a basically economic set of assump-tions. That is, results from social choice theory demonstrate that it is logically impossible to design a mechanistic incentive/control system that convinces every individual in the organization that his or her own inter-ests are best pursued by close devotion to organizational interest. As Holmstrom's quote at the beginning of this essay argues, for every incen-tive system that has other desirable characteristics, there will always be incentives for some individuals to pursue a narrow definition of self-interest over organizational well-being.

If this is the case, then I submit that there will always be a competitive advantage for those organizations whose managers can inspire members to transcend short-term self-interest. This leads to an examination of yet another literature in modern economics: repeated game theory. Indeed, the primary research agenda in repeated game theory in the last few years has been the search for a formula for the evolution of social norms. I will argue that, because of the indeterminacy of repeated game theory, there will necessarily be a role for individual leadership—setting an example of self-denial, instilling ideals of commitment and loyalty, encouraging mutually reinforcing expectations of cooperation, very much as de-scribed by Chester Barnard fifty years ago.

While this paper will end up sounding somewhat negative toward principal-agency theory, and very positive about Chester Barnard, I want to make it clear at the beginning that my criticism of principal-agency theory is not methodological. Just because Chester Barnard's intuitions were relatively sound, I do not want to dismiss attempts to formulate consistent, rigorous theories that are consistent with those intuitions. The development of rigorous deductive theories from a relatively parsi-monious set of initial assumptions is both highly desirable and noticeably lacking in the "organic" view of managers that dominates political sci-ence and social psychology. Indeed, the challenge of these rigorous theo-ries is the primary contribution that economic theory can and has been making to the study of organizations. Political scientists and psycholo-gists can best respond to the challenge of economic analysis by demand-ing that economists make clear the testable implications of their elegant models, by empirically testing those implications, and (when the first theories are inevitably shown to be false at certain points) by providing competing, testable, but equally rigorous models.

## OVERCOMING INEFFICIENCY THROUGH HIERARCHY

As Alchian and Demsetz argue (1972), hierarchies exist because there are important efficiencies to be realized by coordinated group behavior. They capture this notion with the idea of "team production," in which the marginal productivity of one individual is itself a function of the performance of other individuals.

If there were no such interactive effects among individual effort levels and productivity, then there would be no efficiency gain from trying to coordinate their individual behaviors. It would not be possible to improve on an atomistic market situation in which each producer bought inputs from other individuals and sold outputs to other actors farther down the production chain.

In the presence of a team production process, Alchian and Demsetz argue that individual interest will clash with group well-being. The reason is that each individual's effort costs are experienced privately, while the benefits of their efforts are realized as a "public good." In such a case, the production efforts have production "externalities" that result in prisoners' dilemmas just as surely as do consumption externalities. No matter how hard everyone else is working, each individual will equate his own marginal effort cost with his share of the marginal profits generated by his effort. Since each individual normally realizes only a small fraction of the marginal profits generated by his own effort, then equilibrium behavior is inefficient. "Every team member would prefer a team in which no one, not even himself, shirked" (1972, 790).

Team shirking has been documented by social psychologists, who call it "social loafing" (Latane, Williams, and Harkins 1979; Edney 1979). In experiments with shouting and rope-pulling, they have demonstrated a general tendency for individuals to work less the more they believed other individuals were joining in their joint effort. This behavior is not restricted to the social psychology laboratory; it evidently plagued workers whose job it was to tow boats along canals in prerevolutionary China (Cheung 1983).

It should be noted, however, that the concept of "shirking" is not restricted to the problem of laziness or loafing. Even the dictionary definition of shirking means "the avoidance or evasion of duty" (for whatever reason). In the context of our paper, the term denotes a variety of behaviors that might prevent optimal coordination of team members' efforts.

These behaviors may result from contrary policy preferences or from contrary group loyalties, as in professional jealousies and infighting. For economy of presentation I will use the term shirking, but I intend it to denote this broader set of behaviors.

As another example of shirking, let us consider the franchising problem. People go to McDonald's because they want a clean place to eat a fast meal. Customers tend to think that a given McDonald's is clean not necessarily because they have been in that restaurant before, but because they have been in other McDonald's before. But each McDonald's benefits from the fact that other franchise-holders are keeping their restaurants clean. What would happen to one franchise-holder's profits if he cut corners on keeping his own franchise clean? His profits may well go up, because he can cut down his labor costs and still get the customers by relying on the general McDonald's reputation. It is a prisoners' dilemma.

The franchise problem is simply the team-production problem writ large. The franchisers as a group do better by having a national reputation for cleanliness, but without a special disciplining process, each franchiser would have an incentive to "free ride" on the efforts of other franchisers, leaving all of them worse off (Rubin 1978).

Alchian and Demsetz propose that hierarchies solve the shirking problem in the presence of team-production functions. Hierarchies are characterized by the presence of supervisors, or monitoring specialists, whose task is "apportioning rewards, observing the input behavior of inputs as means of detecting or estimating their marginal productivity and giving assignments or instructions in what to do and how to do it" (1972, 782). Thus, the monitor is responsible for CHANGING THE INCENTIVE SYSTEM so that individuals find it in their interest to shirk less.

## INCENTIVE SYSTEMS: IMPOSSIBILITY RESULTS FROM SOCIAL CHOICE THEORY

May a manager devise an incentive system such that the subordinates find it in their interest to coordinate efforts in such a way as to achieve the efficiency gains from team production? Presumably, we are seeking a situation such that the supervisor who creates the incentive system finds it in her own self-interest to impose this ideal incentive system. That is, we would hope that the supervisor, in encouraging efficient production by subordinates, does not have to pay so much for incentives that she herself goes broke. Or more generally, we hope that there is no incentive (when the cost of subordinate rewards and sanctions are considered) for the supervisor to "cheat" by departing from the ideal incentive system.

Unfortunately, the problems of information asymmetry and team production which cause market failure can cause "hierarchical failure" inside the firm. That is, there seem to be no problems in imposing efficient incentive systems in organizations with no team production externalities and no information asymmetries. But either of these conditions for market failure can result in the failure of hierarchically imposed incentives to achieve a perfect alignment of individual incentives and organizational well-being.

## Hidden Action and Inefficiency

The link between information asymmetry and inefficiency has been much discussed in principal-agency theory. If an agent is assumed to be risk-averse, while a principal is assumed to be risk-neutral, then an ideal incentive system would allow the principal to bear the risks associated with agent actions. Such a system is possible as long as it is possible for the agent and principal to contract over the kinds of behaviors that the principal would most desire of the agent. The agent can then be rewarded in the form of a flat salary for performance of the specified behaviors, with punishment in the form of a decrease in wages only for nonperformance.

But very often the principal and agent cannot contract over the agent's actions, because the actions are unobservable. Whenever the agent is hired for a form of specialized expertise, for instance, the principal may not be in a position to tell if the agent has taken the actions that are most likely to lead to a favorable outcome for the principal. The principal and agent then may be in a position to contract only on the outcome, which may be jointly determined by the agent's actions and some external, random variable. In such a situation, payment in the form of a flat salary will be problematic. The agent will be able to blame low performance outcomes on factors other than his own performance. The principal will not be able to know whether low performance outcomes are in fact due to those conditions or to the agent's shirking.

To induce the agent to work as hard as possible, the principal will find it necessary to contract over the performance outcome, which necessarily induces an element of risk into the agent's payoff structure. For instance, a bank manager may have an incentive contra bonus based on that branch's profits, which are a function of the manager's efforts, but also a function of external economic conditions. But in order to induce the normally risk-averse employee to accept greater variation in wage, it will be necessary to increase the mean wage. As a result, the employee is made worse off by the burden of risk he has to bear, and the principal is made worse off by the increment in average incentives she has to pay out. Both could be made better off if the employee could be trusted not to shirk while being paid on the basis of a lower, but flat wage. Without that trust, however, the information asymmetry caused by the inability of the principal to monitor subordinate effort levels directly results in the necessity of a second-best incentive system that leaves both of them worse off.

### Hidden Action: Team Production

In the normal principal/agency model, the inefficiencies are caused by the fact that the outcomes that the principal is interested in are jointly determined by the agent's actions and some exogenous, random variable. This fact makes it more difficult for the principal to monitor the agent's actions directly.

Holmstrom (1982) demonstrates that the same inefficiencies can result simply from team production, even without environmental uncertainty. He uses this result to criticize the Alchian and Demsetz solution to the problem of teams.

He points out that the problem with these organizations is the necessity of dividing the surplus in allocations that alter incentives suboptimally. If the actor who sets the incentives is interested in maximizing the residual profits, then there is no incentive for her to select the right "incentive compatible" incentive scheme. Holmstrom believes that a repository must be found for the surplus generated by team efforts, a repository that is completely outside the organization. Only then will the organization's members have the correct incentives to generate an optimal surplus.

A brief sketch of Holmstrom's proof is instructive. Holmstrom assumes that there are $n$ agents whose actions determine a level of revenue $x$. The actions taken are nonobservable and are costly to each of the agents. In particular, we assume the production function is a team production, in which the productivity of each individual's actions is determined by other individuals' levels of effort.

Holmstrom points out the desirability of a "budget-balancing" incentive system—that is, one which exactly distributes the revenues generated by the actors among the actors. Holmstrom then shows that no budget-balancing incentive system can create incentives for the actors such that their Nash-equilibrium actions are Pareto-optimal.

The reason is that the existence of a Nash equilibrium means that each rational actor has equated her own marginal cost of effort with her own marginal benefit. If the incentive system has allocated her, for example, one-third of the revenues generated by the team, then she will find it rational to increase her effort levels until her marginal cost of effort exactly equals her marginal productivity times that share fraction ($\frac{1}{3}$). But Pareto optimality requires that every individual work until her marginal productivity for the team as a whole is exactly equal to her (private) marginal cost. These two requirements can be reconciled only if each individual gets *all* of the marginal revenue generated by her own efforts, which will necessarily violate the budget-balancing condition.

The existence of a contradiction means that the given assumptions are logically inconsistent. With any budget-balancing incentive scheme that a manager can come up with, there will be a tension between individual self-interest and group efficiency—exactly the tension described by the prisoners' dilemma.

Thus, team production causes a prisoners' dilemma game in hierarchies as well as in the nonhierarchical teams described by Alchian and Demsetz. The team-production function implies production externalities that result in the same fundamental schism between individual and group benefit that consumption externalities produce. And as Hurwicz showed for consumption externalities, no budget-balancing incentive system can overcome the problem.

Intuitively, this is saying that team production externalities create just as much of a "cover" for shirking by employees as environmental uncertainties. This is true whether or not the employees want to shirk—the industrious employees are incapable of proving, in a team-production setting, that a decline in team productivity was not due to their own effort instead of the shirking of the lazy employees. And as Holmstrom points out in the quote that begins this essay, an incentive system that gives everyone an incentive not to shirk is too expensive to impose.

Because the requirement of budget-balancing seems fundamentally inconsistent with efficiency in team production or in revelation of team-member types, Holmstrom proposes an entirely novel solution to the problem of team shirking. In his solution, the team members make a contract with the entrepreneur that would require them to share their revenue if it is as great as the Pareto-optimal outcome; falling short of the efficient outcome, the revenue would all go to the entrepreneur. The entrepreneur's responsibility would not be to monitor, chastise, or sanction subordinates; it would simply be to serve as a "sponge" for the surplus. Such an arrangement also would eliminate the moral hazard problem (Hammond 1983). The rationalization for this system is that it would make every team member's full effort absolutely essential to anyone (and everyone) getting paid. The incentive for shirking disappears because every team member realizes that shirking would deprive everyone (including himself) of all benefit of effort.

This solution works well as long as the "profit sponge"—the non-involved owner who absorbs the residual—remains outside the system. The problem is that the entrepreneur as sponge has no incentive to stay outside the system. Inside, she has every incentive to tamper with employee incentives. Eswaran and Kotwal (1984) argue that the third party would attempt to change the subordinates' incentives with a bribe. The "sponge" realizes that getting one of the subordinates to shirk absolves him of any contractual obligation to pay any of the other workers. Clearly, the "sponge" is best off if he can get all but one of the subordinates to work and pay none of them. He would thus have an incentive to offer a satisfactorily tempting bribe to one of the subordinates. The problem is not that nice incentive systems don't exist, but that the incentive setters don't have an incentive to pick the nice system. Eswaran and Kotwal appropriately term this problem "the moral hazard of budget-breaking" to show the parallelism with the moral hazard problem of shirking by subordinates.

Holmstrom has thus articulated a dilemma without any neat answers. The distribution of revenues generated by team efforts necessarily creates incentives for inappropriate behavior, if not from the employees, then from the manager or the owner of the "residual" profits. There will always be incentives for individuals to shirk, cheat, or follow their own preferences in ways that cumulate to organizational inefficiencies.

### Beyond Incentive-Setting: The Possibilities of Cooperation

Holmstrom's result is all the more disturbing because it suggests the incompleteness of contractarian solutions to collective action problems such as team production. Once the Leviathan is created to correct the deficiencies of collective action, Leviathan itself is found to generate inefficiencies. The very mechanism that makes Leviathan desirable—the authority to change members' incentives—is found to be logically insufficient to guarantee efficiency. The irony, then, is that the managers of a hierarchy will find it desirable to look for modes of inducing *voluntary* cooperation within Leviathan.

## The Evolution of Cooperation

In 1984, Robert Axelrod published his seminal work, *The Evolution of Cooperation*. In this book, Axelrod argues that in repeated plays of prisoners' dilemma games, players can achieve the benefits of the pareto-optimal outcome by playing a strategy of "tit-for-tat." A tit-for-tat multiperiod strategy is defined as playing the cooperative (dominated) alternative in the first play of the game and thereafter repeating the other player's previous choice. Thus, if an opponent fails to cooperate in period 3, his tit-for-tat partner will fail to cooperate in period 4.

Playing tit-for-tat is a way of punishing one's opponent for picking the dominating defect strategy and of rewarding one's opponent for selecting the cooperative strategy. Playing multiple times against a large number of opponents, the tit-for-tat players will do very well when playing against each other. They will also do almost as well as "always-defect" players when playing against "always-defect" players, since they do not allow themselves to be taken advantage of. Can such a theory explain the existence of organizations with a "culture of cooperation"?

As a simple example, let us imagine that there are a large number of supervisors and a large number of subordinates who have to match themselves into two-person organizations. An organization consists of a subordinate and a supervisor who play the game in table 9.1 for one hundred plays. At the end of one hundred plays, the superior and subordinate teams disband and reorganize to play the game another one hundred times with other partners.

Let us assume that there are three types of subordinates. "Lazy" sub-

Table 9.1 Evolution of Cooperation in Hierarchical Dilemmas (Subordinate's payoffs are in boldface)

| Subordinate's Choices | Superior's Choices | | | |
|---|---|---|---|---|
| | Pay Well | | Pay Poorly | |
| Work Hard | **$2,** | $2 | **$0,** | $4 |
| Shirk | **$4,** | $0 | **$1,** | $1 |

| | Payoffs After 100 Repeated Plays in Pairs | | | | | |
|---|---|---|---|---|---|---|
| Subordinate Types | Superior Types | | | | | |
| | Always Pay Poorly | | Tit-for-tat | | Always Pay Well | |
| Always Shirk | **$100,** | $100 | **$103,** | $99 | **$400,** | $0 |
| Tit-for-tat | **$99,** | $103 | **$200,** | $200 | **$200,** | $200 |
| Always Work Hard | **$0,** | $400 | **$200,** | $200 | **$200,** | $200 |

ordinates always select the "shirk" option. "Energetic" workers always select the "work-hard" option. And "tit-for-tat" workers play a tit-for-tat strategy. There are three analogous kinds of superiors: miserly, generous, and tit-for-tat.

Each superior would like to hire an energetic subordinate. Each subordinate would like to work for a generous employer. However, each subordinate has every reason to advertise himself as an energetic subordinate in order to get a job, and each superior has every reason to advertise himself as a generous superior. For all practical purposes then, let us assume that the matching between subordinates and superiors is simply random.

In an environment in which there is an equal number of all three types of individuals, the miserly managers can expect to do better in the long-run than the tit-for-tat managers, who will in turn do better than the always generous managers. Translating this into expectations about performance in a competitive market environment, we can expect that the proportion of always generous managers will decrease.

How well do the employees do? In the original environment, in which there were equal numbers of all three types of managers, then the lazy employees do best, followed by tit-for-tat employees, and then by the industrious employees, who are mercilessly exploited by the miserly managers that they are paired with. In fact, if the proportions of employees in future periods is related to how well each type does in the past, then we might well expect that lazy employees are a diminishing breed. The same thing is true for the generous managers, who are exploited by lazy employees.

However, as the number of "always-generous" managers decreases, then the advantage of being a lazy employee decreases as well. This is because the only large advantage to being a lazy employee comes from exploiting the always-generous managers. Similarly, the only large advantage to being a miserly manager comes from exploiting the industrious subordinates. If we assume that this, too, is a shrinking breed (due to starvation, learning, or other reasons), then what happens?

Let us assume that the number of firms with always-generous managers or with always-working employees has decreased to zero and that there are equal numbers of the two remaining kinds of employers and employees. Then we observe that the tit-for-tat managers and subordinates both do better than their miserly or shirking counterparts. The expected value of playing a miserly strategy against an unknown employee is $101.50, while the expected value of playing a tit-for-tat strategy is $149.50. As the proportion of "suckers" disappears, the advantages of being cooperative become greater.

Let us put this result together with the Holmstrom result. To the extent that hierarchies are unable to impose incentives systems that eliminate all reason for shirking among employees, then those managers who are able to encourage cooperative, tit-for-tat play of the inevitable prisoners' dilemma games within the hierarchy will do better than managers who expect self-interested, short-term maximizing behavior from their subordinates and who themselves play noncooperative strategies against them.

### The Unraveling Problem and the Role of Leadership

There are theoretical problems with the tit-for-tat solution to inefficient Nash equilibria in hierarchies. The most fascinating solution to these theoretical problems get us deep into the meaning of political leadership in hierarchical dilemmas.

Suppose we are playing a prisoners' dilemma tournament like the one described above, in which each pair of players know they are playing together for one hundred plays. What happens when they reach the last play? The advantage of playing tit-for-tat is to induce cooperation in future plays. In the final round, this advantage disappears, and each player is simply faced with the fact that each can do better by playing a "defect" strategy, no matter what the other chooses to do. So if each player is playing tit-for-tat as a way of doing better in the long run, they will abandon tit-for-tat in the final round and each will defect.

But they should anticipate that this will happen in the final round, so that in the penultimate round of the game, the advantage of tit-for-tat has also disappeared, and they should both defect in that round as well. But the unraveling of cooperative play in the second-to-last round implies that it should unravel in the third-to-last round, and so on. Logically, then, tit-for-tat should not be a viable strategy in any round of play. Tit-for-tat strategies should not be available to self-interested rational players who are confident that their partners are also self-interested and rational.

This problem has been addressed by Kreps, Milgrom, Roberts, and Wilson in their paper, "Rational Cooperation in the Finitely Repeated Prisoners' Dilemma" (1982). Their answer, which has immediate application to the managerial dilemmas discussed in this paper, hinges on the existence of some uncertainty on the part of players about the motivations of their opposites.

For the unraveling problem hinges on the perfect confidence on the part of each player that her opposite is in fact rational and will therefore defect in the final round of play. If each player has some uncertainty about the partner's rationality, then that allows these uncertain players to play tit-for-tat rationally.

In particular, suppose one player knows that she herself is rational, but she also knows that in the large population from which her partner has been drawn randomly, there are a few players who are committed to tit-for-tat play, despite the fact that it is ultimately irrational due to the unraveling problem. Then the rational player will have every reason to play tit-for-tat for most of the game in order to get the benefits to be derived from mutual cooperation, even though she knows that she herself, and possibly her partner as well, will abandon tit-for-tat when it gets close to the end of their time together.

In any given pair of players, it only takes a small amount of uncertainty about the other person's possible commitment to tit-for-tat play to make a strategy that is "almost" tit-for-tat rational for the most narrowly self-interested players. The possibility that there are committed tit-for-tat players destroys the "common knowledge" that both players are rational and therefore destroys the necessity of unraveling.

In fact, one player may know that both players in the pair are rational rather than committed tit-for-tat players, but will pretend to believe in a tit-for-tat player in order to keep the mutually beneficial ruse going. The other player may know that his opponent is deceiving him, but may well go along with the deception for most of the game in order to further the cooperative play of the game.

Thus, Kreps et al. demonstrate that even if the possible existence of the committed tit-for-tat player is a myth, it is a socially desirable myth that all sides would do well to go along with. Players might tell each other of tit-for-tat players they have known, as a way of enhancing the viability of the myth. They may advertise themselves as committed tit-for-tat players; and this self-advertisement may be socially useful even if 98 percent of the hearers don't believe it. As long as a few players act as if they believe that other people might be tit-for-tat players, then mutually beneficial tit-for-tat play can be maintained.

## Supporting the Norm of Cooperation

But how can the "myth of the cooperative player" be generated in a population of people playing a prisoners' dilemma tournament? This, it seems to me, is the first clear sign that the role of leader in a firm goes beyond the manipulation of incentives to include the psychological manipulation of popular expectations and myth-building. Because (a) no static incentive system can eliminate self-interested shirking and because (b) tit-for-tat evolution of cooperation may unravel in the absence of appropriate myths and expectations, there is a payoff to leaders who can manipulate psychological expectations on the part of large populations. In particular, a leader who can create in a population a belief in the myth of the cooperative player (or at least create a belief that others in the population believe in the myth of the cooperative player) can thereby prevent the unraveling that leads to mutually destructive noncooperation in the play of prisoners' dilemma tournaments.

Certainly, this coincides dramatically with one traditional definition of managerial responsibility in firms, which has insisted that the central role of leadership in a firm is much different than simply monitoring and rewarding subordinate efforts. Chester Barnard (1938) placed the creation of a willingness to cooperate right at the center of his elaborate scheme. Barnard stated clearly that cooperation was a difficult thing to achieve because of the conflict between individual motives and common purpose: "The inculcation of belief in the real existence of a common purpose is an essential executive function. It explains much education and so-called morale work in political, industrial, and religious organizations that is so often otherwise inexplicable" (p. 87). Indeed, a great deal of organizational resources are spent on efforts to inculcate the belief in a common purpose and the willingness to make sacrifices for that common purpose. And the substance of this "morale work" is primarily the following message: "We are all in this together, and if you will cooperate, everyone else will respond in kind." In other words, the purpose of these rather expensive educational efforts is to create the expectation on the part of the multiple players in a large firm that cooperative behavior will be met in kind—and that it won't all unravel.

## THE INDETERMINACY OF COOPERATION: THE FOLK THEOREM

While Barnard argues that encouraging cooperation is a central role of management, he does not claim that cooperation is in any way inevitable. As Barnard says,

> it is readily believed that organized effort is normally successful, that failure of organization is abnormal. This illusion from some points of view is even useful . . . But in fact, successful cooperation in or by formal organizations is the ab-

normal, not the normal, condition. . . . most cooperation fails in the attempt, or dies in infancy, or is short-lived. . . . Failure to cooperate, failure of cooperation, failure of organization, disorganization, disintegration, destruction of organization—and reorganization—are characteristic facts of human history. This is hardly disputable. Explanations of the fact usually make reference to the perversity of human nature, to egoism, to the combative instinct, to 'false' economic systems, or the struggle for food and the limits of its supply." (pp. 4–5)

But why shouldn't the evolution of cooperation be inevitable? Once again, economics does a very good job of explaining why things can go wrong. And the economic answer is incorporated in the "folk theorem" of repeated games.

## The Folk Theorem

The difficulty lies in the multiplicity of outcomes that are sustainable in repeated games—cooperation is not the only possible outcome that can be reached by rational individuals. The problem is best illustrated for an organizational context by a game devised by Kreps (1984) in his important paper, "Corporate Culture and Economic Theory" (see figure 9.1).

In this game, B faces the temptation of abusing the trust placed in her by player A. Knowing this, player A will choose not to place trust in player B. But this results in both doing worse (zero each) than if both players would do what is irrational.

As Kreps observes, one solution to this problem would be to write a

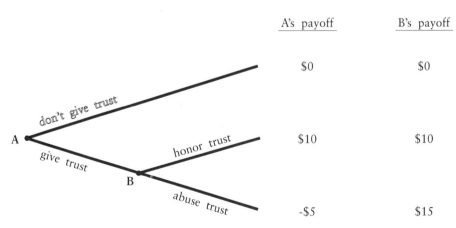

FIGURE 9.1 Game Showing the Indeterminacy of Cooperation in an Organizational Context (from Kreps 1984)

contract that would effectively change the incentives. Under the contract, B could promise to submit to a large (larger than $10) penalty for abusing the trust. A potential problem would be the transactions costs associated with drawing up the contract and hiring a credible enforcer. These transactions costs would eat into the potential gain from escaping the prisoners' dilemma and could make it not worthwhile to write the contract.

An alternative solution is available if the game is repeated. For instance, Kreps imagines a scenario in which at each round, there is a ten-percent chance that the round will be the last. Then, player A could announce a strategy of placing trust in player B until such time as player B abuses the trust. Player B would then have the possible incentive of multiple future rounds of gaining $10 to balance against the $5 incentive to violate the trust in a given period. This makes it viable for player B to honor the trust, simply from a self-interest perspective. This is an equilibrium outcome in the repeated game, in that each player's strategy is best given the other player's strategy.

Kreps notes that this outcome is only one of an infinite number of possible outcomes that can be achieved as equilibrium outcomes in repeated games of this sort. There are other strategy pairs that have the characteristic "each person's strategy is best given the other person's strategy." For instance, player B could announce that he will violate player A's trust one time out of three. If A ever retaliates by choosing not to trust B in any given period, player B will massively retaliate by violating A's trust on *every* subsequent opportunity. Given this announced strategy, player A's best choice is still to trust player B at every opportunity, even knowing that the trust will be violated one time out of three.

This equilibrium outcome is more favorable to player B. The problem for game theorists is that game theory does not give any basis for choosing between these two and a large number of other possible equilibrium outcomes, some favoring A, some favoring B, some efficient, some inefficient. Once the game is played as a repeated game, the folk theorem says that "we can sustain as a noncooperative equilibrium payoff any feasible vector of expected payoffs for players that are sufficiently above the worst that others can inflict upon them" (Kreps 1984, 14).

This means that anything from mutually cooperative, to mutually noncooperative, to one-sided exploitative outcomes can be sustained by rational actors playing the same repeated game. The implications include at least two significant facts: (1) we can't predict what will happen in repeated social interactions using game theory alone, and (2) there is nothing inevitable about the emergence of cooperation in any given organizational setting.

## Empirical Evidence on the Unraveling of Cooperation

The folk theorem suggests that the beliefs of the various players involved about the likely responses of other players are all important: it is this psychological network of mutually reinforcing expectation that makes one perfectly feasible outcome (e.g., cooperation) happen instead of another perfectly feasible outcome ( e.g., noncooperation). This means that we should observe quite *different kinds of outcomes even in hierarchies with identical structures and incentive systems.* Indeed, the same organization may manifest quite different outcomes as a result of different sets of mutually reinforcing psychological expectations.

There seems to be an entire literature in organizational behavior on "sociological dysfunctions" that would illustrate that cooperation is not inevitable and can in fact disintegrate under the impact of changing perceptions and norms. The primary example of this literature is Gouldner's work on the bureaucratic "rigidity cycle" (1954). To explain this concept, let us imagine an organization that is working rather smoothly with a high degree of morale and commitment by employees, which in turn necessitates few rules and little expenditure on tight supervision by managers.

Then imagine that, in one area of performance, management is upset with employee output. How should the manager correct the problem? Gouldner sees the normal, Weberian bureaucratic solution to be the imposition of additional hierarchy and rules: that is, managers set a more tightly proscribed standard of behavior in the problem area and increase supervision to see that the standard is met.

How will employees respond? Gouldner documents that the normal response will be grudging acquiescence in the rules, resentment at the increased levels of supervision, and an increased unwillingness to cooperate beyond the minimal acceptable response as defined by the increasingly defined rule system. Gouldner quotes employees who were responding to a manager's edict that workers could not "punch in early" and thus accumulate some overtime. Said one employee, "Well, if that's the way he wants it, that's the way he wants it. But I'll be damned if I put in any overtime when things get rough and they'd like us to." Another employee said, "OK, I'll punch in just so, and I'll punch in on the nose. But you know you can lead a horse to water and you can lead him away, but it's awful hard to tell just how much water he drinks while he's at it" (Gouldner 1954, 175).

The productivity implications of the last remark are clear. The worker, who might have been willing to put in a good effort while he is on the job, is now going to shirk to the extent that he can get away with it. This could lead to a need for overtime down the road, but employees like the first one quoted will not be willing to respond.

What is the managerial response? It will clearly be that employees are necessarily shirkers who cannot be trusted. The response will be to increase supervision even more and to elaborate more confining work rules. This elicits even more stubborn noncooperativeness on the part of employees, and hence more hierarchy and rules on the part of subordinates. Clearly, the end result is a managerial style in which attempts at cooperation and trust are regarded as a waste of time, and employee behavior is managed by a strict system of incentives in which it is expected that employees will work as little as they can get away with.

This vicious cycle of increasing bureaucratic rigidity is clearly not as efficient as one in which managers give employees some leeway (in regard to punching in and out, for example), and employees respond with high morale and cooperation. The trick is maintaining this outcome as the expected outcome over repeated plays of the prisoners' dilemma. And "trick" is the right word. There is no magic incentive-system formula in which mutual cooperation always emerges as the unique Nash equilibrium behavior. While this outcome is in the feasible set of outcomes in repeated play, it is only one of a large set of outcomes which are feasible. Political leadership in an organization consists of inspiring trust and creating expectations to make such an outcome possible.

## Social Conventions and Norms: How They Supplement Economics

The evidence from Gouldner reinforces the belief that there are multiple possible equilibrium outcomes that are possible under a given incentive system and that one responsibility of the manager is to inculcate the correct set of mutually reinforcing expectations in order to encourage more efficient equilibrium outcomes. The usefulness of social conventions as ways by which groups focus on one possible equilibrium instead of another has been recognized for some years (Lewis 1969; Hardin 1982; Calvert 1987; Leibenstein 1987; Hechter 1987). One outstanding example of this is the convention known as "gift exchange" and its applicability to hierarchical firms.

A long-standing problem in labor economics has been to explain why many firms, often the more efficient firms, pay employees more than the market-clearing equilibrium wage rate. This necessarily results in involuntary unemployment of the sort that would not occur with neoclassical economics, in which the demand and supply for labor were exactly equal at equilibrium.

Economist George Akerlof (1982) explains involuntary unemployment as arising from "gift exchanges" within firms. The gift exchanges described are just those that would be necessary to escape a prisoners' dilemma between superiors and subordinates.

Akerlof was motivated to develop his model by evidence from a study by sociologist George Homans (1954) of a small group of women posting customer cash payments as employees of a utility company. These employees consistently posted an average of about 15 percent more than the minimum work requirement for the company. This level of effort was achieved despite the fact that a failure to achieve the minimum resulted only in a mild reprimand, and exceeding the work requirement resulted in absolutely no wage differential or improved promotional opportunities. On the other hand, all of the employees (both those who exceeded the average and those below the average) were paid more than the level it would take to replace them.

Akerlof is struck by the similarity of the arrangement to the gift-exchange economies studied by anthropologists. In these economies, individuals who do well on a given hunt give gifts to others in the society, in expectation of a comparable gift at a future time. (Akerlof notes the etymological similarity between the words for "gift" and "poison" in several languages, since receiving a gift carries with it the burden of responding in kind.)

Akerlof views the workers as giving a "gift" of effort that is above and beyond that which is called for given the incentive system in place. In return, workers receive the gift of higher-than-market-clearing wages and flexible application of work rules. This gift exchange leaves both sides better off than they would be if the firm refused to pay more than the market-clearing wage and the employees refused to work at more than minimum standards.

A recent paper by Daniel Raff (1988) suggests that this is what Henry Ford had in mind when he made his historic introduction of the $5 per day wage in 1914. The previous wage had been roughly $2.34, and the increase in wages would eat up half of expected profits in the coming year. It occurred at a time when Ford was replacing large numbers of skilled craftsmen with unskilled assembly-line workers. Thus, the motivation was not to attract a "better" type of worker. On the other hand, the motivation was, it seems, to be a sign of commitment to worker well-being, in return for which Ford expected less turnover and more productivity. Both of these expectations were rewarded. Turnover rates dropped from 370 percent in 1913 to 16 percent in 1915. Productivity increased by about 50 percent (Raff 1988, table 6).

One meaning of this is that the account of "rational behavior" in organizations certainly takes on entirely new content. In the market institution, rational behavior consists of individual maximizing behavior. The individual is in fact liberated to undertake simple maximizing behavior by the fact that he is, like everyone else, a price-taker. Being a price-taker means that no individual has to worry about the effects of one's own behavior on anyone else.

In convention-governed coordination games, on the other hand, everyone has to worry about the behavior of everyone else and the effect of their own behavior on the expectations of others. In a repeated prisoners' dilemma game, people worry about the effect of their own deviations from social norms and the effects of those deviations on the viability of the norms, and on the effects of erosion in those norms. "Rational choice" in such a behavior may move an employee to make a "gift" of costly effort—even in the absence of a punishment mechanism—simply because the ultimate effects of deviation from the norm may be large, uncertain, and negative. But if this is true, then the choices of "homo economicus" in repeated, personal, norm-constrained, social interactions becomes virtually indistinguishable from the behavior attributed to "homo sociologicus."

## The Role of Leadership: Building Reputations, Building Culture

This leads us to ask if there is anything left in the classic distinction between economics and sociology: "Economics is about how individuals make choices, and sociology is about how individuals have no choices to make." The gap between economics and sociology has certainly shrunk dramatically as economists have learned to accept the possibility that individual choices in coordination games are rationally constrained by social conventions and norms. However, individuals in social settings constrained by social norms still have important choices to make. The choices they make help determine the expectations that others have about how the game is to be played and help to shape and alter the conventions that govern the outcome of coordination games.

Basically, a convention is just a short-hand term for the perception on the part of a group of players about how the rest of the players are to play a game. That perception is affected all the time by a variety of signals and communications on the part of the players. A player's reputation is a psychological perception on the part of other players about how the given player prefers to play a game. Thus, the employers of a given firm may create a reputation as being "cooperative." They could create a reputation of being willing to pay more than the market-clearing wage for labor in exchange for more than effort-minimizing behavior on the part of laborers. Such a reputation could be created by past play, by public pronouncements, by the imaginative use of symbols and manipulation of myths. The behavioral literature on organizational leadership discusses managers using any and all of these tactics to create and reinforce an appropriate set of organizational conventions.

Peters and Waterman (1984), in their study of *Excellence* in management give as an example Ray Kroc, the head of McDonald's hamburger chain. Kroc recognized that there are enormous profits to be made by having a chain of fast-food restaurants with a reputation for quality hamburgers and clean floors. Kroc also recognized that the same things which make this profit possible create incentives for individual franchise-holders to shirk: by not spending that marginal labor dollar to keep the floors clean twenty-four hours a day, by buying meat that isn't the required quality. Kroc dealt with this problem in part by changing incentives. You can be sure that the contracts with franchise-holders are written in such a way that there is a big penalty for franchise-holders that fail to meet cleanliness and food quality standards.

But Ray Kroc believes the message of the Holmstrom theorem, which is that contract incentives are never sufficient. Instead of relying completely on structural incentives, Kroc says, "I believe that less is more in the case of corporate management; for its size, McDonald's today is the most unstructured corporation I know, and I don't think you could find a happier, more secure, harder working group of executives anywhere." He accomplishes this by a thousand corny techniques to keep morale high and instill an atmosphere of trust and cooperation. These include Hamburger University and the "All-American Hamburger Maker" competition among employees.

What Peters and Waterman document in their book is a willingness on the part of some managers to come out from behind their desks and create a reputation of trustworthiness and caring for their employees. This kind of action wouldn't be necessary, I submit, if it were possible to design the perfect incentive system that perfectly aligned individual and group interests. But it is not possible. And because it is not, managers have to find a way to motivate employees to work when they would rather shirk, to take a chance when it is in their interest to play it safe, to be polite to customers when they get nothing out of it.

Nor are Peters and Waterman the only two organization theorists to document the significance of this noneconomic managerial role. Akin and Hopelain (1986) found the "willingness to work hard" rather than "just putting in time" to be characteristic of highly productive organizations. In these same organizations, managers were found to be highly supportive of workers and engaged in the organization as "participant-observer" rather than outside of the organization as objective machine-designer.

In their classic study of effective managers, McClelland and Burnham (1976) discovered that a desire for "socialized power" was characteristic. While many managers have a desire for organizational power, the most successful managers modified this by developing both a high level of self-control and a desire to work with, rather than at the expense, of other members of the organization. On the other hand, a study of "failed" executives reveals a typical pattern that includes "insensitivity to others," "arrogance," and "betrayal of trust" (McCall and Lombardo 1983).

The message of the Holmstrom theorem is that there is no way to make an organization of diverse individuals into a machine. Managers should look at their organizations as being composed of individuals with diverse interests who will inevitably find themselves in conflict on occasion. Their best response to this problem is to inspire among their own employees a willingness to cooperate and trust each other by setting an example of being concerned and trustworthy themselves.

Nor is "cooperation" in any sense a deterministic, inevitable outcome. The impact of the Folk Theorem is that many (an infinite number) of possible outcomes can be supported as Nash equilibria behaviors. Hierarchies are organic in that we must presume that psychological and political factors go a long way toward explaining which set of outcomes is supported by which set of mutually reinforcing expectations.

## Political Leadership and Culture Building

Political leadership is concerned with the creation of mutually reinforcing expectations concerning which of the infinitely many strategy sets we in this particular organization will play in this particular repeated game. It therefore involves a whole set of psychological and political factors such as the manipulation of symbols, the creation of cultural myths, the facilitation of communication.

For if repeated game theory can lead you to predict and explain any outcome in this entire area, then game theory lacks any predictive power; modern game theory cannot provide a deterministic outcome that is a function simply of the structural characteristics of the game. The role of leadership gives closure where repeated game theory offers none: it is to shape the set of expectations among subordinates that the organization is embarking on just one of the many mutually appropriate strategies. In defining corporate culture, Kreps defines a role for political leadership. To him, "corporate culture" is in part "the means by which a principle [of group decision-making] is communicated to hierarchical inferiors . . . It says 'how things are done, and how they are meant to be done' in the organization" (1984, 5).

This helps to explain why different organizations in the same industry might have quite different cultures. Cultures are affected by the individual choices of members of the organization, especially those in a leadership position who make conscious and sophisticated use of the technology of mass communication. The leadership skills of the members involved make the difference; and the leadership skills would translate into the ability to take the initiative and make a certain strategy pair salient and viable.

## SUMMARY

Hierarchies have their origins in market failure. And rational goal-oriented behavior will look different in hierarchies than in markets because "success" in a hierarchy consists often of establishing mutually enforcing expectations about when cooperation and teamwork are appropriate and how they are to be reciprocated and rewarded in the long-run.

The market failure that leads to hierarchy stems immediately from the existence of team production functions, which make it potentially more efficient for individuals to work together as a team rather than separately. The hierarchical manipulation of incentives can go part of the way toward correctly aligning individual and group incentives. But as Holmstrom shows, no budget-balancing incentive system in a hierarchy can perfectly align individual and group incentives in the presence of team-production externalities.

For this reason, managers who can induce norms of cooperation and trust among employees can realize more of the gains from team production than can managers who rely on formal incentive systems only. While cooperation in a repeated social dilemma is sustainable by rational actors as a Nash equilibrium, so are a variety of noncooperative or exploitative outcomes. Repeated play makes cooperation possible in a team, but not inevitable.

As a result, the successful manager, recognizing the goal-oriented "rationality" of the participants, will consciously adopt strategies that get individuals to depart from the narrow self-interest maximization that constitutes a sufficient definition of rationality in markets. A successful manager will demonstrate trustworthiness in hopes of training subordinates to be trustworthy themselves; she will recognize and encourage a multiplicity of goals, including group acceptance and professional self-actualization, recognizing in these the building blocks of a culture of cooperation. She will train herself and subordinates in an awareness of the dangers of the social dilemma that is inherent in every hierarchy and will shape the awareness of the possibilities of escaping those dangers through the rational evolution of cooperation in the ongoing plays of the hierarchical dilemma.

## References

Akerloff, George. 1982. "Labor Contracts as Partial Gift Exchange." *Quarterly Journal of Economics* 97: 543–69.
Akin, Gib, and David Hopelain. 1986. "Finding the Culture of Productivity." *Organizational Dynamics* 12: 19–32.
Alchian, Armen, and Harold Demsetz. 1972. "Production, Information Costs, and Economic Organization." *American Economic Review* 62: 777–95.
Axelrod, Robert. 1984. *The Evolution of Cooperation.* New York: Basic Books.
Barnard, Chester I. 1938. *The Functions of the Executive.* Cambridge: Harvard University Press.
Calvert, Randall. 1987. "Coordination and Power: The Foundation of Leadership Among Rational Actors." Paper delivered at the American Political Science Association meeting, Chicago.
Cheung, Steven N. 1983. "The Contractual Nature of the Firm." *Journal of Law and Economics* 26: 1–21.
Coase, R. H. 1937. "The Nature of the Firm." *Economica* 4: 386–405.
———. 1960. "The Problem of Social Cost." *Journal of Law and Economics* 3: 1–44.
Edney, Julian J. 1979. "The Nuts Game: A Concise Commons Dilemma Analog." *Environmental Psychology and Nonverbal Behavior* 3: 242–52.
Eswaran, Mukesh, and Ashok Kotwal. 1984. "The Moral Hazard of Budget Breaking." *Rand Journal of Economics* 15: 578–81.
Gouldner, Alvin. 1954. *Patterns of Industrial Bureaucracy.* New York: The Free Press.
Halberstam, David. 1986. *The Reckoning.* New York: Avon Books.
Hammond, Thomas H. 1983. "Notes on the Theory of Corporate Organiza-

tion." Paper presented at the Conference on Adaptive Institutions, Stanford University.

Hardin, Russell. 1982. *Collective Action*. Baltimore: Johns Hopkins University Press.

Hechter, Michael. 1987. *Principles of Group Solidarity*. Berkeley: University of California Press.

Holmstrom, Bengt. 1982. "Moral Hazard in Teams." *Bell Journal of Economics* 13: 324–40.

Homans, George. 1954. "The Cash Posters." *American Sociological Review* 19: 724–33.

Hurwicz, Leonid. 1973. "The Design of Mechanisms for Resource Allocation." *American Economic Association* 63: 1–30.

———. 1979. "On Allocations Attainable Through Nash Equilibria." *Journal of Economic Theory* 21: 140–65.

Jensen, Michael C. 1983. "Organization Theory and Methodology." *Accounting Review* 58: 319–39.

Jensen, Michael C., and W. H. Meckling. 1976. "Theory of the Firm: Managerial Behavior, Agency Costs, and Ownership Structure." *Journal of Financial Economics* 3: 304–60.

Kreps, David M. 1984. "Corporate Culture and Economic Theory." Paper presented to the Second Mitsuibishi Bank Foundation Conference on Technology and Business Strategy.

Kreps, David M., Paul Milgrom, John Roberts, and Robert Wilson. 1982. "Rational Cooperation in the Finitely Repeated Prisoners' Dilemma." *Journal of Economic Theory* 27: 245–52.

Latane, Bibb, Kipling Williams, and Stephen Harkins. 1979. "Social Loafing." *Psychology Today* 12: 104–10.

Leibenstein, Harvey. 1987. *Inside the Firm: The Inefficiencies of Hierarchy*. Cambridge: Harvard University Press.

Lewis, David. 1969. *Convention*. Cambridge: Harvard University Press.

McCall, Morgan W., Jr., and Michael M. Lombardo. 1983. "What Makes a Top Executive?" *Psychology Today* 16: 26–31.

McClelland, David C., and David H. Burnham. 1976. "Power Is the Great Motivator." *Harvard Business Review* 54: 100–110.

Peters, Thomas J., and Robert H. Waterman, Jr. 1984. *In Search of Excellence: Lessons from America's Best-Run Companies*. New York: Warner Communication Co.

Raff, Daniel M. 1988. "Wage Determination Theory and the Five-Dollar Day at Ford." *Journal of Economic History* 48: 387–99.

Rubin, Paul. 1978. "The Theory of the Firm and the Structure of the Franchise Contract." *Journal of Law and Economics* 21: 223–33.

Taylor, Frederick W. 1947. *Scientific Management*. New York: Harper & Bros.

COMMENT: *Applying Rational Choice Theory: The Role of Leadership in Team Production*
Robert H. Bates and William T. Bianco

Gary Miller's paper reminds us once again that intellectual revolutions proceed dialectically. In recent years, "rational choicers" in political science posed as revolutionaries attacking their colleagues in the profession, especially "the behavioralists." Now, Miller suggests, intellectual rewards may be reaped by those who promote the synthesis and reintegration of these traditions, rather than by those who emphasize their differences.

Miller also shows us how difficult the synthesis may prove to be. As he stresses, recent developments provide the technology needed to characterize "soft" phenomena, such as "trust," "reputation," and "norms," and to make concrete predictions about their implications for individual behavior.

Game-theoretic models are of use, however, only if they precisely incorporate the specific factors that drive real-world decisions. What appears to be subtle and unimportant to the observer may have profound effects on behavior—and disastrous effects on the predictions of a game that fails to take them into consideration. While we affirm and highlight the significance of Miller's intellectual program, we nonetheless feel that these difficulties bedevil Miller's work.

Miller uses results from the theory of iterated games—especially games of incomplete information—to explain how real-world leaders motivate followers to cooperate. As Miller notes, these results predict leader success under fairly general conditions; they also suggest that a critical tactic for leaders is to create and sustain a "reputation" of rewarding cooperation and punishing defection.

Our work indicates, however, that Miller's analysis is not complete.[1] In particular, when we employ the tools of game theoretic reasoning to analyze concepts such as retaliation and reputation, we find that the leader of a team possesses far less ability to initiate and sustain team production than Miller would appear to claim.

---

In the spirit of team production, neither Bates nor Bianco is responsible for the errors in this paper. Nor can either take credit for its virtues. The order of the names is therefore alphabetical and does not reflect their relative contributions to this paper.

1. See William T. Bianco and Robert H. Bates, "Cooperation by Design: The Role of Leadership in Collective Dilemmas," *American Political Science Review* 83 (March 1990).

Our work also suggests what is needed to strengthen the analysis: a precise specification of the incentives that motivate leaders and the capabilities that structure—and constrain—their strategies. Some types of leaders, we show, are able to monitor individual follower strategies and target sanctions against shirkers, and these can fulfill the role Miller suggests. By contrast, other types of leaders—those who can monitor only output but not follower effort and who cannot target sanctions—are much less able to initiate and sustain successful team production.

## New Directions in Political Science: Miller's Program

Miller's analysis of team production attempts to unify two traditions in political science: rational choice theory and behavioralism. Within political science, "rational choicers" draw most directly from economics; the "behavioralists" from psychology, sociology, and social psychology. As played out in political science, rational choicers emphasize choice; the behavioralists, constraint.[2] Rational choicers emphasize the capacity of people to process information and make decisions; the behavioralists, their tendency to employ rules of thumb. Behavioralists study the origin and acquisition of preferences; rational choicers, their use in decision making.

The divide between the two traditions is compounded by the association of rational choice theory with economics. *Nothing*, it should be emphasized, should equate the two. The theory of rational choice imputes no content to preferences; they need not be restricted to material goods, profits, or dollars. Nor does the theory make assumptions about how the preference of individuals aggregate into social outcomes; the axioms concerning the behavior of markets stand independently of the axioms of individual choice.

Nonetheless, in political science, an intellectual commitment to rational choice has been equated with a commitment to market economics. The result is a focus on the role of issues and interests in the literature on elections, on divisible goods in the literature on pressure groups, and on material incentives in the literature on bureaucracies. Issue voting has been counterpoised against the role of party identification,[3] selective in-

2. More accurately, rational choice studies choice under constraint. But some of the behavioral sciences so emphasize the strength of norms and structures that the role choice plays is, consequently, quite small.

3. See the famous symposium on "issue voting" in the *American Political Science Review* 66 (June 1972).

centives against solidaristic incentives and civic duty in the literature on pressure groups,[4] and the desire to maximize budgets against the role of "professionalism" in the literature on bureaucracies.[5]

That party identification remains the single strongest determinant of electoral choice; that ideology, religion, and notions of the collective good animated broad-based movements in favor of civil rights, in opposition to the Vietnam War, and on behalf of the preservation of the environment; and that bureaucrats often appear to care a lot about the missions of their organizations and the quality of the services they supply—these remain challenges to the rational choice paradigm. These challenges have been confronted by some,[6] but ignored by far too many.

In earlier days, it was as if the prize went to those who could make the analysis of politics resemble as much as possible economic reasoning.[7] It is likely that in the future the garlands will be bestowed upon those who take instruction from recent results in decision and game theory, those who return to earlier work in sociology and social-psychology, and those who "rationalize" this work, as it were, while using formal technology to tease out the not so obvious implications.

A major contribution of Miller's works is to reveal the power and the promise of freeing the core tools of rational choice theory from their bondage in market economics. He applies these tools to institutions—organizations and bureaucracies—that differ profoundly from markets. And, within the tradition of organization theory, he turns sharply against those who emphasize marketlike properties of incentive systems. While retaining a commitment to rational choice, Miller nonetheless focuses on such "soft" variables as leadership, reputation, and trust.

The significance of Miller's work in political science is that it may mark the next frontier in the extension of the rational choice paradigm: the synthesis and reinterpretation of noneconomic variables that have traditionally been studied by the behavioral sciences.

4. Mancur Olson, *The Logic of Collective Action* (Cambridge, MA: Harvard University Press, 1965).

5. William A. Niskanan, *Bureaucracy and Representative Government* (Chicago: Aldine Atherton, 1971).

6. Morris Fiorina, "An Outline for a Model of Party Choices," *American Journal of Political Science* 21 (August 1977):601–25.

7. See, for example, Warren F. Ilchman and Norman Thomas, *The Political Economy of Change* (Berkeley: University of California Press, 1969).

## LIMITATIONS OF MILLER'S WORK

While underscoring the importance of integrating the rational choice and behavioral traditions, Miller's work also suggests the difficulty of doing so. For, upon careful re-analysis, it becomes clear that key steps in his argument have yet to be established.

Initiating cooperation in an iterated team production game requires that each follower possess a unilateral incentive to begin the game by cooperating. As realized by Miller, this incentive does not exist. As we have shown elsewhere,[8] even if followers were to play trigger strategies of conditional cooperation, no follower would choose to unilaterally initiate cooperation. A trigger strategy of conditional cooperation means a strategy in which a worker reciprocates with cooperation if another initiates cooperation but retaliates with permanent defection if another first defects. Workers can *sustain* cooperation once it is achieved: trigger strategies provide the means to achieve that goal. The problem is to get to cooperation in the first place.

Miller's solution is to introduce a leader whose responsibility it is to distribute the benefits of team production to followers. By rewarding cooperation and punishing defection, the leader is supposed to present followers with an incentive to begin by cooperating and to continue to cooperate in subsequent iterations of the game.

Two problems confound this claim.[9] First, since cooperation is costly, the followers must find the leader's strategy of rewarding cooperation and punishing defection to be credible. A problem of credibility arises if the leader can improve her payoff by either punishing spontaneously or by failing to retaliate. Under complete information, credibility requires that conditional cooperation is the leader's (weakly) dominant strategy; under incomplete information, it can be achieved if the leader can generate and sustain an appropriate "reputation."

Under complete information, however, conditional cooperation is *never* a leader's dominant strategy. In general, it is always possible to construct a set of follower strategies such that a leader can improve her payoff by deviating from her trigger strategy if the followers use these strategies.[10] Thus, under complete information followers will realize that

8. See Bianco and Bates (1990).

9. Bianco and Bates (1990) contains a formal version of this argument.

10. For example, suppose followers use the following strategy:

$t = 0$: Defect

$t > 0$: Cooperate if the leader punished on iteration 0, and defect otherwise.

while conditional cooperation may be a Nash (or subgame perfect) equilibrium strategy, it is not a dominant strategy for the leader. They will therefore not find the leader's pledge to reward on the first iteration, to reward cooperation on subsequent iterations, and to punish defection to be credible. In this case the leader's control of rewards and punishments will not serve to initiate cooperation.

Under incomplete information—that is, where followers are uncertain about the leader's payoffs—the situation is somewhat different. Given this uncertainty, followers may believe that conditional cooperation is the leader's dominant strategy regardless of whether this is actually the case. Moreover, leaders can act to sustain and reinforce these beliefs; the leader can make choices that promote her "reputation" as a conditional cooperator.[11]

However, even if followers are *certain* that the leader will reward and punish according to a conditional cooperation strategy, cooperation may not be their best response. In particular, unless the leader is able to discriminate among the followers and target punishments against those who fail to cooperate, a follower's payoff-maximizing strategy depends upon the strategy of other followers. In the absence of perfect monitoring and enforcement, therefore, conditional cooperation is not a dominant strategy for the followers. Again, leaders may be unable to initiate and sustain team production.

The central image of Miller's work is that of a leader standing amidst a collection of followers, all of whom know that if they could only cooperate, they would all be better off. In Miller's world, the leader leads by employing her reputation as a conditional cooperator; by reinforcing follower beliefs that they will use a trigger strategy, leaders create an incentive for followers themselves to adopt such strategies. Our analysis shows how difficult it is for leaders to act this way.

---

If followers use this strategy, a leader (regardless of type) receives a higher payoff if she punishes on the first iteration and rewards thereafter than if she uses a trigger strategy (which will trigger defection by the followers beginning on iteration 1). The trigger strategy cannot therefore be a dominant strategy for the leader. In addition, under some conditions a leader improves her payoff by punishing followers spontaneously or by not punishing defectors. Both results imply the leader's trigger strategy is not her dominant strategy.

11. A related question concerns the source of follower uncertainty. Miller's analysis is typical of incomplete information games in that worker uncertainty exists by assumption. The authors of this paper are unaware of any research which considers how uncertainties are formed rather than sustained or exploited. The recent attention to informational factors in the study of politics (Miller's work is but one example) makes research into the origin of uncertainties a priority item.

THE INSTITUTIONAL SOURCES OF LEADER POWER

Our analysis also suggests that a leader's (in)ability to initiate and sustain team production depends upon certain definable characteristics of the leader. We focus on three factors: the leader's reward structure, her information about followers' strategies, and her ability to sanction some team members while rewarding others.

One might think of these characteristics as features of an institution—powers or resources that accrue to whoever holds the position of leader. Alternatively, one can think of team members choosing a particular individual to be leader, but also deciding what powers to give to that individual. In either case, the conclusion is the same: a leader's success at initiating and sustaining team production depends partly on her "cleverness" or "reputation" but also on exogenous features of the team production game which the leader does not control.

The first institutional feature that shapes the leader's incentives is: the manner in which the leader is rewarded. The leader may, for example, be a residual claimant of the benefits of team production. Alternatively, she may be rewarded by receiving a fixed share of the benefits produced by team production.

A second feature of the institution is the leader's capabilities: whether she can monitor and reward individual members of the team or only the team as a whole. The first type of capabilities we refer to as enhanced; the second as limited.

Given these distinctions, we derive the topology of leaders shown in table 9.2.

Our analysis establishes that under complete information, all types of leaders are unwilling to unilaterally behave as conditional cooperators; that is, to reward initially, reward subsequent cooperation, and punish defection. Moreover, under incomplete information, leader "reputations" induce cooperation by followers only for leaders of Type B or D.

A leader's claim that she will reward and punish according to a trigger strategy regardless of follower behavior is not credible under complete information. Put simply, it is always possible to construct follower strategies such that the leader prefers to deviate from her trigger strategy.[12] Other problems arise for certain kinds of leaders. Type A leaders (limited capabilities, fixed share) are always unwilling to retaliate against followers unless all followers cease to cooperate following a defection. The

12. The authors are indebted to Randy Calvert of the University of Rochester for his help on clarifying this point.

**Table 9.2** Topology of Leader Types

|  |  | *Capabilities* | |
|---|---|---|---|
|  |  | Limited | Enhanced |
| *Rewards* | Fixed Share | Type A | Type B |
|  | Residual Claimant | Type C | Type D |

same result may be true for Type C leaders (limited capabilities, residual claimant). Only leaders with enhanced capabilities are willing to retaliate against defectors when needed regardless of how other followers will respond.

Other types of leaders may have an incentive to spontaneously punish followers in order to claim all the benefits of team production for themselves. This incentive can arise for leaders who are residual claimants (Types C or D).

Capabilities and reward structure remain important influences on a leader's ability to initiate and sustain cooperation under incomplete information. As described previously, if followers are uncertain about the leader's payoffs, appropriate leader behavior will reinforce follower beliefs that conditional cooperation is the leader's dominant strategy. However, even if followers are *certain* that the leader will behave this way, conditional cooperation may not be their payoff-maximizing response.

Our characterization of leader rewards and capabilities shows that reputations are of no help in achieving team production when the leader possesses limited capabilities (Types A and C). Of course, regardless of the leader's incentives or capabilities, it may be possible to construct follower beliefs such that they believe that the leader is a conditional cooperator; but the leader must possess enhanced capabilities in order for this reputation to cause followers to cooperate.

Consider an extreme example: followers believe with probability 1 that the leader will reward and punish them according to a strategy of conditional cooperation. If the leader also possesses enhanced capabilities, each follower will believe that he will be rewarded if he cooperates and punished if he defects. Given these beliefs, the leader's threats need only be "severe enough" in order to motivate the follower to begin cooperating and to continue to do so regardless of the behavior of other followers.

Let another leader possess the same reputation and "severe-enough" threats, but have limited capabilities. Now the follower's calculation is different: *any* defection by a follower will trigger leader punishment of *all* followers. Under these circumstances, each follower is best off cooperating only if he expects everyone else to do so. Thus, a leader with limited capabilities is unable to provide followers with a unilateral incentive to begin to cooperate—regardless of the severity of his threats or the strength of his reputation.

The effect of a leader's reward structure on her ability to initiate cooperation under incomplete information is less clear. Regardless of how a leader is compensated, it is possible to construct follower beliefs about leader payoffs such that the followers will expect the leader to reward and punish according to a trigger strategy when the game is played. However, rewarding a leader with a fixed share appears to simplify the problem of constructing a reputation which convinces followers that the leader will use a trigger strategy. Fixed-share leaders are always willing to reward followers initially and on subsequent iterations, unless the rewards induce follower defections. In contrast, even if rewards do not induce defections, residual claimant leaders may have an incentive to punish followers initially or to punish spontaneously on subsequent iterations.

These results suggest the origins of the weakness in Miller's argument. His assessment of the power of "soft" incentives, such as reputation and trust, comes from the analysis of two-person games.[13] If the leader can monitor individual followers and target rewards and punishments selectively, then, in effect, she is engaged in a series of two-person games. When the leader has limited capabilities, however, her interactions with one follower are not separable from her interactions with other followers. Under these circumstances, results from two-player games fail to generalize to the multi-player game of team production.

The point is simple: the "rules of the game"—leader incentives and capabilities—are a critical influence on a leader's success at initiating and sustaining successful team production. Only leaders with enhanced capabilities are able to exploit reputation effects to the same end. The structure within which a leader operates shapes and constrains her behavior as well as the success of her efforts.

13. In particular, Miller's argument leans heavily on the two-player games (or games where one player interacts sequentially with many other players) analyzed in David Kreps, Robert Wilson, Paul Milgrom, and John Roberts, "Rational Cooperation in the Finitely Repeated Prisoners' Dilemma," *Journal of Economic Theory* 27 (1982): 245–52 and in David Kreps, "Corporate Culture and Economic Theory," unpublished paper, Stanford University, 1984.

## CONCLUSION

Miller's work heralds, one hopes, the beginning of a new trend in the application of rational choice theory to political science: its divorce from market economics and its application to materials drawn from the behavioral sciences. As Miller recognizes and underscores, in studying organizations other than markets, scholars will have to confront phenomena more often noted by behavioral scientists than by economists: "trust," "reputation," and "norms."

Miller's work suggests the utility of formal models in understanding the impact of institutional structures. As we have shown for team production, a leader's ability to create trust, exploit reputation, and enforce norms varies with the institutional features that determine her strategies, rewards, and information. In formal terms, the leader's power depends on characteristics of the extensive form of the team-production game.

Understanding when leaders make a difference thus requires a marriage between abstract modeling, a feeling for the "human element" in analytic problems, and substantive knowledge. The behavioralists' insights into the determinants of human behavior and information about the rules of real-world interactions—the extensive form—are critical to the success of formal analysis. Only by starting with this information will formal models yield valid accounts of real-world behavior.

Miller has shown that the tools developed by the rational choice theorist offer profound insight into the properties of organizations. While being cautious about the specific claims that Miller advances, we nonetheless remain inspired by the agenda he sets for our discipline.

## 10

# The Social Evolution of Cooperation

### RUSSELL HARDIN

### INTRODUCTION

The central questions of political theory are an explanatory and a normative question: Why does the state work? and How can we justify its working the way it does? Both questions are forced upon us by concern with conflict and the realization that in resolutions of conflict some typically benefit only if others lose.[1] The traditional answers to the first question, why the state works at all, are that it is backed by power and that it depends on cooperation. These answers undergird the conflict and the cohesion models of society, which are commonly taken to be alternative, contrary models. I wish to defend the thesis that they are not contrary models, that power and cooperation are heavily intertwined in the organization of society and government, indeed, that they are mutually reinforcing in the sense that power is based in cooperation and that it also enables cooperation.

The two questions are sometimes reduced to one on the presumption that the explanatory question is answered normatively in the following way. Cooperation is often thought to require normative commitments, and these commitments can be taken to give an answer to the fundamen-

I wish to thank Richard Arneson, David Copp, Haskell Fain, Gilbert Harman, Carol Heimer, Margaret Levi, and several attendees at the Pacific Division meetings of the American Philosophical Association in Los Angeles, March 1986, as well as discussants at the Universities of Colorado, Melbourne, and Washington, and the Australian National University for comments on an earlier draft of this paper. The paper was originally written for presentation as a Henry Stafford Little Lecture, Princeton University, 10 April 1986. I am grateful to the Public Lectures Committee at Princeton for providing a splendid stimulus.

1. There is a major class of exceptions to this claim. Some conflicts are unwanted, as in Hobbes's state of nature. Resolutions of them may take the form of simply eliminating certain perverse incentives. Some societies, such as the Yanomamö of New Guinea, "engage in warfare because among other reasons they cannot stop, not because they necessarily as a culture derive any benefit from fighting. In the absence of any central authority they are condemned to fight for ever" (C. R. Hallpike, "Functionalist Interpretations of Primitive Warfare," *Man* 8 (Sept. 1973): 451–70.

tal normative question of political theory. In this view the cohesion model of society is inherently normative in that it depends on the normative commitments of the members of society. Parsons says, "The famous problem of order ... cannot be solved without a common normative system." [2] Normative cohesion theorists tend to associate power with conflict in the absence of normatively determined cooperation. I wish to argue on the contrary that much of the power of political bodies, of states, arises from cooperation—indeed, from cooperation that is not normatively determined but that is the product of the interest-seeking of the members of society. In this account, a successful answer to the explanatory question above still leaves open the normative question of the justification of the political order that we can explain.

To explore these issues we should turn to the strategic structures of social relations. To speak of strategic structures is to focus on the way in which outcomes are determined by the interactions of choices by several or many actors each trying to achieve certain results that may differ substantially from the outcomes of their interactions. This is the subject of game theory, that wonderful framework for analyzing social relations that was first elaborated at Princeton during the Second World War by John von Neumann and Oskar Morgenstern.[3]

## THE STRUCTURES OF SOCIAL INTERACTION

There are three great categories of strategic interaction: conflict, coordination, and cooperation. If your actions affect my outcome, we are in one of these three kinds of interaction. *Pure conflict interactions* are typified by such games as poker and chess and to some extent by such social interactions as primitive wars of annihilation and the scramble for natural resources. In a pure conflict one party can gain only if another loses. *Coordination interactions* are the virtual opposite of this. In such interactions each party can gain only if others also gain. The most striking example of such interactions is the rule of the road, according to which we all want to drive by the same convention. In most countries we drive on the right. No one really cares whether we all drive right or left—but we all care whether we *all* drive by the same convention. *Cooperation interactions* involve elements of both conflict and coordination. The cen-

2. Talcott Parsons, "Power and the Social System," pp. 94–143 in Steven Lukes, ed., *Power* (New York: New York University Press, 1986), 121. If one could read the notion of "a common normative system" to include rampant egoism, Parsons's view would be true. He clearly means the notion to be a counter to rampant egoism.

3. John von Neumann and Oskar Morgenstern, *Theory of Games and Economic Behavior* (Princeton, NJ: Princeton University Press, 1944, first edition).

tral example of cooperation interactions is exchange: I have something you want and you have something I want. I'd rather have what you have than what I have and you'd rather have what I have. We can both benefit by exchanging. There is conflict because each of us has to give up something in order for the other to gain. And there is coordination because we can both be made better off at once by exchanging.

Much of the discussion of cooperation, both in ordinary language and political theory, runs together the latter two categories that I have called coordination and cooperation. I don't wish to quibble about vocabulary here but I do wish to keep the interactions straight, because the distinction between them is clearly very important in explanations of many social processes and institutions. It is in the explanation of these that I am interested. To avoid some confusion I will often refer to what I have here called cooperation interactions as exchange, although the category of exchange is not as extensive as that of cooperation.

What we exchange may be objects: you give me a book, I give you one. Or it can be actions: you do something for me and I do something for you. This sounds like the very stuff of politics. Or what we exchange can even be abstentions: the United States abstains from building a new weapons system if the Soviet Union abstains from building the same. Exchanges can be perverse in the sense that the element of conflict, of loss, may dominate that of coordination, of gain. For example, you give me the book you wrote and I retort by giving you the book I wrote.

Coordination problems are commonly resolved by conventions. We somehow happen on a way of coordinating that might be one of many plausible ways of coordinating well. Once we have done so, there is little or no incentive to do anything but go along with the convention. This is an account that is given by Hume and articulated in game theoretic terms by David Lewis.[4] For example, the driving convention in the United States may have arisen spontaneously without legal backing, although it is now backed by the force of law. The very orderly convention for time that we now follow first arose almost spontaneously only last century. The morass of diverse local sun times that were the norm in the United States until 1883 were too confusing to keep sensible railway schedules. The railways coordinated on standard railway time and eventually cities, states, and—in living memory—the nation adopted laws to mandate

4. David Hume, *A Treatise of Human Nature,* especially book 3, part 2, section 8, "Of the Source of Allegiance"; David K. Lewis, *Convention* (Cambridge, MA: Harvard University Press, 1969).

standard time.[5] One can see the problem from the fact that still in the 1960s there was a 35-mile bus trip from Steubenville, Ohio, to Moundsville, West Virginia, that required seven time changes.[6]

## COORDINATION AND POWER

Successful social coordination, whether intended or not intended, can create extraordinary power. Even the driving convention carries with it great power to sanction those who violate it, as many who are accustomed to one convention learn to their sorrow when they drive in nations that follow the opposite convention. Each of us may go along with a particular coordination merely because it would be costly not to. But because each of us goes along, the resulting convention may elevate someone to a station of power. This realization is at the core of the nascent theory of the state according to Adam Smith, who—I have it on the authority of certain of my colleagues at the University of Chicago—is every economist's favorite political theorist.

The usual concern with Smith's theory of the state is with his apparent theory of stages of development, from the state of nature through pastoral societies to, eventually, the England of his own time. I am not concerned with this account but only with the way in which Smith implicitly explains the power of government. For example, in a pastoral society he supposes that an individual shepherd will find it in his interest to be part of a group of shepherds because the group or tribe can better protect each individual against various depredations.[7] In a competitive world of pastoralists, one benefits best from association with the most powerful tribe. Hence, if someone rises to capable leadership with a tribe, others will be attracted to join with it. The result eventually will be remarkable power in the control of the leader of the tribe.[8] Combination for the sake of survival then makes it possible not merely to survive but to thrive and even to plunder.

This is essentially an argument from coordination. We coalesce be-

5. Ian R. Bartky and Elizabeth Harrison, "Standard and Daylight Saving Time," *Scientific American* 240 (May 1979): 46–53.

6. Ibid., p. 49.

7. Adam Smith, *An Inquiry into the Nature and Causes of the Wealth of Nations* (Oxford: Clarendon Press, 1976; Indianapolis, Ind.: Liberty Classics, 1981, reprint), book 5, chap. 1, part 2, pp. 711–15.

8. James remarks, "This tendency of organic unities to accumulate when once they are formed is absolutely all the truth I can distill from Spencer's unwieldy account of evolution" (William James, "Herbert Spencer," pp. 107–22 in James, *Essays in Philosophy* [Cambridge, MA: Harvard University Press, 1978; essay first published 1904], 119).

cause it is individually in our interest to do so as long as others do so as well. What we need to guide is in coalescing with others is merely the evidence of sufficient leadership and sufficient members to make our joining them clearly beneficial. If others were coalescing around a different leader or a different group, we would be as pleased to join with them. On this evolutionary theory of the growth of power, fitness leads not merely to survival but also to increasing fitness. Power may not simply be a resource that can be expanded until it is gone; rather it may derive from coordination that recreates itself.[9]

That this is a central part of the power of even modern states can be shown by the answer to an apparent conundrum in John Austin's theory of law, according to which obedience to law is based on the threat of sanction.[10] We may call this the 'gunman theory' of law.[11] The conundrum is that, if we are to be made to obey law by threat of force, then the state will be unable to mount adequate mechanisms of enforcement. Hume says, "No man would have any reason to *fear* the fury of a tyrant, if he had no authority over any but from fear; since, as a single man, his bodily force can reach but a small way, and all the farther power he possesses must be founded either on our own opinion, or on the presumed opinion of others."[12] As a contemporary lawyer puts this argument: "No state could possibly compel people to obey all these rules at gunpoint; there would not be enough soldiers and policemen to hold the guns (a sort of Orwellian vision of society), they would have to sleep sooner or later, and then anarchy might break out."[13] Anarchy *might* indeed break out, but as we all know it generally does not even under far

9. Of course, there may be some conflict in our group. I may wish I were leader in your stead. To become leader, however, I will need to gain a sufficient following to make it the interest of others to recoordinate behind me.

10. John Austin, *The Province of Jurisprudence Determined* (New York: Noonday Press, 1954).

11. This theory is severely criticized by H. L. A. Hart, *The Concept of Law* (Oxford: At the Clarendon Press, 1961).

12. David Hume, "Of the First Principles of Government," pp. 32–36 in Hume, *Essays Moral, Political and Literary,* ed. by Eugene F. Miller (Indianapolis, Ind.: Liberty Press, 1985; essay first published 1741), 34. Many philosophers have followed Hume's view. Although he seems to know better in other places, Hume here fails to note that "the presumed opinon of others" need be only the opinion that they are themselves at risk if they do not support the tyrant. They can take that risk with impunity only if they are relatively sure others will join with them, that is, will coordinate on redefining power. See further, Gregory S. Kavka, *Hobbesian Moral and Political Theory* (Princeton: Princeton University Press, 1986), 254–66. Kavaka cites several references (ibid., p. 257n).

13. Anthony D'Amato, "Is International Law Really 'Law'?" *Northwestern Law Review* 79 (1984–85): 1293–1314, quotation from p. 1295.

less massively controlled circumstances. Why? It is commonly assumed that norms of cooperation and obedience are necessary to keep us in our places.This does not follow, however. To wreck the state, it is not enough that anarchy break out a little bit at a time. If it is to prevail against threatened sanctions, it must break out all at once. It must be pervasive. A moderately organized state can typically keep its citizens under control without going to Orwellian extremes. The Videla regime in Argentina, the Nazi occupation in Czechoslovakia, and many others have kept large populations under control with little more than force simply because it was not actually necessary to invoke the force against everyone at once. Those who would oppose such a regime must coordinate their actions in opposition or be weaker than their numbers.

In a relatively orderly state, most individuals cannot expect to benefit from seriously transgressing the law, because the police, as weak as they may be, can be expected to apprehend a significant proportion of transgressors. That, remarkably, may be all that the gunman theory of the state requires for its success. The gunman theory might well be called the coordination theory of state power or even the dual-coordination theory. It depends on coordination at the level of government and on lack of coordination at the level of any potential popular opposition. The state need not compel everyone at gunpoint, it need merely make it in virtually everyone's clear interest individually to comply with the law.

Note the way coordination works here. It creates power because it makes certain behaviors on the part of relevant others less rewarding than they would be against an uncoordinated group. In turn, this means that the coordinated, powerful group can now do many things at far less cost than doing these things would otherwise have involved. Hence, coordination not only creates power, it also reduces the need to use power.

In the coordination theory of state power and of obedience to law it is relatively easy to understand the remarkable change in allegiance of a populace under certain radical changes in government. For example, we are often treated to agonizing questions about the nature of the German people that they could have given their allegiance to Hitler on short notice and then could quickly have switched their allegiance from Hitler to the puppet governments of the western allies and the Soviet Union. Throughout, most Germans seem to have been model citizens. Most of us would similarly be model citizens under the coercive circumstances of the Germans during and after Hitler's rule. If there were as many genuinely loyal Nazis as we sometimes suspect, it would be odd that they submitted so readily to the postwar governments if obedience really turned on a civic norm of cooperation or a shared commitment to a particular set of values.

In the coordination theory it is also easy to grasp the power of passive disobedience, as in the Indian independence movement or the American civil rights movement, which depends on the power of popular coordination against the limited capacity of a normal state to control its population. That there is differential capacity for coordination is clear. The large population often cannot coordinate except by careful, covert conspiracy while the minions of the state can conspire openly. What makes passive disobedience a rare device is that it too requires open conspiracy, hence widespread moral agreement. But passive disobedience is not anarchy, or at least not chaos. It is generally quite orderly. If there is great disorder, it is often introduced by the state in the effort to rout the orderly resisters.

## EXCHANGE

Perhaps the interaction that most commonly underlies what we call cooperation is that of the game theorist's favorite game, the prisoner's dilemma. This game was discovered or invented—it is not clear which is the more apt term here—by Merrill Flood and Melvin Dresher, two early game theorists who were trying to test bargaining theories with experimental games.[14] Oddly, two of the games with which Flood experimented before the prisoner's dilemma involved simple exchanges—of old cars for money. He seems not to have seen that his prisoner's dilemma game was a simplification and generalization of such exchanges. Unfortunately, this association got lost in the later naming of the game by A. W. Tucker, who saw in the game a perverse analog of American criminal justice, in which prosecutors extract confessions on the promise of reduced sentences.[15] Social theorists have come to see prisoner's dilemmas everywhere in social interaction and many have been surprised by the ubiquity of the game.[16] Had the game originally been named "exchange," we would have *expected* it to be ubiquitous.

14. The unnamed prisoner's dilemma is reported in Merrill Flood, "Some Experimental Games," *Management Science* 5 (October 1958):5–26, especially pp. 11–17. It was less accessibly published in "Some Experimental Games," Rand Corporation Research Memorandum RM-789-1, 20 June 1952. To my knowledge, this is the first instance of the appearance of the prisoner's dilemma.

15. Merrill Flood, private communication, 25 February 1975, reports that Tucker gave the game its present name.

16. Arthur Stinchcombe captures this growing sense in his sly review of work by Jon Elster, "Is the Prisoner's Dilemma All of Sociology?" *Inquiry* 23 (1980): 187–92.

Ordinarily we think of exchange as essentially a two-party affair, as in Flood's games over the sale of used cars in California. But the strategic structure of exchange can be generalized to any number of players. In its many-person or collective guise, exchange is a very interesting problem at the core of the issue of social order. It is in some ways less tractable than the ordinary two-party problem and, indeed, it entails the perversity of what Mancur Olson has called the "logic of collective action." [17] Under this logic, a group of people with a common interest that requires common action may share an interest collectively but not individually. You and I both want cleaner air and we can both contribute to cleaning it up by not burning our leaves or grilling our dinners over charcoal and by paying more for cars that pollute less. Unfortunately, it is in my interest for everyone else to behave well in these ways, but it is not in my interest for *me* to behave well. The best of all worlds for me, egocentric as I am, is that in which you all behave well while I barbecue and otherwise pollute to my heart's content.

This is not unlike the motivations in Flood's and Dresher's original, still unnamed, prisoner's dilemma or in any ordinary exchange. In the best of all worlds for Flood in one of his car-buying games, he would have got the car without having to pay for it. At the level of two-person exchange in our actual world, that might require theft. But if I pollute the air of thousands of asthma sufferers in order to gain a slight pleasure, that is not theft—it is just the dismal logic of collective action. When we want benefits from collective exchange, we are slapped by the back of the invisible hand that coddles us to success in dyadic exchanges on the market.

The problem of pollution is a perverse and in some degree a modern variant of the central problem of collective action in social life. The collective problem of pollution has to do with the failure to control destructive impulses that are individually beneficial. The more urgent problem at the base of social life is that of motivating constructive actions to create order and wealth. The order we enjoy in a well-ordered state is in part the product of large-number exchanges or collective actions in which we individually contribute to the provision of a collective good. Collectively we may create resources that give us collective power. But generally we cannot count on individual generosity to contribute to collective endeavors. We need the motivations of direct benefit to individuals that made Flood's game of buying and selling a used car an easy

17. Mancur Olson, Jr., *The Logic of Collective Action* (Cambridge, MA: Harvard University Press, 1965).

problem. It was easy because neither the buyer nor the seller could get the benefits of the exchange without paying the cost of giving up the money or giving up the car. Often the only way to tie the benefits and costs of *collective* action so directly together is through legal sanctions. Our cars do not pollute as much as they once did because the state forces us to buy cars with pollution control devices. While many people might pay extra for optional safety equipment such as airbags or seatbelts on their cars, presumably few would pay extra for optional pollution control equipment.

Traditional political philosophers suppose that voluntary collective action is hard to motivate. They have commonly argued that we therefore create states with the power to sanction people individually. Not surprisingly, this move is ridiculed as circular because it supposes that we solve the grievous problem of collective action by *collectively* acting to solve it. This would not be a helpful explanatory move. Yet it does seem true that much of the source of a society's power to motivate collective action comes from mutual cooperation. If this is so, must people not finally be motivated primarily by norms rather than by interests when they are concerned with social order? Surely to some extent people *are* motivated by norms. But much of modern social life seems much more heavily to depend on motivations from interest. The extraordinary wealth of industrial societies would be hard to explain if norms were thought to be the central motivators of workers on the job. Then do we partition ourselves and act from norms in politics and from interests in economics? That seems to be the central division for many scholarly accounts and, on the apparent views of some people, it underlies our division into academic disciplines.

Against this way of viewing social cooperation, I think that a large part of the answer to our seeming paradox is that much of the cooperation that is needed to create central power to regulate further cooperation grows out of a substantially different form of collective interaction: it grows out of games of coordination, not out of games of exchange. *Coordination begets power that begets sanctions that motivate collective exchange.* Of course, the causal chain of social life will not typically be so simple and pristine as this. Indeed, there will be no beginning for the chain. In any actual institution we will see an amalgam of resources that are sometimes created by coordination, sometimes by voluntary collective exchange, and sometimes by the use of prior resources to compel further contributions to the collective stores. There may be elements of norm-guided behavior in any of these, especially in voluntary collective exchange. But for many institutions the clear structure of motivations is individual incentives derived largely from the power of coordination.

## CONFUSIONS BETWEEN COORDINATION AND EXCHANGE

Is the distinction between coordination and exchange important for our further understanding of political theory? To see that it is, let us briefly consider several issues. First, let us consider the conceptual issue in the understanding of political power. Debates on power are often confused by the failure to distinguish the sources of it. Then let us turn to three instances of confusion in important political theories that are also based on this failure. These theories are Hobbes's theory of political society, Marx's optimistic theory of revolution, and contemporary explanations of the common law that base the law in arguments from efficiency. Keeping straight the different strategic sources of power in the nature of power and in such theories as these is crucial to political history.

### Power

First, consider conceptual confusions in the notion of power. All too often discussions of power are concerned too soon with what power is rather than with how it comes to be, how it is created. As noted above, political power can be based *directly* in successful coordination of many people. Such coordination may sensibly be called a form of power. Power can also be based *indirectly* in collective exchange, which can produce resources, such as money. People can cooperate in such exchanges either spontaneously or under threat of sanctions. The force of the sanctions may derive from the power of a coordinated body or from the availability of resources to the state or other sanctioner. These resources can be used to manipulate or coerce people to do things unrelated to the original exchange that produced the resources.

It follows that power derived from resources can be used to augment the resources. It can also be expended as the resources are expended, as in war; and, if it is not adequately augmented, it can be exhausted. Power based in coordination can increase as it attracts further people to the coordination. For example, Smith's pastoral leader may be so powerful as to attract others to his following because they seek his protection. Power based in coordination can be destroyed very quickly by recoordination behind a different leader or on a different convention, or even by the collapse of coordination. For example, in Xenophon's account, Cyrus's upstart army was on the verge of victory over Darius's army and might have routed the latter when Cyrus charged into battle against the king and was slain. As the news spread, his army collapsed before an alternative leader could be elevated to its head. Although it had taken months to mold that army, its extraordinary power was dissipated in hours.[18] Darius seemed correctly to infer that victory went to the survivor even if the survivor may have lost most of the battle.

Power based in coordination may be harder to manipulate than that based in resources. It may be more fragile, as the Greeks fighting on the side of Cyrus learned, and it may be more resistant to changes in the uses to which it is put. It is often associated with charisma. Power based in resources extracted from collective exchange or from coerced contributions will be far more fungible. It can often be seized, as in coups.

Power based in coordination is rather like the money system than like exchange. We generally can rely on the intrinsically worthless paper money in our pockets just because virtually everyone else relies on it. If, however, enough of us suddenly were to coordinate in running on our banks to convert our currency into something else—silver, gold, or yen—our currency would suddenly lose its value. Coordination power is similarly a function of reinforcing expectations about the behavior of others. Exchange power is more nearly like the actual goods that are in exchange, either for money or for other goods. It takes the form of deployable resources. It is this dual nature of the sources of power and therefore of the workings of power that make efforts to define it generally unsatisfactory in the vast and vastly disagreeable "power is . . ." literature. For example, contrary to the view of Parsons, there is no "generalized medium" of power analogous to the medium of money in exchange.[19] Coordination power shares the characteristic of money in that it depends on mutually reinforcing expectations. And exchange power shares the sometime characteristic of money that it is backed by real resources.

It is in the coordination view of power that we should analyze many aspects of political life, as for example, political participation. When one is a voter, Brian Barry asks, "Is it better to be powerful or lucky?"[20] He rightly concludes that it is better to be lucky in the sense that what one wants is simply to have one's views be the majority views. If, in the resource view of power, we were to analyze the resources of individual voters to determine their power, these would seem paltry. In the coordination view, it is not the individual voter who is powerful; rather, it is

18. Xenophon, *The Persian Expedition*, book 1, chaps. 8–10, book 2, chap. 1.
19. Parsons, "Power and the Social System," p. 97.
20. Brian Barry, "Is It Better To Be Powerful or Lucky?" *Political Studies* 28 (June and September 1980): 183–94, 338–52.

the coordinated mass of voters who vote together that is powerful. Similarly, it is not the individual herder in Smith's pastoral society who is powerful; rather, it is the coordinated collective of herders under unified leadership. When the coordination breaks, the power dissipates, as it did for Cyrus's army. In game theoretical language, power based in coordination is superadditive, it adds up to more than the sum of the individual contributions to it.

Again, as noted above, successful coordination of a group may radically reduce the group's costs of action in important ways simply because its coordination induces others not to oppose it. Individual or small groups of herders, for example, might have to be constantly on the alert to protect their herds. The members of a large pastoral tribe might rest relatively content in the same environment.

## Leviathan

It is sometimes supposed that Hobbes represents the central problem of political order as a general prisoner's dilemma. If we all voluntarily cooperate in leaving each other's goods and persons alone, we all prosper better than if we all plunder one another's goods and threaten one another's safety. But so long as everyone else is cooperating, I would benefit from taking advantage of them and plundering for my benefit. Indeed, no matter what anyone else does, my interest is better served by my plundering than by my abstinence. This is the structure of the prisoner's dilemma.

Smith's account of the rise of powerful leaders in pastoral societies seems far more plausible than this account, which, in any case, I think is a misreading of Hobbes. Smith supposes that before the rise of herding there could have been little advantage in going after another's property because there could be little property of value.[21] This is not the conceptual point that without a state to define ownership there can be no property but merely the economic point that before herding there could have been little of value to plunder from anyone. The potential benefits of plundering would therefore have been negligible. Moreover, if a plunderer ran some risk of personal harm, then plundering would be worse than not plundering.

That is to say, in the rudest state of economic and political development—not to speak of what philosophers call a "state of nature"—plun-

21. Smith, *Wealth of Nations,* book 5, chap. 1, part 2, p. 709. Also see Smith, *Lectures on Jurisprudence* (Oxford: Clarendon Press, 1978; Indianapolis, Ind.: Liberty Classics, 1982, reprint), 16.

dering no matter what others did was plausibly not the dominant strategy it would be in the supposed prisoner's dilemma of Hobbes. Since the harm that could come from being attacked was likely greater than the gains to be made from attacking, the strategic structure of a rude society is that of a coordination game *if only* it is true that coordination of the many gives protection against attack, as surely it often must. Hence, the problem that Hobbes had to resolve is not a prisoner's dilemma or exchange but a coordination game. The rudimentary state precedes the rise of wealth that would make plundering worthwhile.

The resolution of such a game might seem similar to Hobbes's resolution of his problem in that it might well involve the elevation of someone to a position of powerful leadership. The elevation will not follow by a variant version of a contract to regulate an exchange, however, but will happen merely by coordination, perhaps spontaneously without direction from anyone. And the leader's power can fade as quickly as did the power of Cyrus's army.

Consider an earlier version of the justification of government to overcome prisoner's dilemma interactions, that posed by Glaucon in Plato's *Republic*. Glaucon says that if I could have a ring of Gyges, which would allow me to become invisible at will, I would plunder and rape at will. His theory of obedience to law is simply an early variant of the gunman theory.[22] The problem of the possibility of freely committing crimes and escaping punishment under the law poses a prisoner's dilemma and not merely a coordination problem. It requires the general cooperation of others for me to gain advantage from my own uncooperative behavior. Hence, Glaucon's problem is a problem of incentives *after* order has been established to make production and accumulation of wealth possible. Hobbes's problem in the so-called state of nature is a problem *before* or about the establishment of order. If the order that is established can successfully punish all transgressors, that is, if there is no working equivalent of the ring of Gyges, there will be no sense to the notion of free-riding on that order.

### The Socialist Revolution

The hope of a socialist revolution in Marx and in latter-day Marxists is also commonly seen as the resolution of what appears to be a prisoner's dilemma. But if this is the strategic structure of the problem, then, as

22. Plato, *The Republic*, book 2, 360b–c.

Mancur Olson concludes, *"class-oriented action will not occur if the in-dividuals that make up a class act rationally."*[23] This is merely a specific instance of the more general logic of collective action: all of those who would benefit from a revolution will choose to let others take the risks of fighting it, but then it will not be fought. Marx is commonly thought to see social change as driven by interests, not ideas. Hence, he should agree with Olson.

On this account, Marx is thought simply to have misunderstood the strategic structure of the problem of revolution and to have founded his historicist theory of the coming of socialism on flawed reasoning.[24] One defense of Marx on this point is to suppose that he did not think that class action would be based on narrowly rational or self-interested mo-tivations but would follow from class-oriented motivations. Such an ex-planation elevates normative or altruistic motivations over self-interest motivations in this context. At first it sounds odd to think that what motivates an individual to act against the interest of the individual is the interest of the individual's class. But it is possible that the self-seeking that drives much of our lives retires momentarily in the face of certain opportunities, as it does when we see someone in danger, when we work for the benefit of a child or others, or when we become excessive patriots in times of national crisis.

What is wanted in an explanation of revolution that relies on such a motivation is an account of how individuals come to identify the interests of their class as their own interest. Without this latter explanation, the contemporary efforts to refurbish Marx's prediction of socialist revolu-tion in industrial societies seem like wish fulfillment. They recall the pop-ular Sidney Harris cartoon in which two mathematicians are standing before a blackboard. On the left and right sides of the board are compli-cated formulations that look very different but that one of the mathe-maticians seems to think equivalent. The other mathematician has doubts: he is pointing at the middle of the board and saying, "I think you should be more explicit here in step two." Step two simply says "THEN A MIRACLE OCCURS."

An alternative, less miraculous defense of Marx's view of the possibil-

23. Olson, *The Logic*, p. 105, emphasis in original.
24. A survey of some of the literature on this issue is in Scott Lash and John Urry, "The New Marxism of Collective Action: A Critical Analysis," *Sociology* 18 (February 1984):33–50. To escape the difficulties of basing a theory of revolution on individual inter-ests, Lash and Urry want to focus on the 'causal powers' of social classes.

ity of socialist revolution is to suppose that he did not see the problem as merely a prisoner's dilemma, but also in part as a simple problem of coordination. In particular, the mobilization of large enough numbers on certain occasions reduces the costs of acting against state power. On the actual evidence of earlier events of his lifetime, this would not have been a perverse way to view the problem, although it may later have come to seem implausible. It would be tendentious to claim that Marx held a clear view of the strategic structure of the problem of revolutionary action. But on the evidence of the French Revolution and of the revolutionary events of 1848, it is not implausible to suppose that revolution would be relatively easy *if* it could get coordinated.[25] Once coordinated, it was on these occasions almost a matter of orderly, focussed rioting or mutiny. Once enough people were participating, the costs of participating fell to almost negligible levels.

There was some chance of harm, as there was for street demonstrators in Teheran during the events leading to the abdication of the Shah, but it was slight once the crowds at, say, the Bastille were large. Technically it might typically be true on these occasions that the order of payoffs in the matrix of the game of revolution was strictly that of the prisoner's dilemma, as it may also be for voting in, say, American elections. But successful coordination may so greatly reduce costs that the latter are almost negligible, so that the slightest moral commitment may tip the scales toward action. Just as it would be odd for many Americans in communities in which voting is easy to balk at the minor cost in inconvenience, so it might seem odd for many workers or soldiers or others to balk at joining a crowd to march on the palace or the Bastille. This is not identical to a multiple coordination problem, such as that in the driving convention, in which one simply wants to go with the majority. In the revolutionary coordination, one has an active preference between the outcome of full attack and that of no attack. Still, one prefers to attack if enough others do and not to attack if enough others do not.

This argument would seem to fit well with Marx's analysis. Richard Arneson, however, argues that in his expectations of revolution Marx was really "the German Romantic, not the sober Victorian political economist."[26] Marx characterizes the problem of modern proletarian

25. Marx says that "The February [1848] Revolution was a surprise attack, a *taking* of the old society *unawares*" (Karl Marx, *The 18th Brumaire of Louis Bonaparte* [New York: International Publishers, 1963], 18).

26. Richard J. Arneson, "Marxism and Secular Faith," *American Political Science Review* 79 (September 1985): 627–40, quote on p. 633.

revolutions as one in which the proletariat "recoil ever and anon from the indefinite prodigiousness of their own aims, until the situation has been created which makes all turning back impossible. . . ."[27] Arneson supposes this cannot mean that the proletariat reach a point at which individual benefits from revolutionary action outweigh individual risks. Rather, he says, "a point is reached at which turning back would renege on a commitment to one's most ideal self-image, to be realized in the attainment of the most prodigious aims by heroic means."[28] The florid style of Marx's rhetoric makes it hard to call his account sober rather than romantic. But what seems to make "all turning back impossible" is not romantic attachment to one's "most ideal self-image." Rather it is the eventual development of the necessary class consciousness to know what to do with the state once it has been taken. The revolution will succeed when the proletariat has been prepared for its mission of rule and when it then has momentary opportunity to grasp control in a *coup de main,* an unexpected stroke, such as that of 1848.[29] Coordination without clear enough purpose will soon collapse. Turning back from a coordination once there is clear purpose then is impossible in part because opposing forces cannot naturally regain control after those forces collapse in the face of the revolutionary move.

It was perhaps the startling ease with which spontaneous revolutions took control in cities that led the French under Thiers to put down the Paris Commune with such thoroughgoing brutality as to make it seem more nearly like murder than warfare. The answer to the coordination explanation of revolutionary action is draconian force. This lesson of the Commune has been learned well by many later regimes and leaders in various places, such as the Nazis in Czechoslovakia, Stalin in the Soviet Union, Pinochet in Chile, and Videla in Argentina, with their harsh, blanket suppression of dissenters and potential dissenters. *They raise the likely costs of revolutionary activity enough to change its structure.* Since the time of the Commune, no one can any longer suppose that revolution can be simply a matter of spontaneous coordination in an industrial state. It can occur relatively easily, if at all, only when the state has lost its resources for self-defense, as in Russia in 1917 at the end of a disastrous war, or in Iran during the death agony of the Shah, or in societies with far poorer resources in the state's control. It is this realization that gives the chill to our expectations from current events in South Africa.

27. Marx, *18th Brumaire*, p. 19.
28. Arneson, "Marxism and Secular Faith," p. 633.
29. Marx, *18th Brumaire*, p. 18.

If the old state raises the costs enough to individuals for revolutionary activity, it overcomes the power of coordination to reduce the costs of revolutionary activity. It forces potential revolutionaries to see their problem overwhelmingly as a prisoner's dilemma in which free-riding is in the individuals' interest. Indeed, in recent decades it is hard in many settings to view the prospect of revolution as even a prisoner's dilemma. States often especially and effectively target the leadership of revolutionary groups, so that early leaders cannot sensibly see their cause as one in which they have any hope of benefiting from the collective action even if it eventually succeeds. The state can use the very resources that Marx thinks the revolutionaries want to seize to stop them in their tracks. Then the conflict aspect in the collective interaction of insurgency may severely override its coordination aspect and we should not expect much further revolutionary activity.

## The Common Law

One of the most innovative and interesting scholarly endeavors of the past decade or so has been the renewed effort to give economic interpretations of the nature and content of law. The chief omission in this endeavor to date has been the relative neglect of strategic considerations in the focus on efficiency and wealth maximization.[30] In much of this work, the concern is with the global efficiency of a given state of affairs as compared to some other. This is a relatively static view of the problem not unlike the predominant mode of economic analysis more generally, which focuses on static equilibrium. A major difficulty in a static understanding of efficiency is that our major concern is often with policy, with how to get from the state of affairs in which we find ourselves to another that seems ideally better. This is fundamentally a strategic and dynamic problem.[31] If such dynamic considerations are important in economics, they are crucial in the law.

In general the greatest barrier to achieving ideally efficient outcomes

30. For a survey of this field, see Jules Coleman, "Law and Economics," chapter 5 of Jeffrie Murphy and Jules Coleman, *The Philosophy of Law* (Totowa, NJ: Rowman and Allanheld, 1984); Richard A. Posner, "The Ethical and Political Basis of Wealth Maximization," pp. 88–115 in Posner, *The Economics of Justice* (Cambridge, MA: Harvard University Press, 1981).

31. Posner is, of course, not oblivious of strategic considerations in the common law. See his brief discussion of *stare decisis,* the doctrine of decision according to precedent, in Richard A. Posner, *Economic Analysis of Law* (Boston: Little, Brown, 1977, second edition), 426–27.

in a system of common law, and plausibly also in a system of legislated law, is the weight of what we have already decided and of the institutions we have already created. These structure expectations and overwhelmingly determine the general cast of outcomes. Once they have been in place long enough to do this, they are conventions in the strong game theoretic sense that they resolve coordination problems. Although we can change conventions—that is typically the purpose of legislation that alters part of a regime of common law—we may not be able to do it easily. Moreover, if our concern is with efficiency, it should be partly with dynamic efficiency, with the costs and benefits of making changes—not only with static efficiency, with the costs and benefits of living under one legal regime rather than another.

Once we have a particular legal rule in place, it acquires political force, but it also acquires moral force. Neither of these may be sufficient to block revision of the rule, but they are likely to be serious considerations if the rule is important. One of the important aspects of passive disobedience to a particular law is the demonstration that the moral force of that law is in serious question. Voiding the Jim Crow laws of the American South and passing laws against the Jim Crow practices of much of the nation clearly affected many expectations, no doubt to the detriment of many interests. Some of these expectations were moral on any reasonable account. Blocking them was part of the cost of changing the laws.

More fundamentally, we may ask why have a system of common law at all? The answer is a grand version of the doctrine of *stare decisis:* bcause we already have it. At various early times in the history of the development of any particular legal system, we have opted for various systems. At early enough stages when it might be possible to choose a system, it might be hard to put forth a compelling argument for the general superiority of any one system, whether codified or common law. The choice of *which* system might have been virtually a matter of indifference. But choosing *some* system was not a matter of indifference: we need some system of law to give us decisive resolutions of issues so that we may get on with our lives. Hence, the central problem is to get everyone coordinated on some workable system. If historically we did not come around to choosing a system, that may not have been a serious loss. A system of common law based on precedents is a system that could simply grow up over time even without active creative efforts to devise the best possible system.

## The Normative Question

It would be out of place here to go very extensively into the answers to the normative question of how to justify the state's working the way it does. But I should say something about the implications for that question of the explanatory analysis here. According to a well-known dictum of Hume, objective facts cannot imply values. One who was convinced of this dictum would readily conclude that the foregoing analysis cannot imply anything about the justification of the state's working. To some extent this conclusion would be wrong, for two reasons.

First, there is a related, contrary dictum that "ought" implies "can." If it is not possible for me to do something then it cannot be the case that I morally ought to do it. At the level of a society, this dictum would suggest that if the requisite institutional structure for accomplishing some end cannot be created out of the stuff of actual humans, then it cannot be true that that end ought to be achieved. This is the limited lesson that Bernard Williams thinks we may draw from sociobiology. "The most that sociobiology might do for ethics," he says, is "to suggest that certain institutions or patterns of behavior are not realistic options for human societies."[32]

Second, one answer to the normative question is that, in a narrow sense, might may sometimes make right.[33] For example, once we have successfully coordinated in the same way on a particular, recurring problem, we may have established a convention, as in the discussion of the common law above. Thereafter, we individually have very strong incentive to follow the convention. Moreover, and more important here, we have very strong moral reason to do so to the extent that violating the convention would bring harm to others, as my driving on the left in North America would likely bring harm to others.[34] In this account, efforts to find *a priori* normative justification for many laws and for the system of common law are often wrongheaded. What justifies them is a combination of a historicist explanation of their origin and a consideration of whether they are reasonably, not ideally, workable.

Apart from these two considerations, however, Hume's dictum seems

32. Bernard Williams, *Ethics and the Limits of Philosophy* (Cambridge, MA: Harvard University Press, 1985), 44.

33. See further, Russell Hardin, "Does Might Make Right?" pp. 201–17 in J. Roland Pennock and John W. Chapman, editors, NOMOS 29: *Authority Revisited* (New York: New York University Press, 1987).

34. This is obviously a contingent claim that depends on what coordination opportunities there are.

compelling—we cannot derive an ought from an is. We may explain the state's power as the results of coordination and of the creation of resources through collective exchange, but this explanation yields us no immediate proof of the rightness of what the state may do. Indeed, we may reasonably suppose that resources generated for general purposes may well be corruptly used for particular purposes. This is, of course, the traditional liberal's great fear: that the state will abuse its power. Indeed, no sooner does Smith lay out the nascent theory of the pastoral state discussed above than he notes that the system in which the sovereign dispensed justice for a fee "could scarce fail to be productive of several very gross abuses." [35]

## CONCLUSION

The major forms of cooperation that we see in social and political contexts have their origins in two distinctively different kinds of strategic interactions: coordination and exchange. These typically come together in important institutional arrangements. But in many contexts, such as in Smith's account of the organization of a pastoral society and in many problems of international relations, coordination seems to come first. Is it in fact prior to exchange in explaining widespread social cooperation and institutions? In an explanatory sense it probably is, although in a historical sense it might be impossible to show that it was in actual cases. It is prior because coordination creates a convention—an institution, a norm, or power—and that convention then promotes further coordination.

The force of this explanation is that, although it may sound circular, it is valid. As noted earlier, the problem of collective action cannot sensibly be resolved in the seemingly similar circular manner of supposing we should act collectively in order to resolve our problem of collective action. That just is our problem of collective action. But coordination can come about without intent, without overcoming contrary incentives. It can just happen. And if it just happens the same way a few times the result may be a forceful convention that then governs future behavior by giving us specific incentives for action.

In recent years we have been given very clever evolutionary explanations of cooperation and of altruism. This is an important effort just because an evolutionary perspective would seem to predict a very strong trait of looking out for one's own interest. This trait and any trait for

35. Smith, *Wealth of Nations*, book 5, chap. 1, part 2, p. 716.

altruism clearly conflict in many contexts and we might commonly think interest would dominate in determining much behavior. An alternative to biological evolution is social evolution in the rise of institutions and norms. On an explanation from social evolution we account for strong institutions for cooperation even on the assumption that, biologically, we are wired to be strongly self-seeking. Hence we have cooperation that is consistent with our biologically determined egoism. Through social evolution we build complex institutional structures out of simpler ones. In the end we have an inextricable mixing of exchange and coordination, of power from resources based in exchange and power that is coordination.

COMMENT: *On Russell Hardin's "The Social Evolution of Cooperation"*
Carol A. Heimer

Hardin ingeniously argues that the claims that the state is based on power and that it is based on cooperation need not be contradictory because power both rests on cooperation and, in turn, facilitates cooperation. The key is that simple coordination can create the power needed to create the sanctions to motivate further cooperation. In some cases in which individuals' interests are best served by collective action, conventions that allow individuals to coordinate their actions will be sufficient to create this sort of cooperation. But such collective action may give power to one or another actor around whom the activities of others are coordinated. This newly powerful actor can then introduce sanctions to help overcome the free-riding that undermines other kinds of cooperative ventures (in particular those that have the structure of a prisoner's dilemma). Thus coordination can lead to collective action, which leads to power, which leads to further cooperation.

Further, some kinds of collective action surely cost less when people's activities are carefully coordinated. The paradox of voting would be even more puzzling if, in addition to having to explain why people voted when their individual votes were ineffective in determining the outcome of an election, we also had to explain why they would go to a lot of trouble figuring out how to register their votes if there were not polling places, voting machines, ballots, and easy access to information about candidates, party affiliations, party platforms, and the mechanics of voting. Hardin shows how coordination can sometimes arise spontaneously and suggests how this view of the role of coordination illuminates otherwise murky analyses of the Hobbesian problem of political order, the possibilities of socialist revolution, and the origins of systems of common law based on precedent.

The beauty of this formulation is that it makes the origin of the state considerably less mysterious since "mere" coordination is easier to arrange than cooperation and sometimes comes about spontaneously. Further, it suggests how one might account for some of the observed differences in the strength and stability of political groupings, in the likelihood of collective action, etc. If power and cooperation are partly based on coordination, then one should look at differences in the ease or difficulty of coordination to explain differences between groups in power and cooperative behavior. As Hardin notes (p. 364), "That there is a differential capacity for coordination is clear." The remainder of this comment will suggest how one might turn capacity for coordination into a variable and what kinds of things might cause variations in capacity to coordinate.

I recall recently reading an argument to the effect that the social life of young people in poorer parts of the city is facilitated by the existence of vacant lots. Adolescents can meet here without advance planning and carry on their social lives without extensive supervision from adults. Suburban kids who do not have easy access to vacant lots or equivalent places to meet have to go to great pains to coordinate schedules, to arrange to meet at concerts, etc. We would expect, then, that suburban kids would be less likely to spontaneously meet their friends, but we would also expect that they might develop a different set of skills, namely those that are necessary to the maintenance of a social life when coordination is more difficult. Where there are few vacant lots to coordinate their social lives for them, adolescents learn to make appointments, to phone in advance, to arrive on time, etc.—skills that some might argue will be helpful to them in adult life when they will need to coordinate with employers, co-workers, spouses, and babysitters.

The problem with this example is that it is not clear that coordination is *more* likely in one case than the other, at least after the suburban adolescents learn to use a telephone and an appointment book. All we really know is that coordination is likely to come about in different ways in the two cases. This *may* make coordination, and hence collective action, more likely in one case than in the other, but that is something we would have to investigate.

A parallel contrast can be found between city life in Europe (in Britain especially) and in the United States. In the United States we have few public institutions like pubs that draw people out of their homes and bring them into contact with their neighbors on a regular basis. Pub schedules coordinate the social lives of the British in situations in which Americans would have to send out invitations or leave messages on answering machines to have an equivalent amount of contact with neighbors. This paucity of coordinational materials means that some kinds of collective action are surely more costly in America than in Britain.

Hardin argues that Marx may have seen socialist revolution as a problem of coordination and that Marx's statement about the impossibility of turning back after a certain stage (cited on p. 373) may have been a comment about what happens when coordination and clear purpose are finally brought together. Before coordination and clear purpose are united, coordination can served as a vehicle for many different purposes; after that point, it is much more difficult to harness the coordination to serve different ends. Further support for Hardin's view that Marx may have seen socialist revolution as a coordination problem rather than as a prisoner's dilemma comes from another of Marx's famous insights. Marx also argued that working-class consciousness (and hence the likelihood of revolution) depended strongly on workers being brought together in one place. By coordinating the activities of workers for capitalist ends, employers also facilitate their coordination for other purposes, including collective action on behalf of the working class. So employers may or may not facilitate coordination between workers by bringing them together, and workers whose situations are rich in the materials of coordination may or may not have sufficient sense of purpose so that coordination leads to collective action.

In order to use Hardin's important insight to construct a variable describing variations in the difficulty of coordination in particular time periods, societies, age groups, parts of cities, and so forth, we need some notion about what makes coordination easy. This is the sort of question one would expect Thomas Schelling to have answered, but I do not think he has. Schelling has commented in *The Strategy of Conflict* that there are focal points—twelve noon, round numbers ($100 or $1,000 for example). Presumably some of these common foci of attention are part of nearly universal systems—part of the decimal system, part of the way we keep time, etc. Other points of coordination have to do with the physical layout of our environment, including the prominence of certain features of the landscape or the existence of crossroads and natural meeting places. Here culture and precedent can reinforce geography. A prominent feature of the environment that has been used to coordinate collective action before will be more likely to serve as a setting for collective action in the future. The clock tower at Northwestern's Rebecca Crown

Center is now more likely to be a place for demonstrations after having been used extensively in antiapartheid activities. Though coordination depends partly on physical layout, it also depends on the cultural interpretation of the physical environment, on sharing a culture.

Different societies or parts of societies are differentially rich in the materials of coordination. Some of these differences are naturally occurring, other differences are or could be amplified or created by wise leaders. Coordination is probably facilitated by the existence of landmarks or crossroads that serve as natural gathering places. But leaders can emphasize the precedents associated with particular places and so increase the coordinating effect of the physical environment. Further, as the design of many business establishments and public buildings shows, physical coordination of human activities need not be based on pre-existing features of the environment. Barriers, lines, arrows, signs, etc. are quite effective in getting people to do what they are "supposed" to.

Similarly, coordination is surely facilitated when people share a cultural heritage and is more difficult when there is too much cultural diversity (for example, in ethnically and linguistically mixed societies). But leaders can build on whatever cultural resources there are by stressing those parts of the culture that facilitate coordination. And, of course, appropriate cultural forms can be created, as we see happening in the use of scripts in businesses and their attempts to teach us these scripts, for instance, through advertising.

The extent to which coordination leads to power probably depends on the details of how it takes place. Traffic can be coordinated either by lights and signs or by traffic police. One gives the police a larger role than the other. Bottlenecks and crossroads emphasize the importance of those located at them. Gathering places and events can be named neutrally or named to point to the roles of particular people in important events. Stressing the role of a particular person might increase his or her attractiveness as a leader others might rally around.

One might further expect that some kinds of coordination might be more invulnerable to disruption than others. Coordination that is multilayered might be harder to disrupt than coordination that was based only on a single mechanism. For instance, the ties between adult siblings are much stronger when their parents are alive than after their parents die. After the parents' deaths there is no easy way to coordinate visits, and adults whose parents have died report seeing less of their siblings than they would like. But if a family had coordinated visits not just by gathering periodically at the parents' home but also by gathering at particular holidays, those holidays might serve as a coordination mechanism even after the parents' deaths. When coordination is cued by several stimuli it is harder to disrupt than when it is cued only by one. Hardin cites the example of Cyrus's army falling apart when Cyrus was killed in battle (pp. 367–68). An upstart army is peculiarly vulnerable because its coordination is usually based only on a single mechanism, the leader.

In this comment I have tried to suggest some of the things that will make it more likely that the coordination aspect of collective action will dominate the conflict aspect. While there are naturally occurring variations in the materials that facilitate coordination (for example, cultural forms), leaders can do a lot to facilitate coordination by creatively using pre-existing materials or devising new conventions. Those who would prevent collective action can either increase the difficulty of coordination or increase the costs so that the conflict of interests again dominates the coordination aspect of collective action.

But thinking of power as sometimes stemming from coordination and, in turn, facilitating cooperation makes the social order seem considerably more resilient and less fragile than when one believes that if people were able to see the strategic structure they would all cease to cooperate unless coerced.

# 11

# Institutions and Their Consequences for Economic Performance

## Douglass C. North

From the most primitive tribes to modern societies, human beings have always devised ways to structure human interaction. Institutions, whether solutions to simple problems of coordination (conventions) or to more complex forms of exchange such as those that characterize modern societies, provide a set of rules of the game that define and limit the choice set. They are the humanly devised constraints that shape human interaction so that when we wish to greet friends on the street, drive an automobile, buy oranges, borrow money, form a business, bury our dead, or whatever, we know or can learn easily how to do these things. It is easy to observe that institutions differ when we attempt to do the same things in a different country—Bangladesh for example.

In the sections that follow, I (1) explore the relationship between institutions and the costs of exchange; then examine (2) the nature of institutions, (3) the structure of political institutions, and (4) institutional change; and finally (5) summarize the contribution that institutional analysis can make to economics.

I

Ever since Adam Smith, economics has been built on the firm bedrock of the gains from trade. Until very recently, however, economists have assumed that exchange is costless; and even with the introduction of transaction-cost analysis, the implications of the costliness of transacting have not been understood by the profession. Let me state baldly the implications of transaction analysis for economics. The transaction sector (that part of transaction costs that goes through the market and therefore can be directly measured in monetary terms) made up approximately 45 percent of GNP in 1970 (Wallis and North 1986). Those transaction costs are a large part of the total cost—the sum of the production and trans-

This essay is drawn from, and is a condensation of, parts of a book by the author entitled, *Institutions, Institutional Change and Economic Performance* (Cambridge: Cambridge University Press, 1990).

action costs—of operating an economy or an individual enterprise. Since institutions play a critical role in the cost of transacting (and also help determine production costs) their success in reducing total cost has been and continues to be a critical determinant of economic performance.

Why is it so costly to transact? The short answer is that it takes resources to define and enforce exchange agreements. Even if everyone had the same objective function (for example, maximizing the firm's profits) transacting would take substantial resources; but in the context of individual utility functions, and asymmetric information about the valuable attributes of what is being exchanged (or the performance of agents), the costs arising from transacting are a fundamental influence on economic activity.

A longer explanation of the costliness of transacting requires a more thorough examination of the nature of exchange. We owe to Lancaster (1966) the insight that a good or service is composed of a bundle of valuable attributes. It is only a short additional step to recognize that some attributes are physical (size, shape, color, location, taste, etc.); others are property rights attributes (the right to use, to derive income from, and to exclude others). To the extent that these attributes are separable, they must be defined, that is measured, in order to be transferable in exchange. It is costly to measure and protect the rights over them (Barzel 1982). This argument holds equally for the performance of agents in hierarchical organizations. It is also costly to enforce agreements. If exchange consisted of the transfer of a unidimensional good at an instant of time (implicit features of neoclassical theory) then these issues would be of trivial importance. But enforcing the exchange of multidimensional goods across space and time poses fundamental dilemmas of cooperation, which have rightly been the subject of immense attention in game theoretic models. Successful solutions have entailed the creation of institutions that, in game theoretic terms, raise the benefits of cooperative solutions or raise the costs of defection and that, in transaction-cost terms, lower transaction plus production costs per exchange so that the potential gains from trade become realizable. Regardless of the approach, the key is institutions.

Institutions consist of informal constraints and formal rules and of their enforcement characteristics. Together they provide the rules of the game of human interaction. Let me illustrate by analogy with the rules of the game of a team competitive sport. They too consist of formal written rules and typically informal unwritten codes of conduct that underlie and supplement formal rules, such as not deliberately injuring a key player on the opposing team. These rules and informal codes are sometimes violated and punishment is enacted. Therefore, an essential part of the game is the likelihood of ascertaining violations and the severity (costliness) of punishment. Taken together the formal and informal rules and the effectiveness of enforcement shape the whole character of the game. Some teams are successful as a consequence of (and therefore have the reputation for) constantly violating rules and thereby intimidating the opposing team. Whether that strategy pays off is a function of the effectiveness of monitoring and the severity of punishment. Conversely, sometimes codes of conduct—good sportsmanship—constrain players even though they could get away with successful violations. Now let me return to institutions to elaborate on these common elements.

Informal constraints include conventions that evolve as solutions to problems of coordination and that all parties are interested in having maintained, norms of behavior that are recognized codes of conduct, and self-imposed codes of conduct such as standards of honesty or integrity. Conventions are self-enforcing. Norms of behavior are enforced by a second party (retaliation) or by a third party (societal sanctions or coercive authority), and their effectiveness will depend on the effectiveness of enforcement. Models of such exchange structures make up a large share of the game theory literature.

Self-imposed codes of conduct, unlike conventions and norms of behavior, do not entail wealth-maximizing behavior but rather the sacrifice of wealth or income for other values. Their importance in constraining choices is the subject of substantial controversy—for example in modeling voting behavior in Congress (see Kalt and Zuppan 1984). Most of the controversy has missed the crucial reason of why such behavior can be and is important. And that is that institutions, frequently deliberately, sometimes accidentally, lower the cost of such behavior to individuals. Economists who persist in believing ideas don't matter have simply missed the crucial point that institutions can make them matter a great deal. Votes may not matter individually, but in the aggregate they matter and they cost the voter very little; legislators commonly find enough ways by strategic voting to vote their personal preferences rather than those of the electorate; and judges with lifetime tenure are deliberately shielded from interest-group pressures. In each of the above illustrations the institutional framework has altered the cost to the individual of expressing his or her convictions. In each case the choices that were made were different than they would be if the individual bore the full cost that resulted from those actions. The lower the cost we incur for our convictions (ideas, dogmas) the more they contribute to outcomes (Nelson and Silberberg 1987).

Formal rules differ in degree from informal constraints. On a continuum from taboos, customs, traditions at one end to written constitutions at the other end of the scale, the gradual transition in history has been uneven but unidirectional. Most conspicuously, both the sources and the rate of change are different as between formal rules and informal constraints; this difference has important implications for institutional change.

Formal economic rules are typically nested in a hierarchy, from constitutions to statute and common law to specific contracts and bylaws of organizations; they are more costly to alter as we go higher on the ladder. Formal political rules specify the hierarchy of the polity from basic decision rules to agenda control. Economic rules define property rights, that is the bundle of rights over the use and the income to be derived from property, and the rights of alienation. Both political and economic rules are devised as a consequence of the bargaining strength of those making the decision rules; marginal changes occur with changes in bargaining strength (to be discussed below). But given the initial bargaining strength of the parties, the function of the rules is to facilitate exchange, both political and economic.

The costliness of defining and enforcing agreements reflects the effectiveness of the institutions. The ability at low cost to measure what is being exchanged and to enforce agreements across time and space requires complex institutional structures; conversely, the inability at low cost to measure and enforce agreements has been a consequence of institutional failure and results in economic stagnation. Successful economic growth is the story of the evolution of more complex institutions that make possible cooperative exchange relations extending over long periods of time amongst individuals without personal knowledge of each other. Institutional reliability means we can have confidence in outcomes increasingly remote from our personal knowledge, an essential requirement to realizing the potential of modern technology, which entails immense specialization and division of labor.

The combination of formal rules, informal constraints, and enforcement characteristics of institutions defines the humanly devised constraints and, together with the traditional constraints of standard theory, the choice set. The property rights literature has long since demonstrated that different property rights produce different outcomes; but because it has not taken into account both the effectiveness of enforcement and informal constraints, that approach is incomplete and at least partly mis-leading. The choices as reflected in contracts between exchanging parties actually will reflect not only formal constraints, but also the uncertainties arising from the effectiveness and costliness of enforcement. Equally, con-ventions, informal community sanctions, will play a part in the ex-change. Therefore, to understand the choices available in an exchange one must take into account all the dimensions that make up an institu-tion.

Let me illustrate the relationship between institutions (formal rules, informal constraints, and enforcement characteristics) and transaction costs in a specific example—the exchange of a residential property in modern United States. I examine first the transaction costs incurred in the transfer and then the institutions that determined those costs of trans-acting.

In the seller's utility function are the price, terms, and security of the contractual obligation; that is, the likelihood that the buyer will live up to the contract *ex post*. The value of the residence to the buyer is a func-tion not only of price and credit terms but also of the attributes that are transferred with the sale. Some, such as the legal rights that are and are not transferred, the dimensions of the property and house, are easily measured; others, such as the general features of the property, are readily observed on inspections. But still others, such as the maintenance and upkeep costs and the characteristics of neighbors, may be far more diffi-cult to ascertain. Equally, the security of property against default, expro-priation, uncertain title, or theft will vary according to the difficulty of ascertaining the likelihood of each and therefore its importance. Now in the traditional neoclassical paradigm, with perfect information—that is, zero transaction costs—the value of the asset that is transferred assumes not only perfect information but perfectly secure property rights. In that case, since both buyer and seller have been able to costlessly ascertain the value of all the attributes (both physical and property rights) and there is no uncertainty or insecurity of property rights, the standard sup-ply and demand models of housing with zero transaction costs would define the value of the asset. In fact, because all of the above-mentioned attributes influence the value of the residence to the buyer and seller, the smaller the discount (that is, the smaller the transaction costs incurred) from the idealized neoclassical model, the more perfect the market. It is institutions in the aggregate that define and determine the size of the discount, and it is transaction costs that the buyer and seller incur that reflect that institutional framework.

The particular institutional matrix of this housing market consists first of all of a hierarchy of legal rules derived from the U.S. Constitution and the powers delegated to the states. State laws defining the conveyance characteristics of real property, zoning laws restricting which rights can be transferred, common and statute law undergirding, defining, or restricting a host of voluntary organizations: all of these influence transaction costs. Realtors, title insurance, credit bureaus, savings and loan associations that affect the mortgage market all will be influenced. The efficiency of these organizations is a function of the structure of property rights and enforcement (such as title insurance costs) and the structure of the capital market (including both voluntary organizations and governmental organizations, guarantees, and subsidies).

It should be noted carefully that while many of these institutions lower transaction costs, some—such as rules that restrict entry, require useless inspections, raise information costs, or make property rights less secure—in fact raise transaction costs. Institutions everywhere are a "mixed bag" of those that lower costs and those that raise them. The U.S. residential housing market is a relatively efficient market in which, on balance, the institutions induce low-cost transacting. Had I modeled the same market in a Third World country there would have been a notable lack of those institutions that provide an efficient capital market and security of property rights and equally lots of institutions raising transaction costs.

The uncertainty discount associated with hard-to-measure attributes may be ameliorated by insurance, such as title insurance or insurance against termites for example; or by bonding (by the seller) against certain hard-to-measure maintenance costs. While zoning laws may restrict the degrees of freedom of neighbors from impinging on the buyer's welfare (and restrict the buyer's choice set as well), other uncertain features, such as the characteristic behavior of pets in the neighborhood, whether there are noisy neighbors, the quality of upkeep of adjoining yards, etc. could lower the value of an asset to the buyer. Typically, however, these features, however imperfectly, may be restricted by neighborhood norms and conventions and some may be appropriable by the buyer. (For example, building a fence around the yard to keep out unwanted pets, even though it is a neighborhood in which the norm is to have yards unfenced.) Enforcement characteristics rest not only on an hierarchy of organizations, courts, police, etc., but also on the degree of uncertainty associated with the performance and the effectiveness of enforcement.

The fundamental implication of the foregoing illustration is that the discount from the frictionless exchange envisioned in economic theory will be greater to the degree that the institutional structure allows third parties to influence the value of attributes that are in the utility function of the buyer. These could be the behavior of neighbors, the likelihood of theft, the possibility of changes by local authorities in zoning ordinances that may affect the value of the property, etc. The greater the uncertainty of the buyer, the lower the value of the asset. Likewise, the institutional structure will equally determine the risks to the seller that the contract will be fulfilled or that the seller will be indemnified in case of default. It is worth emphasizing again that the uncertainties described above with respect to security of rights are the critical distinction between the relatively efficient and secure markets of high-income countries and the insecure and costly nature of these transactions in economies both in the past and in the present Third World.

The transaction costs of the transfer are partly market costs, such as legal fees, realtor fees, interest charges, title insurance, credit-rating searches; and partly the costs of time each party must devote to gathering information, the costs of searching, etc. Thus, to the degree that the buyer's utility function is adversely affected by noisy neighbors, pets, etc., it will pay to invest time in ascertaining neighborhood characteristics and conventions about such behavior. Obtaining information about crime rates, police protection, and security systems equally entails search costs for the buyer.

While the contract that will be written in this transaction will specify the transfer of legal rights, penalties for default, and other conditions (such as insurance clauses, etc.), it will clearly be incomplete with respect to a range of attributes that are of value to the buyer, including some in the public domain that may be appropriated by the buyer, or in some cases by a third party. Unforeseen legal claims, the discovery of high levels of radon in the basement, changes in the flight path of commercial aircraft that locate them over the house, a new neighbor who creates a beautiful garden under one's window, are just a few possibilities.

Turning from examining the relationship between institutions and transaction costs in an exchange, let us examine that in the production of goods and services. Institutional structures affect both production and transaction costs. All the usual problems of measurement and enforcement obtain; the structure of property rights, the effectiveness of the courts and the judicial system, and the complementary development of voluntary organization and norms are the basic undergirding of a productive economy.

Specifically the firm's entrepreneur must be able to ascertain the quantity and quality of inputs and outputs. Since in the neoclassical firm these can be obtained costlessly, the contrast between a hypothetical neoclassical firm and a real firm is striking. The former was little more than a production function without any costs of organization, supervision, coordination, monitoring, metering, etc. However a real-life firm must purchase inputs that constantly require measurements and metering if it is to produce output of constant quality, since variability in quality will *ceterus paribus* adversely affect demand for its product. Otherwise consumers (or if it is an intermediate good, producers) must (when quality is variable) devote resources to ascertaining quality; hence, producers who can guarantee constant quality will be favored.[1]

These conditions (namely, costless measurement and enforcement) are implicitly assumed in what we call efficient factor and product markets, but their existence entails a complex set of institutions that encourage factor mobility, the acquisition of skills, uninterrupted production, rapid and low-cost transmission of information, and the invention and innovation of new technologies. Realizing all these conditions is a tall order never completely filled since, as with the institutions of exchange described above, the actual institutional framework is a mixed bag of those institutions that promote productivity-raising activities and those that provide barriers to entry, encourage monopolistic restrictions, and impede the low-cost flow of information. The most decisive evidence of an institutional framework that broadly favors productivity-enhancing activity is not only a well-developed capital market (which reflects effective property rights across time) but also the existence of a variety of informal organizations that supplement and extend formal rules.

It is possible and frequently the case that a technical combination that involves costly monitoring may be less "efficient" than a technique that has lower physical output but less variance in the product quality or lower costs of monitoring the worker. Let me illustrate three different choices arising from the interplay between techniques, institutions, production costs, and transaction costs.

---

1. For a fascinating analysis of the significant resource costs that the producer must engage in to assure constant quality, see the detailed description of the production of peas in Susan Sheehan's essay "Peas" in the *New Yorker*, 17 June 1973. The trouble taken by Green Giant to attempt to eliminate variability in size, tenderness, and sweetness in the production of peas involved enormous monitoring and metering resources that began in the field and did not end until the cans went off to the retailer.

1. A contention of Marxist writers is that deliberate deskilling of the labor force occurred during the early twentieth century in the United States. That is, employers adopted capital-intensive techniques that eliminated the demand for highly skilled workers and replaced them with semiskilled or unskilled workers. The explanation for this choice is that the bargaining power of skilled workers enabled them to strategically disrupt the production process, which, given the "high speed throughput" (Chandler's term, 1977) of modern technology, was enormously costly. Long-run total cost could be reduced by using less skilled workers who were without the bargaining power to disrupt production. In this case, a new technique was introduced to lower transaction costs.

2. Unitizing an oil field, that is creating an organization with the coercive power and monitoring authority to allocate the output of the oil field, raises transaction costs (because of the resources that must be devoted to creating and maintaining an organization and then to monitoring compliance). At the same time it reduces production costs (the result of more efficient pumping and recovery) to an extent that more than offsets the rise in transaction costs (Libecap and Wiggins 1985). In this case, an institutional change lowers production costs.

3. Andrea Shepard (1987) describes the deliberate policy of a semiconductor manufacturer who licenses the design of new chips to competitors so that customers can be assured that the chip manufacturer will not be able to hold up customers who adopt the new design. By alleviating customers' concerns, this policy enhances demand for the product. While this policy lowers transaction costs, it does so at the sacrifice of productive efficiency, since both scale economies and "learning-curve" effects are lost to competing firms.

Informal institutional constraints frequently play a major role with respect to the quantity and quality of labor output. While Marxists long ago recognized that the quantity of labor input could not be mechanically transformed via a production function into the quantity and quality of output, this subject has only recently become a major focus of economists' concern (at least partially a consequence in recent years of the enormous quality difference in labor output between Japanese and American automobile manufacturers). Conventions about output, forms of organization designed to encourage worker participation and cooperation, and attempts to select labor with an ideological commitment to hard work have all become recent research agendas in industrial organization. The unique feature of labor markets is that institutions are de-

391

vised to take into account that the quantity and quality of output is influenced by the attitude of the productive factor (hence investing in persuasion, morale building, etc. is a substitute at the margin for investing in more monitoring).

3

The major focus of the literature on institutions and transaction costs has been on institutions as efficient solutions to problems of organization in a competitive framework (Williamson 1975 and 1985). Thus market exchange, franchising, or vertical integration are efficient solutions to the complex problems confronting the entrepreneur in a competitive environment. Valuable as this work has been, it leaves out the most important contribution institutional analysis can make to economics: to explain the diverse performance of economies. How do we account for the poverty of nations, the failure of some economies to grow, or for that matter the differential performance of sectors in an economy? Institutions structure incentives, which in turn determine the performance of economies. The formal economic constraints (property rights) are specified and enforced by political institutions and the literature described above simply takes those as a given. While there is a large literature on regulation and even modeling political outcomes (for example Becker 1983 and 1985), it is essentially a-institutional and therefore does not confront the critical role that political institutions play in economic performance.

To explain the diverse performance of economies, let me start with a simple model of a polity consisting of a ruler and diverse constituents.[2] In this setting the ruler acts like a discriminating monopolist, offering to different groups of constituents "protection and justice"—or at least the reduction of internal disorder and the protection of property rights—in exchange for tax revenue. Since different constituent groups have different opportunity costs and bargaining power with the ruler, different bargains result. There are economies of scale in the provision of these (semi) public goods of law and enforcement and total revenue is therefore increased. However, the division of the incremental gains between ruler and constituents depends on their relative bargaining strength; changes at the margin, either the violence potential of the ruler or the opportunity cost of the constituents, will result in redivision of the incremental revenue. Moreover the ruler's gross and net revenue differ significantly as a

2. This model is elaborated in "A Neo-Classical Theory of the State," in North 1981.

result of the necessity of developing agents (a bureaucracy) to monitor, meter, and collect revenue. The agents may (depending on the effectiveness of incentives) increase gross revenue and increase or decrease net revenue. All the consequences inherent in agency theory apply at this point.

This model of the polity can become one step more complicated when I introduce the concept of a representative body reflecting the interests of constituent groups which bargains with the ruler. This concept is consistent with the origin of Parliaments and Estates Generales and Cortes in early modern Europe, which evolved as a response to the ruler's need for more revenue. In exchange for this revenue the ruler would agree to provide certain services to constituent groups. The representative body facilitates exchange between the parties. On the ruler's side, this new relationship with constituents leads to the development of a hierarchical structure of agents. This is a major transformation from the simple (if extensive) management of the king's household and estates to a bureaucracy monitoring the wealth and or income of the king's constituents.

When we move from the polities in early modern Europe to modern representative democracy, our story is complicated by the development of multiple-interest groups and by an institutional structure much more complicated but still devised to facilitate (again given relative bargaining strength) the exchange between interest groups. This political transaction-cost model is built on the recognition of the multiplicity of interest groups reflecting concentrations of voters in particular locations. Thus, there are elderly in Florida and Arizona, miners in Pennsylvania and West Virginia, artichoke growers in California, automobile manufacturers in Michigan, etc. Each legislator's district has a concentration of no more than a few of the large number of interest groups. Therefore, legislators cannot succeed acting alone and must make agreements with other legislators with different interests.

What kind of institutions will evolve from such exchange relationships between legislators? Previous work, beginning with Buchanan and Tullock (1962), focused on vote-trading, or log-rolling. This work was certainly a step forward in recognizing the way by which legislators could engage in activities that facilitated exchange. However, such an approach was too simple to solve fundamental problems involved in legislative exchange. It assumed that all bills and payoffs were known in advance, and it had a timeless dimension to it.

In fact, a variety of exchanges arise in which today's legislation can only be enacted by commitments made for a future date. In order to lower the costs of exchange, one must devise a set of institutional arrangements that would allow for exchange across space and time. Note the parallels with economic exchange as described above. How does credible commitment evolve to enable agreements to be reached when the payoffs are in the future and on completely different issues? Self-enforcement is important in such exchange, and in repeat dealings a reputation is a valuable asset. But as in economic exchange, the costs of measurement and enforcement, discovering who is cheating whom, when free-riding will occur, and who should bear the cost of punishing "defectors" make self-enforcement ineffective in many situations. Hence political institutions constitute ex-ante agreements about cooperation among politicians. They reduce uncertainty by creating a stable structure of exchange. The result is a complicated system of committee organization consisting of formal rules and informal constraints that together shape congressional choices. Its evolution in the American Congress is described in a recent study of the structure by Barry Weingast and William Marshall (1988).

While political institutions facilitate exchange amongst bargaining parties, there is no implication of economic efficiency as an outcome. In an earlier study (North 1981), I argued that there were two basic reasons why rulers typically produced inefficient property rights (defined here simply as rules which do not produce increases in output). First, competitive constraint on the ruler means that a ruler will avoid offending powerful constituents with close access to alternative rulers. He will agree to a property-rights structure favorable to those groups regardless of its effects on efficiency. Second, while efficient property rights would lead to higher societal income, they may not lead to more tax revenues because of higher costs of monitoring, metering, and collecting. Granting guilds monopolies in Colbert's France may not have been efficient, but it did improve tax collecting as compared to an unregulated decentralized economy.

The same constraints have obtained throughout history (and continue to obtain). Inefficient (as defined above) economic institutions are the rule not the exception. It is not that political entrepreneurs would not like to have economic growth; it is that the constraints described above seldom make such choices a feasible option. Moreover, the process of institutional change does not result in evolutionary competition weeding out inefficient institutions in favor of efficient ones (or at least the tendency is so weak and diffuse as to permit the persistence of inefficient economies for very long periods of time). Let us see why.

## 4

To understand institutional change we must first recognize that a basic function of institutions is to provide stability and continuity by dampening the effects of relative price changes. It is institutional stability that makes possible complex exchange across space and time. A necessary condition for efficient markets that underlie high-income societies are channels of exchange, both political and economic, which minimize uncertainty. This condition is accomplished by the complexity of the set of constraints that constitute institutions: by rules nested in a hierarchy, each level more costly to change than the previous one. In the United States, the hierarchy moves from constitutional rules to statute law and common law to individual contracts. Political rules are also nested in a hierarchy even at the level of specific bills before Congress. Both the structure of committees and agenda control assure that the status quo is favored over change. Informal constraints are even more important anchors of stability. They are extensions, elaborations, and qualifications of rules that "solve" numerous exchange problems not completely covered by formal rules and hence have tenacious survival ability. They allow people to go about the everyday process of making exchanges without the necessity of thinking out exactly at each point and in each instance the terms of exchange. Routines, customs, traditions, and conventions are words we use to denote the persistence of informal constraints. It is the complex interaction of rules and informal constraints, together with the way they are enforced, that shape our daily living and direct us in the mundane (the very word conjures up images of institutional stability) activities that dominate our lives. It is important to stress that these stability features in no way guarantee that the institutions are efficient (as defined above). Stability is a necessary condition for complex human interaction but it is not a sufficient condition for efficiency.

One major source of institutional change has been fundamental changes in relative prices (see North and Thomas 1973, for illustration) but another has been ideas. I know of no way to explain the demise of slavery in the nineteenth century in an interest-group model. The growing abhorrence on the part of civilized human beings of one person owning another not only spawned the antislavery movements but, through the institutional mechanism of voting, resulted in its elimination. The voter paid only the price of going to the polls to express his conviction and the slaveowner had no feasible way to bribe or pay off voters to prevent them from expressing their beliefs. As noted earlier, institutions make ideas matter.

The agent of change is the entrepreneur—political or economic. So far, I have left organizations and their entrepreneurs out of the analysis and the definition of institutions has focused on the rules of the game rather than the players. Left out was the purposive activity of human beings to achieve objectives, which in turn results in altering constraints. Organizations and learning alter outcomes, but how?

Let me begin with organization. More than half a century ago Coase (1937) argued that transaction costs are the basis for the existence of the firm. That is, if information and enforcement are costless, it is hard to envision a significant role for organization. What is it about transaction costs that leads to organization? The answers have ranged from the firm being a form of exploitation (Marglin 1974), to a response to asset specificity (Williamson 1975 and 1985), to a response to measurement costs (Barzel 1982). Whatever the merits of these alternatives (and they are not altogether mutually exclusive), they all focus on the trees but not the forest. Organizations are a response to the institutional structure of societies, and, in consequence, the major cause of the alteration of that institutional structure. The institutional constraints together with the traditional constraints of economic theory define the potential wealth-maximizing opportunities of entrepreneurs (political or economic). If the constraints result in the highest payoffs in the economy being criminal activity, or the payoff to the firm is highest from sabotaging or burning down a competitor, or to a union from engaging in slowdowns and makework, then we can expect that the organization will be shaped to maximize at those margins. On the other hand, if the payoffs come from productivity-enhancing activities, then economic growth will result. In either case the entrepreneur and his or her organization will invest in acquiring knowledge, coordination, and "learning-by-doing skills" in order to enhance the profitable potential. As the organization evolves to capture the potential returns, it will gradually alter the institutional constraints from within. It will do so either indirectly, via the interaction between maximizing behavior and its effect on gradually eroding or modifying informal constraints; or it will do so directly, via investing in altering the formal rules. The relative rate of return on investing within the formal constraints or devoting resources to altering the constraints will reflect the structure of the polity, the payoffs to altering the rules, and the costs of political investment.

Institutional change therefore is an incremental process in which short-run profitable opportunities cumulatively create the long-run path of change. The long-run consequences are unintended for two reasons. First, the entrepreneurs are not interested in long-run consequences, but the direction of their investment influences the extent to which there is investment in adding to or disseminating the stock of knowledge, encouraging or discouraging factor mobility, etc. Second, there is frequently a significant difference between intended outcomes and actual outcomes. The economist's behavioral assumption makes a direct connection between choices and outcomes with no intervening dilemmas of uncertainty about processing the information or deciphering the complexities of the environment. In fact, outcomes frequently diverge from intentions precisely because of the limited capabilities of individuals and the complexity of the problems to be solved. The path of institutional change that determines the long-run evolution of societies is shaped by constraints derived from the past and the unanticipated consequences of the innumerable incremental choices of entrepreneurs which continually modify those constraints. Path dependence means that history matters, that it is a consequence of incremental institutional change, and that it can account for the divergent paths of economies. Moreover, given the tendency of politics to produce inefficient property rights, economic decline or stagnation can persist since there will not typically develop a feedback that will create organizations with the incentive to invest in productive activity. Instead the "perverse" incentives will generate organizations and hence entrepreneurs with economic and political bargaining strength who will find it profitable to pursue economically inefficient paths.

Institutional change is overwhelmingly incremental, but discontinuous institutional change does occur—in the form of revolution. It would take me far beyond the limits of this essay to deal properly with this topic, but several important points follow from the preceding analysis:

1. Incremental change means that the parties to the exchange recontract to capture some of the potential gains from trade (at least for one of the exchanging parties). This change can range from a simple recontracting to fundamental change in the political rules that resolves a "gridlock" crisis. However, if a blocking coalition is successful in preventing political restructuring, then the potential gains from exchange cannot be realized and "entrepreneurs" will attempt to form a coalition of groups to break out of the deadlock (by violence, strikes, etc.).

2. Path dependency limits the bargaining flexibility of the parties and hence is a major cause of such deadlocks. That is, the choice set for each of the conflicting parties has no intersection so that even though there may be large gains from trade (resolving the disagreements) none is within the feasible choice set of the parties.

3. Since neither party to a dispute is likely to have the "muscle" to win by itself, the parties must form coalitions and make deals with other interest groups. As a result, the final outcome of successful revolutions becomes very uncertain since conflict within the winning coalition over the restructuring of the rules and hence the distribution of rewards will lead to further conflict.

4. Broad support for violent action requires ideological commitment to overcome the free-rider problem (North 1981, chap. 5). The stronger the ideological commitment of the participants, the greater the price they will be willing to pay and hence the more likely the revolution will be successful.

5. Revolutionary change is seldom as revolutionary as it appears on the surface (or in the utopian vision of revolutionaries). The reason is both that the "half-life" of ideological commitment tends to be short and that the formal rules change but the informal constraints do not, and in consequence there develops an ongoing tension between informal constraints and the new formal rules, many of which are inconsistent with each other. The long-run resolution tends to be some restructuring of both and an outcome that retains or even recreates some of the prerevolutionary formal constraints.

5

Let me conclude by summarizing the contribution that institutional analysis can make to economics. I shall not elaborate on the already rich literature that has sprung up from institutional and transaction-cost analysis in industrial organization, public finance, public choice but instead focus on the broader contribution that is still to be undertaken:

1. The most general contribution that institutional modeling can make to economic theorizing is to make clear and explicit the institutionally specific context within which the model holds. Implicit in most economic models are specific political rules, property rights, and enforcement characteristics that are critical to the outcomes. Changes in these would produce different outcomes. Economists, however, seem seldom to be aware of just how specific their model is to the institutional constraints (how it would work in Bangladesh, for example).

2. A self-conscious incorporation of institutions into economic theory will force economists to question the behavioral models that underlie the discipline. If neoclassical economics has no institutions in the models, it is because the behavioral assumption, which incorporates characteristics about human behavior as well as about the information that the players have, does not require it. But since institutions really exist, it is incumbent on the economist to ask searching questions about the implications of institutions for the behavioral model that the economist employs. The role of ideology, for example, plays an important part once we recognize that people have subjective perceptions about the world around them and that expressing convictions in various institutional contexts frequently can be done at negligible cost to the individual. Likewise, when our behavioral models incorporate the incompleteness of our information and our limited ability to process that information, then we will understand why we need to develop the regularized patterns of human interaction that we call institutions and why they may be very inadequate or far from optimal in any sense of the term. The nascent cooperation between psychologists and economists offers the promise of enriching our behavioral models (see Hogarth and Reder 1986).

3. Incorporating institutions in their models should make economists aware that ideas matter. Institutions structure human interaction so that we frequently and in many critical choice contexts can express our ideas, ideologies, and dogmas at little or no cost to ourselves. The result is to frequently produce different outcomes than those derived from interest-group models in economics and public choice.

4. The integration of political and economic theory is essential to much modeling in a world where government plays such an immense role in choices. The key to such integration is the modeling of political and economic institutions that will permit us to explore in theoretical terms the interaction between these two institutions and to derive in consequence real political economy models in macroeconomics and other areas in which government plays a critical role.

5. If an understanding of the nature of institutions can make an important contribution to redefining the parameters and choice set in economic theory, an understanding of institutional change offers the prospect of getting a handle on long-run economic change—something that has so far eluded traditional economics. The central role that institutions play in connecting the past with the present and the future, the incremental character of institutional change, and the path-dependent process together provide an opening wedge to undertake a meaningful exploration

of economic development. Certainly one of the failures of the social sciences in the post–World War II era has been its inability to develop useful models that would account for the poor performance of Third World economies and in consequence provide a policy guide to deal with economic development. Neoclassical economic theory was not intended to account for such poor performance, and it doesn't. It simply assumes away all the relevant issues. It is institutions that provide the key constraints and therefore shape incentives, and it is the path of institutional change that is determining the evolving performance of economies. Institutional theory focuses on the critical problems for development of human organization and the problems of achieving cooperative solutions to human interaction.

It is only appropriate that an economic historian would conclude this essay by making what should by now be an obvious point. Institutional analysis places history in a central role in economics. Central, because the constraints within which choice-making occurs are derived from the past, and without an understanding of the way those constraints have evolved, we cannot understand the choice set today. The study of economic history should provide the economist with an understanding of what the current institutional constraints are. With an understanding of the past incremental process that led to those constraints, the economist can obtain insight into the bargaining strength of organized groups and the consequent forces shaping current institutional evolution and hence incorporate relevant constraints into his or her models.

REFERENCES

Barzel, Y. 1982. "Measurement Costs and the Organization of Markets," *Journal of Law and Economics* 25: 27–48.
Becker, G. S. 1983. "A Theory of Competition among Pressure Groups for Political Influence," *Quarterly Journal of Economics* 98: 371–400.
———. 1985. "Public Policies, Pressure Groups, and Dead Weight Costs," *Journal of Public Economics* 28: 329–47.
Buchanan, J. M., and G. Tullock. 1962. *The Calculus of Consent.* Ann Arbor: University of Michigan Press.
Chandler, Alfred. 1977. *The Visible Hand.* Cambridge, MA: The Belknap Press.
Coase, Ronald. 1937. "The Nature of the Firm," *Economica* 4 (November): 386–405.
Hogarth, R. M., and M. W. Reder, eds. 1986. "The Behavioral Foundations of Economic Theory," *Journal of Business,* volume 57.
Kalt, J. P., and M. A. Zupan. 1984. "Capture and Ideology in the Economic Theory of Politics," *American Economic Review* 74: 279–300.
Lancaster, Kelvin. 1966. "A New Approach to Consumer Theory," *Journal of Political Economy* 93: 690–714.

Libecap, G. D., and S. N. Wiggins. 1985. "The Influence of Private Contractual Failure on Regulation: The Case of Oil Field Utilization," *Journal of Political Economy* 93: 690–714.

Marglin, S. 1974. "What Do Bosses Do?" *Review of Radical Political Economy* 6: 60–112.

Nelson, D., and E. Silberberg. 1987. "Ideology and Legislator Shirking," *Economic Inquiry* 25: 15–25.

North, Douglass C. 1981. *Structure and Change in Economic History.* New York: W. W. Norton and Company.

North, D. C. and R. Thomas. 1973. *The Rise of the Western World: A New Economic History.* Cambridge, MA: The University Press.

North, D. C., and J. Wallis. 1986. "Measuring the Transaction Sector in the American Economy, 1870–1979." In S. L. Engerman and R. E. Gallman, eds. *Long-Term Factors in American Economic Growth.* Chicago: University of Chicago Press.

Shepard, A. 1987. "Licensing to Enhance Demand for New Technologies," *Rand Journal of Economics* 18: 360–68.

Weingast, B. R., and W. J. Marshall. 1988. "The Industrial Organization of Congress; or, Why Legislatures, Like Firms, Are Not Organized as Markets," *Journal of Political Economy* 96: 132–63.

Williamson, O. E. 1975. *Markets and Hierarchy.* New York: The Free Press.

———. 1985. *The Economic Institutions of Capitalism.* New York: The Free Press.

# 12

# A Logic of Institutional Change

## Margaret Levi[1]

The people of the institution-free Hobbesian world have equality of bargaining power but no social order. In a world endowed with institutions that resolve societal conflicts, there is social order but unequal bargaining power and unequal access to coercive resources. These facts are the basis of both the rigidities and the instabilities we observe in institutional arrangements. The capacity to resolve conflicts both in society and within the institution itself rests on a structure of coercive and bargaining resources that enable some actors to effectively delimit the decisions of others. Those exercising such power have the means and the interest in maintaining current institutional arrangements that suit their purposes and in reforming those that do not. Individuals subject to such power will acquiesce only as long as there are gains from trade, the costs of withdrawal are too high, or they are unable to perceive an alternative.

Institutions are often hard to transform or destroy. Nonetheless, transformations do occur. A central question raised by the preceding papers is the cause of secular institutional change, that is, a major transformation or destruction of an institution. The debate hinges on whether the best explanation rests in models of biological evolution, social evolution, contracting and recontracting, leadership, or some combination.

I start with the assumption that individuals create institutions, which then constrain the subsequent choices of the same individuals or future generations. In other words, there is path dependence. I next assume that those making decisions often have divergent interests from those whom their decisions affect. I further assume that there is an unequal distribution of power among those who constitute the institution. By that I mean there is unequal access both to the coercive capacity of the institution

1. I wish to thank Yoram Barzel, James Caporaso, Robert Keohane, Peter Kollock, Ian Lustick, Stephen Majeski, Douglass C. North, Jodi O'Brien, Helena Silverstein, and the members of PEDDS (Political Economy Drinks and Discussion Society) for comments.

and to resources on which others depend. From these assumptions it is obvious that one source of institutional change is the redistribution of the coercive and bargaining resources of power within the institution. But what causes a shift in power, and under what circumstances are the relatively weak able to affect the direction of change? My claim is that the behavioral withdrawal of acquiescence with or consent to current institutional arrangements is one source of institutional change and an important "weapon of the weak." [2]

## DEFINING INSTITUTIONS

Before attempting to elaborate this possible logic of institutional change, it is necessary first to establish what an institution is. Much of the now extensive literature on institutions does not even bother to define the term. Shepsle and Weingast (1987) and March and Olsen (1984) claim institutions are a key to understanding politics but fail to tell us what exactly an institution is. Kiser and Ostrom (1982) emphasize rules as the definitional characteristic of institutional arrangements, in particular "the rules used by individuals for determining who and what are included in decision situations, how information is structured, what actions can be taken and in what sequence, and how individual actions will be aggregated into collective decisions" (p. 179).

The only author among those in this volume who offers a definition is Douglass North. In North's view, an institution is characterized by its capacity to delimit choices and its possession of enforcement mechanisms. Institutions, and this is part of North's claim, reduce certain transaction costs, that is, the costs of making and keeping a contract, while raising others. Institutions reduce the uncertainty that arises from otherwise unpredictable behavior and, therefore, make it easier to identify appropriate trading partners and to write contracts that take into account most eventualities (see also, Schotter 1981, 11; Heiner 1983, 573; and Kreps 1984). However, North also notes how institutions can raise transaction costs by, for example, increasing the number of bargaining partners and interactions.

To the extent institutions have been defined, the emphasis is on rules that regulate recurrent behavior. One additional feature of institutions that is probably assumed but certainly not captured by this characteri-

---

2. Michels (1962 [1919]) originally coined this term to describe organization of the relatively powerless. More recently, Scott (1985) has appropriated the term to refer to various forms of routine and everyday resistance by peasants in contemporary Malaysia.

zation is relative durability (Keohane 1988).[3] It is their durability that makes institutions so hard to transform and that makes major transformations, when they occur, so interesting to study.

The emphasis on rules begins to get at what an institution is and not just what it does. Nonetheless, it obfuscates crucial distinctions between institutions and other arrangements for aggregating individual behavior. In particular, the line between an institution and a norm becomes extremely thin if only the nature of the rule is considered.[4] Certainly, sanctions tend to exist against those who "break the norms" of a group, but the most important incentives and disincentives for compliance with norms are cognitive and social. Institutions, on the other hand, have a legalistic aspect and rely on a relatively clear structure of enforcement. The subset of institutions with which I am primarily concerned also possess personnel and are generally characterized as well by a division of labor among those personnel. Punishable offenses, penalties, and the responsibility for taking punitive action are fairly well-defined. Some actor or set of actors has the task of monitoring institutional behavior, and the same or some other actors has the task of punishing those who are caught.[5]

The prevailing characterization of institutions as sets of rules also tends to obscure variations among different kinds of institutions. In common usage, the term institution refers to, among other possibilities, decision procedures (be they in primitive communities or advanced capitalist democracies), families, firms, schools, hospitals, prisons, the courts, legislatures, markets, and the state as a whole. Since they are all given the same label, the implication is that they are different examples of the same phenomenon, yet treating such very distinct forms of regulation as basically similar makes analysis difficult. Without clearer definitional or at least typological criteria, the already difficult task of explaining the

3. In a paper presented to the 1988 International Political Science Association Meetings in Washington, D.C., Ken Shepsle also stressed the relative durability of institutions. His notion of "structure-induced equilibrium" (see, e.g. Shepsle and Weingast 1987) tries to capture this aspect of institutions.

4. There are theorists, including North, who do not find it useful to distinguish between an institution and a norm. However, common language makes the distinction for good reason. Although the two phenomena tend to reinforce each other, treating them as the same phenomenon obfuscates some crucial analytical issues discussed throughout this volume and below.

5. Michael Taylor's work and the works of some of the international political economists (e.g., Keohane 1988) are particularly concerned with institutions without a central power-holder. Even in these kinds of institutions, however, there are mechanisms for monitoring and enforcement, as the authors themselves note.

creation, maintenance, and transformation of institutions becomes in-tractable. One strategy is to develop an abstract schema of the compo-nents of all institutions (e.g., Ostrom 1986). An alternative is a typology of institutions.

Indeed, what we have come to call institutions diverge in, among other ways, the number of persons the rules encompass, the behaviors covered by the rules, and the extent to which internal institutional enforcement rests on the power of an external institution such as the state. Different kinds of institutions possess significantly different arrangements for monitoring and enforcing decisions. It is one thing to require two or three children to be home by a certain hour, quite another to impose a curfew on an entire population, and something else again to impose the death penalty or to make foreign policy. This is not to claim that a family lacks significant power relative to its members but that its powers are qualitatively—and quantitatively—different than that of a state. The provision of health care, of justice, or of government services requires more elaborated mechanisms for coordination, service delivery, and en-forcement and more material resources than a family that is the center of nurturance, socialization, and welfare for a relatively few people.

The focus of this paper is on a particular subset of institutions, those characterized by formal arrangements for aggregating individuals and regulating their behavior through the use of explicit rules and decision processes enforced by an actor or set of actors formally recognized as possessing such power. Whether the rules are written as law, written at all, or represent verbal or customary agreements varies, but in all cases the behavioral expectations are relatively clear. Examples of formal in-stitutions include the state, hospitals, educational facilities, and firms.

By definition, the institutions I am investigating are sets of relatively durable and formal rules that allocate resources of power, constrain the choices of the personnel and the clients, citizens, or subjects of the insti-tution, and possess internal enforcement mechanisms. Externalized, ex-plicit rules and hierarchies of personnel distinguish formal institutions from other organizational arrangements and from norms that also reg-ulate behavior through the use of incentives and disincentives. This defi-nition excludes customs and culture even though they may regulate "re-petitive interactions among individuals." Nor can most pressure and interest groups and protest movements be labeled institutions. Although they may well affect outcomes, they are unable to enforce their decisions on those they hope to affect. Moreover, they tend to possess a transient quality. Over time, of course, some collective action organizations, such as political parties, become institutionalized (e.g., Michels [1919] 1949), implying the development of hierarchy and relative permanence.

To understand institutions is to understand that they represent concessions of power by one group of actors to at least one other individual in order to resolve potentially major conflicts among strategic actors. Hardin stresses this point, although he gives more credit to Adam Smith than to Thomas Hobbes for theorizing the initial scenario of the grant of power. North also acknowledges the role institutions play in delimiting choices so as to avoid or, when necessary, resolve societal conflicts. He is building on the transaction cost literature, in which an institution, including the firm, is no longer a black box but a complex of analyzable contractual relationships.[6] The work of transaction cost scholars, mostly economists, moves the discussion forward considerably by revealing the behavioral effects of contract terms and monitoring arrangements. They tend, however, to reduce what institutions do to expediting and delimiting potential contracts that facilitate gains from trade and cut transaction costs. This approach serves to reinforce a Candidian view of institutions as "the best of all possible worlds."[7]

Formal institutions not only have internal hierarchies of enforcement and decisionmaking, they are also likely to establish and reinforce the bargaining and coercive power of certain members of a society relative to others. This power is then used to distribute services, to coordinate the actions of individuals with a common interest, to ensure that the already powerful can continue to accrue benefits,[8] or to arbitrate inevitable conflicts in a way that reduces the costs to the participants and to

6. It took many years for analysts to develop the transaction cost perspective, initially presented by Coase (1937), but Fama (1980), Jensen and Meckling (1976), North (1981), and Williamson (1985) are among those who have begun to usefully apply it to the behavior of firms and organizations. The principal-agent literature is one result.

7. See the special issue of *Politics & Society,* edited by Levi and Bates (1988). The claim some economists make that institutional arrangements evolve toward a Pareto-optimal equilibrium is at best contentious. What I am arguing is that stability rests on a situation in which the nature of the available strategic choices make a move from the current equilibrium unlikely. Thus, while there may be a Nash equilibrium, the result need not make everyone better off and may make some worse off, as in many collective action situations.

8. The emphasis on how institutions, particularly the state, enable the already powerful to secure more than the market rent through the winning of monopolies and regulations that favor them is what distinguishes the rent-seeking models from other approaches derived from neoclassical economics. See, especially, Buchanan, Tollison, and Tullock (1980). However, as I have argued elsewhere (Levi 1988, 23–25), the application of rent-seeking models tends to be used to support a normative critique of state intervention. It is the normative critique that drives the analysis and thus blinds many of its advocates to the diversity of effects of state regulation of the economy.

others affected by the conflict. Some institutions serve the interests of the many, some the interests of the few, but all facilitate and regulate the resources of power. A definition of institutions that ignores this fact fails to capture part of what is distinct about institutions, namely that the mechanisms for limiting choices, including contractual choices, reflect the distribution of power.

Institutions resolve collective action problems by eliciting contributions from individuals who cannot attain their ends unless someone (or ones) has the power to coordinate or coerce or by mobilizing a group of people to act together. They establish the terms and delimit the outcomes of controversies.[9] The level of conflicts some institutions potentially resolve and the kinds of power resources they sometimes create cover a long continuum. Despite their differences, however, institutions generally are characterized by the duality of both containing and creating power, a fact most of the authors in this volume, and certainly Marx and Hobbes, recognize.

## ANALYZING INSTITUTIONAL CHANGE: THE ARGUMENT

This definitional discussion was the necessary prologue to the central question I wish to pose. What causes institutional change? By institutional change I mean a shift in the rules and enforcement procedures so that different behaviors are constrained or encouraged. Given my characterization of formal institutions as socially constructed rules that reflect a particular distribution of power resources, it follows that formal institutions become susceptible to change as the distribution of resources changes. Change is most likely when there is an increase in the effectiveness of individuals seeking change and a decrease in the blocking power of individuals whose interests are served by the current institutional arrangements.

My aim is to outline one possible logic of formal institutional change in which the analytical focus is on institutional decisions that have the unintended consequence of undermining what I call contingent consent[10] and, thus, of raising the cost of enforcement. The withdrawal of contingent consent precipitates change when it enhances the bargaining power

9. Ralf Dahrendorf (1957) coined the rather neat term "the institutionalization of conflict" to describe how collective bargaining circumscribes the relationship between workers and employers.

10. Contingent consent is a more inclusive term than "quasi-voluntary compliance" used in *Of Rule and Revenue* (1988).

of those who no longer comply or devalues the coercive resources currently in use. In analyzing the impact of the withdrawal of contingent consent, I consider only the relations among institutional actors: managers, employees, and clients, in some cases; subjects, or citizens, in others. It is their resources and their actions that determine the nature of the institutional change.[11]

I have argued elsewhere (Levi 1988) that if an institution depends only on coercion for the successful implementation of its policies, the costs of enforcement will be unsupportably high. Thus, institutional leaders will search for alternative means to create compliance. Rational choice theory reveals that coercion and side payments are principal means by which to induce individuals to comply. Sociologists add norms. I am clarifying the traditional three-fold schema[12] and adding a fourth dimension: contingent consent.

The effectiveness of selective incentives, whether negative in the form of coercion or positive in the form of side payments, is based on straightforward utilitarian calculations. Both coercion and side payments affect the relative weight of costs and benefits in the choice to comply with institutional rules. They do not tell the whole story, however. Even taking into account nontangible forms of rewards and punishments, such as the bestowal or withdrawal of esteem, there is more compliance than selective incentives explain. More people refrain from jaywalking or littering, pay their taxes, or join the armed services than the theory predicts.

11. If this perspective is more widely applied, nearly all sources of change become endogenous—with the possible exception of external conquest. Revolution may well be an effect of internal institutional decisions. So might technical change. Analysts within the Schumpeterian tradition contend that technical change has its roots in factors external to the institution. Brilliant innovators and entrepreneurs appear who offer a better alternative. Inventors can come up with better machines, medical researchers can develop new practices, administrators can reorganize, a Henry Ford or Frederick Livingston Taylor can uncover new methods for coordinating or coercing the labor force. All such developments have radical consequences for the institutions their ideas affect. Despite the appeal of the Schumpeterian argument, I find North's (1981) account of endogenously generated technical change to be more persuasive. Derived from an interpretation of Marx, North's arguments are certainly consistent with at least some contemporary Marxian approaches (e.g., Cohen 1978). From this perspective, technical innovations are products of institutions that facilitate experimentation. Change occurs when the innovations threaten the relationships on which the institution is based, usually by stimulating new resources and incentives for change among a particular set of actors in whose interest it is to challenge the status quo.

12. For example, Etzioni (1961) distinguishes among coercive, utilitarian, and normative compliance. We are principally in agreement on the meaning of coercion, but he restricts utilitarian compliance to remuneration and normative compliance to the vague category of symbolic rewards. One author whose approach is closer to my own and from whom I have drawn, particularly in regard to the strategic basis of compliance, is Oran Young (1979).

Political economists—of all persuasions—have recently focused on the role of what some call ideology and some call norms of behavior in inducing voluntary compliance. Without question the most effective institutional arrangements incorporate a normative system of informal and internalized rules. However, several different phenomena seem to be encompassed by the term norms. On the one hand, there are moral principles that encourage people to comply (or to refrain from complying) whatever the costs, the information, or the behavior of others. For example, some men will sign up for military service once war is declared no matter who the enemy is or how justified the war is. Others will refuse to fight in any war. Such patriots and pacifists are unaffected by incentives and disincentives, by who the enemy is, or by the behavior of government or other citizens. I suspect that moral principles, as I have defined them, actually influence the behavior of a relatively small proportion of the population, but this remains an empirical question.

There is another kind of norm that I think is far more widespread in inducing compliance. The norm of fairness regulates behavior by offering a rule for when one should comply. It generates a kind of compliance that possesses both a normative and a utilitarian element: what I label contingent consent. If current arrangements represent an acceptable bargain and if others are doing what they can reasonably be expected to do to uphold the bargain, the institutional arrangements can be considered "fair." If individuals are convinced that the norm of fairness is operating, they are more likely to act in accordance with rules of conduct the norm of fairness implies. A norm of fairness is always collectively informed and adopted. More clearly than a moral principle, the norm of fairness develops through a social process and in a social context; it is relational and contextual.

Compliance as consent is contingent upon two kinds of factors: (1) approval of the social bargain; and (2) the compliance of those providing and the others contributing to the provision of the service. The first represents a normative evaluation. The second reflects the fact that part of contingent consent is conditional cooperation (Taylor [1976] 1987) in which low discount rates, repeated interactions, knowledge of others and reciprocity over time permit the emergence of rational decisions to comply. In the case of formal institutions, an individual's cooperation or compliance is conditional upon the provision of promised benefits by institutional managers and personnel and upon the continued compliance of others. No one wants to be a sucker. Thus, any particular individual's decision to comply is based on confidence that others are doing their share.

From this perspective, institutions represent a social bargain in which there are returns for compliance. Not everyone benefits equally, and there are those who do not benefit at all. Nonetheless, without gains from trade for a substantial number of individuals, the institution is untenable simply because compliance will be impossible to attain. Given that institutions resolve collective action problems among strategic actors, positive returns from compliance are an essential ingredient in building an institution. But so, I claim, are assurances that others are following the same norm.

In the logic of institutional change that follows from this argument, a breakdown in the factors on which compliance is contingent leads to a withdrawal of consent, which, in turn, increases the costs of enforcement. Those seeking change use noncompliance as a bargaining resource. Those protecting the status quo can no longer rely on the same level of coercive resources. In response, institutional practice is likely to change. New rules must be developed, additional coercive resources must be brought to bear, or both.

Under what conditions then is contingent consent withdrawn? Institutions tend to continuity, but they are also subject to instabilities that derive from the inequality of power resources. Subordinates, even if there are initial gains from trade, may develop an interest in changing the rules that constitute the institution so as to achieve a more favorable outcome. This is most likely to occur if they have acquired new resources of power, if new information has made them aware of resources they had hitherto failed to recognize or use, or if new circumstances make them question a hitherto acceptable bargain. The introduction of Communist Party organizers into the peasant communities of Vietnam is an example of an increase in resources that led to challenges of the existing political and economic arrangements (Popkin 1979). The Women's Movement provided new resources to some groups of women, but for others its influence lay in its ideology, an ideology that offered new information about what rights women have. The movement raised questions, not previously asked, about employer and spouse practices and thus precipitated demands for change. An example of the effect of circumstances is the reevaluation of unemployment programs during depressions.

Approval of the social bargain may decline with an increase in resources that permit a group to reject the current bargain. An equally important impetus to challenges of the status quo may be a change in consciousness that alters a group's perception of what it is due or how it should be treated.

Contingent consent may also be withdrawn when there is erosion of confidence in the compliance of others. This can occur when those who possess institutional power are caught abusing that power, that is, breaking the social bargain; or when it is apparent that other individuals are failing to comply. Such knowledge is made possible by coordination, as Hardin notes, conditional cooperation, or a combination of the two.[13] It also requires that such behaviors be publicly observable.

The decision to withdraw consent is an individual act that is collectively informed by an evaluation of the effectiveness of the norm of fairness in guiding the behavior of others. Acceptance of the bargain is affected by ideology, that is one's understanding of what is one's due, as well as by resources, that is one's actual probability of achieving a given end. However, the norm is also behaviorally defined and behaviorally observed. If others are not acting in accordance with the norm, its force as a rule is weakened.

Considerable work already exists on how changes in resources and consciousness increase the probability of collective mobilization (see especially Piven and Cloward 1977; Zald and McCarthy 1987). My focus will be, therefore, on how the behavior of institutional managers and personnel, on the one hand, and citizens, subjects, and clients, on the other, affect contingent consent.

There is in fact both a hierarchy of enforcement and an inequality of resources among the actors within a formal institution. Who would doubt that the owner, boss, or administrator has greater coercive capacity than others in the institution? Differential access to information and greater power in policy making, personnel decisions, and enforcement enable principals to follow their own interests, even when they diverge from those of their employees and clients. The opportunism that the principal-agent literature (e.g., Jensen and Meckling 1976; Williamson 1985) focuses on among agents can also infect principals. Pareto attempts to capture this phenomenon in his notion of "spoliation," in which government leaders engage in personal gain at the expense of the general welfare (1966, esp. pp. 114–20).

The fact that the opportunism of principals has not been of major

13. In chapter three in *Of Rule and Revenue* (Levi 1988), I discuss in more detail how rulers can establish coordination and conditional cooperation to enable them to create what I call there quasi-voluntary compliance. The effect is to reduce the costs of collecting revenue and enhance their legitimacy.

concern among most transaction cost theorists is not surprising. The principal-agent research tends to be management-oriented. Its driving concern is to discover the most efficient form of organization, especially what incentive structure gets the best work effort out of employees. Productivity, compliance, and other such institutional requirements are enhanced when principals are able to constrain the behavior of agents and when, as in the case of social service, health, taxing, and protective agencies, the employees are able to constrain the behavior of those populations over whom they have charge. Although few of the principal-agent theorists have actually bothered to contemplate the nature of or necessity for constraints on principals,[14] abuse of power issues can be absorbed into the transaction cost perspective as another species of inefficiency.

Transaction cost theorists may have ignored possible abuses of power by principals, but institution builders have not. The constitutions of nearly all governments, firms, and public and nonprofit agencies recognize the necessity for controls on those within the institution who have power over others. Most contain procedures for ensuring that rulers, agency heads, or corporate executives are unable to use their unequal access to coercion, information, and other resources for unauthorized personal ends.

Cases of principals or managers engaging in abuses of power abound. Again drawing from my book, publicity meant to deter tax avoidance in Australia in the 1970s may or may not have had the intended effect, but it certainly did stimulate popular mobilization against the tax system (1988, chap. 7). The government responded with a serious attempt at tax reform. In such cases, the actions of institutional policymakers have the unintended consequences of strengthening potential opposition who then use the increase in their power to transform the institution.[15]

Intelligent policymakers and institutional managers will try to rectify mistakes and rescind decisions whose unintended consequences are harmful to their aims. Philip the Fair, a thirteenth-century monarch of France, discovered soon enough that the cost of refusing to return a war subsidy for a war that never took place was protest and an incapacity to collect additional revenues. Subsequently, he acted in accordance with a revised assessment of probable constituent reactions to his war and tax

14. North (1981) is a notable exception. Also, see Levi (1988).

15. Hilton Root (1987) provides a very interesting example of this phenomenon. He argues that seventeenth-century decision-makers of the central French state revitalized local communities in order to enhance their tax base and power relative to the seigneurial class. In achieving that goal, the central state actors also succeeded in creating the base for revolutionary collective action.

policies (Levi 1988, 107). Sometimes, however, an election or coup takes place before the institutional leadership can respond to what it learns.

So far I have been exploring only the decisions of institutional policymakers. Also important are the decisions by employees, clients, and subjects to comply with institutional rules. These decisions, I have argued, often represent a mixture of motives: they may be responses to coercion and side payments but also have an important strategic component based on calculations of how others will behave. It is the interdependence of decisions among institutional actors that make the choices strategic, but it is the inequality of power that conditions the choice of strategy. Noncompliance is an individual decision, but it can be part of either an individual or collective action. It can take the form of a positive act of defiance such as burning one's draft card or of a non-effort such as is represented by shirking or free-riding.

Following North, I claim there is a contractual element even within the most oppressive institutional frameworks. If those being asked to comply are not receiving even the best of a bad bargain, they may compel institutional leadership to resort to ever more costly forms of enforcement. The end result will be a weakening of the institution and its transformation through revolution or reform.

It is incontrovertible that individuals who find themselves badly served by an institution will try to change it—if they can. Thus, workers form unions and peasants rebel. However, collective action by the relatively weak and powerless is notoriously difficult. The probability of success by groups that do succeed in organizing is also low. They lack the resources to maintain themselves, to wage a fight, and to hold onto the gains of victory.[16] Nor does success in influencing change in any way ensure that the changes will be the ones sought.

The model of formal institutional change I have presented should help illuminate when the relatively weak and powerless have some likelihood of success in their attempts to transform institutional arrangements. In the best case scenario for them, they would take advantage of any new resources that come their way or any reduction in the relative bargaining power of those who control the institutional framework to influence decisions and policies favorable to them. However, given that these are actors who are initially poor in bargaining and coercive resources and likely to remain so, they will have to create bargaining resources from what few tools they have: the capacity to organize collectively and the

16. Discussions of the difficulties confronting the poor and powerless abound. Of especial interest are Piven and Cloward (1977) and Zald and McCarthy (1987).

ability to refuse compliance. Often, individual—but collectively informed—noncompliance is easier. It circumvents collective action problems, and it may enable the noncompliant to evade repression. Given the operation of the norm of fairness, however, the withdrawal of contingent consent is most likely when there is a breaking of the social bargain on which the institution rests.

Decidedly structuralist works on institutional change, such as Skocpol (1979), and more anthropological accounts, such as Scott (1985), both fit within this framework. Skocpol illustrates cases of sufficient weakening of the powerful so that subjects have questions about the capacity of existing institutional arrangements to deliver on promised benefits. At the same time, the deterioration of the coercive power of the institutional managers gives the opposition an opportunity to take over. Scott claims that one of the most important "weapons of the weak" is the ability to withdraw compliance. This can take a passive form, such as shirking, or an active form, such as rebellion. In either case, it reduces the effective power of those who enforce institutional rules and is most prevalent when a social contract is being broken.

Both of these important books on institutional transformation stress exogenous factors as what initially sets in process the decisions that ultimately lead to alterations in the relationships of power and the capacity to effect change. According to Skocpol, war drains the state of military and fiscal resources and weakens both the capacity and the legitimacy of the state to enforce domestic compliance with its policies. With Scott, the Green Revolution in agriculture reduces the reliance of landlords on peasant labor and thus alters the incentives for maintaining their traditional—but institutionalized—relationship. In the first case, the decisions of high-level state actors in response to war ultimately weakens them relative to their agents and subjects. In the second case, the introduction of machinery enhances the bargaining power of the landlords. In both cases, there is a decline in the approval of existing social arrangements and in confidence that others will keep their bargains. As the revised choices of the actors alter or increase their power, the institution undergoes transformation.

The withdrawal of contingent consent is but one—and not always the most analytically important—basis for altering the distribution of power resources within an institution. Often, more important is the generation or discovery of new resources by challengers or the deterioration of the resources of those currently defining the institutional arrangements. For example, in cases of successful social revolution, it is necessary both that the rebels increase their capacity to engage in effective collective action and that there is a concomitant decrease in the capacity of state actors to block such change (see, e.g., Skocpol 1979).

Most institutional change is incremental rather than totally reconstructive or destructive, however. Once established, institutions tend to take on a life of their own. The process of institutional creation is also a process that tends to enhance their survival. Most formal institutions are established by law and their continuity backed by law. Incorporation of firms and businesses and public regulations to establish health and welfare services are examples of how law, and therefore government, enforces the very existence of the institution. This makes it difficult—although not impossible—to dissolve such an institution. However, they remain susceptible to change that is the consequence of internal institutional decisions that alter, often subtly, the distribution of resources.

Sometimes such change results from the intentional actions of institutional managers. Louis XIV, Henry VIII, Franklin D. Roosevelt, Lee Iacocca, and Robert Moses are but a few of the names that come to mind among the many historical and contemporary examples of chiefs of state and of executives of agencies or firms who have acted purposively to increase their power in order to transform the institutions they run to better suit their ends. Such ends range from greater institutional efficiency to personal venality. I offer several extended illustrations of such actions in *Of Rule and Revenue* (1988). For example, I document (chap. 4) a number of fundamental transformations of the tax system brought about by Roman military leaders. Increased revenues enabled them to defeat enemies and extend territory. The effect, over several centuries, was a total alteration of the Roman institutions of governance.

Some of the most historically important institutional transformations have incrementally evolved from the unintended consequences of routine decisions. Marx's theory of historical materialism presents such an account, particularly in his analysis of capitalism. Marx demonstrates how the actions of capitalists to further their own interests both undermines their resources of power and enhances that of the working class.[17] Brenner (1982), North (1981), and Levi (1988) apply this sort of analysis to problems of long-term secular change.

Often the important catalysts to incremental institutional change are decisions of institutional managers and staff that have the unintended

---

17. See, especially *Capital*, vol. 1 (Marx 1906 [1863]), and the first part of the "Manifesto" (Marx and Engels 1978 [1848]). For recent discussions of Marx's historical materialism, see Cohen (1978) and Elster (1985).

consequences of undermining their power. Many a military dictatorship has been overthrown by an army developed in order to increase the power of the dictator. Certainly the War on Poverty was not meant to enhance the ability of relatively poor and powerless people to engage in militant collective actions against government. Since many decisions are based on a strategic consideration of how others will behave, a faulty prediction can lead to unanticipated results. This, in turn, will lead to institutional change if the institutional policymakers are unable, probably because of lack of time (or, possibly, because of stupidity), to redress the problem and if the resulting reallocation of power resources to the challenger is sufficient.

From North's perspective, a change in the relative prices of particular institutional arrangements brings about an alteration of power. This is so, but the language of price and contracting obscures the social struggle that goes into setting this "price" or bargaining that "contract." Non-market interactions can be translated into supply, demand, and gains from trade, but the institutional outcome may bear little resemblance to the market clearing price encompassed in an indifference curve.

Bates and Bianco assert strongly, and I concur, that rational choice is not simply economics applied more generally. Neoclassical economists assume that all actors are self-interested, and many neoclassical economists equate self interest with wealth maximization. For rational choice theorists, the content of preference functions depends on the actors and the context. In discussing rulers, I specified their preferences as maximizing revenues to the state, but I imputed no such content to the preferences of the taxpayers (Levi 1988). Neoclassical economists focus on the market as the mechanism by which preferences are aggregated into collective choices. Rational choice theorists consider a range of possible mechanisms of aggregation. Most important for the case I am making here, neoclassical economists tend to elide over the effect of unequal access to the resources that determine the contract or the price. For some rational choice theorists, particularly those who label themselves "analytical Marxists" (see, e.g., Roemer 1986), unequal bargaining and coercive power are at the heart of explanations of conflict and historical change.

What are the implications of what I have argued for the investigation of institutional change? To analyze institutional change, it is necessary to understand not only the distribution of power within the institution but also the consequences, intended and unintended, of individual decisions in the context of strategic interactions. Moreover, I hope to have shown that the maintenance of compliance is crucial to the maintenance of institutions. The power of institutional decision-makers rests on their ability to offer benefits in exchange for compliance and on their ability to monitor and coerce the noncompliant. Also crucial is their ability to evoke trust through demonstrating that the social bargain is a good one and through demonstrating that the bargain is being kept.

## REFERENCES

Brenner, Robert. 1982. "The Agrarian Roots of European Capitalism." *Past and Present* 97: 16–113.

Buchanan, James M., Robert D. Tollison, and Gordon Tullock, eds. 1980. *Toward a Theory of a Rent-Seeking Society.* College Station, Texas: Texas A&M University Press.

Coase, Ronald. 1937. "The Nature of the Firm." *Economica* (November): 386–407.

Cohen, G. A. 1978. *Karl Marx's Theory of History: A Defense.* Princeton: Princeton University Press.

Dahrendorf, Ralf. 1957. *Class and Class Conflict in Industrial Society.* Stanford: Stanford University Press.

Elster, Jon. 1985. *Making Sense of Marx.* New York and Cambridge: Cambridge University Press.

Etzioni, Amitai. 1961. *A Comparative Analysis of Complex Organizations.* New York: The Free Press of Glencoe.

Fama, Eugene F. 1980. "Agency Problems and the Theory of the Firm." *Journal of Political Economy* 88, no. 21: 288–307.

Heiner, Ronald A. 1983. "The Origin of Predictable Behavior." *American Economics Review* 73 (September): 560–95.

Jensen, M. C., and W. H. Meckling. 1976. "Theory of the Firm: Managerial Behavior, Agency Costs, and Ownership Structure." *Journal of Financial Economics* 3, no. 4 (October): 306–60.

Keohane, Robert O. 1988. "International Institutions: Two Approaches." *International Studies Quarterly.* 32, no. 4: 379–96.

Kiser, Larry, and Elinor Ostrom. 1982. "The Three Worlds of Action: A Metatheoretical Synthesis of Institutional Approaches." In *Strategies of Political Inquiry,* edited by Elinor Ostrom, 179–222. Beverly Hills: Sage Publications.

Kreps, David M. 1984. "Corporate Culture and Economic Theory." Manuscript. Stanford University Graduate School of Business.

Levi, Margaret. 1988. *Of Rule and Revenue.* Berkeley: The University of California Press.

Levi, Margaret, and Robert Bates, eds. 1988. "The Political Economy of French and English Development." *Politics & Society* 16 nos. 2–3.

March, James G., and Johan P. Olsen. 1984. "The New Institutionalism: Organizational Factors in Political Life." *APSR* 78 (September): 734–49.

Marx, Karl. [1863] 1906. *Capital.* New York: Modern Library.

Marx, Karl, and Friedrich Engels. [1848] 1978. "Manifesto of the Communist Party." In *The Marx-Engels Reader,* edited by Robert Tucker, 469–500. New York: W. W. Norton.

Michels, Robert. [1919] 1949. *Political Parties*. New York: Free Press.

North, Douglass C. 1981. *Structure and Change in Economic History*. New York: Norton.

Ostrom, Elinor. 1986. "A Method of Institutional Analysis." In *Guidance, Control, and Evaluation*, edited by G. X. Kaufmann, G. Majone, and V. Ostrom, 229–44. Berlin and New York: Walter de Gruyter.

Ostrom, Elinor. 1990. *Governing the Commons: The Evolution of Institutions for Collective Action*. New York: Cambridge University Press.

Pareto, Vilfedo. 1966. *Sociological Writings*. Edited by S. E. Finer and translated by Derick Mirfin. New York: Praeger.

Piven, Frances Fox, and Richard Cloward. 1977. *Poor People's Movements*. New York: Vintage Books.

Popkin, Samuel. 1979. *The Rational Peasant*. Berkeley: University of California.

Roemer, John, ed. 1986. *Analytical Marxism*. New York: Cambridge University Press.

Root, Hilton. 1987. *Peasants and King in Burgundy: Agrarian Foundations of French Absolutism*. Berkeley: University of California Press.

Schotter, Andrew. 1981. *The Economic Theory of Social Institutions*. New York: Cambridge University Press.

Scott, James C. 1985. *Weapons of the Weak: Everyday Forms of Peasant Resistance*. New Haven: Yale University Press.

Shepsle, Kenneth A., and Barry R. Weingast. 1987. "The Institutional Foundations of Committee Power." *APSR* 81 (March): 85–104.

Skocpol, Theda. 1979. *States and Social Revolutions*. New York: Cambridge University Press.

Taylor, Michael. [1976] 1987. *The Possibility of Cooperation*. Cambridge and New York: Cambridge University Press.

Williamson, Oliver E. 1985. *The Economic Institutions of Capitalism*. New York: The Free Press.

Young, Oran R. 1979. *Compliance and Public Authority: A Theory with International Applications*. Baltimore: The Johns Hopkins University Press.

Zald, Mayer N., and John D. McCarthy. 1987. *Social Movements in an Organizational Society*. New Brunswick and Oxford: Transaction Books.

# CONTRIBUTORS

ANDREW ABBOTT is an associate professor in the Department of Sociology at Rutgers University. He is the author of *The System of Professions* (University of Chicago Press, 1988).

ROBERT H. BATES is Luce Professor of Political Economy at Duke University. His most recent book is *Beyond the Miracle of the Market* (Cambridge University Press, 1989).

GARY S. BECKER is University Professor of Economics and Sociology at the University of Chicago. He is the author of *The Economic Approach to Human Behavior* (University of Chicago Press, 1976) and *A Treatise on the Family* (Harvard University Press, 1981).

WILLIAM T. BIANCO is an assistant professor of political science at Duke University. His most recent publication is "Doing the Politically Right Thing: Results, Behavior, and Vote Trading," *Journal of Politics* 51 (November 1989).

GEOFFREY BRENNAN is Professorial Fellow, Director's Office, Research School of Social Sciences, The Australian National University. He is the co-author, with James Buchanan, of *The Reason of Rules* (Cambridge University Press, 1985).

JOHN BROOME is reader in economics at the University of Bristol. He is the author of *Weighing Goods* (Blackwell, 1990).

JAMES S. COLEMAN is University Professor of Sociology at the University of Chicago. He is the author of *The Foundations of Social Theory* (Harvard University Press, 1990).

KAREN S. COOK is professor of sociology at the University of Washington. She has recently edited *Social Exchange Theory* (Sage Publications, 1987) and *The Future of Sociology* (Sage Publications, 1988, with Edgar Borgatta).

JON ELSTER is professor of political science at the University of Chicago. One of his recent books is *The Cement of Society* (Cambridge University Press, 1989).

HOWARD A. FAYE, recently a visiting scholar at Pembroke College, is a doctoral student in political science at the University of Washington. His dissertation focuses on center-periphery relations in the United States and the United Kingdom.

ROBERT E. GOODIN is Professorial Fellow, Department of Philosophy, Research School of Social Sciences, The Australian National University. He is the author of numerous books, including *Reasons for Welfare: The Political. Theory of the Welfare State* (Princeton University Press, 1988).

RUSSELL HARDIN is Mellon Foundation Professor of Political Science and Philosophy at the University of Chicago. He is the author of *Morality within the Limits of Reason* (University of Chicago Press, 1988).

MICHAEL HECHTER is professor of sociology at the University of Arizona. His most recent book is *The Principles of Group Solidarity* (University of California Press, 1987).

CAROL A. HEIMER is associate professor of sociology at Northwestern University. She is the author of *Reactive Risk and Rational Action* (University of California Press, 1985).

DANIEL KAHNEMAN is professor of psychology at the University of California, Berkeley. He is the co-editor, with Paul Slovic and Amos Tversky, of *Judgment under Uncertainty* (Cambridge University Press, 1982).

MARGARET LEVI is professor of political science at the University of Washington. *Of Rule and Revenue* (University of California Press, 1988) is her most recent book.

MARK J. MACHINA is professor of economics in the Department of Economics at the University of California, San Diego. He is co-founder of the *Journal of Risk and Uncertainty,* published by Kluwer Academic Publishers in Boston.

STEPHEN J. MAJESKI is associate professor of political science at the University of Washington. He has published recently (with David Sylvan) several articles regarding United States foreign policy. They are working currently on a manuscript entitled *United States Foreign Policy: A Computational Approach.*

GARY J. MILLER is Reuben C. Taylor, Jr., and Anne Carpenter Taylor Professor of Political Economy in the Olin School of Business at Washington University. He is the co-author, with Jack H. Knott, of *Reforming Bureaucracy: The Politics of Institutional Choice* (Prentice-Hall, 1987).

DOUGLASS C. NORTH is Luce Professor of Law and Liberty at Washington University. He is the author of *Structure and Change in Economic History* (Norton, 1981).

JODI A. O'BRIEN is a doctoral student in sociology at the University of Washington. The title of her dissertation is "Action and Ideology: A Case Study of the Mormons."

CHARLES R. PLOTT is Edward F. Harkness Professor of Economics and Political Science in the California Institute of Technology. He is the co-author, with David M. Grether and R. Mark Isaac, of *The Allocation of Scarce Resources* (Westview Press, 1989).

GEORGE J. STIGLER is professor of economics at the University of Chicago. A number of his classic articles have been collected recently in *The Essence of Stigler* (Hoover Institution Press, 1986).

ARTHUR L. STINCHCOMBE is professor of sociology at Northwestern University. He is the author of *Economic Sociology* (Academic Press, 1983).

MICHAEL TAYLOR is professor of political science at the University of Washington. He is the author of *The Possibility of Cooperation* (Cambridge University Press, 1987).

AMOS TVERSKY is Davis-Brack Professor in the Behavioral Sciences and professor of psychology at Stanford University. He is the co-editor, with Daniel Kahneman and Paul Slovic, of *Judgment under Uncertainty* (Cambridge University Press, 1982).

# INDEX

Milgrom, Paul, 335–36
Mill, John Stuart, 201–2
Moral hazard, 307
Morality, 171–72
Morgenstern, Oskar, 133, 359
Motivations, 34–38
Müller-Lyer illusion, 75

Neumann-Morgenstern theory, 134
Noncooperative bargaining theory, 40n30
Nonexistence of rational choice. *See* Indeterminacy
Non-expected utility models of preferences, 104–9
Nonlinear functional models of risky choice, 81–82
Nontransitive models of risky choice, 81–82
Nontransparent dominance, 73–75
Normative, defined, 291–92
Normative behavior, and theory of agency, 287
Normative privilege of rationality, 41–42
Normative rules, hierarchy of, 61–63
Normative systems, reasoning in, 289–94
Norm-generating structures, 250–80
Norms: and the collective action problem, 238–40; emergence of, in a social system, 250–80; generation and maintenance of, 273–80; and institutions, 404; and preference formation, 189–281; with sanctions, 254–55; and social conventions, 341–43
North, Douglass C., 403, 406, 415–16

Olsen, Johan P., 403
Olson, Mancur, 233–34, 365
Ordinal utility function, 92
Organizational control, 324
Ostrom, Elinor, 403

Parsons, Talcott, 289, 302
Pascal-Fermat expected value approach, 93
Peters, Thomas J., 344–45
Political entrepreneurs, 233–35
Political institutions, and economic performance, 392–94

Political leadership, in hierarchies, 324–47, 349–57
Power: and cooperation, 367–69; coordination and, 361–64; institutional sources of leader, 354–56; political, 367
Prediction, Popperian view of, 19n
Preference formation, and norms, 189–281
Preference hypothesis, testability of, 146
Preference reversal, 141–43, 181; and the cognitive basis of motivations, 37–38; phenomenon, 109–15
Preference transitivity experiments, 146
Preferences: non-expected utility models of, 104–9; theory of induced, 122. *See also* Tastes
Principal-agency theory, 324–25, 329–32
Prisoners' Dilemma, 241; and the collective action problem, 222–24, 226–29, 231–33; and exchange, 364–67; and norms, 239, 254–56; and populations of strategic actors in interaction, 252–54
Probabilistic beliefs, 111
Probabilities, subjective, manipulation of, 122–25
Probability theory, 91, 122–25
Professional ethics, and reason, 302
Property rights, 235–38
Prospect theory, 62–72, 82–83, 179–80
Pseudocertainty and certainty, 75–81
Psychology, and the preference reversal phenomenon, 114–15
Pure conflict interactions, 359–60

Raff, Daniel, 342–43
Ramsey, Frank, 133
Rational action: and the failure of rational choice theory, 20–24; reasoning in, 289–94
Rational choice models, 170–72
Rational expectations, and indeterminacy, 28–29
Rationality: alternatives to, 39–47; assumptions of, and a research agenda, 83–86; and expected utility theory, 134–38; failures of, 47–56, 84–86
Rational model, advantage of, 82–83
Reason, 285–315, 317–23